THEOH 4 4 5

D1005448

The Religious Personality

The Religious Personality

Edited by

Donald Capps
University of Chicago

and

Walter H. Capps
University of California, Santa Barbara

Wadsworth Publishing Company, Inc.
Belmont, California

L. C. Cat. Card No.: 76-125185

Printed in the United States of America

1 2 3 4 5 6 7 8 9 10—74 73 72 71 70

Dedicated in gratitude
to our parents

Preface

Societies may be formed out of shared religious convictions. Cultures exhibit religious components. Churches can particularize religious communal feeling. Traditions can lend support to religious ideas. World-views may rest on religious presuppositions. But initially and finally it is men that are religious. In its elemental sense, the word "religious" gives primacy to men.

If the word "religious" in the elemental sense belongs primarily to men, the substance of religion ought to be accessible in man's self-portrayals. Therefore, we have here compiled a series of self-portrayals by men who can be identified as religious. Our purpose is to show that religious factors are traceable in human affairs—particularly in the formation of a personal history. Thus we have focused on a variety of life-styles formed by religious sensitivity. *The Religious Personality* is a sourcebook of personal stories of men for whom a religious factor was conscious.

There is no way of knowing in advance what might result from a disciplined examination of personal documents. Nor can we anticipate how this approach might affect the long-standing issues surrounding *homo religiosus*. But a number of introductory statements can be made simply on the basis of the selections in this anthology. For example, the reader will recognize that religious men aspire to an uncommon sort of personal resoluteness—a profound singleness of mind and purpose which gains expression in fidelity to a resolve or faithfulness to a vision. He will note that religious men have asked themselves, "What is the one thing necessary?" and then have gone on to secure their own authenticity in these terms. He will also discover, as Erik H. Erikson has documented, that many religious men have been cultural workers—ideological innovators—who have used their sensitivities to reform their own cultural epochs. On the other hand, he will see that religious men frequently exercise a certain caution or reserve in their relations with others, based on feelings that they are destined for momentous tasks or are privileged observers of extra-ordinary events. Their enthusiasms are often directed to the numinous elements in human experience, sometimes centering on a personal God and often extending to the source of a divine transcendence. Further, the reader will discover through these personal documents that being human and being religious are interdependent. Thus he will discern a variety of patterns by which these individuals maximize self-assertions or self-denials, and weave life-affirmations and life-negations together. In some instances such patterns result in an established integrity and, in other cases, in a residue of discontent.

The fundamental purpose of this book, then, is to create a propitious setting and to provide resourceful materials for discoveries of this kind. To ensure that the materials themselves sustain the setting, we have guarded against intermediaries. There are neither interlocutors nor second-order negotiators. We trust that the subject will be communicated because the proper mood and format have been provided.

A word about format. Much thought was given to the table of contents—to the items which should be included in the collection of personal documents. We did not choose individuals or documents so that all of them would illustrate the same phenomenon. Nor did we want to restrict the scope to specific geographical locations or eras. Rather, we tried to bring together many individuals from earlier as well as recent times. The selection was deliberate, although somewhat arbitrary. We tried to imagine a symposium on the subject of "the religious personality," then drew up a list of people to invite for participation. The criteria were multiple. Some persons suggested were generally regarded by other people as being "religious." Others summoned had put forth their own religious claims. Others were asked to attend in spite of their own disclaimers to being religious. On occasion invitations were issued to persons not recognized by their contemporaries for their religiosity, but whose lives foretold new religious styles. In short, we wanted a truly representative symposium, enabling us to observe the development of the religious personality over a significant span of time.

We decided to group the works according to four fundamental *dispositional factors*. Because our study falls within at least two fields—religion and psychology—we developed a classification which allows the materials to register within both of these fields without violating either. Through the pattern we have chosen, the two fields can touch each other. They touch, we believe, because they have been given a common ground.

Our four dispositional factors are not intended to be exhaustive. There is nothing complete or final about them. However, these four factors stand out in the self-concepts of the individuals included in this anthology. Thus each group of individuals for whom a certain factor is dominant is designated a type of "self." The four types we have observed are (1) the resigned self, (2) the chastised self, (3) the fraternal self, and (4) the aesthetic self.

The subjects of a discussion, however, can only be previewed in its preface. Thus, the editors must step aside to place the symposium in the able care of its participants and witnesses. This we must do, while reiterating the hope that our approach has broken the ground for a new paradigm and new method of study-ing the "religious." But this is implicit if the religious autobiography is in fact a particular genre of literature—a unique "symbolic form"—with its intrinsic grammar and a recurrent structural design.

We would like to thank the following reviewers for their many valuable comments: Professor John Bash, Chico State College; Professor C. W. Hovland, Oregon State University; Professor Leland Jamison, Syracuse University; and Professor Thomas Love, San Fernando Valley State College. We also express our gratitude to Carol A. Carrig for conscientious assistance, especially in preparing some of the bibliographical references which are appended to the selections, and, of course, to the students who inspired this book and for whom we prepared it.

Contents

Introduction

Because the word "religious" can be used in a variety of senses, approaches to the study of religion are numerous. One examines the histories of selected religious traditions—Christianity, Judaism, Islam, Buddhism, Hinduism, Taoism, or Shintoism. Another seeks to isolate the components of cultic religious experience: the myths and rites, the sacrificial and sacramental practices. A third distinguishes different strands of religious experience—the ethical, mythological, doctrinal, societal, mystical. In addition to these, some approaches build upon religion's interaction with the humanities and social sciences, and others stress the function of religious factors in selected societies and cultures. Because the word "religious" pertains to many frames of reference, none of these approaches is cancelled by the one employed in *The Religious Personality*.

At the same time, the word "religious" gives primacy to men and this fact has significant methodological implications. If *men* are most fundamentally identified as "religious," men should be our object of direct study. The approaches to religion indicated above have detected some fundamental truths about the components of man's religious experience. They have shown, for example, that religious communities possess social agency as well as influence and expression, and churches lend a cohesive group-identity structure to belief and action. Similarly, they have disclosed that theologies give conceptual arrangement to religious affirmations and truth claims, and religious traditions can be utilized to locate the great systems of cultic experience and cultural order. In the same way, they have discovered religious overtones in the symbolic forms—music, art, mythology, literature, philosophies of history—and religious suppositions in the sciences of man. But if the word "religious" in the elemental sense belongs primarily to men, the substance of religion ought to be accessible in man's self-portrayals.

In many colleges and universities, on certain occasions students invite their professors to deliver a "last lecture." The invitation itself specifies the intention. The students are asking the professor to talk to them on a different kind of

Do paper on ourselves, biblography

1

subject from the one on which he usually lectures in the classroom. Or, if they allow him to speak on a topic which lies within his area of professional competence, they are requesting that he do so with nonprofessional considerations in mind. To facilitate the mood, they require the professor to put himself in the position of having an hour—one hour only, one last hour—in which to talk about whatever is of vital importance to him. Or, to put it in another way, to make certain that communication will occur in the first person, and that it will be of the first order, the students ask the professor to talk about himself. They bid him raise these questions with himself: If this were my last opportunity to speak, about what would I speak? What should I say? What ought I to communicate? For what would I choose to be remembered? By assigning the request in this way, the students cultivate a certain methodological deliberateness in assuring that whatever is communicated will come with immediacy, intimacy, intensity, and involvement. And, to prevent the professor from straying from his assignment (and lapsing back into a classroom performance), they charge his "lecture" with finality.

As editors of *The Religious Personality*, we have sought to take advantage of similar methodological ploys. It was beyond our power to stage a series of "last lectures." But we could arrange for specimen instances of a provocative functional likeness, selected from the personal documents of men who seem to qualify as religiously sensitive men. In terms of basic intention, the personal document (defined by Gordon W. Allport as "any self-revealing record that intentionally or unintentionally yields information regarding the structure, dynamics, and functioning of the author's mental life") is similar to the "last lecture." Its format as well as the rapport which it establishes both imply, for instance, that the content to be communicated is to be gathered from a personal history. A man may write or talk about a great range of subjects in his professional capacity—depending on training, talent and bent, obligations, reputation, responsibilities, and a host of other factors. But in his diary, journal, and autobiographical recordings he can be expected to turn and return to the interests which prompt him most directly and which do not cease even after his professional rounds have been made. These are the interests, from day to day, which form his personal history. Furthermore, the autobiographical account implies an immediacy and intimacy, a self-consciousness and first-order sensitivity which no other mode of communication can guarantee or duplicate. In his journal, diary, or autobiography, a man will write about himself; the subject is assigned from nowhere else. In addition, the first canons for interpreting the personal document are supplied by the very one for whom the events and interests are most decisive, namely, the one who experienced those events and interests as his own. The evaluation does not come from outside. There is no additional external source of arrangement. Through the entries in his personal records, the man affected by religious factors can chronicle what it feels like to be thus affected. The responses are recorded by the one for whom the experience is most real. The autobiographical account consists of a personal story which is arranged by means of self-interpretation. Like the "last lecture," its form and materials prevent its author (and subject) from lapsing into modes of expression which destroy directness and intensity. The personal document guards against the extrapolations and deviations which are appropriate to other sorts of symbolic sets. This capacity is based on the fact that the autobiographical account is formed by a certain mood which normalizes involvement, immediacy, intimacy, and finality. Thus, we have selected this as the most effective mode for conveying what it is to experience a religious life.

The collection of autobiographical statements we have chosen for *The Religious Personality* cuts across several lines of classification. Hence there are a number of ways by which we could have arranged the table of contents. Because we feel that religion and psychology are the two disciplines most relevant to our study, however, we have devised a scheme of order which primarily relates to these two areas of study. We have asked ourselves, in the case of each selection, what self-concept most dominated the author's view of his experience and the world. Four distinct self-concepts emerged. In order of their presentation, they are (1) the resigned self, (2) the chastised self, (3) the fraternal self, and (4) the aesthetic self.

Before describing these types in greater detail, we need to indicate at the outset some of the methodological limitations of this typology. First, in making judgments as to which factor predominated in a given case, we let the selection itself rather than external historical facts about that person govern the choice. Thus, Dietrich Bonhoeffer's suffering and eventual death at the hands of Nazis would certainly qualify him as the chastised self. But the feeling that seemed to predominate in our selection from his prison papers was that of the fraternal self deeply involved in the fate of Germany and, through it, Christendom and Western culture. In consequence, we placed him in the category titled "the fraternal self." Contrariwise, Elie Wiesel's identification with the fate of Jews in World War II qualifies him for the fraternal-self category. Yet the dominant theme of the selection was that of chastisement, especially suffering at the hands of a vindictive deity. Thus, we placed Wiesel in the category of "the chastised self." Our typology is therefore primarily useful as a means of structuring the anthology. This does not mean, however, that there is no sense of continuity between our typology and the real historical figures. It simply means that our typology cannot articulate all dimensions of the individual's personality simultaneously.

This suggests a second methodological limitation of the typology. Some of the individuals, *on the basis of the selection itself*, could easily fit into more than one category. For example, on the basis of the selection, C. G. Jung would have fit the aesthetic-self as well as resigned-self category. In such cases, the judgment as to which factor predominates was somewhat arbitrary. The reader may well want to quarrel with the final assignments in certain cases. However, this problem merely attests to the fact that the personalities included in this volume possess a richness and complexity that finally resist a typological analysis such as we have attempted here. It would be a total misconception of our objectives in constructing this anthology if it were assumed that this informal factor-analysis implied any kind of psychological reductionism. Nonetheless, of all possible ways of arranging the materials, the attempt to extrapolate certain dominant dispositional factors remains the most suggestive and the least fraught with methodological problems of another sort.

The Resigned Self

The dispositional factor which we have designated "the resigned self" is exhibited in that individual who feels especially torn between two conflicting courses. He frequently refers to himself as possessing two "opposing wills." He recognizes that this opposition must ultimately be resolved. The manner in which the conflict becomes distinctively religious is quite obvious. He senses that God or Providence stands on one side of the issue. Thus, the selection of one alternative over the other is experienced as a submission or resignation to the will of God. While his commitment to this alternative is usually perceived as a personal sacrifice of a major kind, the decision is followed by a sense of peace, of a quieted conscience. Frequently, the resolution of this conflict is experienced as a divine intervention—usually a disclosure, revelation, or illumination which confirms his decision.

Each of the figures included in this section manifests an intense conflict followed by submission to divine or other suprahuman intervention. Augustine is the classic case. Torn between Christianity and Manicheanism, between sexual continence and marriage, he experiences a divine intervention (the voice of a child instructing him to read the scriptures and the appearance of Continence in the form of a chaste queen) and submits to the Christian faith and sexual continence. John Wesley is similarly torn between his affection for Miss Sophy, a young American girl, and faithfulness to his high calling. While his choice has agonizing and even humiliating consequences, he nonetheless experiences divine confirmation of his decision on his return to England. William Cowper faces a disturbing vocational dilemma, a professional commitment which literally terrifies him. Jung, whose case is somewhat more complicated, is torn between faithfulness to the religious tradition of his father and his sense of being called to affirm a more personally compelling "myth." Again, in Jung's case, the resolution of the dilemma comes as a kind of divine intervention in the form of a dramatic illumination. In short, we have designated as "the resigned self" that individual for whom an intense and prolonged conflict is resolved through extraordinary intervention.

The Chastised Self

The dispositional factor which we have called "the chastised self" applies to that individual who feels himself subject to the reproach of other men, God, or both. When reproached by other men, he typically believes that they are jealous or envious of his attainments. On the other hand, he feels that he himself has an inordinate amount of self-pride. He concludes, therefore, that God is using the blandishments, slander, and treachery of other men to break his pride. In this way, he perceives that these chastisements are meant for good. Through these sufferings and persecutions, as inexplicable as they may seem, he is being prepared for a higher purpose.

There is a subtle but extremely critical difference in the manner in which the chastised self and the resigned self understand the will of God. The resigned self does not question God's power over human events. He knows that God or Providence controls human affairs. He therefore believes that the problem (the disjuncture between man and God) is due to his own obstinacy, blindness, or sin. He knows that he must submit himself to the divine plan, or, failing to do so, he will be broken by the sheer force of the working out of this plan in human history. If God, in His severity, weans him from the wrong path (usually away from the pleasures of this world), He does so in order to save the individual from being torn asunder. In contrast, the chastised self expresses a certain doubtfulness of God's control over human affairs. Or, if he acknowledges that God is very much in control, he doubts His benevolence. As a result, he frequently expresses impatience with God: What is the meaning of these sufferings? Are my sufferings essential to the divine plan? Are God's chastisements simply vindictive? Could God, if He chose, put a stop to the assaults by other people? Thus, for the chastised self, the problem or conflict includes dimensions which are partly external to him and which he does not directly control.

Each of the individuals included in this category experienced intense or prolonged physical and mental suffering. In the course of their sufferings, some dared to reproach God. Abelard confesses, "I, in my madness, reproached You, and in anger accused You often repeating the complaint of Blessed Anthony: 'Good Jesus, where were You?' " Madame Guyon questions God's wisdom: "I could not understand your conduct, O my God, which, while setting me free, had yet more strongly bound me by giving me two children immediately before the death of my husband." But while they reproach God, both Abelard and Madame Guyon affirm their ultimate trust in Him. Elie Wiesel is different. He is not amenable to suggestions that human suffering is God's way of preparing men for a higher purpose or destiny: "How could I say to him: 'Blessed art thou, Eternal, Master of the Universe, who chose us from among the races to be tortured day and night, to see our fathers, our mothers, our brothers, end in the crematory? Praise be thy holy name, thou who hast chosen us to be butchered on thine altar?' " Wiesel therefore rejects both the traditional view that one's sufferings are due to his previous sins and the notion that these sufferings have some higher meaning or purpose. The Jewish experience in World War II, which Wiesel records and articulates, demonstrates that suffering is morally absurd. With the exception of Wiesel, however, the figures included in this section prove willing to view their sufferings as part of God's holy purpose, even as evidence that they have been given a significant role in this providential design. Cotton Mather views his sufferings as "being really my honors." Madame Guyon realizes that through her sufferings God revealed "that he destined me to be the mother of a great people." Finally, therefore, the very fact that one suffers becomes evidence that human existence is something more than capricious, that one's own existence has meaning and purpose.

The Fraternal Self

The dispositional factor which we have designated "the fraternal self" applies to that individual who clearly identifies his own spiritual pilgrimage or religious ventures with that of a larger group of individuals. This larger group may be a particular ethnic complex within a pluralistic culture, or it may be a whole nation. For the fraternal self, there is a direct, intimate relationship between his own religious aspirations and those of the community with which he identifies. His detractors frequently accuse him of projecting his personal conflicts onto the ethnic or national community. But the fraternal self perceives the situation differently. He senses that his own personal conflicts are already inherent in the identity of the group. Thus, the basic impetus behind his words and actions is not projection, but the recognition of his formative place in the destiny of his people.

The fraternal self has much in common with the chastised self. He, too, often feels compelled to dispute the belief that human affairs are moving necessarily in accordance with a divinely constituted plan. His actions are frequently impelled by the conviction that it is necessary for man himself to ensure that such a plan becomes operative in any particular set of historical circumstances. In addition, the fraternal self often believes that suffering (either his own or that of the group) is essential to the working out of the destiny of the group or nation. The difference between these two types, therefore, is largely a matter of emphasis. For the chastised self, the problem of suffering is fundamental. For the fraternal self, the problem of the relation of personal and group identity is fundamental. Thus, for the chastised self, the suffering may be closely tied to the destiny of the group (as in the case of Elie Wiesel). But the suffering may also be a highly individual matter (as in the cases of Abelard and Madame Guyon). Similarly, the fraternal self may find that suffering, including fasting, imprisonment, or even martyrdom, is essential to the growth of the community with which he has identified. This was true for both Gandhi and

Bonhoeffer. But suffering need not be fundamental to the individual's understanding of his group's destiny. In Benjamin Franklin's scheme of things, suffering can be avoided and perhaps even eliminated through the creation of moral order. Suffering is not essential to the creation of that order.

Each of the figures included in this section manifests an identification with the problems and communal aspirations of his people. Benjamin Franklin, for example, invested himself in the fate of the young rising nation of America in its formative period, identifying himself with those who had come in order to be "cultivators of the earth." He resists any divisiveness that would threaten the basic objective of building a nation. Thus he criticizes the clergyman who concentrates on making men Presbyterians instead of "good citizens." He adopts a theological perspective which is deliberately nonsectarian, based on "the essentials of every religion." Good citizenship therefore takes precedence over sectarian, divisive interests. While affirming the overriding importance of good citizenship, Mohandas Gandhi has a somewhat different conception of it. For Gandhi, the good citizen is the one who obeys the laws of his society, considering this his sacred duty. But because he obeys these laws scrupulously, "he is in a position to judge as to which particular rules are good and just and which unjust and iniquitous." Thus, the principle of civil disobedience emerges out of the fraternal impetus of good citizenship. And, as we have already indicated, Dietrich Bonhoeffer sensed that the total fate of Germany in World War II was focused in his existence.

Richard L. Rubenstein is the fraternal self in another sense. Rather than identifying with national aspirations, he identifies primarily with a particular ethnic group within a pluralistic society. In this sense, he has much in common with Martin Luther King, Jr. and Malcolm X. For Rubenstein, the question of whether that identification should be thoroughgoing is especially problematic; it was a matter of intense soul-searching. At length he realizes that rejection of his Jewish identity would in fact imply his acceptance of "the irrational mythology that the Christian world has constructed of the Jew." He carries this fraternal identification so far as to become a rabbi, the recognized leader of the Jewish community. Similarly, Malcolm X identifies with the communal problems and aspirations of the black minority in America. For him, the effort to achieve for black people a viable alternative to a "mixed, diluted and weakened ethnic identity" leads to a number of profoundly dramatic and richly symbolic acts. Not only is he instrumental in affecting a major religious realignment (from Christianity to Islam) for many of those with whom he identified, but he is also compelled on his own behalf to take a new personal name. Finally, the story of Black Elk illustrates identification with a group that is threatened by plundering invaders. In a vision Black Elk is told that he has been given ancestral power to "make over" the Sioux nation. When, subsequently, the tribe is defeated in battle, its worth and dignity devastated, Black Elk laments that the dream of his people died and the entire earth has lost its center.

The Aesthetic Self

The dispositional factor which we have designated "the aesthetic self" applies to those individuals for whom harmony, order, or the absence of internal dissonance is particularly crucial. The aesthetic self is especially sensitive to the contradictions and contrarieties of human existence. He feels strongly impelled to transcend these contradictions, either in his personal life or through his creative work. His attempts to rise above or penetrate through these contradictions, however, are only partially or temporarily successful. Kierkegaard, in describing an experience in which he felt a sense of inner unity, exclaimed: "Lucky is the man to whom that is possible at every moment of his life; in whose breast those two factors have not only come to an agreement but have joined hands and been wedded." For the aesthetic self, the sense of inner harmony and congruence is the rare occurrence, the peak experience.

The aesthetic self shares much in common with the resigned self. Both feel themselves "torn asunder," pulled in conflicting directions. And both long for respite from this sense of being pulled apart, of being, as Strindberg puts it, "like an unhappy married couple who cannot get a divorce." But the resigned self is persuaded that, if he is willing to relinquish one dimension of his existence, then the sense of contradiction can be overcome. The aesthetic self does not submit himself in this way. He maintains the two or more conflicting dimensions as a perennial tension. He consoles himself with the belief that this tension is essential to his creativity. Thus, if the aesthetic self longs for harmony and order, this order will derive from the dialectic of the conflicting dimensions rather than from the rejection of one or the other. As Andre Gide says, "I surrendered then to this provisional disorder . . . believing . . . that the disorder itself was less dangerous for my soul than an arbitrary and necessarily artificial order." And Goethe, in recognizing that this dialectical pattern remains beyond human perception, turns his attention to the human response to this ambiguous situation. He suggests that the proper human response when confronted with the incomprehensible is not submission, but bravery and composure. There is a sense in which the resigned self betrays a fundamental weakness that the aesthetic self finds offensive.

Each of the figures included in the section designated "the aesthetic self" manifests a longing for harmony, order, or congruence. But each expresses this longing in rather idiosyncratic ways. Nietzsche attempted to recover his "lost integrity" through love for a woman: "While I was with Lou Salome my center of awareness moved from my head to my heart, and all the Lutheran contradictions in my nature fused to a single passion of love for the Jewish people and all peoples. . . . This priestess of Isis interiorized my knowledge; I began to know life as a living experience, as the harmonious blending of the seen and the unseen, as an artistic activity in tune with cosmic forces that filled me with the splendor and desolation of godlike existence." Goethe sought inner harmony through nature—through intimacy with the God of nature. He discovered early, however, that nature is enigmatical, "manifested in contradictions." He could not look at nature as manifesting a single divine plan, a providential development. Rather, nature resembled both chance and providence. It was both beneficent and malicious. For Goethe this contradiction remained unresolved. Paul Tillich was most impressed with the ambiguities of human existence. He found it possible to portray his entire life in terms of the boundary between a series of alternative possibilities. For Tillich there was no finite overcoming of the opposing principles; their resolution is left to an ultimate transcendence, an act which he reserves for the Eternal.

Soren Kierkegaard, who saw himself progressing through the aesthetic and ethical to the religious stages of personal development, would probably have resisted inclusion in this group. Nonetheless, he fits very nicely into the category of those for whom harmony and unity are fundamentally desirable but strangely elusive. In coming to terms with this elusiveness, he attributes his unusual intellectual gifts to a "disproportion between soul and body." Thus, "because of the strained relation between soul and body my mind has received a tensile strength that is rare." In a similar way, Gide acknowledges that such unity is impossible to attain. As we have noted, he resists the temptation "to form . . . the artificial unity of my life." To resign oneself to an artificial unity would be accepting a premature closure. He concludes, therefore, that "only in movement can I find my equilibrium." August Strindberg, viewing himself as a young man about to enter professional life, asks whether his "character" consists of any meaningful unity: "And where is the self—which is supposed to constitute one's character? Here and there and every place at once. One's ego is not a unity in itself; it is a conglomeration of reflexes, a complex of urges, drives, instincts, alternately suppressed and unleashed." Thus, he reflects on "the conflicting elements in his family," the kaleidoscopic range of experiences he has had, and he concludes from this that he is "a rich mixture of all sorts of material, but all disorganized." He faced his entrance into professional life, therefore, aware of the rich complexity of his character but without a sense of unity, harmony, or order.

In the foregoing pages we have sketched the scheme by which the materials in our anthology are arranged. We have distinguished four types of self by reference to their respective dominant dispositional factors. We have also given some consideration to distinctions between the four types and to some of the ways in which they tend to overlap. It would be useful to push the typology further, and to explore more of its suggestions. It may well be that we can utilize its ingredients in speaking about the influence of historical factors on personality formation. We could then perhaps go on to correlate the occurrences of the selfs with particular social and cultural situations. The chastised self, for example, seems to feed on oppression, and the fraternal self appears to respond to the identity needs of a community within a larger group context. Perhaps these contextual affiliations lend some credence to the suggestion advanced by Robert Lifton that a new type of self has emerged in recent decades. That is the self who, like the mythical Proteus, feels internally compelled to keep pace with the changes and varieties of human existence at the risk of personal disequilibrium. In contrast to the new type of self, the resigned self is likely to experience no more than one major ideological switch in his lifetime, Lifton points out, and "that one would be remembered as a significant individual turning-point, accompanied by profound soul-searching and conflict" ("The Protean Man," in *Partisan Review*, Winter 1968). Furthermore, for the aesthetic self, the capacity to sustain prolonged and frequently intense intellectual and vocational conflicts without being torn asunder appears to be the mark of the genuinely human. At the same time, our analysis of the aesthetic self suggests that this capacity for sustaining conflict is accompanied by a residual nostalgia or longing for harmony, order, the absence of dissonance. Perhaps, then, the religious personality in modern times is characterized by a sense of composure or equilibrium in a conflict-ridden universe.

Let us turn, however, to the selections themselves, and to the various ways in which the One has manifested itself to men of religious concern.

Part One

The Resigned Self

St. Augustine

The Confessions

*So the winds blew and shifted and
drove my heart this way and that, and
time went by and I was slow in turning
to the Lord. . . . And you, Lord, in
the secret places of my soul, stood
above me in the severity of your mercy,
redoubling the lashes of fear and
shame, so that I should not give way
once more.*

St. Augustine was born in 345 A.D. and died in 430. He was alive during the last days of the Roman Empire and witnessed its fall. He is known as the chief architect of mediaeval culture, the one who provided the means of transition from the Graeco-Roman period to the Middle Ages.

Author of at least 80 works, including *The Confessions, The City of God*, and *On The Trinity*, Augustine established the religious creed and moral code of mediaeval Christianity. For many, the beliefs he articulated persist to this day. As Alfred North Whitehead called Western philosophy "a footnote to Plato," so can it be argued that Western theology is "a footnote to Augustine." No one (with the possible exception of Thomas Aquinas in the thirteenth century) has had greater influence than Augustine. Protestants and Catholics alike trace many of their characteristic convictions and attributes to him.

The selection from *The Confessions* which is included here concerns those events which led to Augustine's conversion. Though much abbreviated, the account enables the reader to observe a significant portion of Augustine's childhood, the strong influence of his mother Monica, his waywardness and temptation to steal fruit and take on a mistress, his attraction to a number of religious and philosophical schools and positions, and his separation from and re-attachment to his mother, as well as the circumstances surrounding his conversion experience. After 387, the last year described in our selection,

Augustine went on to study theology more formally and became a skillful defender of the faith against detractors and heretics. Eventually, for some 34 years, Augustine served as Bishop of Hippo in northern Africa. He was killed when the Vandals besieged the city of Hippo.

St. Augustine, in his theological reflections, corresponds very well to what we have called "the resigned self." His chief work, *The City of God* (written to answer the charge that the capture of Rome by the Visigoths in 410 was a punishment for Rome's acceptance of Christianity), outlines the histories of two opposing cities (the city of God and city of earth) in terms of the opposition between forms of authority which are present in the two cases. As Augustine views them, these two kinds of authority have been contending for man's allegiance since the beginning of creation. One is responsible for earthly society; the other provides the motivation for the heavenly kingdom. One is the basis of civil power, and the other is the basis of ecclesiastical power. One represents man's attempt to claim all that is his due; the second shows how grace operates so that the self is denied or at least submits to providential rule. *Humilitas* re-establishes the perfect relationship between God and man as well as the harmonious ordering of all things earthly and heavenly.

In recent years, psychological analysis has been applied to St. Augustine's "personal documents." (See, for example, the two sets of essays on Augustine in the *Journal for the Scientific Study of Religion*, Vol. V, Nos. 1 and 2, 1965.) St. Augustine's life-style—particularly the premium which he placed on self-denial—has been accepted by many in the Western world as the highest religious ideal. Others, regarding such great self-denial as being destructive of ego-strength, have suggested that Augustine is responsible for both religious and psychological retardation. According to his detractors, Augustine's pervasive influence is only made possible by the immaturity of mankind.

In any case, human agency, sexuality, and procreation are major issues in *The Confessions*, since Augustine is determined not to preempt the prerogatives of God. As David Bakan has written, "Central in the discourse of Augustine there runs the thread of awareness of the relationship between sexuality and existence. It would seem that his major struggle is that between the agency of man in his sexual role in the creation of human beings on the one hand, and the role of God in the creation of human beings on the other." From any vantage point, Augustine's life-style and his theology agree with and reflect each other. No other life has had a greater influence on Western religious self-consciousness.

Confessions

Conflicting Parental Influences

I will now call to mind my past foulness, and the carnal corruptions of my soul; not because I love them, but that I may love Thee, O my God. For love of

From St. Augustine, *The Confessions*, translated by Edward B. Pusey (Oxford: J. H. Parker, 1843). Slightly edited.

Thy love I do it; reviewing my most wicked ways in the very bitterness of my remembrance, that Thou mayest grow sweet unto me (Thou sweetness never failing, Thou blissful and assured sweetness); and gathering me again out of that my dissipation, wherein I was torn piecemeal, while turned from Thee, the One Good, I lost myself among a multiplicity of things. For I even burnt in my youth heretofore, to be satiated in things below; and I dared to grow wild again, with these various and shadowy loves: my beauty consumed away, and I stank in Thine eyes; pleasing myself; and desirous to please in the eyes of men.

For that year were my studies intermitted: whilst after my return from Madaura (a neighbour city, whither I had journeyed to learn grammar and rhetoric), the expenses for a further journey to Carthage were being provided for me; and that rather by the resolution than the means of my father, who was but a poor freeman of Thagaste. To whom tell I this? not to Thee, my God; but before Thee to mine own kind, even to that small portion of mankind as may light upon these writings of mine. And to what purpose? that whosoever reads this, may think out of what depths we are to cry unto Thee. For what is nearer to Thine ears than a confessing heart, and a life of faith? Who did not extol my father, for that beyond the ability of his means, he would furnish his son with all necessaries for a far journey for his studies' sake? For many far abler citizens did no such thing for their children. But yet this same father had no concern how I grew towards Thee, or how chaste I were; so that I were but copious in speech, however barren I were to Thy culture, O God, who art the only true and good Lord of Thy field, my heart.

But while in that my sixteenth year I lived with my parents, leaving all school for a while (a season of idleness being interposed through the narrowness of my parents' fortunes), the briers of unclean desires grew rank over my head, and there was no hand to root them out. When that my father saw me at the baths, now growing towards manhood, and endued with a restless youthfulness, he, as already hence anticipating his descendants, gladly told it to my mother; rejoicing in that tumult of the senses wherein the world forgetteth Thee its Creator, and becometh enamoured of Thy creature, instead of Thyself, through the fumes of that invisible wine of its self-will, turning aside and bowing down to the very basest things. But in my mother's breast Thou hadst already begun Thy temple, and the foundation of Thy holy habitation, whereas my father was as yet but a catechumen, and that but recently. She then was startled with a holy fear and trembling; and though I was not as yet baptised, feared for me those crooked ways in which they walk who turn their back to Thee, and not their face.

Woe is me! and dare I say that Thou heldest Thy peace, O my God, while I wandered further from Thee? Didst Thou then indeed hold Thy peace to me? And whose but Thine were these words which by my mother, Thy faithful one,

Thou sangest in my ears? Nothing whereof sunk into my heart, so as to do it. For she wished, and I remember in private with great anxiety warned me, "not to commit fornication; but especially never to defile another man's wife." These seemed to me womanish advices, which I should blush to obey. But they were Thine, and I knew it not: and I thought Thou wert silent and that it was she who spake; by whom Thou wert not silent unto me; and in her wast despised by me, her son, the son of Thy handmaid, Thy servant. But I knew it not; and ran headlong with such blindness, that amongst my equals I was ashamed of a less shamelessness, when I heard them boast of their flagitiousness, yea, and the more boasting, the more they were degraded: and I took pleasure, not only in the pleasure of the deed, but in the praise. What is worthy of dispraise but vice? But I made myself worse than I was, that I might not be dispraised; and when in any thing I had not sinned as the abandoned ones, I would say that I had done what I had not done, that I might not seem contemptible in proportion as I was innocent; or of less account, the more chaste.

Behold with what companions I walked the streets of Babylon, and wallowed in the mire thereof, as if in a bed of spices and precious ointments. And that I might cleave the faster to its very centre, the invisible enemy trod me down, and seduced me, for that I was easy to be seduced. Neither did the mother of my flesh (who had now fled out of the centre of Babylon, yet went more slowly in the skirts thereof), and she advised me to chastity, so heed what she had heard of me from her husband, as to restrain within the bounds of conjugal affection (if it could not be pared away to the quick) what she felt to be pestilent at present and for the future dangerous. She heeded not this, for she feared lest a wife should prove a clog and hindrance to my hopes. Not those hopes of the world to come, which my mother reposed in Thee; but the hope of learning, which both my parents were too desirous I should attain; my father, because he had next to no thought of Thee, and of me but vain conceits; my mother, because she accounted that those usual courses of learning would not only be no hindrance, but even some furtherance towards attaining Thee. For thus I conjecture, recalling, as well as I may, the disposition of my parents. The reins, meantime, were slackened to me, beyond all temper of due severity, to spend my time in sport, yea, even unto dissoluteness in whatsoever I affected. And in all was a mist, intercepting from me, O my God, the brightness of Thy truth; and mine iniquity burst out as from very fatness.

Theft is punished by Thy law, O Lord, and the law written in the hearts of men, which iniquity itself effaces not. For what thief will abide a thief? not even a rich thief, one stealing through want. Yet I lusted to thieve, and did it, compelled by no hunger, nor poverty, but through a cloyedness of well-doing, and a pamperedness of iniquity. For I stole that, of which I had enough, and much better. Nor cared I to enjoy what I stole, but joyed in the theft and sin itself. A pear tree there was near our vineyard, laden with fruit, tempting neither for colour nor taste. To shake and rob this, some lewd young fellows of us went,

The Resigned Self

late one night (having according to our pestilent custom prolonged our sports in the streets till then), and took huge loads, not for our eating, but to fling to the very hogs, having only tasted them. And this, but to do what we liked only, because it was misliked. Behold my heart, O God, behold my heart, which Thou hadst pity upon in the bottom of the bottomless pit. Now, behold let my heart tell Thee what it sought there, that I should be gratuitously evil, having no temptation to ill, but the ill itself. It was foul, and I loved it; I loved to perish, I loved mine own fault, not that for which I was faulty, but my fault itself. Foul soul, falling from Thy firmament to utter destruction; not seeking aught through the shame, but the shame itself . . . .

Thus doth the soul commit fornication, when she turns from Thee, seeking without Thee, what she findeth not pure and untainted, till she returns to Thee. Thus all pervertedly imitate Thee, who remove far from Thee, and lift themselves up against Thee. But even by thus imitating Thee, they imply Thee to be the Creator of all nature; whence there is no place whither altogether to retire from Thee. What then did I love in that theft? and wherein did I even corruptly and pervertedly imitate my Lord? Did I wish even by stealth to do contrary to Thy law, because by power I could not, so that being a prisoner, I might mimic a maimed liberty by doing with impunity things unpermitted me, a darkened likeness of Thy Omnipotency? Behold, Thy servant, fleeing from his Lord, and obtaining a shadow. O rottenness, O monstrousness of life, and depth of death! could I like that I might not, only because I might not?

What then was this feeling? For of a truth it was too foul: and woe was me, who had it. But yet what was it? Who can understand his errors? It was the sport, which as it were tickled our hearts, that we beguiled those who little thought what we were doing, and much disliked it. Why then was my delight of such sort that I did it not alone? Because none doth ordinarily laugh alone? ordinarily no one? yet laughter sometimes masters men alone and singly when no one whatever is with them, if anything very ludicrous presents itself to their senses or mind. Yet I had not done this alone; alone I had never done it. Behold my God, before Thee, the vivid remembrance of my soul; alone, I have never committed that theft wherein what I stole pleased me not, but that I stole; nor had it alone liked me to do it, nor had I done it. O friendship too unfriendly! thou incomprehensible inveigler of the soul, thou greediness to do mischief out of mirth and wantonness, thou thirst of others' loss, without lust of my own gain or revenge: but when it is said, "Let's go, let's do it," we are ashamed not to be shameless.

Who can disentangle that twisted and intricate knottiness? Foul is it: I hate to think on it, to look on it. But Thee I long for, O Righteousness and Innocency, beautiful and comely to all pure eyes, and of a satisfaction unsating. With Thee is rest entire, and life imperturbable. Whoso enters into Thee, enters into the joy of his Lord: and shall not fear, and shall do excellently in the All-Excellent. I sank away from Thee, and I wandered, O my God, too much astray from Thee my stay, in these days of my youth, and I became to myself a barren land.

Pursued by His Mother

To Carthage I came, where there sang all around me in my ears a cauldron of unholy loves. I loved not yet, yet I loved to love, and out of a deep-seated want, I hated myself for wanting not. I sought what I might love, in love with loving, and safety I hated, and a way without snares. For within me was a famine of that inward food, Thyself, my God; yet, through that famine I was not hungered; but was without all longing for incorruptible sustenance, not because filled therewith, but the more empty, the more I loathed it. For this cause my soul was sickly and full of sores, it miserably cast itself forth, desiring to be scraped by the touch of objects of sense. Yet if these had not a soul, they would not be objects of love. To love then, and to be beloved, was sweet to me; but more, when I obtained to enjoy the person I loved. I defiled, therefore, the spring of friendship with the filth of concupiscence, and I beclouded its brightness with the hell of lustfulness; and thus foul and unseemly, I would fain, through exceeding vanity, be fine and courtly. I fell headlong then into the love wherein I longed to be ensnared. My God, my Mercy, with how much gall didst Thou out of Thy great goodness besprinkle for me that sweetness? For I was both beloved, and secretly arrived at the bond of enjoying; and was with joy fettered with sorrow-bringing bonds, that I might be scourged with the iron burning rods of jealousy, and suspicions, and fears, and angers, and quarrels.

And Thou sentest Thine hand from above, and drewest my soul out of that profound darkness, my mother, Thy faithful one, weeping to Thee for me, more than mothers weep the bodily deaths of their children. For she, by that faith and spirit which she had from Thee, discerned the death wherein I lay, and Thou heardest her, O Lord; Thou heardest her, and despisedst not her tears, when streaming down, they watered the ground under her eyes in every place where she prayed; yea Thou heardest her. For whence was that dream whereby Thou comfortedst her; so that she allowed me to live with her, and to eat at the same table in the house, which she had begun to shrink from, abhorring and detesting the blasphemies of my error? For she saw herself standing on a certain wooden rule, and a shining youth coming towards her, cheerful and smiling upon her, herself grieving, and overwhelmed with grief. But he having (in order to instruct, as is their wont not to be instructed) enquired of her the causes of her grief and daily tears, and she answering that she was bewailing my perdition, he bade her rest contented, and told her to look and observe, "That where she was, there was I also." And when she looked, she saw me standing by her in the same rule. Whence was this, but that Thine ears were towards her heart? O Thou Good omnipotent, who so carest for every one of us, as if Thou caredst for him only; and so for all, as if they were but one!

Whence was this also, that when she had told me this vision, and I would fain bend it to mean, "That she rather should not despair of being one day what I was"; she presently, without any hesitation, replies: "No; for it was not told me that, 'where he, there thou also'; but 'where thou, there he also'?" I confess to Thee, O Lord, that to the best of my remembrance (and I have oft spoken of this), that Thy answer, through my waking mother,—that she was not perplexed by the plausibility of my false interpretation, and so quickly saw what was to be seen, and which I certainly had not perceived before she spake,—even then moved me more than the dream itself, by which a joy to the holy woman, to be fulfilled so long after, was, for the consolation of her present anguish, so long before foresignified. For almost nine years passed, in which I wallowed in the mire of that deep pit, and the darkness of falsehood, often assaying to rise, but dashed down the more grievously. All which time that chaste, godly, and sober widow (such as Thou lovest), now more cheered with hope, yet no whit relaxing in her weeping and mourning, ceased not at all hours of her devotions to bewail my case unto Thee. And her prayers entered into Thy presence; and yet Thou sufferedst me to be yet involved and reinvolved in that darkness. . . .

And Thou, O God, from afar perceivedst me stumbling in that slippery course, and amid much smoke sending out some sparks of faithfulness, which I showed in that my guidance of such as loved vanity, and sought after leasing, myself their companion. In those years I had one,—not in that which is called lawful marriage, but whom I had found in a wayward passion, void of understanding; yet but one, remaining faithful even to her; in whom I in my own case experienced what difference there is betwixt the self-restraint of the marriage-convenant, for the sake of issue, and the bargain of a lustful love, where children are born against their parents' will, although, once born, they constrain love. . . .

But Thou, my refuge and my portion in the land of the living; that I might change my earthly dwelling for the salvation of my soul, at Carthage didst goad me, that I might thereby be torn from it; and at Rome didst proffer me allurements, whereby I might be drawn thither, by men in love with a dying life, the one doing frantic, the other promising vain, things; and, to correct my steps, didst secretly use their and my own perverseness. For both they who disturbed my quiet were blinded with a disgraceful frenzy, and they who invited me elsewhere savoured of earth. And I, who here detested real misery, was there seeking unreal happiness.

But why I went hence, and went thither, Thou knewest, O God, yet showedst it neither to me, nor to my mother, who grievously bewailed my journey, and followed me as far as the sea. But I deceived her, holding me by force, that either she might keep me back or go with me, and I feigned that I had a friend whom I could not leave, till he had a fair wind to sail. And I lied to my mother, and such a mother, and escaped: for this also hast Thou mercifully forgiven me, preserving me, thus full of execrable defilements, from the waters of the sea, for the water of Thy Grace; whereby when I was cleansed, the streams of my mother's eyes should be dried, with which for me she daily watered the ground under her face. And yet refusing to return without me, I scarcely persuaded her to stay that night in a place hard by our ship, where was an Oratory in memory of the blessed Cyprian. That night I privily departed, but she was not behind in weeping and prayer. And what, O Lord, was she with so many tears asking of Thee, but that Thou wouldest not suffer me to sail? But Thou, in the depth of Thy counsels and hearing the main point of her desire, regardest not what she then asked, that Thou mightest make me what she ever asked. The wind blew and swelled our sails, and withdrew the shore from our sight; and she on the morrow was there, frantic with sorrow, and with complaints and groans filled Thine ears, Who didst then disregard them; whilst through my desires, Thou wert hurrying me to end all desire, and the earthly part of her affection to me was chastened by the allotted scourge of sorrows. For she loved my being with her, as mothers do, but much more than many; and she knew not how great joy Thou wert about to work for her out of my absence. She knew not; therefore did she weep and wail, and by this agony there appeared in her the inheritance of Eve, with sorrow seeking what in sorrow she had brought forth. And yet, after accusing my treachery and hardheartedness, she betook herself again to intercede to Thee for me, went to her wonted place, and I to Rome.

And lo, there was I received by the scourge of bodily sickness, and I was going down to hell, carrying all the sins which I had committed, both against Thee, and myself, and others, many and grievous, over and above that bond of original sin, whereby we all die in Adam. For Thou hadst not forgiven me any of these things in Christ, nor had He abolished by His Cross the enmity which by my sins I had incurred with Thee. For how should He, by the crucifixion of a phantasm, which I believed Him to be? So true, then, was the death of my soul, as that of His flesh seemed to me false; and how true the death of His body, so false was the life of my soul, which did not believe it. And now the fever heightening, I was parting and departing for ever. For had I then parted hence, whither had I departed, but into fire and torments, such as my misdeeds deserved in the truth of Thy appointment? And this she knew not, yet in absence prayed for me. But Thou, everywhere present, heardest her where she was, and, where I was, hadst compassion upon me; that I should recover the health of my body, though frenzied as yet in my sacrilegious heart. For I did not in all that danger desire Thy baptism; and I was better as a boy, when I begged it of my mother's piety, as I have before recited and confessed. But I had grown up to my own shame, and I madly scoffed at the prescripts of Thy medicine, who wouldst not suffer me, being such, to die a double death. With which wound had my mother's heart been pierced, it could never be healed. For I cannot express the affection she bore to me, and with how much more vehement anguish she was now in labour of me in the spirit, than at her childbearing in the flesh. . . .

O Thou, my hope from my youth, where wert Thou to me, and whither wert Thou gone? Hadst not Thou created me, and separated me from the beasts

The Resigned Self

of the field, and fowls of the air? Thou hadst made me wiser, yet did I walk in darkness, and in slippery places, and sought Thee abroad out of myself, and found not the God of my heart; and had come into the depths of the sea, and distrusted and despaired of ever finding truth. My mother had now come to me, resolute through piety, following me over sea and land, in all perils confiding in Thee. For in perils of the sea, she comforted the very mariners (by whom passengers unacquainted with the deep, use rather to be comforted when troubled), assuring them of a safe arrival, because Thou hadst by a vision assured her thereof. She found me in grievous peril, through despair of ever finding truth. But when I had discovered to her that I was now no longer a Manichee, though not yet a Catholic Christian, she was not overjoyed, as at something unexpected; although she was not assured concerning that part of my misery, for which she bewailed me as one dead, though to be reawakened to Thee, carrying me forth upon the bier of her thoughts, that Thou mightest say to the son of the widow, Young man, I say unto thee, Arise; and he should revive, and begin to speak, and Thou shouldest deliver him to his mother. Her heart then was shaken with no tumultuous exultation, when she heard that what she daily with tears desired of Thee was already in so great part realised; in that, though I had not yet attained the truth, I was rescued from falsehood; but, as being assured, that Thou, Who hadst promised the whole, wouldest one day give the rest, most calmly, and with a heart full of confidence, she replied to me, "She believed in Christ, that before she departed this life, she should see me a Catholic believer." Thus much to me. But to Thee, Fountain of mercies, poured she forth more copious prayers and tears, that Thou wouldest hasten Thy help, and enlighten my darkness; and she hastened the more eagerly to the Church, and hung upon the lips of Ambrose, praying for the fountain of that water, which springeth up unto life everlasting. But that man she loved as an angel of God, because she knew that by him I had been brought for the present to that doubtful state of faith I now was in, through which she anticipated most confidently that I should pass from sickness unto health, after the access, as it were, of a sharper fit, which physicians call "the crisis."

Marriage Plans

Being led, however, from this to prefer the Catholic doctrine, I felt that her proceeding was more unassuming and honest, in that she required to be believed things not demonstrated (whether it was that they could in themselves be demonstrated but not to certain persons, or could not at all be), whereas among the Manichees our credulity was mocked by a promise of certain knowledge, and then so many most fabulous and absurd things were imposed to be believed, because, they could not be demonstrated. Then Thou, O Lord, little by little with most tender and most merciful hand, touching and composing my heart, didst persuade me, that not they who believed Thy Books (which Thou hast established in so great authority among almost all nations), but they who believed them not, were to be blamed; and that they were not to be heard, who should say to me, "How knowest thou those Scriptures to have been imparted unto mankind by the Spirit of the one true and most true God?" For this very thing was of all most to be believed, since no contentiousness of blasphemous questionings, of all that multitude which I had read in the self-contradicting philosophers, could wring this belief from me, "That Thou art" whatsoever Thou wert (what I knew not), and "That the government of human things belongs to Thee. . . ."

". . .But wait! Even those things are pleasant; they have some, and no small sweetness. We must not lightly abandon them, for it were a shame to return again to them. See, it is no great matter now to obtain some station, and then what should we more wish for? We have store of powerful friends, if nothing else offer, and we be in much haste, at least a presidentship may be given us: and a wife with some money, that she increase not our charges: and this shall be the bound of desire. Many great men, and most worthy of imitation, have given themselves to the study of wisdom in the state of marriage."

While I went over these things, and these winds shifted and drove my heart this way and that, time passed on, but I delayed to turn to the Lord; and from day to day deferred to live in Thee, and deferred not daily to die in myself. Loving a happy life, I feared it in its own abode, and sought it, by fleeing from it. I thought I should be too miserable, unless folded in female arms; and of the medicine of Thy mercy to cure that infirmity I thought not, not having tried it. As for continency, I supposed it to be in our own power (though in myself I did not find that power), being so foolish as not to know what is written, None can be continent unless Thou give it; and that Thou wouldest give it, if with inward groanings I did knock at Thine ears, and with a settled faith did cast my care on Thee.

Alypius indeed kept me from marrying; alleging that so could we by no means with undistracted leisure live together in the love of wisdom, as we had long desired. For himself was even then most pure in this point, so that it was wonderful; and that the more, since in the outset of his youth he had entered into that course, but had not stuck fast therein; rather had he felt remorse and revolting at it, living thenceforth until now most continently. But I opposed him with the examples of those who as married men had cherished wisdom, and served God acceptably, and retained their friends, and loved them faithfully. Of whose greatness of spirit I was far short; and bound with the disease of the flesh, and its deadly sweetness, drew along my chain, dreading to be loosed, and as if my wound had been fretted, put back his good persuasions, as it were the hand of one that would unchain me. Moreover, by me did the serpent speak unto Alypius himself, by my tongue weaving and laying in his path pleasurable snares, wherein his virtuous and free feet might be entangled.

For when he wondered that I, whom he esteemed not slightly, should stick so fast in the birdlime of that pleasure, as to protest (so oft as we discussed it) that I could never lead a single life; and urged in my defence when I saw him wonder, that there was a great difference between his momentary and scarce-remembered knowledge of that life, which so he might easily despise, and my continued acquaintance whereto if but the honourable name of marriage were added, he ought not to wonder why I could not contemn that course; he began also to desire to be married; not as overcome with desire of such pleasure, but out of curiosity. For he would fain know, he said, what that should be, without which my life, to him so pleasing, would to me seem not life but a punishment. For his mind, free from that chain, was amazed at my thraldom; and through that amazement was going on to a desire of trying it, thence to the trial itself, and thence perhaps to sink into that bondage whereat he wondered, seeing he was willing to make a covenant with death; and he that loves danger, shall fall into it. For whatever honour there be in the office of well-ordering a married life, and a family, moved us but slightly. But me for the most part the habit of satisfying an insatiable appetite tormented, while it held me captive; him, an admiring wonder was leading captive. So were we, until Thou, O Most High, not forsaking our dust, commiserating us miserable, didst come to our help, by wondrous and secret ways.

Continual effort was made to have me married. I wooed, I was promised, chiefly through my mother's pains, that so once married, the health-giving baptism might cleanse me, towards which she rejoiced that I was being daily fitted, and observed that her prayers, and Thy promises, were being fulfilled in my faith. At which time verily, both at my request and her own longing, with strong cries of heart she daily begged of Thee, that Thou wouldest by a vision discover unto her something concerning my future marriage; Thou never wouldest. She saw indeed certain vain and fantastic things, such as the energy of the human spirit, busied thereon, brought together; and these she told me of, not with that confidence she was wont, when Thou showedst her any thing, but slighting them. For she could, she said, through a certain feeling, which in words she could not express, discern betwixt Thy revelations, and the dreams of her own soul. Yet the matter was pressed on, and a maiden asked in marriage, two years under the fit age; and, as pleasing, was waited for . . . .

A Tortured Conscience

And how Thou didst deliver me out of the bonds of desire, wherewith I was bound most straitly to carnal concupiscence, and out of the drudgery of worldly things, I will now declare, and confess unto Thy name, O Lord, my helper and my redeemer. Amid increasing anxiety, I was doing my wonted business, and daily sighing unto Thee . . . .

And I had thought that I therefore deferred from day to day to reject the hopes of this world, and follow Thee only, because there did not appear aught certain, whither to direct my course. And now was the day come wherein I was to be laid bare to myself, and my conscience was to upbraid me. "Where art thou now, my tongue? Thou saidst that for an uncertain truth thou likedst not to cast off the baggage of vanity; now, it is certain, and yet that burden still oppresseth thee, while they who neither have so worn themselves out with seeking it, nor for ten years and more have been thinking thereon, have had their shoulders lightened, and received wings to fly away." Thus was I gnawed within, and exceedingly confounded with a horrible shame, while Pontitianus was so speaking. And he having brought to a close his tale and the business he came for, went his way; and I into myself. What said I not against myself? with what scourges of condemnation lashed I not my soul, that it might follow me, striving to go after Thee! Yet it drew back; refused, but excused not itself. All arguments were spent and confuted; there remained a mute shrinking; and she feared, as she would death, to be restrained from the flux of that custom, whereby she was wasting to death.

Then in this great contention of my inward dwelling, which I had strongly raised against my soul, in the chamber of my heart, troubled in mind and countenance, I turned upon Alypius. "What ails us?" I exclaim: "what is it? what heardest thou? The unlearned start up and take heaven by force, and we with our learning, and without heart, lo, where we wallow in flesh and blood! Are we ashamed to follow, because others are gone before, and not ashamed not even to follow?" Some such words I uttered, and my fever of mind tore me away from him, while he, gazing on me in astonishment, kept silence. For it was not my wonted tone; and my forehead, cheeks, eyes, colour, tone of voice, spake my mind more than the words I uttered. A little garden there was to our lodging, which we had the use of, as of the whole house; for the master of the house, our host, was not living there. Thither had the tumult of my breast hurried me, where no man might hinder the hot contention wherein I had engaged with myself, until it should end as Thou knewest, I knew not. Only I was healthfully distracted and dying, to live; knowing what evil thing I was, and not knowing what good thing I was shortly to become. I retired then into the garden, and Alypius, on my steps. For his presence did not lessen my privacy; or how could he forsake me so disturbed? We sat down as far removed as might be from the house. I was troubled in spirit, most vehemently indignant that I entered not into Thy will and covenant, O my God, which all my bones cried out unto me to enter, and praised it to the skies. And therein we enter not by ships, or chariots, or feet, no, move not so far as I had come from the house to that place where we were sitting. For, not to go only, but to go in thither was nothing else but to will to go, but to will resolutely and thoroughly; not to turn and toss, this way and that, a maimed and half-divided will, struggling, with one part sinking as another rose.

Lastly, in the very fever of my irresoluteness, I made with my body many such motions as men sometimes would, but cannot, if either they have not the limbs, or these be bound with bands, weakened with infirmity, or any other way hindered. Thus, if I tore my hair, beat my forehead, if locking my fingers I clasped my knee; I willed, I did it. But I might have willed, and not done it; if the power of motion in my limbs had not obeyed. So many things then I did, when "to will" was not in itself "to be able;" and I did not what both I longed incomparably more to do, and which soon after, when I should will, I should be able to do; because soon after, when I should will, I should will thoroughly. For in these things the ability was one with the will, and to will was to do; and yet was it not done: and more easily did my body obey the weakest willing of my soul, in moving its limbs at its nod, than the soul obeyed itself to accomplish in the will alone this its momentous will.

Whence is this monstrousness? and to what end? Let Thy mercy gleam that I may ask, if so be the secret penalties of men, and those darkest pangs of the sons of Adam, may perhaps answer me. Whence is this monstrousness? and to what end? The mind commands the body, and it obeys instantly; the mind commands itself, and is resisted. The mind commands the hand to be moved; and such readiness is there, that command is scarce distinct from obedience. Yet the mind is mind, the hand is body. The mind commands the mind, its own self, to will, and yet it doth not. Whence this monstrousness? and to what end? It commands itself, I say, to will, and would not command, unless it willed, and what it commands is not done. But it willeth not entirely: therefore doth it not command entirely. For so far forth it commandeth, as it willeth: and, so far forth is the thing commanded, not done, as it willeth not. For the will commandeth that there be a will; not another, but itself. But it doth not command entirely, therefore what it commandeth, is not. For were the will entire, it would not even command it to be, because it would already be. It is therefore no monstrousness partly to will, partly to nill, but a disease of the mind, that it doth not wholly rise, by truth upborne, borne down by custom. And therefore are there two wills, for that one of them is not entire: and what the one lacketh, the other hath.

Let them perish from Thy presence, O God, as perish vain talkers and seducers of the soul: who observing that in deliberating there were two wills, affirm that there are two minds in us of two kinds, one good, the other evil. Themselves are truly evil, when they hold these evil things; and themselves shall become good when they hold the truth and assent unto the truth, that Thy Apostle may say to them, Ye were sometimes darkness, but now light in the Lord. But they, wishing to be light, not in the Lord, but in themselves, imagining the nature of the soul to be that which God is, are made more gross darkness through a dreadful arrogancy; for that they went back farther from Thee, the true Light that enlightened every man that cometh into the world. Take heed what you say, and blush for shame: draw near unto Him and be enlightened, and your faces shall not be ashamed. Myself when I was deliberating upon serving the Lord my God now, as I had long purposed, it was I who willed, I who nilled, I, I myself. I neither willed entirely, nor nilled entirely. Therefore was I at strike with myself, and rent asunder by myself. And this rent befell me against my will, and yet indicated, not the presence of another mind, but the punishment of my own. Therefore it was no more I that wrought it, but sin that dwelt in me; the punishment of a sin more freely committed, in that I was a son of Adam.

For if there be so many contrary natures as there be conflicting wills, there shall now be not two only, but many. If a man deliberate whether he should go out to their conventicle or to the theatre, these Manichees cry out, Behold, here are two natures: one good, draws this way; another bad, draws back that way. For whence else is this hesitation between conflicting wills? But I say that both be bad: that which draws to them, as that which draws back to the theatre. But they believe not that will to be other than good, which draws to them. What then if one of us should deliberate, and amid the strife of his two wills be in a strait, whether he should go to the theatre or to our church? would not these Manichees also be in a strait what to answer? For either they must confess (which they fain would not) that the will which leads to our church is good, as well as theirs, who have received and are held by the mysteries of theirs: or they must suppose two evil natures, and two evil souls conflicting in one man, and it will not be true, which they say, that there is one good and another bad; or they must be converted to the truth, and no more deny that where one deliberates, one soul fluctuates between contrary wills.

Let them no more say then, when they perceive two conflicting wills in one man, that the conflict is between two contrary souls, of two contrary substances, from two contrary principles, one good, and the other bad. For Thou, O true God, dost disprove, check, and convict them; as when, both wills being bad, one deliberates whether he should kill a man by poison or by the sword; whether he should seize this or that estate of another's, when he cannot both; whether he should purchase pleasure by luxury, or keep his money by covetousness; whether he go to the circus or the theatre, if both be open on one day; or, thirdly, to rob another's house, if he have the opportunity; or, fourthly, to commit adultery, if at the same time he have the means thereof also; all these meeting together in the same juncture of time, and all being equally desired, which cannot at one time be acted: for they rend the mind amid four, or even (amid the vast variety of things desired) more, conflicting wills, nor do they yet allege that there are so many divers substances. So also in wills which are good. For I ask them, is it good to take pleasure in reading the Apostle? or good to take pleasure in a sober Psalm? or good to discourse on the Gospel? They will answer to each, "it is good." What then if all give equal pleasure, and all at once? Do not divers wills distract the mind, while he deliberates which he should rather choose? yet are they all good, and are at variance till one be chosen, wither the one entire will may be borne, which before was divided into many. Thus also,

The Resigned Self

when, above, eternity delights us, and the pleasure of temporal good holds us down below, it is the same soul which willeth not this or that with an entire will; and therefore is rent asunder with grievous perplexities, while out of truth it sets this first, but out of habit sets not that aside.

Thus soul-sick was I, and tormented, accusing myself much more severely than my wont, rolling and turning me in my chain, till that were wholly broken, whereby I now was but just, but still was, held. And Thou, O Lord, pressedst upon me in my inward parts by a severe mercy, redoubling the lashes of fear and shame, lest I should again give way, and not bursting that same slight remaining tie, it should recover strength, and bind me the faster. For I said within myself, "Be it done now, be it done now." And as I spake, I all but enacted it: I all but did it, and did it not: yet sunk not back to my former state, but kept my stand hard by, and took breath. And I essayed again, and wanted somewhat less of it, and somewhat less, and all but touched and laid hold of it; and yet came not at it, nor touched nor laid hold of it; hesitating to die to death and to live to life; and the worse whereto I was inured, prevailed more with me than the better whereto I was unused: and the very moment wherein I was to become other than I was, the nearer it approached me, the greater horror did it strike into me; yet did it not strike me back, nor turned me away, but held me in suspense.

The very toys of toys, and vanities of vanities, my ancient mistresses, still held me; they plucked my fleshy garment, and whispered softly, "Dost thou cast us off? and from that moment shall we no more be with thee for ever? and from that moment shall not this or that be lawful for thee for ever?" And what was it which they suggested in that I said, "this or that," what did they suggest, O my God? Let Thy mercy turn it away from the soul of Thy servant. What defilements did they suggest! what shame! And now I much less than half heard them, and not openly showing themselves and contradicting me, but muttering as it were behind my back, and privily plucking me, as I was departing, but to look back on them. Yet they did retard me, so that I hesitated to burst and shake myself free from them, and to spring over whither I was called; a violent habit saying to me, "Thinkest thou, thou canst live without them?"

But now it spake very faintly. For on that side whither I had set my face, and whither I trembled to go, there appeared unto me the chaste dignity of Continency, serene, yet not relaxedly, gay, honestly alluring me to come and doubt not; and stretching forth to receive and embrace me, her holy hands full of multitudes of good examples: there were so many young men and maidens here, a multitude of youth and every age, grave widows and aged virgins; and Continence herself in all, not barren, but a fruitful mother of children of joys, by Thee her Husband, O Lord. And she smiled on me with a persuasive mockery, as would she say, "Canst not thou what these youths, what these maidens can? or can they either in themselves, and not rather in the Lord their God? The Lord their God gave me unto them. Why standest thou in thyself, and so standest not? cast thyself upon Him, fear not He will not withdraw Himself that thou

St. Augustine

shouldest fall; cast thyself fearlessly upon Him, He will receive, and will heal thee." And I blushed exceedingly, for that I yet heard the muttering of those toys, and hung in suspense. And she again seemed to say, "Stop thine ears against those thy unclean members on the earth, that they may be mortified. They tell thee of delights, but not as doth the law of the Lord thy God." This controversy in my heart was self against self only. But Alypius sitting close by my side, in silence waited the issue of my unwonted emotion.

But when a deep consideration had from the secret bottom of my soul drawn together and heaped up all my misery in the sight of my heart; there arose a mighty storm, bringing a mighty shower of tears. Which that I might pour forth wholly, in its natural expressions, I rose from Alypius: solitude was suggested to me as fitter for the business of weeping; so I retired so far that even his presence could not be a burden to me. Thus was it then with me, and he perceived something of it; for something I suppose I had spoken, wherein the tones of my voice appeared choked with weeping, and so had risen up. He then remained where we were sitting, most extremely astonished. I cast myself down I know not how, under a certain fig-tree, giving full vent to my tears; and the floods of mine eyes gushed out an acceptable sacrifice to Thee. And, not indeed in these words, yet to this purpose, spake I much unto Thee: and Thou, O Lord, how long? how long, Lord, wilt Thou be angry for ever? Remember not our former iniquities, for I felt that I was held by them. I sent up these sorrowful words: How long, how long, "to-morrow, and to-morrow?" Why not now? why not is there this hour an end to my uncleanness?

So was I speaking and weeping in the most bitter contrition of my heart, when, lo! I heard from a neighboring house a voice, as of boy or girl, I know not, chanting, and oft repeating, "Take up and read; Take up and read." Instantly, my countenance altered, I began to think most intently whether children were wont in any kind of play to sing such words: nor could I remember ever to have heard the like. So checking the torrent of my tears, I arose; interpreting it to be no other than a command from God to open the book, and read the first chapter I should find. For I had heard of Antony, that coming in during the reading of the Gospel, he received the admonition, as if what was being read was spoken to him: Go, sell all that thou hast, and give to the poor, and thou shalt have treasure in heaven, and come and follow me: and by such oracle he was forthwith converted unto Thee. Eagerly then I returned to the place where Alypius was sitting; for there I had laid the volume of the Apostle when I arose thence. I seized, opened, and in silence read that section on which my eyes first fell: Not in rioting and drunkenness, not in chambering and wantonness, not in strife and envying; but put ye on the Lord Jesus Christ, and make not provision for the flesh, in concupiscence. No further would I read; nor needed I: for instantly at the end of this sentence, by a light as it were of serenity infused into my heart, all the darkness of doubt vanished away.

The Resigned Self

Then putting my finger between, or some other mark, I shut the volume, and with a calmed countenance made it known to Alypius. And what was wrought in him, which I knew not, he thus showed me. He asked to see what I had read: I showed him; and he looked even further than I had read, and I knew not what followed. This followed, him that is weak in the faith, receive; which he applied to himself, and disclosed to me. And by this admonition was he strengthened; and by a good resolution and purpose, and most corresponding to his character, wherein he did always very far differ from me, for the better, without any turbulent delay he joined me. Thence we go in to my mother; we tell her; she rejoiceth: we relate in order how it took place; she leaps for joy, and triumpheth, and blesseth Thee, Who are able to do above that which we ask or think; for she perceived that Thou hadst given her more for me, than she was wont to beg by her pitiful and most sorrowful groanings. For thou convertedst me unto Thyself, so that I sought neither wife, nor any hope of this world, standing in that rule of faith, where Thou hadst showed me until her in a vision, so many years before. And Thou didst convert her mourning into joy, much more plentiful than she had desired, and in a much more precious and purer way than she erst required, by having grandchildren of my body.

Suggestions for Further Reading

Karl Adam, *St. Augustine. The Odyssey of His Soul* (New York: Macmillan, 1932).

David Bakan, "Some Thoughts on Reading Augustine's *Confessions*," *Journal for the Scientific Study of Religion* V, 1 (1965), 149-52.

Gerald Bonner, *St. Augustine of Hippo. Life and Controversies* (Philadelphia: Westminster, 1963).

Peter Brown, *Augustine of Hippo: A Biography* (Berkeley: University of California Press, 1967).

Walter H. Clark, "Depth and Rationality in Augustine's *Confessions*," *Journal for the Scientific Study of Religion* V, 1 (1965), 144-48.

Herbert A. Deane, *Political and Social Ideas of St. Augustine* (New York: Columbia University Press, 1963).

James E. Dittes, "Continuities Between the Life and Thought of Augustine," *Journal for the Scientific Study of Religion* V, 1 (1965), 130-40.

E. R. Dodds, "Augustine's Confessions: A Study of Spiritual Maladjustment," *Hibbert Journal* XXVI (1927-28), 459-73.

Jean Guitton, *The Modernity of St. Augustine*, trans. A. V. Littledale (London: Geoffrey Chapman, 1959).

Ralph Harper, "Remembering Eternity: St. Augustine and Proust," *Thought.* XXXIV (1959), 569-606.

Joseph Havens, "Notes on Augustine's *Confessions*," *Journal for the Scientific Study of Religion* V, 1 (1965), 141-43.

Charles Kligerman, "A Psychoanalytic Study of the Confessions of St. Augustine," *Journal of the American Psychoanalytic Association* V, 3 (1957), 469-84.

Henri I. Marrou, *St. Augustine and His Influence Through the Ages,* trans. Patrick Hepburne-Scott (New York: Harper, 1957).

Arthur D. Nock, *Conversion: The Old and the New in Religion from Alexander the Great to Augustine of Hippo* (London: Oxford University Press, 1933).

Regin Prenter, "Metaphysics and Eschatology in the Sacramental Teaching of St. Augustine," *Studia Theologica* I (1948), 5-26.

Paul W. Pruyser, "Psychological Examination: Augustine," *Journal for the Scientific Study of Religion* V, 2 (1966), 284-89.

W. H. Temple, "Some Letters of St. Augustine," *Bulletin of the John Rylands Library* XXXIII (1930), 111-30.

Frederik van der Meer, *Augustine the Bishop. The Life and Work of a Father of the Church,* trans. Brian Battershaw and G. R. Lamb (New York: Harper, 1965).

M. Versfeld, "St. Augustine as Psychotherapist," *Blackfriars* XLV (1964), 98-110.

Robert I. Watson, *Great Psychologists* (New York: J. P. Lippincott, 1963), pp. 88-96.

Philip Woollcott, Jr., "Some Considerations of Creativity and Religious Experience in St. Augustine of Hippo," *Journal for the Scientific Study of Religion* V, 2 (1966), 273-83.

Hemme Hayen

The Autobiography of a Seventeenth-Century Pietist

*I was hardly ever without inner
conflict which arose from
reproaches, however small they
might appear, which I made myself
daily, and so much unaccountable
distress from outside caught
inwardly at my heart so hard that
this conflict grew even more heated,
getting more and more persistent,
pressing me inwardly harder and
harder until finally the will was
impelled to patience.*

     This instance of late seventeenth (and early eighteenth) century Dutch piety was included in Johann Henrich Reitz' 1200-page *History of the Reborn* (1717), a compilation of the life stories of exemplary religious persons. Recounting the "mystical experiences" of Hemme Hayen (b. 1633), it was written as an edification to others. This function is indicated by its subtitle: "Examples of pious Christians of both sexes, well-known and named as well as unknown and unnamed, from all stations of life. How the same were first drawn by God to him and converted, and, after many trials and tribulations were brought by God's Spirit and Word to faith and a quiet conscience." Hayen's autobiography traces the process of regeneration and shows the obstacles which must be surmounted in achieving the quiet conscience.

     Pietism arose in Protestant—chiefly Lutheran—circles as a reaction against the gradual but increasing departure of Reformation communities from the Reformation faith. It was opposed to dogmatism and the formalization of the religious life and wanted to be sure that piety was a thing of the heart and not simply of the intellect. Its adherents were devoted to the Bible alone and tried to apply the words of Scripture to their own lives. They attempted to cultivate sensitivity to the workings of the Holy Spirit and strove above all to keep their inner lives fresh and vital. Much of the inspiration for the movement came from the efforts of Philip Jacob Spener (1635-1705), author of *Pia desideria*, or *Earnest Desires for a Reform of the True Evangelical Church*. The movement was anticipated by Johann Arndt, author of *True Christianity*, and also lists August Hermann Francke as one of its principal leaders.

In this setting, Hayen's account, like the other personal documents in Reitz' collection, served to record, mark out, and interpret the significant events in the process of individual religious regeneration. It reflects the highs and lows, the temperamental turmoils and triumphs, of a consciousness which understands itself to be under the direct influence of the Spirit of God and which asks nothing less of itself than complete singleness of mind. It was presented as an edifying devotional manual, a model for the religious life. Several affirmations are made repeatedly: religion involves change of heart; holiness is a practical ideal; and the fruits of faith are simplicity, self-control, and complete commitment to the things of the spirit.

Autobiography

My father, by name Haye Lieben, and my mother, Elisabeth Seels, lived as peasants in East Friesland towards the north, in a village called Engerhofen. There I was born in 1633 about Michaelmas.

When I was eighteen months old my father died, and after another eighteen months I acquired a stepfather, a certain Intse Reinders, one of the Netherlandish Anabaptists: he was a bargee plying between Engerhofen and Emden, trading in herbs.

About my tenth year, at an age when I was very fond of running about, I twisted my leg so badly that I've been lame ever since. This gradually drew me away from games and childish vanity; and God has since clearly shown me how very useful this trouble has been to humble me and incline me to Him. For immediately, and some time after, I was continually concerned about the true fear of God and the amendment of man's sinful life. And yet earthly things nevertheless regained the upper hand with me. But my stepfather, a God-fearing man, continually admonished me to be virtuous, often saying: 'Whoever wants to get to Heaven, must act as if he were alone,' and that, as Moses says

From Hemme Hayen, "The Autobiography of a Seventeenth-Century Pietist," translated and edited by D. E. Bowman and G. M. Burnett, *The Downside Review*, Vol. 87 (January 1969), pp. 26-45. Reprinted by permission.

(Exodus xxiii, 2), a man must not follow the multitude to do evil. And I must confess that God awoke him to a special instrument of my conversion.

Along with him, my mother also instructed me in the fear of God and liked to see me reading the Bible and other books, especially *The Soul's Treasury* and *a Kempis's Imitation of Christ*, which little book I have often read through since and still enjoy reading. Also I was at the beginning of my illumination, of which I am about to tell, informed by the spirit that both authors of these books had entered into the gracious light of God, as also the author of *The Migrating Souls*, and others too. My mother was glad I spent my time reading these books, even though other tasks, however necessary, were sometimes neglected as a result.

On 1st May 1658, I married in my twenty-fifth year a young woman named Ime Lamperts who according to my reckoning was then about twenty years of age and an orphan, the daughter of Lampert Gouckes and Esse Handschen of West Friesland, who used to live on a farm at Upgant where I afterwards lived with my wife.

During my courtship I committed my ways continually to God, wishing no other than what was pleasing to His mercy, handing over the whole affair in prayer to Him. When people asked me if I did not find it wearisome the affair dragging on so, I would answer it was all one to me just as long as the will of God was done. A year before I had wooed a girl in vain, but even then I was quite unperturbed. On that occasion, with the parents well disposed towards me and willing to persuade their daughter into it, I required them not to say anything since I had committed the affair to God and was well content.

In the twenty-three years that I have lived with my wife we have had twelve children, but never more than three alive at any one time, and the three final survivors are—our first-born daughter Esse and two sons, Haye and Lampert.

Meanwhile we were continually visited by many hard outward chastisements. I was hardly ever without inner conflict which arose from reproaches, however small they might appear, which I made myself daily, and so much unaccountable distress from outside caught inwardly at my heart so hard that this conflict grew even more heated, getting more and more persistent, pressing me inwardly harder and harder until finally the will was impelled to patience, since it found that the whole business would not be settled by pleasure or anything outward but would that way only be made worse, and that no peace might be obtained except through complete submission.

Amongst temptations the following was quite exceptional. I had a daughter about twelve years old who drowned in the well behind our house. I have no doubt the Lord allowed this to happen specially in order to try us, otherwise He could have let her die quietly in her bed when her time came. My son Haye also once fell into the very same well, but I promptly rescued him. Further we were crossed by many head of cattle dying, which made business go downhill considerably for us: it pleased God thereby to free my heart from the shadows to which it still cleaved, so that they should not be a hindrance to us.

I always used to say it seemed easy getting money and goods, but the Lord soon made this easy matter impossible, taking away, through persistent bodily infirmities, any desire I might have for them. My wife too had had for many years a severe pain in all her limbs from child-bearing, which got worse and worse, whatever remedies we used. With all these bodily infirmities which also evoked the sympathy of our neighbours, it often happened that my wife, when her heart was brimming over with pain, would say to me: 'My dear husband! How shall it all end with us? If the Lord deprives us of all our goods, what shall we do then?' Whereupon I would reply: 'Child, be of good cheer! God will do everything just as He pleases, which is best. And even if the Lord should choose to end our mortal lives, well, He has done that to other pious folk as well! How are we any better than those who come to our door begging their bread?' Once I placed the example of Job and all his sufferings before her, whereupon she answered with all the fear that was in her: 'Job's suffering never lasted so long! It may have been very great, but it did end one day and he afterwards received more than he had ever had before. But our suffering has no end; it presses harder and harder and is always with us.'

Whenever she happened to be worried I might die before her, I would comfort her with the example of the poor widow who on God's command received help from Elisha. 'True,' she would say, 'God may have done that then, but would He ever do the same for us?' but I would only say to her: 'Yes, God is now just as mighty as then!' And with that she would be content. When, even after my illumination, she was still very worried that she might survive me, I told her by divine revelation that she would die before me, which indeed was confirmed by God. I was very happy with my wife and the place where we dwelt was all I could desire. But my heart could find no contentment in it all, since it was being urged on to something better.

Not long before, I had started going to the Lutheran Church, but on consideration of the common frailties that are in it I became deeply depressed, because of which I thought of joining the Mennonites. My mind was set on the lowest of them, those called the 'Fine Ones.' For I was interested in taking up with whatever was best, whatever was pleasing to God. But after some time had elapsed, I noticed more and more that even amongst these folk the full measure of true Christian love and faithfulness was not to be found. Nevertheless my longing to be one of them still remained right up to the time of my illumination.

Meanwhile I would occasionally call in on our preacher, Benjamin Potinius of Marienhofen. He possessed some of the writings of Jakob Böhme and amongst them his book *The Way to Christ*. It so happened about six months before my illumination that he spoke to me of this man and of his lofty illumination and I said to him: 'What do you think, preacher? Could a man still receive such illumination and grace?' And when he saw that I said this with heartfelt

The Resigned Self

earnestness, he laid his hand on my shoulder and said something very significant: 'Hemme, a great light will shortly arise for you! Do not forget to let me know, when the time comes!'

Prior to my illumination, I had not read any of Böhme's writings; instead I had read very carefully those of which I spoke at the beginning. One day while I was reading I came across the text: 'one must not love God for the sake of Heaven'. This struck me as very strange and seemed to be a fiction. 'What!' said I, 'should a man not love God for the sake of Heaven?' But since then I have learnt better, that you must love God for God's sake and His sake only. (This is the so-called *amour désintéressé* which has been the subject of so much discussion in France among the Quietists.)

As the time of my illumination approached, all who belonged to my household were well-nigh overwhelmed by outward visitations. I would often say to myself: 'Whenever God afflicts us that means He is thinking of us'. Indeed, when we were without trouble for a spell, which was seldom the case, I would think: 'Our dear Lord must not like us because He is not chastening us!' In particular our household was affected with great physical infirmities in just that very week that God revealed His light of grace to me, and, as I have already said, I myself was at that time still weighed down by depression, which was impelling me to join the fine Mennonites. Now it happened that my son sprained his ankle on one of those days, and so on the Saturday I sent for one of the aforementioned Mennonites from Oldeborg, a village near Opgant, to come and have a look at my son's bad foot, also in order that I might speak with him about his religion. But by the time he came on Sunday morning to Opgant, God had already graciously visited me with His healing light. For in the year 1666, on 4th February in the early hours, I was woken up by the power of this light, and my thoughts immediately fell upon certain biblical texts which I can now no longer quote exactly, but which I then straightway understood spiritually, and I had a very deep vision such as had never happened to me before. I thought of several passages of the Holy Scriptures and straightway understood them very clearly. Indeed, whatever my senses happened to light upon, that I grasped directly in a spiritual fashion and was filled with such a supernatural, quite inexpressible, indeed utterly superhuman, heavenly sweetness in my soul and communion with the ground of being, that I cried aloud from the excess of this joy, unable to restrain myself from doing so. Then right away I nudged my wife and said, joyful as I was: 'Child, are you awake?' She, however, was amazed that I was so happy and said: 'Aye, I am awake and can hear you all right. What's the matter?' I answered: 'Our dear Lord is now granting me what I have so long been asking for!' Hereupon she was equally delighted with me and sweetly pleased, saying: 'Ah! Have you now received it? That is good. But why are you shouting so?' I answered: 'I'm shouting for joy'. I kept on shouting the whole time, the joy was so unutterably great that I could not restrain myself from shouting.

After this had gone on for some time I gradually began to relax a little, until I could get up and put on my clothes, something I would hardly have managed before on account of the great glory of this grace. Meanwhile the Mennonite man came from Oldenborg, looked at my son's leg, bound it up and, as he had arrived at noon, stayed with us for dinner. After the meal I went part of the way back with him and we fell into conversation about Jakob Böhme, for this inspired man was at that time constantly in my mind. Immediately my companion asked me, using a phrase current amongst these folk: 'Was Jakob Böhme one of ours?' His meaning was—'of his persuasion'. It annoyed and depressed me greatly, the way he wanted to restrict godliness exclusively to his community; and the light was hidden from me during the time we were speaking together, only some ardour still remained. After we had parted from each other I returned home not knowing if more was yet to follow. But the working was so strong inwardly that I could not go out for three days because of it. During these days, especially on Monday and Tuesday, I was extremely restless. One minute I would be sitting, next minute I would be fidgeting about the house like a pregnant woman about to be delivered. It was in a way almost like a pain and yet I would really say it was more a sweetness than a pain for there was no discomfort to it, rather a quite exceptional supernatural joy. Even my body was at that time filled, as it were, with the new spirit and I felt as if it were being moved inwardly by the same.

On Sunday evening I went to bed and slept right through the night. On the Monday I got up early and took a day off work. And since I was rather animated I read Isaiah, chapters 55 to 61 inclusive. Then I understood all, even to the inner core, and saw very clearly how the spirit of God does not speak only of the coming of Christ in the flesh but more especially of His coming according to the spirit. For at that time I felt, as St. Paul says: 'I henceforth knew no man after the flesh'. Indeed, whatever I read directly grew bright in my mind and I thought to myself: how could I ever have been so blind before as not to see this! Afterwards I could not read any more for a while because my inner working was so great; I did try but it was no use.

This grace was growing all the time. In particular it manifested itself very intensely and with great power on the Tuesday in a very pleasant taste or rather such unutterable sweetness as is to be found in nothing earthly. The nights from Monday to Tuesday and from Tuesday to Wednesday I had no sleep at all, as on the three following nights, aye, even during that between Saturday and Sunday I hardly slept a wink. I may have had some soft sweetnesses and easings, but they could not be called sleep. The delectable working that was in my mind made it impossible for me to sleep.

But I must now return to what I have by-passed in my story. When on Wednesday morning the ferment in me had settled for a while, about 8 or 9 o'clock that morning I went over to Marienhofen again, to have a word with the preacher, Benjamin Potinius, of whom I have already spoken. But his

The Resigned Self

brother, the preacher of Dornum, happened to be with him, which prevented me from speaking to him right away, so instead I sat by the fire for a while with them, with some annoyance however, since I desired to speak to the preacher alone and tell him what had happened to me. It so chanced that the preacher's little boy, then a child of about three years of age—he is still alive—asked me for an apple, for he was used to me bringing him something whenever I came, but this time I had not given it a thought, my mind was too full. Then the father got up and went to his study to fetch an apple for me to give to the child. I followed hard on his heels into his study, saying very joyfully and eagerly, indeed I could not restrain myself: 'Pastor! Now our dear Lord is showing me the favour which I've so long asked Him for.' He said: 'How do you mean, Hemme Hayen?' I said: 'Because I now know and understand how a man can come to God, that it doesn't depend on the sects but simply on a man's whole-heartedly fearing and searching after God. Also as regards the millennium which we were talking about recently, when I was astonished that there were such opinions in Christendom, simply because I was ignorant of the matter—well, it's been borne in on me that it means a time which runs through and under other time but which can only be felt and known by those to whom God shows this favour. And I have now clearly seen that there are many men who are actually and essentially living their lives in this most blessed time.'

When the preacher heard this he was so moved that he cried out for joy, the tears running down his cheeks. I also cried out with him, indeed I hardly left off crying aloud, except when I restrained myself forcibly in company. We wiped away our tears and went back into the kitchen to sit by the fire with the other preachers, and because it was midday the preacher invited me to dine with him, which I did. But from that day on I ate nothing during the nine days and nights following, though I did however need an occasional drink to refresh myself, for I was thirsty from time to time. This seemed to signify the thirst that was in me after righteousness. On which account I also said to my domestic servants: 'You people should also therefore thirst equally after righteousness!' But as regards food, at that time it was too coarse for me. During the time we were at the preacher's table the two teachers were discussing various passages from the Scriptures. This seemed strange to me and I said to myself: 'How is it? These things aren't like that at all—they're so clear. How is it that they can't understand?'

After the meal I went home, enjoying continual sweet communion with God. The following day, which was the Thursday, it occurred to me to announce this good news to my sister who lived in Engerhofen, an hour's journey south of Opgant. I set off there about 8 a.m. by my reckoning, and as I was going through the fields and coming onto the heath, my tongue became, as it were, loose and stammering in my mouth and I spoke, but not I, for it was none of my doing, rather divine power alone spoke out of or through me. And while my tongue was thus touched, the Holy Ghost said: *Cyre Christi Leo Mea*, and immediately I also saw the same words set out in Latin capitals before my eyes in a very beautiful shining light as if they were written in gold, but much more beautiful and resplendent. For the heavenly far excels in beauty the earthly. Behind these words a number lies hidden. But the interpretation which God gave me of it was this: *Cyre* means in fact the fall of Adam; *Christi* in such a fashion however that he could be saved again by Christ; the latter was *Leo*, the lion of the stem of Juda. Then came the question: what then has He saved? To which the answer was: *Mea*, me! But even though these four words are to be taken literally, nevertheless they are neither Latin (which, however, they most resemble) nor any other tongue. Not long after the meaning of the numbers which make up 1257 was also shown to me. These refer to the time to come, through which I still had to pass. For seven of the letters are numbers: CC is 200, V is 5, II is 2, L is 50, M is 1000, as is common knowledge. Since then it has also been revealed to me why my number was not complete, i.e. 1260, three days being missing. For the number 1260, as treated in the Revelation, means a time of testing, although these days are not confined to any one time. The designation of time is only a lid to stop reason from getting at the matter. Then I also saw that the days should be fulfilled, but only, as it were, in a glimpse; I was not at liberty to speak more explicitly of the matter.

This happened to me when I was near Oldenburg which lies between Opgant and Engerhofen, where dwelt the Mennonite man who had treated my son's foot. When I arrived at his house I told him a little of these things and also spoke of godliness, but it was immediately snatched away from him and did not get through. I then went on to my sister's with this great joy always in my mind. As I entered her house, she was sitting by the hearth, working something with her hands. The first thing I said to her was: 'Sister, I'm in Heaven'. For the joy was so great that I burst out with it, being unable to restrain myself. My sister, startled at this, asked: 'What is it, brother? Are you out of your mind? Have you been reading too much?' 'Don't be frightened', I said, 'I haven't been reading too much, but our dear Lord is doing me the favour of granting me what I have so long asked Him for.' Hereupon her husband comes in from lying down (he had been away the previous day and so had slept on rather longer than usual) and was very angry, mainly because I had been talking so loud. For because of my excitement I had been speaking very loud at the time. Also another of my old acquaintances came in; the man said: 'Why have you been keeping to yourself so much? We used to have good times together, didn't we?' I answered: 'Well, let this be of some consolation to you—that I who was such a poor sinner have been so pardoned by God that you should also prepare to repent!' Thereupon a rich man entered and said: 'O Hemme Hayen! If only I didn't have so many possessions!' I answered: 'Don't let the fact that you've got many possessions hold you back! Turn your heart from them and seek to be rich in God!'—and other such words.

By that time it was noon and the company were going in to dinner. But I did not stir. My sister, surprised at this, prevailed upon me, urging me strongly to eat with the others. But I refused, saying: 'I won't eat now, but I'll drink with you instead'. With that she left off trying, gave me something to drink and they ate without me. The whole time we held sweet converse and towards evening I returned home, my sister accompanying me part of the way. During which I said to her: 'A time has been appointed for something remarkable to happen to me!' without my knowing how, what or when it should be and come about. I felt it playing in my mind, as it were, and would sometimes come out with words before I realized what I was saying.

Hereupon I took my leave and walked on all alone, enjoying such utterly inexpressible joy that the thought occurred to me: what if some gold pieces were now to lie before you on the path? Would you break off so much time from this heavenly sweetness as to pick them up? And straightway I replied to myself: 'No!' Indeed I even now almost believe that were the whole path to have been strewn with gold pieces, pearls and diamonds, I would not even have turned to look at them, so infinitely sweet was that divine inner feeling; everything is contemptible by comparison.

On the way it was inwardly revealed to me that the preacher Potinius of Marienhofen was at my house. And after I had gone a bit further I was again told that he had already left. Soon after I arrived home, and the first thing I said to my wife was: 'Why did the preacher go away so soon?' She was amazed at this question and answered: 'How did you know the preacher had been here?' I said: 'I know the preacher has been here and has gone away. I must speak to him this evening!' But I set out right away to go and see him, and when I arrived I went in and sat with him for a while and spoke through God's strange providence of various things without my knowledge or deliberation. I spoke the same in foreign words, so that the preacher said: 'That's Hebrew, that's Greek, that's Latin'. I said: 'I don't know what it is, but that's how things are'. When we had thus spoken together for a while, he urged me to eat something, but I refused and returned home, quite exalted with joy and inwardly so inspired and inflamed beyond measure that I thought I must die with the glory of it. For the body is too weak to bear such a blaze. Then I prayed, saying: 'Lord, no more or my breast will burst asunder!' So I walked on sweetly homewards. It had then reached its highest pitch, and with my bodily frailty could not possibly have risen any higher.

When I got home, I found our whole household in bed and went to sit down and undress myself. Immediately I was shown on a flat brick at the side of the hearth a circular spot as large as a *Reichsthaler* which was very bright and transparently clear like a crystal: my mind was filled anew with gladness at it. I doubted however, if this was something special and not rather something ordinary, and went to the window to see if it might not have been caused by the moonlight. But when I looked I saw the moon was not shining. Then I went back to it and looked at it with great amazement and inwardly I was told very distinctly: 'This is a particle of the new earth'. And after I had gone round it many times and looked my fill of it, it disappeared from sight.

Behold, these things and the foregoing never failed to amaze me anew, whenever I considered such great matters and then contrasted my littleness with them. With that I went to bed. During one of these nights—I do not actually know which, except that it was immediately before Passiontide—I received an utterly sweet sensation in my outer senses. Sight was very clear and hearing so delectable that the sound I heard excelled incomparably all worldly melodies and music and fully proved it was heavenly. Smell seemed very fragrant to me—and to my wife too, even though she was not aware of the other properties. For she said to me: 'What pleasant smell is this?' I said: 'You smell it too, eh?' 'Yes', she said; and I was glad she could also enjoy it with me. For at that moment I smelt various cordial and sweet smells as if they'd been apothecaries' preparations, only much more pleasant and rare. The smell consisted of a strange sweetness and was like a mixture of many divers kinds of fragrance, the rarest imaginable. Touch was also pleasant beyond measure. All was so heavenly and absolutely perfect that it is impossible to describe it to anyone, the way it was. Only those who one day find or already have found it, can understand.

Next morning, early on Good Friday, as soon as it was light, I said to my wife: 'Get up and make a big fire! For it has been revealed to me that something remarkable is going to happen.' I actually did not know what, only that something would occur—so much the spirit had intimated. Thereupon my wife got up and did as I said. I got up straight after her, got dressed, and went and sat by the fire. And at once a conversation was held within me as if between a father and son which lasted about three hours, very clear and vocal, all of which I had to utter and answer in my natural speech. My housemates who were present did not hear the divine voice even though it was performing loud and clear in me, and so I had to repeat what it said. The conversation proceeded without the least reflection on my part in such a lively and joyful manner as is impossible to express, grasp or believe. Its sound also varied according to whether the father or the son was speaking. At the very beginning it was conducted softly inside me, not vocally but as thoughts, and only afterwards did it become loud and vocal. The speeches that were made then are too lofty for me to reveal here. Much of it has gone from my mind; but what I do still remember and it is permissible to express, I shall tell.

Amongst other things the son said (he was now the new man who had been reborn in me): 'My father, are you now playing this way with your children, are you so near to us? How did you come to be so far from us before?' The father answered: 'I have always been with you. But what think you of these things?' Then I said, 'Lord, thou knowest, and I trust that thou art he and dost this, and no other'. Again the Lord said: 'What think you? Have you attained

The Resigned Self

this of yourself or through your own works?' I answered, 'No, Lord, only thy grace and mercy can do this'. Thereupon my soul withdrew into the utmost and profoundest lowliness and humility and confessed entirely and freely that it was not worthy of itself thus to receive even the smallest benefits of the Lord. Thereupon the Lord let me see inwardly very clearly how all types of religions were as if journeying to a city which represented blessedness and amongst which certain men, in consideration of their outer lowliness and humility, were preferred. But they, like the others, stopped at the gates of the city, though some of many different kinds, who by all accounts did not appear likely, were going in.

Now it sometimes happened, since we were farmers, that our labourers occasionally asked me about outward things. But I would then say briefly and kindly to them: 'Why children! Do as you think fit for the time being. I mustn't bother myself with worldly matters, I have now got something far better and nobler.' And thereupon they would leave me in peace.

Hereupon the passion of our Lord Jesu was revealed from beginning to end, in such fashion that I too had physically to submit to standing with my arms and hands seemingly bound like His. And when the Lord Jesu's death was to be accomplished in me, my arms and hands being thus stretched out, I actually, specifically felt a pain that was indescribable. My son Haye just then dropped an earthenware dish which broke in pieces, and the fall made me feel as if I had been thrust through and killed physically and palpably by a sword, so that the sweat broke out on my face. And from this crucifixion I got and still bear in my right hand a mark of the cross, which marks are otherwise rare.

Hereupon the tempting of Abraham came into my mind, God saying to me: 'If your little boy (a child of about three years of age) were to fall into the fire, would you then cease to trust in me to save him, and take it upon yourself to help?' I said, 'No, Lord!' Nor did I make as if to do so but committed the matter entirely to God the Lord. Meanwhile my little boy comes in, falls, and it seems as if he might fall into the fire, but he fell to one side. It would seem as if it was meant to shake me, but it could not, for I did not even help up my little boy and yet he was still preserved without my aid and came out of it safe and sound.

Hereupon Potinius the preacher came into my house to speak with me. And I asked him: 'Where have you been all this time?' He said, 'How do you know I've been some time coming?' I answered 'I know that since you left home to come and speak to me, your journey has taken you a long time'. He said: 'A man came up to me who delayed me against my will with his talk'. Then I said to him: 'You mustn't come here until this is accomplished'. So he sat only a little while, then went away again. And, just as he himself said afterward, he could not possibly have stayed long in our house at that time.

When the preacher had gone, the spirit said to me: 'Put your shoes on (for I was wearing slippers) but don't fasten the left shoe!' I did as I was told. Again this voice, which was very distinct, spoke: 'Go forth!' Without my knowing whither, I went out of our front door, and my wife too without question, but I closed the door (as was necessary) behind me. Once I was outside I was led by a person who talked to me incessantly—it was the Lord Jesus Himself; He also revealed Himself to me clearly and explicitly, saying, 'Be not afraid! It is I!' While I was being thus led, I walked with my hands clasped together, and He held His hand over them and so drew me on. Thus I went along, secure in His conduct, right through the middle of our land towards the Venne. Now there was in the middle a river of water, and He led me through it; I also went boldly with Him through it, even going up to my knees in it. But so far as I know, I did not get wet at all, nor did our household notice the slightest thing amiss. When I had almost got to the other side, the Lord commanded me to wash just my face. I did so, drying myself with one of my coat-tails. But while I was drying myself I was suddenly taken aback, thinking I had gone too far, and said: 'Lord, I didn't realise!' Then the Lord said: 'In this too I've purposely let you go your own way'. What was the deeper significance of this I did not know then, nor do I know even yet—I mean the drying part. But washing signifies the washing away of sins and the renewal of the spirit through baptism or the grace of the holy spirit—as I was assured by the spirit in my mind. So I went on, led by Him right to the end of the land. And there strange things were spoken which are not for the telling. And when I had by this time become rather weak inwardly, I began to wonder if I should go on and what I should do now. Thereupon the voice straightway answered: 'Turn round three times towards the sun and then go back home by the most direct route you can find. But do not look back, neither enter in at the door you went out at!' Just as I was about to turn towards the sun, it happened that the ground I stood on turned south, the sun itself standing still. But there are other deep mysteries to this which I have now forgotten. I went round the house and re-entered by the back door which I found open (the other I had gone out by was locked, as I have already said), and went back and sat by the fire, and my wife with me. Then a loud voice rang out in my mind, saying: 'Put your feet in the fire!' I was then impelled as before to utter what it said. And when my wife heard this she asked: 'Me too?' Then the voice continued in me: 'Yes, you too!' And when I had repeated this as before, we each put our right foot straight into the fire, which was quite big at the time and burning high. But we both drew them out again unscathed, unscorched and unharmed. Then the voice spoke: 'Since your wife has been so patient in everything, she shall also be allowed to enjoy everything with you!' All of which I had to repeat.

When we had thus sat a little together and my wife had got up, I looked at my left foot particularly closely and noticed that outside on the tongue of my left shoe, where it is usually tied but was then loose, there was something green from my passage through the water. Thereupon the voice ordered me to take it and hang it over my head, which I did. And the voice spoke: 'Now it's a snake!' I

The Resigned Self

said, 'Lord, can I have a look at it?' But He answered me 'No! For I have trodden the snake's head underfoot. But you shall hear it!' Meanwhile I heard three times a loud blowing noise just like when I've heard adders hissing. Thereupon I went back to the fire and then I suddenly saw a mass, as it were, of sparks flying up out of the fire, and a voice spoke: 'These are the fixed stars!' And immediately I saw some more, though not so many in number, but the sparks were bigger. And during this I heard: 'These are the planets!' After there appeared in the fire as in a mirror my own person in the same shape as when I was sitting before in the chair, dressed in my clothes. When it was gone, a flower could be seen in the light in front, half-lily and half-rose, marked with letters that were hitherto unknown to me.

After I had got through the Friday and evening had come, I betook myself to bed and though I slept but little yet I rested softly with my eyes closed and continued lying quiet in bed the following Saturday and the night after until Sunday morning. And the sweet rest which lasted forty hours signified the burial of the Lord Jesus who had lain forty hours in the grave before He rose, just as Adam slept the same number of hours before he got Eve.

On the Sunday morning before I got up it happened that I saw at one side of the foot of my bed on which I was lying, Aaron's rod, standing against the wall near the bedroom door (the spirit told me that is what it was), and I saw it grow green, blossom and bear almonds so distinctly that, even though I had never seen an almond-tree, the preacher Potinius three days after, when he visited me, could tell from what I said and recognize very clearly and accurately that it was indeed an almond-tree.

Then I got up and went out, as proof of the resurrection of the Lord Christ, but I straightway came back in again and went to bed and lay until the nine days were accomplished, of which I have already spoken.

After the lapse of these nine days my wife and children urged me strongly to eat something, even though I had no need of any earthly food at that time. And finally it pleased the Lord that I should eat. I very much regretted that it had happened and said: 'Ah! Ah! I wish I hadn't eaten after all!' For I felt that my mind was hampered thereby. And then it began to grow worse, which after a while made me feel very poorly, and I asked God whether that sweet delectation might not stay with me; but all I received of His kindness in answer was: 'Without struggle and labour you cannot attain it!'

After that first dawning of God's light of grace many remarkable things have happened to me: for instance, not long after I saw in an ecstasy at the head and foot of my bed two small human figures a hand high in incomparable celestial distinctness and of such excelling beauty as is impossible to express. One was a man, the other a woman. The latter, however, was not human and not of the flesh and its corruptions. The two signified the bridegroom Christ with his bride, the Faithful. This story I hardly ever tell on account of its special glory and great mystery. Some time after this I heard that some people were anxious to know whether King Solomon had also been saved. 'Mm!' I thought, 'I wonder if he was?' And as I lay in bed I happened to look at the wall; and I saw everything very clearly and transparently; and God showed me Solomon on a lofty throne with steps leading up to it, and he had a considerable number of princesses on his right and a smaller number of concubines on his left. Then a loud voice spoke in me: 'Behold, this is Solomon!' And this was a clear and complete assurance that he and his wives were saved.

Shortly after I got a very strong urge to search into all outer things. This came about because I had not been concerned in the past with investigating anything by means of reason—and I had to give it up. My imaginings grew so great that once even the stellar spirit itself revealed itself to me corporeally, covered in scales like a fish, and its colour like filings of spinel: it was in the shape of a tall man—all in order to frighten me off. But it could not overpower me. Nevertheless this was one of the severest temptations I have ever had.

Again I experienced another ecstasy, and came to a place where stood a table laid, at which four persons were sitting, and on the table stood a very beautiful lily, at which I was astonished. Immediately one of the four comes and takes a vial and places it over the lily. This saddened me very much. Then the person said: 'Don't let this sadden you so! For when the light is burning that is lit at the fire of love, then you shall see clearly the same lily again.'

Once I lay in bed in the morning in broad daylight, wide awake, and my mind was in deep contemplation; then I became enraptured and my new man parted, as it were, at my bedside from the old one and left the latter lying like a lifeless log. I turned and saw my natural body lying thus dead and once again fell into a great glory surrounded by a very bright light, and the new body I bore was so bright and splendid that the glory far exceeded that of the sun. I believe without a shadow of doubt that if anyone had then found my outer body he would have regarded the same none otherwise than as dead, as long as the ecstasy lasted.

Another time I lay in bed one morning and on waking fell into an ecstasy; then I felt a man catch hold of me from behind. I looked over my shoulder at him, saying: 'Is it you, my lord?' For it was the Lord Jesus and with that He was gone. I felt however His hands and fingers quite distinctly, especially upon my left side. And when in great joy I felt the spot, I thought I would find a mark from Him, but there was not one.

About this time it also pleased the Lord to grant my wife the favour which He had promised her through me. For almost at the end of her life she received a very pleasant illumination, which it would take too long to relate here. I will however mention something instructive and comforting about it. Beside the indwelling grace which brings to man's heart an inexpressible sweetness and which greatly cheered my wife, it also happened in an ecstasy that God showed her a lily and in the lily a pearl, thereby indicating that some may well obtain the lily but few the pearl. She was then in a weak state physically and became weaker and weaker until on the morning of 7th August 1683 she finally departed this life with special joy and consolation.

When the writer of this narrative further urged the narrator to go on and tell more, he said, 'Well, I'll tell you one more thing and with that I'll close. To God above all belongs the praise and honor! For His grace is infinite.' After the death of my wife, in 1684 shortly after Epiphany, I had the three-day fever three times very bad and when it coming on a fourth time I ordered the bed to be warmed as soon as the fever started. And I got in into the warm as soon as I felt it, in order to ease the coldness with this warmth. But the coldness got so bad that I thought I would suffer death from it. And as I was thinking this, I was carried away. While I was thus transported out of myself, a man comes up to me and says: 'I can take away your fever!' 'Can you really?' said I. 'Yes', he said. 'I can take away the fever from all men.' 'Why', said I, 'how do you do that?' 'I first make them well in their souls', he said, 'and then they're soon better'. While he was saying this about healing the soul, I realised who he was and said, 'My Lord Jesus! Please don't go away from Thy servant, or first deign to speak with him a little.' And He spoke to me of remarkable lofty matters which concern the state of souls. Afterwards I came to and was quite fresh and well, got up immediately, and from that day to this have never had a fever again.

Well, all these things which are thus related in detail were consoling to me beyond measure, but they could not be expressed fittingly. Nor is it possible to signify to anyone in words the sweet fellowship that a man who fears God, enjoys with the Lord—only to wish it him. Blessed, yea a thousand times blessed is the man who finds it for himself! But this requires a total dying to the world, an utter denial of all created things, a complete subjection to God out of pure love, and absolute obedience to Him in all things!

This man Hemme Hayen died a few years ago in Amsterdam. Before his death he made a point of visiting a friend, because he realized his end was near, as indeed he remarked to him: 'Fever makes the children grow, but kills the old ones off.' He died there quietly, and his treasures which he revealed beforehand to a close friend without ever thinking that they should see the light of day here to the amazement of all, passed away with him. His friends according to the bond of faith afterwards frequently requested him to tell them further of God's works and wonders and would like to have written them down; but he refused them, saying: 'The Lord won't let me, I am like a locked garden. The Lord comes in, whenever He pleases; and when He goes away again, He takes the key with Him. But others will bring His wonders to light. For should I write what I could write, then people would kill me out of incredulity.' His fever and illness were short and the work of the Lord on him inward and secret. He kissed farewell in a cordial manner to all those of his acquaintance who visited him. And thus in all quiet he passed over into eternity.

John Wesley

Extracts from the Savannah Journal: A Romantic Episode

*"My heart sank in me like a
stone. I felt how bitter a thing it
is for a spirit of an unbounded
appetite to be left a prey to its
own desires. But it was not long.
For I no sooner stretched forth my
hands to Heaven and bewailed my
having departed from Him, than God
sent me help from his holy place,
and my soul received comfort."*

John Wesley was the founder of Methodism, a religious movement which was to provide the model for virtually all subsequent revivalist movements. Born in 1703, he was the son of a former Dissenter who later became a minister in the Church of England. A critical event when Wesley was six years old led him to believe he was destined to follow in his father's footsteps; narrowly rescued from a fire which completely destroyed the Wesley home, he referred to himself in the words of the prophets Amos and Zechariah as a "brand plucked from the burning." (Later, as the following selection shows, he viewed "burning" and sexual passion as somewhat synonymous.) After graduation from Oxford University in 1724, Wesley did in fact become a minister.

Five years after his graduation, however, he was called back to Oxford as a tutor. On his return, he joined the religious study group which his brother Charles had initiated. Within months he had assumed leadership of the group. Then, in 1735, a turning point occurred in his career. He accepted an invitation to go to America as minister to the newly-founded colony of Georgia. His

The Resigned Self

willingness to go was due in part to the fact that it was becoming difficult for him to maintain control of the religious study group. In the following selection, based on his American experience, he recounts the romantic troubles which necessitated his hasty return to England. He returned to England in February of 1738 without any future prospects.

The next critical event in his life was his conversion in May, three months after his return. His experiences in Georgia, signifying a professional failure, weighed heavily on his mind and clearly provided the context for his conversion experience. It took place in Aldersgate Street in London, where a religious society, probably composed of Moravians, was meeting under the auspices of the Church of England. That evening, Luther's preface to Paul's Letter to the Romans was being read, and Wesley, as he tells it, "felt my heart strangely warmed, I felt I did trust in Christ, Christ alone for salvation; and an assurance was given me, that he had taken away *my* sins, even *mine*, and saved *me* from the law of sin and death." This experience at Aldersgate confirmed Wesley's faith in the religious work which followed. He now directed his attention toward organizing religious societies patterned after the Holy Club at Oxford and the Moravian meetings. In 1739, however, George Whitefield persuaded Wesley that small group evangelization was insufficient, pointing instead to his own success in open-air meetings. Wesley's adoption of field preaching "opened the door through which the full strength of Wesley began to stride forth" (Francis McConnell). When he overcame his reluctance to adopt the unorthodox procedure of preaching outside the churches, Wesley's Methodist revival became a reality.

What was distinctive about Wesley's message? W. R. Cannon suggests that "The Wesleyan Revival arose . . . as a positive affirmation of scriptural Christianity in the face of the rationalistic and deistic philosophy which characterized the intellectual temper of the eighteenth century." Cannon also suggests that the Wesleyan revival emerged "as the moral counterpart of the immoral and corrupt tendencies which characterized the eighteenth century." Fusing both the scriptural and the moral emphases of Methodism, Wesley himself said that it was raised up "to spread Scriptural holiness over the land." Perhaps his most distinctive contribution to Christian thought and practice was therefore his emphasis on Christian perfection, by which he meant the holiness or purity of motive entirely free from the corruptions of self-interest and natural desire. In his view, this perfection is "the grand depositum which God has lodged with the people called Methodist; and for the sake of propagating this chiefly he appeared to have raised us up."

The episode which follows, recounting Wesley's struggle to resign himself to the life of the spirit, may be viewed as part of his lifelong preoccupation with the possibility of Christian perfection. In Georgia, far removed from the moral restraints of pious parents and godly friends, he found the temptations of self-interest and natural desire extremely acute.

Savannah Journal

October 1736

We set out about noon. The afternoon, and so the greater part of the following days, we spent partly in using Bishop Patrick's *Prayers*, and partly in reading the first volume of Fleury's *History of the Church*, a book I chose for her sake chiefly, as setting before her such glorious examples of truth and patience, in the sufferings of those ancient worthies, 'who resisted unto blood, striving against sin.'

In the evening we landed on an uninhabited island, made a fire, supped, went to prayers together, and then spread our sail over us on four stakes, to keep off the night dews. Under this on one side were Miss Sophy, myself, and one of our boys who came with me from Savannah; on the other, our boat's crew. The north-east wind was high and piercingly cold, and it was the first night she had ever spent in such a lodging. But she complained of nothing, appearing as satisfied as if she had been warm upon a bed of down.

The next morning, as we crossed Doboy Sound, the wind being high and the sea rough, I asked her, 'Miss Sophy, are not you afraid to die?' She answered calmly, 'No, I don't desire to live any longer. Oh that God would let me go now! Then I should be at rest. In the world I expect nothing but misery.'

In the evening, the wind being contrary, we landed on the south end of St. Katherine's Island. And here we were obliged to stay till Friday; so that I had time to observe her behavior more nearly. And the more I observed, the more was I amazed. Nothing was ever improper or ill-timed. All she said and did was equally tinctured with seriousness and sweetness. She was often in pain, which she could not hide; but it never betrayed her into impatience. She gave herself up to God, owning she suffered far less than she deserved.

Wed. 27. In the afternoon we fell into a conversation on 'Lying in order to do good.' She owned she used to think there was no harm in it, and that she had herself sometimes done it to me; but added, 'she was now convinced no lying was lawful, and would therefore watch against all kinds of it for the future.'

Thurs. 28. In the afternoon, after walking some time, we sat down in a little thicket by the side of a spring. Here we entered upon a close conversation on Christian holiness. The openness with which she owned her ignorance of it, and the earnest desire she showed for fresh instruction, as it much endeared her to me, so it made me hope she would one day prove an eminent pattern of it.

From *The Journal of the Rev. John Wesley, A.M.*, edited by Nehemiah Curnock, Vol I (London: The Epworth Press, 1909).

Fri. 29. We ventured to set out, though the wind was very high. The waves dashed over the boat every moment, and the cold was extremely piercing. She showed no concern, nor made any complaint, but appeared quite cheerful and satisfied.

It was not without some difficulty that in the afternoon we landed on St. Katherine's again. Observing in the night, the fire we lay by burning bright, that Miss Sophy was broad awake, I asked her, 'Miss Sophy, how far are you engaged to Mr. Mellichamp?' She answered, 'I have promised him either to marry him or to marry no one at all.' I said (which indeed was the expression of a sudden wish, not of any formed design), 'Miss Sophy, I should think myself happy if I was to spend my life with you.' She burst out into tears and said, 'I am every way unhappy. I won't have Tommy; for he is a bad man. And I can have none else.' She added, 'Sir, you don't know the danger you are in. I beg you would speak no word more on this head.' And after a while, 'When others have spoken to me on the subject, I felt an aversion to them. But I don't feel any to you. We may converse on other subjects as freely as ever.' Both my judgment and will acquiesced in what she said, and we ended our conversation with a psalm.

Sat. 30. In the afternoon we landed on Bear Island, and walked together for near two hours. Here again Miss Sophy expressed the strongest uneasiness, and an utter aversion to living at Mr. Causton's, saying, with many tears, 'I can't live in that house: I can't bear the shocks I meet with there.' I said, 'Don't be uneasy, Miss Sophy, on that account. If you don't care to be at Mr. Causton's, you are welcome to a room in our house; or, which I think would be best of all, and your aunt once proposed it, you may live in the house with the Germans.' She made little reply.

About five we took our boat again, and in the evening came to Rattonpossom, another uninhabited island about thirty miles from Savannah. Here our provisions failed; neither could we find any firewood, except one old stump of a tree, nor so much as two or three stakes to prop up our sail. Miss Sophy hung her apron on two small sticks, which kept off a little of the north wind from her head, and lay down on the ground under the canopy of heaven, with all the signs of perfect content.

Sun. 31. We came to Thunderbolt. Here we agreed that I should walk to Savannah and meet her at the landing. She went to Mr. Causton's directly. About five Mr. Causton came to my house, largely protesting his obligations to me, and repeated again and again that whatever I desired with regard to Miss Sophy he would consent to. After talking again with her upon it, I desired, (1) that she should come to my house every morning and evening; (2) that at his house she should come into no company but by her own choice; (3) that she should be no more upbraided with Mellichamp, nor should he be mentioned before her.

Nov. 1, Mon. She was eighteen years old. And from the beginning of our intimate acquaintance till this day, I verily believe she used no guile: not only because even now I know no instance to the contrary, nor only because the simplicity of her behavior was a constant voucher for her sincerity; but because of the entire openness of all her conversation, answering whatever questions I proposed, without either hesitation or reserve, immediately and directly. Another thing I was much pleased with in her was, that whenever we were conversing or reading, there was such a stillness in her whole behavior, scarce stirring hand or foot, that 'she seemed to be, all but her attention, dead.' Yet at other times she was all life—active, diligent, indefatigable; always doing something, and doing with all her might whatever her hand found to do. For indeed, if the weakness of her body did not, her sense of honor would not hinder her doing anything.

Nor did she at all favor herself on account of that weakness; she could not remove, she would not indulge it. Softness and tenderness of this kind she would not know, having left the delicacy of the gentlewoman in England. She utterly despised those inconveniences which women of condition in England would think worse than death. With bread to eat and water to drink she was content; indeed she never used any drink beside water. She was patient of labor, of cold, heat, wet, or badness of food or of want; and of pain to an eminent degree, it never making any alteration in her speech or behavior, so that her frequent headache was only to be discerned by her paleness and dullness of her eyes.

Little of a gentlewoman in delicacy and niceness, she was still less so, if possible, in love of dress. No philosopher would have despised her love of adornment. Though always neat, she was always plain. And she was equally careless of finery in other things. It was use she considered, not show; nor novelty either, being as little concerned for new as for fine or pretty things. The same disregard she had for what are called diversions, such as balls, dancing, visiting; having no desire either to see or be seen, unless in order to be wiser and better.

Not that her love of retirement or want of curiosity was owing, as some supposed, to want of sense. Her constant, even seriousness was very far from stupidity. Indeed, her understanding was not of a piece with her years. Though unimproved, it was deep and strong. It reached the highest things and the lowest. It rose to the greatest, yet stooped to the least. With fine sense she had a large share of common sense, and particularly of prudence, suiting herself readily to all persons and occasions, nature in her supplying the place of experience. Her apprehension was so quick that there was scarce ever need to repeat a thing twice to her, and so clear as to conceive things the most remote from common life without any mistake or confusion. But she was by no means fond of showing her sense; seldom speaking when she could decently avoid it, and then in few words, but such as were clear and pertinent, and contained much in little compass. One reason of her speaking so seldom was the mean opinion she had of herself, particularly of her own understanding, which was also the great cause of her constant eagerness for instruction, and indeed for improvement of every kind, as she was very sensible of her want of all. Hence too it was that she was so teachable in things either of a speculative or practical nature, so readily convinced of any error in her judgment or oversight in her behavior, and so easily persuaded to lay aside her own designs or measures and pursue those which others advised. Indeed, one would almost have thought she had no such ingredient in her nature as self-will.

As her humility was, so was her meekness. She seemed to have been born without anger. Her soul appeared to be wholly made up of mildness, gentleness, longsuffering. Then especially, when she had to do with those who had injured her beyond the manner of men, she stayed for no entreaty before she forgave; but of one thing she was not easily convinced, that any one needed her forgiveness or had done ill either to her or any other. She was with difficulty induced to believe any evil which she did not see. And even when she could not help believing, still she took care 'to speak evil of no man.'

And as her greatest enemies, so much more the greatest strangers had a share in her good will and affection. She was a friend to human kind. To whomever was distressed she was all sympathy, tenderness, compassion. But to any whom she particularly called a friend her behavior can only be conceived, not expressed. Such was the spirit of gratitude that ran through it; such the softness, the sweetness of every part of it; yet still preserving in all that yielding easiness a modesty pure as the light.

The temper of her heart towards God is best known by Him 'who seeth in secret.' What appeared of it was a deep, even reverence, ripening into love, and a resignation unshaken in one of the severest wrung from her a murmuring word. She saw the hand of God and was still. She said indeed, 'If it be possible, Father!' But added, 'Not as I will, but as Thou wilt!'

Such was the woman, according to my closest observation, of whom I now began to be much afraid. My desire and design still was to live single; but how long it would continue I knew not. I therefore consulted my friends whether it was not best to break off all intercourse with her immediately. They expressed themselves so ambiguously that I understood them to mean that I ought not to break it off. And accordingly she came to me (as had been agreed) every morning and evening.

The time she was at my house was spent thus. Immediately after breakfast we all joined in Hickes's *Devotions*. She was then alone till eight. I taught her French between eight and nine, and at nine we joined in prayer again. She then read or wrote French till ten. In the evening I read to her and some others select parts of Ephrem Syrus, and afterwards Dean Young's and Mr. Reeve's *Sermons*. We always concluded with a psalm.

This I began with a single eye. But it was not long before I found it a task too hard for me to preserve the same intention with which I began, in such intimacy of conversation as ours was. . . .

January 1737

Mon. 31. After having been detained several days on Sapolo Island by mists and contrary winds, at last I came to Savannah. Finding Miss Sophy was with Mrs. Musgrove at the Cowpen, a place where I doubted she would learn little good, I went up thither the same evening. She took boat and came down with me immediately, as it was not her custom to deny me anything. For indeed from March 13, 1736, the day I first spoke to her, till that hour, I cannot recollect so much as a single instance of my proposing anything to her, or expressing any desire, which she did not fully comply with.

Feb. 1, Tues. Being the anniversary feast, on account of the first convoy's landing in Georgia, we had a sermon and the Holy Communion.

The next morning, being informed of Miss Bovey's design to marry shortly, I went to her, and told her with all plainness my thoughts of Mr. Burnside and of the whole affair. Though we did not entirely agree in our judgment, she took it as it was intended. Here is one woman in America in whom to this day I have found no guile.

Thurs. 3. I was now in a great strait. I still thought it best for me to live single. And this was still my design; but I felt the foundations of it shaken more and more every day. Insomuch that I again hinted at a desire of marriage, though I made no direct proposal. For indeed it was only a sudden thought, which had not the consent of my own mind. Yet I firmly believe, had she (Miss Sophy) closed with me at that time, my judgment would have made but a faint resistance. But she said 'she thought it was best for clergymen not to be encumbered with worldly cares, and that it was best for her, too, to live single, and she was accordingly resolved never to marry.' I used no argument to induce her to alter her resolution.

Upon reflection, I thought this a very narrow escape; and after much consideration, I went to Mr. Toltschig, the pastor of the Moravians, and desired his advice, whether I had not best, while it was yet in my power, break off so dangerous an acquaintance. He asked, 'What do you think would be the consequence if you should?' I said, 'I fear her soul would be lost, being surrounded with dangers, and having no other person to warn her of and arm her against them.' He added, 'And what do you think would be the consequence if you should not break it off?' I said, 'I fear I should marry her.' He replied short, 'I don't see why you should not.'

The Resigned Self

I went home amazed to the last degree; and it was now first that I had the least doubt whether it was best for me to marry or not, which I never before thought would bear a question. I immediately related what had occurred to Mr. Ingham and Delamotte. They utterly disapproved of Mr. Toltschig's judgment, and in the evening went, as I desired they would, and talked largely with him and Antone (the Moravian Bishop Seifart) about it. It was midnight when I went to them; but even then they did not seem to be fully assured. Mr. Ingham still insisted I had not sufficient proof of her sincerity and religion, since the appearance of it might be owing partly to an excellent natural temper, partly to her desire of marrying me. I asked, 'How he could reconcile such a desire with what she had said on Thursday.' He said, 'Very well; she would soon recall those words, if I made a direct proposal.' He added that I could not judge coolly of these things while I saw her every day, and therefore advised me 'to go out of town for a few days.' I clearly saw the wisdom of this advice, and accordingly went to Irene the next day, four miles from Savannah. But first I wrote two or three lines which I desired Miss Bovey to give Miss Sophy. They were, I think, in these words: '*Feb. 6.* I find, Miss Sophy, I can't take fire into my bosom, and not be burnt. I am therefore retiring for a while to desire the direction of God. Join with me, my friend, in fervent prayer, that He would show me what is best to be done.'

When I came to Irene, I did not care to ask counsel of God immediately, being 'a man of so unclean lips.' I therefore set aside *Monday* the 7th for self-examination; adding only that general prayer, whenever thoughts arose in my heart concerning the issue of things, 'Lord, Thou knowest! If it be best, let nothing be allowed to hinder; if not, let nothing be allowed to affect it.' And this exercise I continued for several hours with some measure of cheerfulness. But towards evening God hid His face, and I was troubled. My heart sank in me like a stone. I felt how bitter a thing it is for a spirit of an unbounded appetite to be left a prey to its own desires. But it was not long. For I no sooner stretched forth my hands to Heaven and bewailed my having departed from Him, than God sent me help from His holy place, and my soul received comfort.

Tues. 8. The next morning I was obliged to go down to Savannah. There I stayed about an hour; and there again I felt, and groaned under the weight of, an unholy desire. My heart was with Miss Sophy all the time. I longed to see her, were it but for a moment. And when I was called to take boat, it was as the sentence of death; but believing it was the call of God, I obeyed. I walked awhile to and fro on the edge of the water, heavy laden and pierced through with many sorrows. There One came to me and said, 'You are still in doubt what is best to be done. First, then, cry to God, that you may be wholly resigned, whatever shall appear to be His will.' I instantly cried to God for resignation. And I found that and peace together. I said, 'Sure it is a dream.' I was in a new world. The change was as from death to life. I went back to Irene wondering and rejoicing;

but withal exceeding fearful, lest my want of thankfulness for this blessing, or of care to improve it, might occasion its being taken away.

I was now more clear in my judgment every day. Beside that I believed her resolve, never to marry, I was convinced it was not expedient for me, for two weighty reasons: (1) because it would probably obstruct the design of my coming into America, the going among the Indians; and (2) because I was not strong enough to bear the complicated temptations of a married state.

Sat. 12. Of this informed my friends at my return to Savannah.

Mon. 14. About seven in the morning, I told her in my own garden, 'I am resolved, Miss Sophy, if I marry at all, not to do it till I have been among the Indians.'

Tues. 15. The next morning she told me, 'People wonder what I can do so long at your house; I am resolved not to breakfast with you any more. And I won't come to you any more alone.'

Wed. 16. She said, 'I don't think it signifies for me to learn French any longer.' But she added, 'My uncle and aunt, as well as I, will be glad of your coming to our house as often as you please.' I answered, 'You know, Miss Sophy, I don't love a crowd, and there is always one there.' She said, 'But we needn't be in it.'. . .

Calling at Mrs. Causton's (Saturday 16th), she was there alone. This was indeed an hour of trial. Her words, her eyes, her air, her every motion and gesture, were full of such a softness and sweetness! I know not what might have been the consequence had I then but touched her hand. And how I avoided it I know not. Surely God is over all!

Sun. 27. After all the company but Miss Sophy was gone, Mr. Delamotte went out and left us alone again. Finding her still the same, my resolution failed. At the end of a very serious conversation, I took her by the hand, and, perceiving she was not displeased, I was so utterly disarmed, that that hour I should have engaged myself for life, had it not been for the full persuasion I had of her entire sincerity, and in consequence of which I doubted not but she was resolved (as she had said) 'never to marry while she lived.'

A moment's reflection when she was gone convinced me that I had done foolishly. And I once more resolved by God's help to be more wary for the future. Accordingly, though I saw her every day in the following week, I touched her not. Yet on Thursday evening (March 3), after we came from her, Mr. Delamotte was deeply concerned. I had never seen him in such uneasiness before. He said, with many tears, 'He found we must part, for he could not live in that house when I was married to Miss Sophy.' I told him, 'I had no intention to marry her.' He said, 'I did not know my own heart; but he saw clearly it

The Resigned Self

would come to that very soon, unless I broke off all intercourse with her.' I told him, 'This was a point of great importance, and therefore not to be determined suddenly.' He said, 'I ought to determine as soon as possible; for I was losing ground daily.' I felt what he said to be true, and therefore easily consented to set aside the next day for that purpose.

March 4, Fri. Having both of us sought God by deep consideration, fasting, and prayer, in the afternoon we conferred together, but could not come to any decision. We both apprehended Mr. Ingham's objection to be the strongest, the doubt whether she was what she appeared. But this doubt was too hard for us to solve. At length we agreed to appeal to the Searcher of hearts. I accordingly made three lots. In one was written 'Marry'; in the second, 'Think not of it this year.' After we had prayed to God to 'give a perfect lot,' Mr. Delamotte drew the third, in which were these words, 'Think of it no more.' Instead of the agony I had reason to expect, I was enabled to say cheerfully, 'Thy will be done.' We cast lots once again to know whether I ought to converse with her any more; and the direction I received from God was, 'Only in presence of Mr. Delamotte.'

I saw and adored the goodness of God, though what He required of me was a costly sacrifice. It was indeed the giving up at once whatever this world affords of agreeable—not only honor, fortune, power (which indeed were nothing to me, who despised them as the clay in the streets), but all the truly desirable conveniences of life—a pleasant house, a delightful garden, on the brow of a hill at a small distance from the town; another house and garden in the town; and a third a few miles off, with a large tract of fruitful land adjoining to it. And above all, what to me made all things else vile and utterly beneath a thought, such a companion as I never expected to find again, should I live one thousand years twice told. So that I could not but cry out: *O Lord God, Thou God of my fathers, plenteous in mercy and truth, behold I give Thee, not thousands of rams or ten thousands of rivers of oil, but the desire of my eyes, the joy of my heart, the one thing upon earth which I longed for! O give me Wisdom, which sitteth by Thy throne, and reject me not from among Thy children! . . .*

Mon. 7. Mr. Causton asked me to ride with him to his plantation, four miles from Savannah. I was quite struck with the pleasantness of the situation: the hill, the river, the woods, were delightful, and shot a softness into my soul which had not left me when at our return he asked me to drink a dish of tea at his house. Soon after I came in, Miss Sophy went out and walked to and fro between the door and the garden. I saw she wanted to speak to me, but remembered my resolutions, especially that to converse with her only in Mr. Delamotte's presence. Yet after a short struggle, the evil soul prevailed in me, and I went. Immediately she caught hold of both my hands, and with the most engaging gesture, look, and tone of voice said, 'You never denied me anything that I desired yet and you shall not deny me what I desire now.' I said, 'Miss Sophy, I will not; what is it?' She answered, 'Don't say anything to her that offered me the letter the other day. My refusing it has given her pain enough already.' I replied, 'I will not. And if you had told me of it before, I would not have told your uncle of it, as Mr. Williamson did.' She said, 'Did he? Well, I find what you have often said is true. There is no trusting any but a Christian. And for my part, I am resolved never to trust any one again who is not so.' I looked upon her, and should have said too much had we had a moment longer. But in the instant Mr. Causton called us in. So I was once more 'snatched as a brand out of the fire.'

Tues. 8. Miss Sophy and Mr. Delamotte breakfasting with me, I asked her what she now thought of Mr. Mellichamp. She said, 'I thank God I have entirely conquered that inclination.' After some serious conversation interposed, I said, 'I hear Mr. Williamson pays his addresses to you. Is it true?' She said, after a little pause, 'If it were not I would have told you so.' I asked, 'How do you like him?' She replied, 'I don't know; there is a great deal in being in the house with one. But I have no inclination for him.' I said, 'Miss Sophy, if you ever deceive me, I shall scarce ever believe any one again.' She looked up at me and answered with a smile, 'You will never have that reason for distrusting any one; I shall never deceive you.' When she was going away, she turned back and said, 'Of one thing, sir, be assured: I will never take any step in anything of importance without first consulting you.'

She went, and I saw myself in the toils. But how to escape I saw not. If I continued to converse with her, though not alone, I found I should love her more and more. And the time to break it off was past. I felt it was now beyond my strength. My resolutions indeed remained. But how long? Yet a little longer, till another shock of temptation, and then I well knew they would break in sunder as a thread of tow that has touched the fire. I had many times prayed that if it was best our intercourse should break off, and that if I could not do it she might. But this too I saw less and less reason to expect. So that all these things were against me, and I lay struggling in the net; nay, scarcely struggling, as even fearing to be delivered.

After evening prayers, Miss Bovey came (as usual) to my house, with Miss Sophy, who was in the utmost consternation. She begged me to go and pacify her aunt. I went and found Mrs. Causton in great disorder, with an open letter in her hand, which she gave me to read, telling me she had just intercepted it. It was written by Mr. Mellichamp to Miss Sophy. I told her I hoped things were not so ill as she apprehended; and when she was a little more composed, I went at her desire to make some further inquiries. In half an hour I returned and found Mrs. Causton chiding Miss Sophy very sharply. Some of her expressions were, 'Get you out of my house; I will be plagued with you no longer.' And turning to me she said, 'Mr. Wesley, I wish you would take her; take her away with you.' I said, 'Miss Sophy answered only with tears. About ten I went home, though with such an unwillingness and heaviness as I had scarce ever felt before.'

Wed. 9. About ten I called on Mrs. Causton. She said, 'Sir, Mr. Causton and I are exceedingly obliged to your for all the pains you have taken about Sophy. And so is Sophy too; and she desires you would publish the banns of marriage between her and Mr. Williamson on Sunday.' She added, 'Sir, you don't seem to be well pleased. Have you any objection to it?' I answered, 'Madam, I don't seem to be awake. Surely I am in a dream.' She said, 'They agreed on it last night between themselves after you were gone. And afterwards Mr. Williamson asked Mr. Causton's and my consent, which we gave him; but if you have any objection to it, pray speak. Speak to her. She is at the Lot. Go to her. She will be very glad to hear anything Mr. Wesley has to say. Pray go to her and talk to her yourself.' I said, 'No, madam; if Miss Sophy is engaged, I have nothing to say. It will not signify for me to see her anymore.' I then offered to leave; but she pressed me to stay, at least till the rain was over. The burden of her conversation was still, 'Why are you uneasy?' and 'Go and talk with her yourself.'

I doubted whether all this were not artifice, merely designed to quicken me. But though I was uneasy at the very thought of her marrying one who, I believed, would make her very unhappy, yet I could not resolve to save her from him by marrying her myself. Besides, I reasoned thus, 'Either she is engaged or not; if she is, I would not have her if I might: if not, there is nothing in this show which ought to alter my preceding resolution.'

Thus was I saved purely by my ignorance; for though I did doubt, I would not believe. I thought it unkind and unjust to believe an artifice of which I had not full proof. Oh, let no one ever fear the being lost by thinking no evil! Had I known the snare, I had perished thereby. All the world could not have saved me. Had I then seen the real case to be this—'She is engaged, but conditionally only. Mr. Williamson shall marry her if you will not'—I could not have stood that shock. I should have incurred any loss rather than she should have run that hazard, of losing both her body and soul in hell.

From Mrs. Causton I went home full of perplexity. After some time spent in prayer, I desired Mr. Delamotte to go to the Lot, and ask if my company would be agreeable. In the meantime, seeing nothing but clouds before me, I had recourse to the oracles of God. I received two answers. The first was, 'Blessed be thou of the Lord, my daughter; for thou hast showed more kindness at the latter end than at the beginning.' The other (which was part of the Morning Lesson on Saturday, August 27, following the Court-day on which I expected my trial) was in these words: 'If I be an offender or have committed anything worthy of death, I refuse not to die. But if there be none of these things whereof they accuse me, no man may deliver me unto them.'

Soon after Mr. Delamotte came back I went. Mr. Williamson and she were together. She began with her usual sweetness, 'Why would you put yourself to the trouble of sending? What need of that ceremony between us? You know your company is always welcome to me.' Then silence ensued, which Mr. Williamson broke thus: 'I suppose, sir, you know what was agreed on last night between Miss Sophy and me.' I answered, 'I have heard something; but I could not believe it, unless I should hear it from Miss Sophy herself.' She replied, 'Sir, I have given Mr. Williamson my consent—unless you have anything to object.' It started into my mind, 'What if she means, unless you will marry me?' But I checked the thought with, 'Miss Sophy is so sincere: if she meant so, she would say so'; and replied, 'If you have given your consent, the time is past; I have nothing to object.' Mr. Williamson desired me, if I had, to speak, and then left her and me together. 'Tis hard to describe the complication of passions and tumult of thought which I then felt: fear of her approaching misery, and tender pity; grief for my own loss; love shooting through all the recesses of my soul, and sharpening every thought and passion. Underneath there was a faint desire to do and suffer the will of God, which, joined to a doubt whether that proposal would be accepted, was just strong enough to prevent my saying plainly (what I wonder to this hour I did not say), 'Miss Sophy, will you marry me?' As soon as I could speak, I reminded her of her resolution, 'If she married at all, to marry one but a religious man,' and desired her to consider whether Mr. Williamson was such. She said, 'She had no proof to the contrary.' I told her, 'That was not enough. Before she staked so much upon it, she ought to have full, positive proof that he was religious.' She said again, 'I no otherwise consented, than if you had nothing to object.' Little more was said, tears in both supplying the place of words. More than an hour was spent thus. About two Mr. Williamson came again. I think it was just as he came she said, 'I hope I shall always have your friendship.' I answered, 'I can still be your friend, though I should not stay in America.' She said, 'But I hope you won't leave us.' I said, 'I can't at all judge how God will dispose of me.' She added, 'However, you will let me have your correspondence?' I replied, 'I doubt it cannot be.' I then exhorted them both to 'assist each other in serving God with all their strength'; and her in particular 'to remember the many instructions and advices I had given her.' I kissed them both, and took my leave of her as one I was to see no more.

I came home and went into my garden. I walked up and down, seeking rest but finding none. From the beginning of my life to this hour I had not known one such as this. God let loose my inordinate affection upon me, and the poison thereof drank up my spirit. I was as stupid as if half awake, and yet in the sharpest pain I ever felt. To see her no more: that thought was as the piercings of a sword; it was not to be borne, nor shaken off. I was weary of the world, of light, of life. Yet one way remained, to seek to God—a very present help in time of trouble. And I did seek after God, but I found Him not. I forsook Him before: now He forsook me. I could not pray. Then indeed the snares of death

The Resigned Self

were about me; the pains of hell overtook me. Yet I struggled for life; and though I had neither words nor thoughts, I lifted up my eyes to the Prince that is highly exalted, and supplied the place of them as I could: and about four o'clock He so far took the cup from me that I drank so deeply of it no more.

Soon after I wrote a note to Mr. Causton, who came to me about five o'clock and told me, 'I don't approve of this match. Mr. Williamson asked my consent this morning; but I have neither denied nor given it. Indeed I have often promised Sophy, so she would not have Mellichamp, she should have whom she would beside. But what passed between her and you at the Lot?' I told him without any disguise. He said, 'If you loved her, how could you possibly be so overseen as not to press her when she was so much moved?' He added, 'I will tell her my thoughts of it once more, and, if you please, so may you. But if she is not then convinced I must leave her to herself.'

Had he then said plainly, 'If you please, you may have her still; but if you won't, another will,' I know not what might have been the event; or had Mr. Delamotte left us alone, when she came to my house after evening prayers. Mr. Williamson begged her not to stay after the rest of the company. But she did very readily. He walked to and fro on the outside of the house, with all the signs of strong uneasiness. I told her, 'Miss Sophy, you said yesterday you would take no steps in anything of importance without first consulting me.' She answered earnestly and many times over, 'Why, what could I do? I can't live in that house. I can't bear these shocks. This is quite a sudden thing. I have no particular inclination for Mr. Williamson. I only promised if no objection appeared. But what can I do?' Mr. Williamson, coming in abruptly, took her away, and put a short end to our conversation.

However, in the morning I called once more at Mr. Causton's and desired to speak with her. Mr. Williamson told me, 'Sir, you shall speak with her no more till we are married. You can persuade her to anything. After you went from the Lot yesterday, she would neither eat nor drink for two hours; but was crying continually, and in such an agony she was fit for nothing.' I said, 'Tomorrow, sir, you may be her director, but today she is to direct herself.' I desired a piece of paper and wrote these words, 'Miss Sophy, will you see me or not?' Mr. Causton bade Mrs. Causton carry it up, and Miss Sophy immediately came down. We went into the garden and I asked, 'Are you fully determined?' She said, 'I am.' I replied, 'Take care you act upon a right motive. The desire of avoiding crosses is not so. Beside, you can't avoid them. They will follow and overtake you in every state.' Mr. Williamson then coming to us, I advised them to have the banns regularly published, exhorted them to love and serve God, told them they might always depend on my friendship and assistance, and went home easy and satisfied.

In the afternoon Mr. Delamotte and I went to the Lot, where I read them Bishop Hall's *Meditation on Heaven*; during which Miss Sophy fixed her eyes on Mr. Williamson and me alternately for above half an hour, with as steady an observation as if she had been drawing our pictures. Mr. Williamson afterwards told me, 'He should always be glad of my advice, and hoped I would still favor them with my conversation, which he should look upon as a particular happiness both to her and him.' I answered, 'I hope we shall all be happy in the place we have been reading of.' Of which indeed I had so strong a persuasion that I returned rejoicing and wondering at myself. The next morning she set out for Purrysburg, and on Saturday, March 12, 1737, was married there; this being the day which completed the year from my first speaking to her! . . .

January 1738

On *Monday* the 9th, and the following days, I reflected much on that vain desire, which had pursued me for so many years, of being in solitude in order to be a Christian. I have now, thought I, solitude enough. But am I therefore the nearer being a Christian? Not if Jesus Christ be the model of Christianity. I doubt, indeed, I am much nearer that mystery of Satan which some writers affect to call by that name, so near, that I had probably sunk wholly into it, had not the great mercy of God just now thrown me upon reading St. Cyprian's works. 'O my soul, come not thou into their secret!' Stand thou in the good old paths. . . .

Suggestions for Further Reading

Henry Bett, *The Spirit of Methodism* (London: Epworth Press, 1943).

Mabel Richmond Brailsford, *A Tale of Two Brothers: John and Charles Wesley* (London: Hart-Davis, 1954).

Sidney R. Brett, *John Wesley* (London: A. and C. Black, 1958).

Robert W. Burtner and Robert E. Chiles, eds., *A Compendium of Wesley's Theology* (Nashville: Abingdon Press, 1954).

William Ragsdale Cannon, *The Theology of John Wesley* (New York: Abingdon Press, 1946).

Horton Davies, *Worship and Theology in England, from Watts and Wesley to Maurice, 1690-1850* (Princeton: Princeton University Press, 1961), esp. pp. 143-209.

Bonamy Dobree, *Three Eighteenth Century Figures: Sara Churchill, John Wesley, and Giacomo Casanova* (New York: Oxford University Press, 1962).

Vivian H. H. Green, *John Wesley* (London: Nelson, 1964).

Ingvar Haddal, *John Wesley: A Biography* (Nashville: Abingdon Press, 1961).

F.E. Maser, "Preface to Victory: An Analysis of John Wesley's Mission to Georgia," *Religion in Life*, XXV (1956), pp. 280-93.

Francis J. McConnell, *John Wesley* (New York: Abingdon Press, 1939).

E. Gordon Rupp, *Six Makers of English Religion, 1500-1700* (London: Hodder and Stroughton, 1957).

Martin Schmidt, *John Wesley: A Theological Biography*, trans. Norman P. Goldhawk (Nashville: Abingdon Press, 1963).

L. Tyerman, *Life and Times of John Wesley*. 3 vols. (New York: Harper, 1872).

William Cowper

Memoir

I was enabled to trust in him that
careth for the stranger, to roll my
burden upon him, and to rest assured
that wherever he might cast my lot
the God of all consolation would
still be with me.

William Cowper's memoir is based primarily on his attempted suicide and subsequent commitment to an asylum. John N. Morris has described it as an account of "his passage through madness and despair to faith and relative (and temporary) serenity." Attempted suicides generally prompt us to ask what precipitated the crisis and why the attempted self-destruction failed. A brief account of Cowper's life prior to his suicide attempt at the age of 32 will not enable us to answer these questions, but it will help us to view this attempted act of self-destruction within the context of his total history.

Cowper, a poet and hymn writer, was born in 1731. His father, an Anglican clergyman, was chaplain to George II. Cowper's mother died when he was six years old, and his father immediately placed him in a boarding school in London. When he was 18 he entered law college. While studying law he began to experience the extreme dejection and melancholy that clouded his whole adult life. After a year of struggling unsuccessfully against despair, he accompanied friends to Southhampton for an extended vacation. One morning in the course of this vacation he suddenly felt his "sorrow and vexation of spirit" dispelled. He attributed this improvement, however, to "nothing but a change of scene and the amusing varieties of the place." Later, he perceived that this initial misinterpretation of his improvement was the work of Satan and felt instead that the experience revealed the "life-giving countenance" of God.

On his return to London, Cowper engaged in a variety of activities, including work on translations of Horace and Voltaire. But the most significant indication of his improved spirits was his romantic attachment to his cousin

Theodora. However, her father opposed the match on the grounds of Cowper's lack of professional prospects and his mental instability. In the same year that his relationship to Theodora was thwarted (1756) Cowper's father died, leaving him a modest inheritance, which dwindled in the course of the next few years. In 1763 a relative, Major William Cowper, came to his assistance and offered him a patronage position as Clerk of the Journals of the House of Lords. Cowper's attempted suicide occurred on the day prior to the qualifying examinations for the position. This was only the first of a number of episodes in his life when the fear of imminent professional or familial commitments precipitated a mental crisis. It happened again, for example, prior to his proposed marriage in 1773.

Besides demonstrating his lack of self-confidence in the face of professional responsibility, the appointment to the clerkship also precipitated in Cowper a severe sense of guilt. He had expressed the wish for the death of the incumbent clerk so that he (Cowper) "might be provided for," and hence he felt he had coveted the post "in the spirit of a murderer." Morris suggests, therefore, that "Cowper's autobiography may be described as an account of the attempt to wrest meaning from the experience of guilt." Intensely guilt-ridden, Cowper felt himself "totally dependent on and totally hopeless of God's mercy."

This sense of dependence on God is also revealed in his relations with other people. It was reflected in his lifelong financial reliance on friends and relatives. On the other hand, his personal relationships were also marked by a profound hopelessness, beginning with his father's decision to send him to boarding school the same year his mother died. But perhaps hopelessness is not a sufficiently strong word to capture Cowper's despair. Morris sees in his extreme anxiety, as he anticipated the examination before the House of Lords, an inordinate "terror" in the face of paternal authority. This terror was evident in his violent struggle, during and following his attempted suicide, to overcome a persistent notion that he was predestined to eternal damnation.

Cowper's passage from despair to faith depended, therefore, on his capacity to perceive the "life-giving countenance" of God behind the threat of abandonment. As he wrote in a poem: "The clouds ye so much dread are big with mercy.... Behind a frowning Providence He hides a smiling face." Such moments of faith, however, were infrequent clearings in a life predominantly clouded with despair. In 1796, four years before his death, he gradually sank into a lethargy and depression from which he never emerged.

Memoir

The Hellish Purpose of Self-Murder

I cannot recollect that till the month of December in the thirty-second year of my life I had ever any serious impressions of the religious kind or at all

From Maurice J. Quinlan, "Memoir of William Cowper: An Autobiography Edited with an Introduction," *Proceedings of the American Philosophical Society*, Vol. 97, No. 4 (1953), pp. 359-382. Excerpts. Published by the American Philosophical Society. Reprinted by permission.

bethought myself of the things of my salvation, except in two or three instances. . . .

[But at] this time, my patrimony being well spent and there being no appearance that I should ever repair the damage by a fortune of my own getting, I began to be a little apprehensive of approaching want. It was, I imagine, under some apprehensions of this kind that I one day said to a friend of mine, if the clerk to the journals of the House of Lords should die I had some hopes that my kinsman who had the place in his disposal would appoint me to succeed him. We both agreed that the business of that place, being transacted in private, would exactly suit me, and both expressed an earnest wish for his death that I might be provided for. Thus did I covet what God had commanded me not to covet and involved myself in still deeper guilt by doing it in the spirit of a murderer. It pleased the Lord to give me my heart's desire and with it an immediate punishment for my crime. The poor man died and by his death not only the clerkship of the journals became vacant but it became necessary to appoint officers to two other places jointly as deputies to Mr. De Grey, who at this time resigned. These were the office of reading clerk and the clerkship of the committees—of much greater value than that of the journals. The patentee of these appointments (whom I pray to God to bless for his benevolent intention to serve me) called on me at my chambers and having invited me to take a turn with him in the garden there made me an offer of the two most profitable places, intending the other for his friend. . . . Dazzled by so splendid a proposal and not immediately reflecting upon my incapacity to execute a business of so public a nature, I at once accepted it, but at the same time (such was the will of Him whose hand was in the whole matter) seemed to receive a dagger in my heart. The wound was given and every moment added to the smart of it. All the considerations by which I endeavored to compose my mind to its former tranquillity did but torment me the more, proving miserable comforters and counsellors of no value. I returned to my chambers thoughtful and unhappy; my countenance fell; and my friend was astonished, instead of that additional cheerfulness he might so reasonably expect, to find an air of deep melancholy in all I said or did.

Having been harassed in this manner by day and night for the space of a week, perplexed between the apparent folly of casting away the only visible chance I had of being well provided for and the impossibility of retaining it, I determined at length to write a letter to my friend, though he lodged in a manner at the next door and we generally spent the day together. I did so and therein begged him to accept my resignation and to appoint Mr. A. to the places he had given me, and permit me to succeed Mr. A. I was well aware of the disproportion between the value of his appointment and mine; but my peace was gone; pecuniary advantages were not equivalent to what I had lost; and I flattered myself that the clerkship of the journals would fall fairly and easily within the scope of my abilities. Like a man in a fever, I thought a change of posture would relieve my pain, and, as the event will show, was equally disappointed. At length I carried my point—my friend in this instance preferring the gratification of my desires to his own interest, for nothing could be so likely to bring a suspicion of bargain and sale upon his nomination, which the Lords would not have endured, as his appointment of so near a relative to the least profitable office while the most valuable was allotted to a stranger.

The matter being thus settled, something like a calm took place in my mind. I was indeed not a little concerned about my character, being aware that it must needs suffer by the strange appearance of my proceedings. This, however, being but a small part of the anxiety I had laboured under, was hardly felt when the rest was taken off. I thought my path to an easy maintenance was now plain and open and for a day or two was tolerably cheerful. But behold the storm was gathering all the while, and the fury of it was not the less violent for this gleam of sunshine.

In the beginning a strong opposition to my friend's right of nomination began to show itself. A powerful party was formed among the Lords to thwart it in favor of an old enemy of the family, though one much indebted to its bounty; and it appeared plain that if we succeeded at last it would only be by fighting our ground by inches. Every advantage I was told would be sought for and eagerly seized to disconcert us. I was bid to expect an examination at the bar of the House touching my sufficiency for the post I had taken. Being necessarily ignorant of the nature of that business, it became expedient that I should visit the office daily in order to qualify myself for the strictest scrutiny. All the horror of my fears and perplexities now returned. A thunderbolt would have been as welcome to me as this intelligence. I knew to demonstration that upon these terms the clerkship of the journals was no place for me. To require my attendance at the bar of the House that I might there publicly entitle myself to the office was in effect to exclude me from it. In the meantime the interest of my friend, the honor of his choice, my own reputation and circumstances all urged me forward; all pressed me to undertake that which I saw to be impracticable. They whose spirits are formed like mine to whom a public examination of themselves on any occasion is mortal poison may have some idea of the horrors of my situation; others can have none.

My continual misery at length brought on a nervous fever: quiet forsook me by day and peace by night; a finger raised against me was more than I could stand against. In this posture of mind I attended regularly at the office, where, instead of a soul upon the rack, the most active spirits were essentially necessary for my purpose. I expected no assistance from anybody there, all the inferior clerks being under the influence of my opponent, and accordingly I received none. The journal books were indeed thrown open to me—a thing which could not be refused, and from which perhaps a man in health and with a head turned to business might have gained all the information he wanted—but it was not so with me. I read without perception and was so distressed that had every clerk in the office been my friend it could have availed me little, for I was not in a condition to receive instruction, much less to elicit it out of manuscripts without direction. Many months went over me thus employed—constant in the use of means, despairing as to the issue.

The feelings of a man when he arrives at the place of execution are probably much like mine every time I set my foot in the office, which was every day for more than half a year together.

At length, the vacation being pretty far advanced, I made shift to get into the country and repaired to Margate. There by the help of cheerful company, a new scene, and the intermission of my painful employment I presently began to recover my spirits, though even here for sometime after my arrival (notwithstanding perhaps that the preceding day had been spent agreeably and without any disturbing recollection of my circumstances) my first reflections when I awoke in the morning were horrible and full of wretchedness. I looked forward to the approaching winter and regretted the flight of every moment which brought it nearer like a man borne away by a rapid torrent into a stormy sea whence he sees no possibility of returning and where he knows he cannot subsist. At length, indeed, I acquired such a facility of turning away my thoughts from the ensuing crisis that for weeks together I hardly adverted to it at all, but the stress of the tempest was yet to come and was not to be avoided by any resolution of mine to look another way.

"How wonderful are the works of the Lord and his ways past finding out!" Thus was he preparing me for an event which I least of all expected—even the reception of his blessed gospel working by means which in all human contemplation must needs seem directly opposite to that purpose but which in his wise and gracious disposal have, I trust, effectually accomplished it.

About the beginning of October, 1763, I was again required to attend the office and prepare for the push. This no sooner took place than all my misery returned; again I visited the scene of ineffectual labours; again I felt myself pressed by necessity on either side with nothing but despair in prospect. To this dilemma was I reduced: either to keep possession of the office to the last extremity and by so doing expose myself to a public rejection for insufficiency (for the little knowledge I had acquired would have quite forsaken me at the bar of the House); or else to fling it up at once and, by this means, run the hazard of ruining my benefactor's right of appointment by bringing his discretion into question. In this situation such a fit of passion has sometimes seized me when alone in my chambers that I have cried out aloud and cursed the hour of my birth, lifting up my eyes to heaven at the same time not as a suppliant but in the hellish spirit of rancorous reproach and blasphemy against my Maker. A thought would sometimes come across my mind that my sins had perhaps brought this distress upon me, that the hand of divine vengeance was in it, but in the pride of my heart I presently acquitted myself and thereby implicitly charged God with injustice, saying, "What sins have I committed to deserve this?"

The Resigned Self

I saw plainly that God alone could deliver me, but was firmly persuaded that he would not and therefore omitted to ask it. Indeed at *his* hands I would not, but as Saul sought to the witch, so did I to the physician Dr. Heberden and was as diligent in the use of drugs as if they would have healed my wounded spirit or have made the rough places plain before me. I made indeed one effort of a devotional kind, for having found a prayer or two, I said them a few nights but with so little expectation of prevailing that way that I soon laid aside the book and with it all thoughts of God and hopes of a remedy.

I now began to look upon madness as the only chance remaining. I had a strong kind of foreboding that so it would one day fare with me, and I wished for it earnestly and looked forward to it with impatient expectation. My chief fear was that my senses would not fail me in time enough to excuse my appearance at the bar of the House of Lords, which was the only purpose I wanted it to answer. Accordingly the day of decision drew near and I was still in my senses, though in my heart I had formed many wishes and by word of mouth expressed many expectations to the contrary.

Now came the grand temptation, the point to which all the while Satan had been driving me, the dark and hellish purpose of self-murder. I grew more sullen and reserved, fled from all society, even from my most intimate friends, and shut myself up in my chambers. The ruin of my fortune, the contempt of my relations and acquaintance, the prejudice I should do my patron were all urged on me with irresistible energy. Being reconciled to the apprehension of madness, I began to be reconciled to the apprehension of death. Though formerly in my happiest hours I had never been able to glance a single thought that way without shuddering at the idea of dissolution, I now wished for it and found myself but little shocked at the idea of procuring it myself. Perhaps, thought I, there is no God; or if there be, the scriptures may be false; if so then God has nowhere forbidden suicide. I considered life as my property and therefore at my own disposal. Men of great name, I observed, had destroyed themselves, and the world still retained the profoundest respect for their memories. *Moral III*

But above all I was persuaded to believe that if the act were ever so unlawful and even supposing Christianity to be true, my misery in hell itself would be more supportable. I well recollect, too, that when I was about eleven years of age my father desired me to read a vindication of self-murder and give him my sentiments upon the question. I did so and argued against it. My father heard my reasons and was silent, neither approving or disapproving, from whence I inferred that he sided with the author against me, though all the time, I believe, the true motive for his conduct was that he wanted, if he could, to think favorably of the state of a departed friend who had some years before destroyed himself and whose death had struck him with the deepest affliction. But this solution of the matter never once occurred to me, and the circumstance now weighed mightily with me.

William Cowper

At this time I fell into company at a chop-house with an elderly well-looking gentleman whom I had often seen there before but had never spoken to; he began the discourse and talked much of the miseries he had suffered. This opened my heart to him; I freely and readily took part in the conversation. At length self-murder became the topic, and in the result we agreed that the only reason why some men were content to drag on their sorrows with them to the grave and others were not was that the latter were endued with a certain indignant fortitude of spirit teaching them to despise life which the former wanted. Another person whom I met at a tavern told me that he had made up his mind about that matter and had no doubt about his liberty to die as he saw convenient, though, by the way, the same person, who has suffered many and great afflictions since, is still alive. Thus were the emissaries of the throne of darkness let loose upon me. Blessed be the Lord who has brought much good out of all this evil! This concurrence of sentiment in men of sense unknown to each other I considered as a satisfactory decision of the question and determined to proceed accordingly.

One evening in November, 1763, as soon as it was dark, affecting as cheerful and unconcerned an air as possible, I went into an apothecary's shop and asked for an half ounce phial of laudanum. The man seemed to observe me narrowly, but if he did I managed my voice and countenance so as to deceive him. The day that required my attendance at the bar of the House being not yet come and about a week distant, I kept my bottle close in my side-pocket, resolved to use it when I should be convinced there was no other way of escaping. This indeed seemed evident already, but I was willing to allow myself every possible chance of that sort and to protract the horrid execution of my purpose till the last moment, but Satan was impatient of delay.

The day before the period above mentioned arrived, being at Richard's coffee-house at breakfast, I read the newspaper and in it a letter which the further I perused it the more closely engaged my attention. I cannot now recollect the purport of it, but before I had finished it, it appeared demonstratively true to me that it was a libel or satire upon me. The author appeared to be acquainted with my purpose of self-destruction and to have written that letter on purpose to secure and hasten the execution of it. My mind probably at this time began to be disordered; however it was, I was certainly given up to a strong delusion. I said within myself, "your cruelty shall be gratified; you shall have your revenge," and flinging down the paper in a fit of strong passion I rushed hastily out of the room, directing my way towards the fields where I intended to find some house to die in, or, if not, determined to poison myself in a ditch when I should meet with one sufficiently retired.

Before I had walked a mile in the fields a thought struck me that I might yet spare my life—that I had nothing to do but to sell what I had in the funds (which might be done in an hour), go on board a ship, and transport myself to France. There, when every other way of maintenance should fail, I promised

The Resigned Self

myself a comfortable asylum in some monastery, an acquisition easily made by changing my religion. Not a little pleased with this expedient, I returned to my chambers to pack up all that I could at so short a notice, but while I was looking over my portmanteau my mind changed again, and self-murder was recommended to me once more in all its advantages.

Not knowing where to poison myself, for I was liable to continual interruption in my chambers from my laundress and her husband, I laid aside that intention and resolved upon drowning. For that purpose I immediately took a coach and ordered the man to drive to Tower Wharf, intending to throw myself into the river from the Custom-house Quay. It would be strange should I omit to observe here how I was continually hurried away from such places as were most favorable to my design to others where it must be almost impossible to execute it—from the fields, where it was improbable that any thing should happen to prevent me, to the Custom-house Quay, where every thing of that kind was to be expected; and this by a sudden impulse which lasted just long enough to call me back again to my chambers and was immediately withdrawn. Nothing ever appeared more feasible than the project of going to France till it had served its purpose, and then in an instant it appeared impracticable and absurd even to a degree of ridicule.

My life which I had called my own and claimed a right to dispose of was kept from me by him whose property indeed it was and who alone had a right to dispose of it. This is not the only occasion on which it is proper to make this remark; others will offer themselves in the course of this narrative so fairly that the reader cannot overlook them.

I left the coach upon the Tower Wharf, intending never to return to it, but upon coming to the Quay I found the water low and a porter seated upon some goods there, as if on purpose to prevent me. This passage to the bottomless pit being mercifully shut against me, I returned back to the coach and ordered it to return to the Temple. I drew up the shutters, once more had recourse to the laudanum, and determined to drink it off directly; but God had otherwise ordained. A conflict that shook me to pieces suddenly took place—not properly a trembling but a convulsive agitation which deprived me in a manner of the use of my limbs, and my mind was as much shaken as my body.

Distracted between the desire of death and the dread of it, twenty times I had the phial to my mouth and as often received an irresistible check; and even at the time it seemed to me that an invisible hand swayed the bottle downwards as often as I set it against my lips. I well remember that I took notice of this circumstance with some surprise, though it affected no change in my purpose. Panting for breath and in an horrible agony, I flung myself back into the corner of the coach. A few drops of laudanum which had touched my lips besides the fumes of it began to have a stupefying effect upon me. Regretting the loss of so fair an opportunity yet utterly unable to avail myself of it, I determined not to live; and already half dead with anguish I once more returned to the Temple.

Instantly I repaired to my room and having shut both the outer and inner door prepared myself for the last scene of the tragedy. I poured the laudanum into a small basin, set it on a chair by the bedside, half undressed myself, and laid down between the blankets, shuddering with horror at what I was about to perpetrate. I reproached myself bitterly with folly and rank cowardice for having suffered the fear of death to influence me as it had done and was filled with disdain at my own pitiful timidity: but still something seemed to overrule me and to say *"Think what you are doing! Consider and live."*

At length, however, with the most confirmed resolution, I reached forth my hand towards the basin, when the fingers of both hands were as closely contracted as if bound with a cord and became entirely useless. Still, indeed, I could have made shift with both hands, dead and lifeless as they were, to have raised the basin to my mouth, for my arms were not at all affected: but this new difficulty struck me with wonder; it had the air of a divine interposition. I lay down in bed again to muse about it and while thus employed heard the key turn in the outer door and my laundress's husband came in. By this time the use of my fingers was restored to me: I started up hastily, dressed myself, hid the basin, and, affecting as composed an air as I could, walked out into the dining-room. In a few minutes I was left alone; and now unless God had evidently interposed for my preservation I should certainly have done execution upon myself, having a whole afternoon before me.

Both the man and his wife being gone, outward obstructions were no sooner removed than new ones arose within. The man had just shut the door behind him when the convincing Spirit came upon me and a total alteration in my sentiments took place. The horror of the crime was immediately exhibited to me in so strong a light that, being seized with a kind of furious indignation, I snatched up the basin, poured away the laudanum into a phial of foul water, and, not content with that, flung the phial out of the window. This impulse having served, the present purpose was withdrawn.

I spent the rest of the day in a kind of stupid insensibility, undetermined as to the manner of dying but still bent on self-murder as the only possible deliverance. That sense of the enormity of the crime which I had just experienced had entirely left me; and unless my Eternal Father in Christ Jesus had interposed to disannul my covenant with death and my agreement with hell that I might hereafter be admitted into the covenant of mercy, had by this time been a companion of devils and the just object of his boundless vengeance.

In the evening a most intimate friend called upon me and felicitated me on a happy resolution which he had heard I had taken to stand the brunt and keep the office. I knew not whence this intelligence arose but did not contradict it. We conversed awhile with a real cheerfulness on his part and an affected one on mine, and when he left me I said in my heart I shall see thee no more!

Behold into what extremities *a good sort of man* may fall! Such was I in the estimation of those who knew me best; a decent outside is all a

The Resigned Self

good-natured world requires. Thus equipped, though all within be rank atheism, rottenness of heart, and rebellion against the blessed God, we are said to be good enough; and if *we* are damned, alas! who shall be saved! Reverse this charitable reflection and say, if *a good sort of man* be saved, who then shall perish? And it comes much nearer the truth, but this is a hard saying and the world cannot bear it.

I went to bed, as I thought, to take my last sleep in this world. The next morning was to place me at the bar of the House, and I determined not to see it. I slept as usual and awoke about three o'clock. Immediately I arose and by the help of a rushlight found my penknife, took it into bed with me, and lay with it for some hours directly pointed against my heart. Twice or thrice I placed it upright under my left breast, leaning all my weight upon it, but the point was broken off and would not penetrate.

In this manner the time passed till the day began to break. I heard the clock strike seven, and instantly it occurred to me there was no time to be lost; the Chambers would soon be opened and my friend would call upon me to take me with him to Westminster. "Now is the time," thought I, "this is the crisis, no more dallying with the love of life." I arose and, as I thought, bolted the inner door of my chambers but was mistaken; my touch deceived me and I left it as I found it. My preservation, indeed, as it will appear, did not depend upon that incident; but I mention it to show that the good providence of God watched over me to keep open every way of deliverance that nothing might be left to hazard.

Not one hesitating thought now remained, but I fell greedily to the execution of my purpose. My garter was made of a broad scarlet binding with a sliding buckle being sewn together at the ends; by the help of the buckle I made a noose and fixed it about my neck, straining it so tight that I hardly left a passage for my breath or for the blood to circulate; the tongue of the buckle held it fast. At each corner of the bed was placed a wreath of carved work fastened by an iron pin which passed up through the midst of it. The other part of the garter which made a loop I slipped over one of these and hung by it some seconds, drawing up my feet under me that they might not touch the floor; but the iron bent, the carved work slipped off, and the garter with it. I then fastened it to the frame of the tester, winding it round and tying it in a strong knot. The frame broke short and let me down again.

The third effort was more likely to succeed. I set the door open, which reached within a foot of the ceiling; by the help of a chair I could command the top of it, and the loop, being large enough to admit a large angle of the door, was easily fixed so as not to slip off again. I pushed away the chair with my feet and hung at my whole length. While I hung there I distinctly heard a voice say three times, *"'Tis over!"* Though I am sure of the fact and was so at the time, yet it did not at all alarm me or affect my resolution. I hung so long that I lost all sense, all consciousness of existence.

William Cowper   71

When I came to myself again I thought myself in hell; the sound of my own dreadful groans was all that I heard, and a feeling like that of flashes was just beginning to seize upon my whole body. In a few seconds I found myself fallen with my face to the floor. In about half a minute I recovered my feet and reeling and staggering I stumbled into bed again.

By the blessed providence of God the garter which had held me till the bitterness of temporal death was past broke just before eternal death had taken place upon me. The stagnation of the blood under one eye in a broad crimson spot and a red circle about my neck showed plainly that I had been on the brink of eternity. The latter, indeed, might have been occasioned by the pressure of the garter, but the former was certainly the effect of strangulation, for it was not attended with the sensation of a bruise, as it must have been had I in my fall received one in so tender a part. And I rather think the circle around my neck was owing to the same cause, for the part was not excoriated nor at all in pain.

Soon after I got into bed I was surprised to hear a noise in the dining-room, where the laundress was lighting a fire; she had found the door unbolted, notwithstanding my design to fasten it, and must have passed the bed-chamber door while I was hanging on it and yet never perceived me. She heard me fall and presently came to ask if I was well, adding she feared I had been in a fit.

I sent her to a friend to whom I related the whole affair and dispatched him to my kinsman at the coffee-house. As soon as the latter arrived I pointed to the broken garter, which lay in the middle of the room, and apprised him also of the attempt I had been making. His words were, "My dear Mr. Cowper, you terrify me; to be sure you cannot hold the office at this rate—where is the deputation?" I gave him the key of the drawers where it was deposited; and his business requiring his immediate attendance he took it away with him; and thus ended all my connexion with the Parliament House.

To this moment I had felt no concern of a spiritual kind. Ignorant of original sin, insensible of the guilt of actual transgression, I understood neither the law nor the gospel—the condemning nature of the one nor the restoring mercies of the other. I was as much unacquainted with Christ in all his saving offices as if his blessed name had never reached me. Now, therefore, a new scene opened upon me. Conviction of sin took place, especially of that just committed; the meanness of it as well as its atrocity were exhibited to me in colours so inconceivably strong that I despised myself with a contempt not to be imagined or expressed for having attempted it. This sense of it secured me from the repetition of a crime which I could not now reflect on without abhorrence.

Before I arose from bed it was suggested to me that there was nothing wanted but murder to fill up the measure of my iniquities, and that though I had failed in my design yet I had all the guilt of that crime to answer for. A sense of God's wrath and a deep despair of escaping it instantly succeeded. The fear of death became much more prevalent in me than ever the desire of it had been. . . .

The Resigned Self

In a State of Desertion

My sins were now set in an array against me, and I began to see and feel that I had lived without God in the world. As I walked to and fro in my chamber I said within myself, "There never was so abandoned a wretch, so great a sinner." All my worldly sorrows seemed as though they had never been; the terrors which succeeded them seemed so great and so much more afflicting. One moment I thought myself shut out from mercy by one chapter; the next by another. The sword of the Spirit seemed to guard the tree of life from my touch and to flame against me in every avenue by which I attempted to approach it. I particularly remember that the parable of the barren fig-tree was to me an inconceivable source of anguish; and I applied it to myself with a strong persuasion in my mind that when the Saviour pronounced a curse upon it he had me in his eye and pointed that curse directly at me.

Having an obscure notion about the efficacy of faith, I resolved upon an experiment to prove whether I had faith or not. For this purpose I resolved to repeat the Creed; when I came to the second period of it, all traces of the former were struck out of my memory nor could I recollect one syllable of the matter. While I endeavored to recover it and when just upon the point, I perceived a sensation in my brain like a tremulous vibration in all the fibres of it. By this means I lost the words in the very instant when I thought to have laid hold of them. This threw me into an agony, but growing a little calmer I made an attempt for the third time; here again I failed in the same manner as before.

I considered it as a supernatural interposition to inform me that, having sinned against the Holy Ghost, I had no longer any interest in Christ or in the gifts of the Spirit. Being assured of this with the most rooted conviction, I gave myself up to despair. I felt a sense of burning in my heart like that of real fire and concluded it was an earnest of those eternal flames which would soon receive me. I laid myself down, howling with horror while my knees smote against each other.

In this condition my brother found me, and the first words I spoke to him were, "Oh! Brother, I am damned! think of eternity and then think what it is to be damned!" I had indeed a sense of eternity impressed upon my mind which seemed almost to amount to a full comprehension of it.

My brother, pierced to the heart with the sight of my misery, tried to comfort me, but all to no purpose, I refused comfort, and my mind appeared to me in such colors that to administer it to me was only to exasperate me and to mock my fears.

While I traversed the apartment in the most horrible dismay of soul, expecting every moment that the earth would open her mouth and swallow me, my conscience scaring me, the avenger of blood pursuing me, and the city of refuge out of reach and out of sight, a strange and horrible darkness fell upon me. If it were possible that a heavy blow could light on the brain without

William Cowper

touching the skull, such was the sensation I felt. I clapped my hand to my forehead and cried aloud through the pain it gave me. At every stroke my thoughts and expressions became more wild and incoherent; all that remained clear was the sense of sin and the expectation of punishment. These kept undisturbed possession all through my illness without interruption or abatement.

My brother instantly observed the change and consulted with my friends on the best manner to dispose of me. It was agreed among them that I should be carried to St. Albans, where Dr. Cotton [Nathaniel Cotton, 1705-1788, a poet-physician who had established an asylum "Collegium Insanorum" in St. Albans] kept a house for the reception of such patients, and with whom I was known to have a slight acquaintance. Not only his skill as a physician recommended him to their choice but his well known humanity and sweetness of temper. It will be proper to draw a veil over the secrets of my prison-house; let it suffice to say that the low state of body and mind to which I was reduced was perfectly well calculated to humble the natural vain-glory and pride of my heart.

These are the efficacious means which Infinite Wisdom thought meet to make use of for that purpose. A sense of self-loathing and abhorrence ran through all my insanity. Conviction of sin and expectation of instant judgment never left me from the 7th of December, 1763, until the middle of July following. The accuser of the brethren was ever busy with me night and day, bringing to my recollection in dreams the commission of long-forgotten sins and charging upon my conscience things of an indifferent nature as atrocious crimes.

All that passed in this long interval of eight months may be classed under two heads—conviction of sin and despair of mercy. But blessed be the God of my salvation for every sign I drew, for every tear I shed, since thus it pleased him to judge me here that I might not be judged hereafter.

After five months of continual expectation that the divine vengeance would plunge me into the bottomless pit, I became so familiar with despair as to have contracted a sort of hardiness and indifference as to the event. I began to persuade myself that while the execution of the sentence was suspended it would be for my interest to indulge a less horrible train of ideas than I had been accustomed to muse upon. "Eat and drink for tomorrow thou shalt be in hell" was the maxim on which I proceeded. By this means I entered into conversation with the Doctor, laughed at his stories, and told him some of my own to match them—still, however, carrying a sentence of irrevocable doom in my heart.

In about three months more (July 25, 1764) my brother came from Cambridge to visit me. Dr. C. having told him that he thought me greatly amended, he was rather disappointed at finding me almost as silent and reserved as ever, for the first sight of him struck me with many painful sensations both of sorrow for my own remediless condition and envy of his happiness.

As soon as we were left alone he asked me how I found myself; I answered, "As much better as despair can make me." We went together into the garden. Here on expressing a settled assurance of sudden judgment, he protested to me that it was all a delusion and protested so strongly that I could not help giving some attention to him. I burst into tears and cried out, "If it be a delusion then am I the happiest of beings." Something like a ray of hope was shot into my heart, but still I was afraid to indulge it. We dined together, and I spent the afternoon in a more cheerful manner. Something seemed to whisper to me every moment, "Still there is mercy.". . .

I went to bed and slept well. In the morning I dreamed that the sweetest boy I ever saw came dancing up to my bedside; he seemed just out of leading-strings, yet I took particular notice of the firmness and steadiness of his tread. The sight affected me with pleasure and served at least to harmonize my spirits, so that I awoke for the first time with a sensation of delight on my mind. Still, however, I knew not where to look for the establishment of the comfort I felt; my joy was as much a mystery to myself as to those about me. The blessed God was preparing me for the clearer light of his countenance by this first dawning of that light upon me. . . .

Having risen with somewhat of a more cheerful feeling, I repaired to my room, where breakfast waited for me. While I sat at table I found the cloud of horror which had so long hung over me was every moment passing away, and every moment came fraught with hope. I was continually more and more persuaded that I was not utterly doomed to destruction. The way of salvation was still, however, hid from my eyes; nor did I see it at all clearer than before my illness. I only thought that if it would please God to spare me I would lead a better life, and that I would yet escape hell if a religious observance of my duty would secure me from it. . . .

But the happy period which was to shake off my fetters and afford me a clear opening of the free mercy of God in Christ Jesus was now arrived. I flung myself into a chair near the window and, seeing a Bible there, ventured once more to apply to it for comfort and instruction. The first verse I saw was the 25th of the 3rd of Romans: "Whom God hath set forth to be a propitiation through faith in his blood to declare his righteousness for the remission of sins that are past through the forbearance of God."

Immediately I received strength to believe it, and the full beams of the Sun of Righteousness shone upon me. I saw the sufficiency of the atonement he had made, my pardon sealed in his blood, and all the fulness and completeness of his justification. In a moment I believed and received the gospel. . . . Unless the Almighty arm had been under me, I think I should have died with gratitude and joy. My eyes filled with tears and my voice choked with transport, I could only look up to heaven in silent fear, overwhelmed with love and wonder. But the work of the Holy Ghost is best described in his own words. It is "joy unspeakable and full of glory." Thus was my heavenly Father in Christ Jesus pleased to give me the full assurance of faith and out of a strong, stony, unbelieving heart to raise up a child unto Abraham. How glad should I now have been to have spent every moment in prayer and thanksgiving!

William Cowper

I lost no opportunity of repairing to a throne of grace, but flew to it with an earnestness irresistible and never to be satisfied. Could I help it? Could I do otherwise than love and rejoice in my reconciled Father in Christ Jesus? The Lord had enlarged my heart, and I ran in the way of his commandments. For many succeeding weeks tears were ready to flow if I did but speak of the gospel or mention the name of Jesus. To rejoice day and night was all my employment. Too happy to sleep much, I thought it was but lost time that was spent in slumber. Oh that the ardor of my first love had continued! But I have known many a lifeless and unhallowed hour since—long intervals of darkness interrupted by short returns of peace and joy in believing. . . .

I repaired to Huntingdon the Saturday after my arrival at Cambridge. My brother who had attended me there had no sooner left me than, finding myself surrounded by strangers and in a strange place, my spirits began to sink and I felt (such was the backslidings of my heart) like a traveller in the midst of an inhospitable desert, without a friend to comfort or a guide to direct me. I walked forth towards the close of the day in this melancholy frame of mind, and having wandered about a mile from the town I found my heart at length so powerfully drawn towards the Lord that, having gained a retired and secret nook in the corner of a field, I kneeled down under a bank and poured forth my complaints before him. It pleased my Saviour to hear me in that this oppression was taken off, and I was enabled to trust in him that careth for the stranger, to roll my burden upon him, and to rest assured that wherever he might cast my lot the God of all consolation would still be with me. But this was not all. He did for me more than either I had asked or thought. . . .

One day, however, towards the expiration of this period I found myself in a state of desertion. That communion which I had so long been able to maintain with the Lord was suddenly interrupted. I began to dislike my solitary situation and to fear I should never be able to weather out the winter in so lonely a dwelling. Suddenly a thought struck me which I shall not fear to call a suggestion of the good providence which had brought me to Huntingdon. A few months before I had formed an acquaintance with the Rev. Mr. Unwin's family. His son, though he had heard that I rather declined society than sought it, and though Mrs. Unwin herself dissuaded him from visiting me on that account, was yet so strongly inclined to it that, notwithstanding all objections and arguments to the contrary, he one day engaged himself as we were coming out of church after morning prayers to drink tea with me that afternoon. To my inexpressible joy I found him one whose notions of religion were spiritual and lively—one whom the Lord had been training up from his infancy for the service of the temple. We opened our hearts to each other at the first interview, and when we parted I immediately retired to my chamber and prayed the Lord who had been the author to be the guardian of our friendship and to grant it fervency and perpetuity even unto death, and I doubt not that my gracious Father heard this prayer also.

The Sunday following I dined with him. That afternoon while the rest of the family was withdrawn I had much discourse with Mrs. Unwin. I am not at

often WC takes symbol as real.

The Resigned Self

liberty to describe the pleasure I had in conversing with her because she will be one of the first who will have the perusal of this narrative. Let it suffice to say I found we had one faith and had been baptised with the same baptism.

When I returned home I gave thanks to God who had so graciously answered my prayers by bringing me into the society of Christians. She has since been a means in the hand of God of supporting, quickening, and strengthening me in my walk with him. It was long before I thought of any other connection with this family than as a friend and neighbour. On the day, however, above mentioned, while I was revolving in my mind the nature of my situation and beginning for the first time to find an irksomeness in such retirement, suddenly it occurred to me that I might probably find a place in Mr. Unwin's family as a boarder. A young gentleman who had lived with him as a pupil was the day before gone to Cambridge. It appeared to me at least possible that I might be allowed to succeed him. From the moment this thought struck me such a tumult of anxious solicitude seized me that for two or three days I could not divert my mind to any other subject. I blamed and condemned myself for want of submission to the Lord's will, but still the language of my mutinous and disobedient heart was, "Give me the blessing or else I die."

About the third evening after I had determined upon this measure I at length made shift to fasten my thoughts upon a theme which had no manner of connection with it. While I was pursuing my meditations—Mr. Unwin and family quite out of sight—my attention was suddenly called home again by the words which had been continually playing in my mind and were at length repeated with such importunity that I could not help regarding them:—"The Lord God of truth will do this." I was effectually convinced that they were not of my own production, and accordingly I received from them some assurance of success; but my unbelief and fearfulness robbed me of much of the comfort they were intended to convey, though I have since had many a blessed experience of the same kind for which I can never be sufficiently thankful. I immediately began to negotiate the affair and in a few days it was entirely concluded.

I took possession of my new abode Nov. 11, 1765. I have found it a place of rest prepared for me by God's own hand, where he has blessed me with a thousand mercies and instances of his fatherly protection, and where he has given me abundant means of furtherance in the knowledge of our Lord Jesus, both by the study of his own word and communion with his dear disciples. May nothing but death interrupt our union!

Peace be with the reader through faith in our Lord Jesus Christ. Amen!

Suggestions for Further Reading

Gamaliel Bradford, "Diversions of a Lost Soul," *Atlantic Monthly*, CXXXIV (1924), pp. 361-370.

William Cowper

David Cecil, *The Stricken Deer, or The Life of Cowper* (London: Collins, 1965).

Edward M. Chapman, *Dawn of a New Day: English Literature in Account with Religion* (Boston: Houghton-Mifflin, 1910).

Hoosag K. Gregory, "The Prisoner and His Crimes: Summary Comments on a Longer Study of the Mind of William Cowper," *Literature and Psychology*, VI (1956), pp. 53-59.

John N. Morris, *Versions of the Self* (New York: Basic Books, 1966).

Maurice J. Quinlan, *William Cowper: A Critical Life* (Minneapolis: University of Minnesota Press, 1953).

_____, "William Cowper and the Unpardonable Sin," *Journal of Religion*, (1943), pp. 110-16.

Charles Ryskamp, *William Cowper of the Inner Temple, Esq. A Study of His Life and Works to the Year 1768* (Cambridge, Eng.: Cambridge University Press, 1959).

Donald A. Stauffer, *The Art of Biography in the Eighteenth Century* (Princeton, N.J.: Princeton University Press, 1941).

George E. Woodberry, *Three Men of Piety. Makers of Literature* (New York: Macmillan, 1907). Deals with Bunyan, Channing, and Cowper (pp. 271-301).

Carl G. Jung

Memories, Dreams, Reflections

*The wisdom and goodness of God had
been revealed to me now that I had
yielded to His inexorable command.
. . . When I endured these assaults
of the unconscious I had an
unswerving conviction that I was
obeying a higher will.*

Carl G. Jung, the only son of a Protestant clergyman, was born in 1875 in Kessuil, Switzerland. Both his paternal and maternal forebears had religious careers, as either pastors or theologians. His father's father, raised a Catholic, was converted to Protestantism by Friedrich Schleiermacher in 1813. In addition to its strong religious concern, the family was also involved in the medical profession. Jung's paternal grandfather founded the first mental hospital in the city of Basel.

Jung himself embarked on a medical career at the University of Basel and in 1902 accepted a position as assistant physician at Burgholzli Psychiatric Clinic at the University of Zurich. His dissertation for his medical degree centered on the psyche's tendency to strive for wholeness or integration. His early psychiatric investigations of what he called "complexes," a term which has since become common parlance, brought his work to the attention of Sigmund Freud. Their collaboration began in 1907 and lasted until 1913. Jolande Jacobi, a noted Jungian, suggests that Jung's split with Freud was due in large part to his attempt to discover the symbolic meaning of unconscious materials (especially dreams) by interpreting them in the light of historical and mythological parallels.

In the same year that he separated from Freud, Jung relinquished his position at Zurich and engrossed himself in the study of religious myth and symbolism. The following selection from his autobiography is based on this period of his life. In overcoming his resistance to "plunging" into his own unconscious, he experienced a kind of spiritual "grace" not unlike that experienced in religious conversions. With the publication of *Psychological Types* in 1921, he emerged from this self-imposed personal and professional exile and in the course of the next few years carried out an extensive and energetic travel-study project. His travels took him to American Indian reservations in Arizona and New Mexico in 1924, to Kenya in 1925, and to Egypt in 1926.

These travels marked the beginning of his professional shift from psychology to cultural analysis. While he continued to be recognized for his contributions to personality theory and psychotherapy, Jung's most enduring contribution has been his investigation of the myths and symbols of both Eastern and Western cultures. In the course of his travels he became increasingly convinced of the spiritual poverty of modern Western man. He discovered that the Pueblo Indian possessed a dignity and tranquil composure missing in the modern Westerner. He observed that the African, while possessing the same demonic, violent urges as modern Western man, was able to control these urges through his rituals. The trip from Africa to the East "was a kind of drama of the birth of light. That drama was intimately connected with me, with my psychology." Jung found especially that the Easterner was "able to integrate so-called 'evil' without 'losing face.'" In contrast, Western man, as World War I clearly demonstrated, had lost the mythical and symbolic means of containing evil.

In *Modern Man in Search of a Soul*, he pointed out that the modern Western world, having broken with Christianity, "is in quest of a new myth, which alone could enable it to draw upon fresh spiritual resources and renew its creative powers" (Mircea Eliade). Our dreams reveal our disorientation at having been cut off from our symbolic roots. Especially in individuals who find orthodox religious belief impossible, the unconscious, through dreams, reveals man's effort to replace the failing myth of Christianity with his own myth, a new symbolic integration. In Jung's view, this new myth struggling to be born will derive its content from "the world of the ancestors." Hence the importance of studying those mythic materials which shaped the religious imagination of the ancestors of European man (but which have since been obscured by Christian dogmatism).

In the following selection, Jung relates his dramatic disaffection from the religious orthodoxy of his childhood, followed by his own search for a personally compelling myth. As the resigned self, he submitted to a higher will in relinquishing the faith of his paternal tradition in favor of his own personal myth. By this submission fresh spiritual resources were made available to him. He had experienced illumination.

The Resigned Self

Memories, Dreams, Reflections

The Experience of Grace

[My twelfth year was indeed a fateful one for me.] One fine summer day that . . . year I came out of school at noon and went to the cathedral square. The sky was gloriously blue, the day one of radiant sunshine. The roof of the cathedral glittered, the sun sparkling from the new, brightly glazed tiles. I was overwhelmed by the beauty of the sight, and thought: "The world is beautiful and the church is beautiful, and God made all this and sits above it far away in the blue sky on a golden throne and . . ." Here came a great hole in my thoughts, and a choking sensation. I felt numbed, and knew only: "Don't go on thinking now! Something terrible is coming, something I do not want to think, something I dare not even approach. Why not? Because I would be committing the most frightful of sins. What is the most terrible sin? Murder? No, it can't be that. The most terrible sin is the sin against the Holy Ghost, which cannot be forgiven. Anyone who commits that sin is dammed to hell for all eternity. That would be very sad for my parents, if their only son, to whom they are so attached, should be doomed to eternal damnation. I cannot do that to my parents. All I need do is not go on thinking."

That was easier said than done. On my long walk home I tried to think all sorts of other things, but I found my thoughts returning again and again to the beautiful cathedral which I loved so much, and to God sitting on the throne—and then my thoughts would fly off again as if they had received a powerful electric shock. I kept repeating to myself: "Don't think of it, just don't think of it!" I reached home in a pretty worked-up state. My mother noticed that something was wrong, and asked, "What is the matter with you? Has something happened at school?" I was able to assure her, without lying, that nothing had happened at school. I did have the thought that it might help me if I could confess to my mother the real reason for my turmoil. But to do so I would have to do the very thing that seemed impossible: think my thought right to the end. The poor dear was utterly unsuspecting and could not possibly know that I was in terrible danger of committing the unforgivable sin and plunging myself into hell. I rejected the idea of confessing and tried to efface myself as much as possible.

That night I slept badly; again and again the forbidden thought, which I did not yet know, tried to break out, and I struggled desperately to fend it off. The next two days were sheer torture, and my mother was convinced that I was ill. But I resisted the temptation to confess, aided by the thought that it would cause my parents intense sorrow.

On the third night, however, the torment became so unbearable that I no longer knew what to do. I awoke from a restless sleep just in time to catch myself thinking again about the cathedral and God. I had almost continued the thought! I felt my resistance weakening. Sweating with fear, I sat up in bed to shake off sleep. "Now it is coming, now it's serious! *I must think.* It must be thought out beforehand. *Why* should I think something I do not know? I don't want to, by God, that's sure. But *who* wants me to? Who wants to force me to think something I don't know and don't want to know? Where does this terrible will come from? And why should I be the one to be subjected to it? I was thinking praises of the Creator of this beautiful world, I was grateful to him for this immeasurable gift, so why should *I* have to think something inconceivably wicked? I don't know what it is, I really don't, for I cannot and must not come anywhere near this thought, for that would be to risk thinking it at once. *I* haven't done this or wanted this, it has come on me like a bad dream. Where do such things come from? This has happened to me without my doing. Why? After all, I didn't create myself, I came into the world the way God made me—that is, the way I was shaped by my parents. Or can it have been that my parents wanted something of this sort? But my good parents would never have had any thoughts like that. Nothing so atrocious would ever have occurred to them."

I found this idea utterly absurd. Then I thought of my grandparents, whom I knew only from their portraits. They looked benevolent and dignified enough to repulse any idea that they might possibly be to blame. I mentally ran through the long procession of unknown ancestors until finally I arrived at Adam and Eve. And with them came the decisive thought: Adam and Eve were the first people; they had no parents, but were created directly by God, who intentionally made them as they were. They had no choice but to be exactly the way God had created them. Therefore they did not know how they could possibly be different. They were perfect creatures of God, for He creates only perfection, and yet they committed the first sin by doing what God did not want them to do. How was that possible? They could not have done it if God had not placed in them the possibility of doing it. That was clear, too, from the serpent, whom God had created before them, obviously so that it could induce Adam and Eve to sin. God in His omniscience had arranged everything so that the first parents would have to sin. *Therefore it was God's intention that they should sin.*

This thought liberated me instantly from my worst torment, since I now knew that God Himself had placed me in this situation. At first I did not know whether He intended me to commit my sin or not. I no longer thought of praying for illumination, since God had landed me in this fix without my willing it and had left me without any help. I was certain that I must search out His

The Resigned Self

intention myself, and seek the way out alone. At this point another argument began.

"What does God want? To act or not to act? I must find out what God wants with me, and I must find out right away." I was aware, of course, that according to conventional morality there was no question but that sin must be avoided. That was what I had been doing up to now, but I knew I could not go on doing it. My broken sleep and my spiritual distress had worn me out to such a point that fending off the thought was tying me into unbearable knots. This could not go on. At the same time, I could not yield before I understood what God's will was and what He intended. For I was now certain that He was the author of this desperate problem. Oddly enough, I did not think for a moment that the devil might be playing a trick on me. The devil played little part in my mental world at that time, and in any case I regarded him as powerless compared with God. But from the moment I emerged from the mist and became conscious of myself, the unity, the greatness, and the superhuman majesty of God began to haunt my imagination. Hence there was no question in my mind but that God Himself was arranging a decisive test for me, and that everything depended on my understanding Him correctly. I knew, beyond a doubt, that I would ultimately be compelled to break down, to give way, but I did not want it to happen without my understanding it, since the salvation of my eternal soul was at stake.

"God knows that I cannot resist much longer, and He does not help me, although I am on the point of having to commit the unforgivable sin. In His omnipotence He could easily lift this compulsion from me, but evidently He is not going to. Can it be that He wishes to test my obedience by imposing on me the unusual task of doing something against my own moral judgment and against the teachings of my religion, and even against His own commandment, something I am resisting with all my strength because I fear eternal damnation? Is it possible that God wishes to see whether I am capable of obeying His will even though my faith and my reason raise before me the specters of death and hell? That might really be the answer! But these are merely my own thoughts. I may be mistaken. I dare not trust my own reasoning as far as that. I must think it all through once more."

I thought it over again and arrived at the same conclusion. "Obviously God also desires me to show courage," I thought. "If that is so and I go through with it, then He will give me His grace and illumination."

I gathered all my courage, as though I were about to leap forthwith into hell-fire, and let the thought come. I saw before me the cathedral, the blue sky. God sits on His golden throne, high above the world—and from under the throne an enormous turd falls upon the sparkling new roof, shatters it, and breaks the walls of the cathedral asunder.

So that was it! I felt an enormous, an indescribable relief. Instead of the expected damnation, grace had come upon me, and with it an unutterable bliss such as I had never known. I wept for happiness and gratitude. The wisdom and goodness of God had been revealed to me now that I had yielded to His inexorable command. It was as though I had experienced an illumination. A great many things I had not previously understood became clear to me. That was what my father had not understood, I thought; he had failed to experience the will of God, had opposed it for the best reasons and out of the deepest faith. And that was why he had never experienced the miracle of grace which heals all and makes all comprehensible. He had taken the Bible's commandments as his guide; he believed in God as the Bible prescribed and as his forefathers had taught him. But he did not know the immediate living God who stands, omnipotent and free, above His Bible and His Church, who calls upon man to partake of His freedom, and can force him to renounce his own views and convictions in order to fulfill without reserve the command of God. In His trial of human courage God refuses to abide by traditions, no matter how sacred. In his omnipotence He will see to it that nothing really evil comes of such tests of courage. If one fulfills the will of God one can be sure of going the right way.

God had also created Adam and Eve in such a way that they had to think what they did not at all want to think. He had done that in order to find out whether they were obedient. And He could also demand something of me that I would have had to reject on traditional religious grounds. It was obedience which brought me grace, and after that experience I knew what God's grace was. One must be utterly abandoned to God; nothing matters but fulfilling His will. Otherwise all is folly and meaninglessness. From that moment on, when I experienced grace, my true responsibility began. Why did God befoul His cathedral? That, for me, was a terrible thought. But then came the dim understanding that God could be something terrible. I had experienced a dark and terrible secret. It overshadowed my whole life, and I became deeply pensive.

The experience also had the effect of increasing my sense of inferiority. I am a devil or a swine, I thought; I am infinitely depraved. But then I began searching through the New Testament and read, with a certain satisfaction, about the Pharisee and the publican, and that reprobates are the chosen ones. It made a lasting impression on me that the unjust steward was praised, and that Peter, the waverer, was appointed the rock upon which the Church was built.

The greater my inferiority feelings became, the more incomprehensible did God's grace appear to me. After all, I had never been sure of myself. When my mother once said to me, "You have always been a good boy," I simply could not grasp it. I a good boy? That was quite new to me. I often thought of myself as a corrupt and inferior person.

With the experience of God and the cathedral I at last had something tangible that was part of the great secret—as if I had always talked of stones falling from heaven and now had one in my pocket. But actually, it was a shaming experience. I had fallen into something bad, something evil and sinister, though at the same time it was a kind of distinction. Sometimes I had an overwhelming urge to speak, not about that, but only to hint that there were some curious things about me which no one knew of. I wanted to find out whether other people had undergone similar experiences. I never succeeded in discovering so much as a trace of them in others. As a result, I had the feeling that I was either outlawed or elect, accursed or blessed.

It would never have occurred to me to speak of my experience openly, nor of my dream of the phallus in the underground temple, nor of my carved manikin. As a matter of fact, I did not say anything about the phallus dream until I was sixty-five. I may have spoken about the other experiences to my wife, but only in later years. A strict taboo hung over all these matters, inherited from my childhood. I could never have talked about them with friends.

My entire youth can be understood in terms of this secret. It induced in me an almost unendurable loneliness. My one great achievement during those years was that I resisted the temptation to talk about it with anyone. Thus the pattern of my relationship to the world was already prefigured: today as then I am a solitary, because I know things and must hint at things which other people do not know, and usually do not even want to know.

In my mother's family there were six parsons, and on my father's side not only was my father a parson but two of my uncles also. Thus I heard many religious conversations, theological discussions, and sermons. Whenever I listened to them I had the feeling: "Yes, yes, that is all very well. But what about the secret? The secret is also the secret of grace. None of you know anything about that. You don't know that God wants to force me to do wrong, that He forces me to think abominations in order to experience His grace." Everything the others said was completely beside the point. I thought, "For Heaven's sake, there must be someone who knows something about it; somewhere there must be the truth." I rummaged through my father's library, reading whatever I could on God, the Trinity, spirit, consciousness. I devoured the books, but came away none the wiser. I always found myself thinking, "They don't know either." I even searched about in my father's Luther Bible. Unfortunately, the conventional "edifying" interpretation of Job prevented me from taking a deeper interest in this book. I would have found consolation in it, especially in chapter 9, verses 30ff.: "Though I wash myself with snow water . . . yet shalt thou plunge me in the mire."

Later my mother told me that in those days I was often depressed. It was not really that; rather, I was brooding on the secret. At such times it was strangely reassuring and calming to sit on my stone. Somehow it would free me of all my doubts. Whenever I thought that I was the stone, the conflict ceased. "The stone has no uncertainties, no urge to communicate, and is eternally the same for thousands of years," I would think, "while I am only a passing phenomenon which bursts into all kinds of emotions, like a flame that flares up quickly and then goes out." I was but the sum of my emotions, and the Other in me was the timeless, imperishable stone.

At that time, too, there arose in me profound doubts about everything my father said. When I heard him preaching about grace, I always thought of my own experience. What he said sounded stale and hollow, like a tale told by someone who knows it only by hearsay and cannot quite believe it himself. I wanted to help him, but I did not know how. Moreover, I was too shy to tell him of my experience, or to meddle in his personal preoccupations. I felt myself to be on the one hand too little, and on the other hand I was afraid to wield that authority which my "second personality" inspired in me.

Later, when I was eighteen years old, I had many discussions with my father, always with the secret hope of being able to let him know about the miracle of grace, and thereby help to mitigate his pangs of conscience. I was convinced that if he fulfilled the will of God everything would turn out for the best. But our discussions invariably came to an unsatisfactory end. They irritated him, and saddened him. "Oh nonsense," he was in the habit of saying, "you always want to think. One ought not to think, but believe." I would think, "No, one must experience and know," but I would say, "Give me this belief," whereupon he would shrug and turn resignedly away. . . .

Children react much less to what grown-ups say than to the imponderables in the surrounding atmosphere. The child unconsciously adapts himself to them, and this produces in him correlations of a compensatory nature. The peculiar "religious" ideas that came to me even in my earliest childhood were spontaneous products which can be understood only as reactions to my parental environment and to the spirit of the age. The religious doubts to which my father was later to succumb naturally had to pass through a long period of incubation. Such a revolution of one's world, and of the world in general, threw its shadows ahead, and the shadows were all the longer, the more desperately my father's conscious mind resisted their power. It is not surprising that my father's forebodings put him in a state of unrest, which then communicated itself to me.

I never had the impression that these influences emanated from my mother, for she was somehow rooted in deep, invisible ground, though it never appeared to me as confidence in her Christian faith. For me it was somehow connected with animals, trees, mountains, meadows, and running water, all of which contrasted most strangely with her Christian surface and her conventional assertions of faith. This background corresponded so well to my own attitude that it caused me no uneasiness; on the contrary, it gave me a sense of security and the conviction that here was solid ground on which one could stand. It never occurred to me how "pagan" this foundation was. [It] . . . offered me the strongest support in the conflict then beginning between parental tradition and the strange, compensatory products which my unconscious had been stimulated to create.

Looking back, I now see how very much my development as a child anticipated future events and paved the way for modes of adaptation to my father's religious collapse as well as to the shattering revelation of the world as we see it today—a revelation which had not taken shape from one day to the next, but had cast its shadows long in advance. Although we human beings have our own personal life, we are yet in large measure the representatives, the victims and promoters of a collective spirit whose years are counted in centuries. We can well think all our lives long that we are following our own noses, and may never discover that we are, for the most part, supernumeraries on the stage of the world theater. There are factors which, although we do not know them, nevertheless influence our lives, the more so if they are unconscious. Thus at least a part of our being lives in the centuries. . . . That it is not an individual curiosity is proved by the religion of the West, which expressly applies itself to this inner man and for two thousand years has earnestly tried to bring him to the knowledge of our surface consciousness with its personalistic preoccupations: *"Non foras ire, in interiore homine habitat veritas"* (Go not outside; truth dwells in the inner man). . . .

Confronting the Unconscious

After the parting of the ways with Freud, a period of inner uncertainty began for me. It would be no exaggeration to call it a state of disorientation. I felt totally suspended in mid-air, for I had not yet found my own footing. Above all, I felt it necessary to develop a new attitude toward my patients. I resolved for the present not to bring any theoretical premises to bear upon them, but to wait and see what they would tell of their own accord. My aim became to leave things to chance. The result was that the patients would spontaneously report their dreams and fantasies to me, and I would merely ask, "What occurs to you in connection with that?" or, "How do you mean that, where does that come from, what do you think about it?" The interpretations seemed to follow of their own accord from the patients' replies and associations. I avoided all theoretical points of view and simply helped the patients to understand the dream-images by themselves, without application of rules and theories.

Soon I realized that it was right to take the dreams in this way as the basis of interpretation, for that is how dreams are intended. They are the facts from which we must proceed. Naturally, the aspects resulting from this method were so multitudinous that the need for a criterion grew more and more pressing—the need, I might almost put it, for some initial orientation.

About this time I experienced a moment of unusual clarity in which I looked back over the way I had traveled so far. I thought, "Now you possess a key to mythology and are free to unlock all the gates of the unconscious psyche." But then something whispered within me, "Why open all gates?" And promptly the question arose of what, after all, I had accomplished. I had explained the myths of peoples in the past; I had written a book about the hero, the myth in which man has always lived. But in what myth does man live nowadays? In the Christian myth, the answer might be, "Do *you* live in it?" I asked myself. To be honest, the answer was no. For me, it is not what I live by." "Then do we no longer have any myth." "No, evidently we no longer have any myth." "But then what is your myth—the myth in which you do live?" At this point the dialogue with myself became uncomfortable, and I stopped thinking. I had reached a dead end.

Then, around Christmas of 1912, I had a dream. In the dream I found myself in a magnificent Italian loggia with pillars, a marble floor, and a marble balustrade. I was sitting on a gold Renaissance chair; in front of me was a table of rare beauty. It was made of green stone, like emerald. There I sat, looking out into the distance, for the loggia was set high up on the tower of a castle. My children were sitting at the table too.

Suddenly a white bird descended, a small sea gull or a dove. Gracefully, it came to rest on the table, and I signed to the children to be still so that they would not frighten away the pretty white bird. Immediately, the dove was transformed into a little girl, about eight years of age, with golden blond hair. She ran off with the children and played with them among the colonnades of the castle.

I remained lost in thought, musing about what I had just experienced. The little girl returned and tenderly placed her arms around my neck. Then she suddenly vanished; the dove was back and spoke slowly in a human voice. "Only in the first hours of the night can I transform myself into a human being, while the male dove is busy with the twelve dead." Then she flew off into the blue air, and I awoke.

I was greatly stirred. What business would a male dove be having with twelve dead people? In connection with the emerald table the story of the Tabula Smaragdina occurred to me, the emerald table in the alchemical legend of Hermes Trismegistos. He was said to have left behind him a table upon which the basic tenets of alchemical wisdom were engraved in Greek.

I also thought of the twelve apostles, the twelve months of the year, the signs of the zodiac, etc. But I could find no solution to the enigma. Finally I had to give it up. All I knew with any certainty was that the dream indicated an unusual activation of the unconscious. But I knew no technique whereby I might get to the bottom of my inner processes, and so there remained nothing for me to do but wait, go on with my life and pay close attention to my fantasies.

One fantasy kept returning: there was something dead present, but it was also still alive. For example, corpses were placed in crematory ovens, but were then discovered to be still living. These fantasies came to a head and were simultaneously resolved in a dream.

I was in a region like the Alyscamps near Arles. There they have a lane of sarcophagi which go back to Merovingian times. In the dream I was coming from the city, and saw before me a similar lane with a long row of tombs. They were pedestals with stone slabs on which the dead lay. They reminded me of old

The Resigned Self

church burial vaults, where knights in armor lie outstretched. Thus the dead lay in my dream, in their antique clothes, with hands clasped, the difference being that they were not hewn out of stone, but in a curious fashion mummified. I stood still in front of the first grave and looked at the dead man, who was a person of the eighteen-thirties. I looked at his clothes with interest, whereupon he suddenly moved and came to life. He unclasped his hands; but that was only because I was looking at him. I had an extremely unpleasant feeling, but walked on and came to another body. He belonged to the eighteenth century. There exactly the same thing happened: when I looked at him, he came to life and moved his hands. So I went down the whole row, until I came to the twelfth century—that is, to a crusader in chain mail who lay there with clasped hands. His figure seemed carved out of wood. For a long time I looked at him and thought he was really dead. But suddenly I saw that a finger of his left hand was beginning to stir gently.

Of course I had originally held to Freud's view that vestiges of old experiences exist in the unconscious. But dreams like this, and my actual experiences of the unconscious, taught me that such contents are not dead, outmoded forms, but belong to our living being. My work had confirmed this assumption, and in the course of years there developed from it the theory of archetypes.

The dreams, however, could not help me over my feeling of disorientation. On the contrary, I lived as if under constant inner pressure. At times this became so strong that I suspected there was some psychic disturbance in myself. Therefore I twice went over all the details of my entire life, with particular attention to childhood memories; for I thought there might be something in my past which I could not see and which might possibly be the cause of the disturbance. But this retrospection led to nothing but a fresh acknowledgment of my own ignorance. Thereupon I said to myself, "Since I know nothing at all, I shall simply do whatever occurs to me." Thus I consciously submitted myself to the impulses of the unconscious.

The first thing that came to the surface was a childhood memory from perhaps my tenth or eleventh year. At that time I had had a spell of playing passionately with building blocks. I distinctly recalled how I had built little houses and castles, using bottles to form the sides of gates and vaults. Somewhat later I had used ordinary stones, with mud for mortar. These structures had fascinated me for a long time. To my astonishment, this memory was accompanied by a good deal of emotion. "Aha," I said to myself, "there is still life in these things. The small boy is still around, and possesses a creative life which I lack. But how can I make my way to it?" For as a grown man it seemed impossible to me that I should be able to bridge the distance from the present back to my eleventh year. Yet if I wanted to re-establish contact with that period, I had no choice but to return to it and take up once more that child's life with his childish games. This moment was a turning point in my fate, but I gave in only after endless resistances and with a sense of resignation. For it was a painfully humiliating experience to realize that there was nothing to be done except play childish games.

Nevertheless, I began accumulating suitable stones, gathering them partly from the water. And I started building: cottages, a castle, a whole village. The church was still missing, so I made a square building with a hexagonal drum on top of it, and a dome. A church also requires an altar, but I hesitated to build that.

Preoccupied with the question of how I could approach this task, I was walking along the lake as usual one day, picking stones out of the gravel on the shore. Suddenly I caught sight of a red stone, a four-sided pyramid about an inch and a half high. It was a fragment of stone which had been polished into this shape by the action of the water—a pure product of chance. I knew at once: this was the altar! I placed it in the middle under the dome, and as I did so, I recalled the underground phallus of my childhood dream. This connection gave me a feeling of satisfaction.

I went on with my building game after the noon meal every day, whenever the weather permitted. As soon as I was through eating, I began playing, and continued to do so until the patients arrived; and if I was finished with my work early enough in the evening, I went back to building. In the course of this activity my thoughts clarified, and I was able to grasp the fantasies whose presence in myself I dimly felt.

Naturally, I thought about the significance of what I was doing, and asked myself, "Now, really, what are you about? You are building a small town, and doing it as if it were a rite!" I had no answer to my question, only the inner certainty that I was on the way to discovering my own myth. For the building game was only a beginning. It released a stream of fantasies which I later carefully wrote down. . . . Toward the autumn of 1913 the pressure which I had felt was in *me* seemed to be moving outward, as though there were something in the air. The atmosphere actually seemed to me darker than it had been. It was as though the sense of oppression no longer sprang exclusively from a psychic situation, but from concrete reality. This feeling grew more and more intense.

In October, while I was alone on a journey, I was suddenly seized by an overpowering vision: I saw a monstrous flood covering all the northern and low-lying lands between the North Sea and the Alps. When it came up to Switzerland I saw that the mountains grew higher and higher to protect our country. I realized that a frightful catastrophe was in progress. I saw the mighty yellow waves, the floating rubble of civilization, and the drowned bodies of uncounted thousands. Then the whole sea turned to blood. This vision lasted about one hour. I was perplexed and nauseated, and ashamed of my weakness.

Two weeks passed; then the vision recurred, under the same conditions, even more vividly than before, and the blood was more emphasized. An inner voice spoke. "Look at it well; it is wholly real and it will be so. You cannot doubt it." That winter someone asked me what I thought were the political prospects of the world in the near future. I replied that I had no thoughts on the matter, but that I saw rivers of blood.

I asked myself whether these visions pointed to a revolution, but could not really imagine anything of the sort. And so I drew the conclusion that they had to do with me myself, and decided that I was menaced by a psychosis. The idea of war did not occur to me at all. . . .

On August 1 the world war broke out. Now my task was clear: I had to try to understand what had happened and to what extent my own experience coincided with that of mankind in general. Therefore my first obligation was to probe the depths of my own psyche. I made a beginning by writing down the fantasies which had come to me during my building game. This work took precedence over everything else.

An incessant stream of fantasies had been released, and I did my best not to lose my head but to find some way to understand these strange things. I stood helpless before an alien world; everything in it seemed difficult and incomprehensible. I was living in a constant state of tension; often I felt as if gigantic blocks of stone were tumbling down upon me. One thunderstorm followed another. My enduring these storms was a question of brute strength. Others have been shattered by them—Nietzsche, and Hölderlin, and many others. But there was a demonic strength in me, and from the beginning there was no doubt in my mind that I must find the meaning of what I was experiencing in these fantasies. When I endured these assaults of the unconscious I had an unswerving conviction that I was obeying a higher will, and that feeling continued to uphold me until I had mastered the task.

I was frequently so wrought up that I had to do certain yoga exercises in order to hold my emotions in check. But since it was my purpose to know what was going on within myself, I would do these exercises only until I had calmed myself enough to resume my work with the unconscious. As soon as I had the feeling that I was myself again, I abandoned this restraint upon the emotions and allowed the images and inner voices to speak afresh. The Indian, on the other hand, does yoga exercises in order to obliterate completely the multitude of psychic contents and images.

To the extent that I managed to translate the emotions into images—that is to say, to find the images which were concealed in the emotions—I was inwardly calmed and reassured. Had I left those images hidden in the emotions, I might have been torn to pieces by them. There is a chance that I might have succeeded in splitting them off; but in that case I would inexorably have fallen into a neurosis and so been ultimately destroyed by them anyhow. As a result of my experiment I learned how helpful it can be, from the therapeutic point of view, to find the particular images which lie behind emotions.

I wrote down the fantasies as well as I could, and made an earnest effort to analyze the psychic conditions under which they had arisen. But I was able to do this only in clumsy language. First I formulated the things as I had observed them, usually in "high-flown language," for that corresponds to the style of the archetypes. Archetypes speak the language of high rhetoric, even of bombast. It is a style I find embarrassing; it grates on my nerves, as when someone draws his nails down a plaster wall, or scrapes his knife against a plate. But since I did not know what was going on, I had no choice but to write everything down in the style selected by the unconscious itself. Sometimes it was as if I were hearing it with my ears, sometimes feeling it with my mouth, as if my tongue were formulating words; now and then I heard myself whispering aloud. Below the threshold of consciousness everything was seething with life.

From the beginning I had conceived my voluntary confrontation with the unconscious as a scientific experiment which I myself was conducting and in whose outcome I was vitally interested. Today I might equally well say that it was an experiment which was being conducted on *me*. One of the greatest difficulties for me lay in dealing with my negative feelings. I was voluntarily submitting myself to emotions of which I could not really approve, and I was writing down fantasies which often struck me as nonsense, and toward which I had strong resistances. For as long as we do not understand their meaning, such fantasies are a diabolical mixture of the sublime and the ridiculous. It cost me a great deal to undergo them, but I had been challenged by fate. Only by extreme effort was I finally able to escape from the labyrinth.

In order to grasp the fantasies which were stirring in me "underground," I knew that I had to let myself plummet down into them, as it were. I felt not only violent resistance to this, but a distinct fear. For I was afraid of losing command of myself and becoming a prey to the fantasies—and as a psychiatrist I realized only too well what that meant. After prolonged hesitation, however, I saw that there was no other way out. I had to take the chance, had to try to gain power over them; for I realized that if I did not do so, I ran the risk of their gaining power over me. . . .

It was during Advent of the year 1913—December 12, to be exact— that I resolved upon the decisive step. I was sitting at my desk once more, thinking over my fears. Then I let myself drop. Suddenly it was as though the ground literally gave way beneath my feet, and I plunged down into dark depths. I could not fend off a feeling of panic. But then, abruptly, at not too great a depth, I landed on my feet in a soft, sticky mass. I felt great relief, although I was apparently in complete darkness. After a while my eyes grew accustomed to the gloom, which was rather like a deep twilight. Before me was the entrance to a dark cave, in which stood a dwarf with a leathery skin, as if he were mummified. I squeezed past him through the narrow entrance and waded knee deep through icy water to the other end of the cave where, on a projecting rock, I saw a glowing red crystal. I grasped the stone, lifted it, and discovered a hollow underneath. At first I could make out nothing, but then I saw that there was running water. In it a corpse floated by, a youth with blond hair and a wound in the head. He was followed by a gigantic black scarab and then by a red, newborn sun, rising up out of the depths of the water. Dazzled by the light, I wanted to replace the stone upon the opening, but then a fluid welled out. It was blood. A thick jet of it leaped up, and I felt nauseated. It seemed to me that the blood continued to spurt for an unendurably long time. At last it ceased, and the vision came to an end.

I was stunned by this vision. I realized, of course, that it was a hero and solar myth, a drama of death and renewal, the rebirth symbolized by the Egyptian scarab. At the end, the dawn of the new day should have followed, but instead came that intolerable outpouring of blood—an altogether abnormal phenomenon, so it seemed to me. But then I recalled the vision of blood that I had had in the autumn of that same year, and I abandoned all further attempt to understand.

Six days later (December 18, 1913), I had the following dream. I was with an unknown, brown-skinned man, a savage, in a lonely, rocky mountain landscape. It was before dawn; the eastern sky was already bright, and the stars fading. Then I heard Siegfried's horn sounding over the mountains and I knew that we had to kill him. We were armed with rifles and lay in wait for him on a narrow path over the rocks.

Then Siegfried appeared high up on the crest of the mountain, in the first ray of the rising sun. On a chariot made of the bones of the dead he drove at furious speed down the precipitous slope. When he turned a corner, we shot at him, and he plunged down, struck dead.

Filled with disgust and remorse for having destroyed something so great and beautiful, I turned to flee, impelled by the fear that the murder might be discovered. But a tremendous downfall of rain began, and I knew that it would wipe out all traces of the dead. I had escaped the danger of discovery; life could go on, but an unbearable feeling of guilt remained.

When I awoke from the dream, I turned it over in my mind, but was unable to understand it. I tried therefore to fall asleep again, but a voice within me said, "You *must* understand the dream, and must do so at once!" The inner urgency mounted until the terrible moment came when the voice said, "If you do not understand the dream, you must shoot yourself!" In the drawer of my night table lay a loaded revolver, and I became frightened. Then I began pondering once again, and suddenly the meaning of the dream dawned on me. "Why, that is the problem that is being played out in the world." Siegfried, I thought, represents what the Germans want to achieve, heroically to impose their will, have their own way. "Where there is a will there is a way!" I had wanted to do the same. But now that was no longer possible. The dream showed that the attitude embodied by Siegfried, the hero, no longer suited me. Therefore it had to be killed.

After the deed I felt an overpowering compassion, as though I myself had been shot: a sign of my secret identity with Siegfried, as well as of the grief a man feels when he is forced to sacrifice his ideal and his conscious attitudes. This identity and my heroic idealism had to be abandoned, for there are higher things than the ego's will, and to these one must bow.

These thoughts sufficed for the present, and I fell asleep again.

The small, brown-skinned savage who accompanied me and had actually taken the initiative in the killing was an embodiment of the primitive shadow. The rain showed that the tension between consciousness and the unconscious was being resolved. Although at the time I was not able to understand the meaning of the dream beyond these few hints, new forces were released in me which helped me to carry the experiment with the unconscious to a conclusion . . . .

When I look back upon it all today and consider what happened to me during the period of my work on the fantasies, it seems as though a message had come to me with overwhelming force. There were things in the images which concerned not only myself but many others also. It was then that I ceased to belong to myself alone, ceased to have the right to do so. From then on, my life belonged to the generality. The knowledge I was concerned with, or was seeking, still could not be found in the science of those days. I myself had to undergo the original experience, and, moreover, try to plant the results of my experience in the soil of reality; otherwise they would have remained subjective assumptions without validity. It was then that I dedicated myself to service of the psyche. I loved it and hated it, but it was my greatest wealth. My delivering myself over to it, as it were, was the only way by which I could endure my existence and live it as fully as possible.

Today I can say that I have never lost touch with my initial experiences. All my works, all my creative activity, has come from those initial fantasies and dreams which began in 1912, almost fifty years ago. Everything that I accomplished in later life was already contained in them, although at first only in the form of emotions and images.

My science was the only way I had of extricating myself from that chaos. Otherwise the material would have trapped me in its thicket, strangled me like jungle creepers. I took great care to try to understand every single image, every item of my psychic inventory, and to classify them scientifically—so far as this was possible—and, above all, to realize them in actual life. This is what we usually neglect to do. We allow the images to rise up, and maybe we wonder about them, but that is all. We do not take the trouble to understand them, let alone draw ethical conclusions from them. This stopping-short conjures up the negative effects of the unconscious.

It is equally a grave mistake to think that it is enough to gain some understanding of the images and that knowledge can here make a halt. Insight

The Resigned Self

into them must be converted into an ethical obligation. Not to do so is to fall prey to the power principle, and this produces dangerous effects which are destructive not only to others but even to the knower. The images of the unconscious place a great responsibility upon a man. Failure to understand them, or a shirking of ethical responsibility, deprives him of his wholeness and imposes a painful fragmentariness on his life.

In the midst of this period when I was so preoccupied with the images of the unconscious, I came to the decision to withdraw from the university, where I had lectured for eight years as *Privatdozent* (since 1905). My experience and experiments with the unconscious had brought my intellectual activity to a standstill. After the completion of *The Psychology of the Unconscious* I found myself utterly incapable of reading a scientific book. This went on for three years. I felt I could no longer keep up with the world of the intellect, nor would I have been able to talk about what really preoccupied me. The material brought to light from the unconscious had, almost literally, struck me dumb. I could neither understand it nor give it form. At the university I was in an exposed position, and felt that in order to go on giving courses there I would first have to find an entirely new and different orientation. It would be unfair to continue teaching young students when my own intellectual situation was nothing but a mass of doubts.

I therefore felt that I was confronted with the choice of either continuing my academic career, whose road lay smooth before me, or following the laws of my inner personality, of a higher reason, and forging ahead with this curious task of mine, this experiment in confrontation with the unconscious. But until it was completed I could not appear before the public.

Consciously, deliberately, then, I abandoned my academic career. For I felt that something great was happening to me, and I put my trust in the thing which I felt to be more important *sub specie aeternitatis.* I knew that it would fill my life, and for the sake of that goal I was ready to take any kind of risk.

What, after all, did it matter whether or not I became a professor? Of course it bothered me to have to give this up; in many respects I regretted that I could not confine myself to generally understandable material. I even had moments when I stormed against destiny. But emotions of this kind are transitory, and do not count. The other thing, on the contrary, is important, and if we pay heed to what the inner personality desires and says, the sting vanishes. That is something I have experienced again and again, not only when I gave up my academic career. Indeed, I had my first experiences of this sort as a child. In my youth I was hot-tempered; but whenever the emotion had reached its climax, suddenly it swung around and there followed a cosmic stillness. At such times I was remote from everything, and what had only a moment before excited me seemed to belong to a distant past.

The consequence of my resolve, and my involvement with things which neither I nor anyone else could understand, was an extreme loneliness. I was going about laden with thoughts of which I could speak to no one: they would only have been misunderstood. I felt the gulf between the external world and the interior world of images in its most painful form. I could not yet see that interaction of both worlds which I now understand. I saw only an irreconcilable contradiction between "inner" and "outer."

However, it was clear to me from the start that I could find contact with the outer world and with people only if I succeeded in showing—and this would demand the most intensive effort—that the contents of psychic experience are real, and real not only as my own personal experiences, but as collective experiences which others also have. Later I tried to demonstrate this in my scientific work, and I did all in my power to convey to my intimates a new way of seeing things. I knew that if I did not succeed, I would be condemned to absolute isolation. It was only toward the end of the First World War that I gradually began to emerge from the darkness.

During those years, between 1918 and 1920, I began to understand that the goal of psychic development is the self. There is no linear evolution; there is only a circumambulation of the self. Uniform development exists, at most, only at the beginning; later, everything points toward the center. This insight gave me stability, and gradually my inner peace returned. . . .

Some years later (in 1927) I obtained confirmation of my ideas about the center and the self by way of a dream. . . . I found myself in a dirty, sooty city. It was night, and winter, and dark, and raining. I was in Liverpool. With a number of Swiss—say, half a dozen—I walked through the dark streets. I had the feeling that there we were coming from the harbor, and that the real city was actually up above, on the cliffs. We climbed up there. It reminded me of Basel, where the market is down below and then you go up through the Totengässchen ("Alley of the Dead"), which leads to a plateau above and so to the Petersplatz and the Peterskirche. When we reached the plateau, we found a broad square dimly illuminated by street lights, into which many streets converged. The various quarters of the city were arranged radially around the square. In the center was a round pool, and in the middle of it a small island. While everything round about was obscured by rain, fog, smoke, and dimly lit darkness, the little island blazed with sunlight. On it stood a single tree, a magnolia, in a shower of reddish blossoms. It was as though the tree stood in the sunlight and were at the same time the source of light. My companions commented on the abominable weather, and obviously did not see the tree. They spoke of another Swiss who was living in Liverpool, and expressed surprise that he should have settled here. I was carried away by the beauty of the flowering tree and the sunlit island, and thought, "I know very well why he has settled here." Then I awoke.

On one detail of the dream I must add a supplementary comment: the individual quarters of the city were themselves arranged radially around a central point. This point formed a small open square illuminated by a larger street lamp, and constituted a small replica of the island. I knew that the "other Swiss" lived in the vicinity of one of these secondary centers.

The Resigned Self

This dream represented my situation at the time. I can still see the grayish-yellow raincoat, glistening with the wetness of the rain. Everything was extremely unpleasant, black and opaque—just as I felt then. But I had had a vision of unearthly beauty, and that was why I was able to live at all. Liverpool is the "pool of life." The "liver," according to an old view, is the seat of life—that which "makes to live."

This dream brought with it a sense of finality. I saw that here the goal had been revealed. One could not go beyond the center. The center is the goal, and everything is directed toward that center. Through this dream I understood that the self is the principle and archetype of orientation and meaning. Therein lies its healing function. For me, this insight signified an approach to the center and therefore to the goal. Out of it emerged a first inkling of my personal myth.

. . . The dream depicted the climax of the whole process of development of consciousness. It satisfied me completely, for it gave a total picture of my situation. I had known, to be sure, that I was occupied with something important, but I still lacked understanding, and there had been no one among my associates who could have understood. The clarification brought about by the dream made it possible for me to take an objective view of the things that filled my being.

Without such a vision I might perhaps have lost my orientation and been compelled to abandon my undertaking. But here the meaning had been made clear. When I parted from Freud, I knew that I was plunging into the unknown. Beyond Freud, after all, I knew nothing; but I had taken the step into darkness. When this happens, and then such a dream comes, one feels it as an act of grace . . . .

Suggestions for Further Reading

Gerhard Adler, *Studies in Analytical Psychology* (New York: G.P. Putnam's Sons, 1966).

Maud Bodkin, *Studies of Type-Images in Poetry, Religion, and Philosophy* (London: Oxford University Press, 1951).

Joseph Campbell, *The Hero with a Thousand Faces* (Cleveland: Meridian Books, 1956).

Avis M. Dry, *The Psychology of Jung* (London: Methuen and Company, Ltd., 1961).

Freida Fordham, *An Introduction to Jung's Psychology* (Baltimore: Penguin Books, 1953).

Michael Fordham, *New Developments in Analytical Psychology* (London: Routledge and K. Paul, 1957).

Julius Heuscher, *A Psychiatric Study of Fairy-Tales* (Springfield: Thomas, 1963).

Raymond Hostie, *Religion and the Psychology of C. G. Jung* (New York: Sheed and Ward, 1957).

Carl Kerenyi and C. G. Jung, *Essays in a Science of Mythology* (New York: Harper Torchbooks, 1963).

Morris Philipson, *Outline of a Jungian Aesthetics* (Evanston, Ill.: Northwestern University Press, 1963).

Ira Progoff, *Jung's Psychology and Its Social Meaning* (New York: Julian Press, 1953).

————, *The Death and Re-Birth of Psychology* (New York: Dell Publishing Company, 1956).

Hans Schaer, *Religion and the Cure of Souls in Jung's Psychology* (New York: Pantheon Books, 1950).

The Resigned Self

Part Two

The Chastised Self

Abelard

The Story of My Adversities

And since everything occurs by divine ordinance, let every faithful soul under every affliction find consolation in the thought that God in His great goodness never permits anything to occur outside His plan and that no matter what wrongdoing is done, He makes it work to the best issue.

Peter Abelard was born in 1079 in Le Pallet (near Nantes). Although probably remembered most for his love affair with Heloise, Abelard was also a superb logician, a competent philosopher, a fine teacher, and an innovative theologian. A student under Roscellin, William of Champeaux, and Anselm of Canterbury, Abelard gained fame by his ability to challenge and threaten his instructors. His life seems to have been formed by the challenges he posed to his superiors. He was in almost constant conflict with the ecclesiastical authorities and in perpetual disagreement with the prevailing intellectual views. Each conflict produced a crisis which worked itself out according to the following pattern: Abelard was brought to trial—openly or subversively, officially or informally—and, whether he was vindicated or condemned, forced to leave for another locale, where in due time the sequence would repeat itself.

Peter Abelard was the first-born son in a prominent family but gave up his inheritance when he entered the priesthood. Later, while teaching logic and theology at Notre Dame in Paris, Abelard in 1114 met Heloise, the niece of

Fulbert, Canon of Notre Dame. For a time she was his student, and during the course of her studies they fell in love. Subsequently, Heloise bore Abelard's child, after which they were married secretly. When the news broke, Fulbert's anger was so great that he incited others to subject Abelard to physical emasculation. In 1118 Abelard retired to the monastery of St. Denis, and Heloise entered a convent. But Abelard's difficulties were not over. In addition to the castigation he received because of his relationship with Heloise, he was also cited for incorrect theological teachings. He was first condemned for his heretical views at Soissons in 1121 and again by the Council of Sens in 1141. At the latter trial Abelard was convicted of having taught that the faith could be explained logically. He died while en route to Rome to defend his position before the highest ecclesiastical authority, the Pope, on April 21, 1142. During his lifetime he had managed to alienate most of the respected teachers in Christendom, as well as St. Bernard of Clairveaux, the famous mediaeval mystic.

Abelard's personal papers reveal a man who was well aware of his own genius and great capacity for challenging the social, intellectual, and moral status quo. At times he emphasizes his own genius and agency; at other times he wants to honor the conviction that both genius and agency are prerogatives of God alone. This is the only way in which he can understand why he should be chastised for seeking to outstrip human capabilities. Abelard's story is the private case history of a man who is caught in the tension between the several sets of directives which make up the mediaeval world view. It is a story one might expect to find in an Augustinian world—a world which supposes that the "earthly city" is dependent upon the "heavenly city" for both reality and goodness.

Abelard's Adversities

Professional Injustices

Please understand, then, that I was born in a certain town called Palets which was built on the way into Brittany, about eight miles east, I think, from the city of Nantes. Such is the nature of that country, or, perhaps of those who dwell there, that my mind bent itself easily to the study of letters. Furthermore, I had a father who had a smattering of literary knowledge before he was girded with the soldier's belt. His love of knowledge was so strong that he saw to it that each son of his should be taught in letters even earlier than in the management of arms. And because I was his first born, and for that reason the more dear to him, he sought with double diligence to have me wisely taught. For my part, the

From Peter Abelard, *Historia Calamitatum: The Story of My Misfortunes: An Autobiography*, translated by Henry Adams Bellows (Saint Paul: Thomas A. Boyd, 1922). Slightly revised and amended by the editors.

The Chastised Self

more success and facility I acquired in the study of letters, the greater became my devotion to them, until I was so enthralled by my passion for learning that, gladly leaving to my brothers the pomp of glory in arms, the right of heritage, and all the honours that should have been mine as the eldest born, I fled from the court of Mars that I might win learning in the bosom of Minerva. And since I found the armory of logical reasoning more to my liking than the other forms of philosophy, I exchanged all other weapons for these, and to the prizes of victory in war I preferred the battle of minds in debate. From then on, journeying through many provinces, and debating as I went, going wherever I heard that the study of my chosen art flourished most, I became like one of the Peripatetics.

I came finally to Paris, where in those days the art of dialectics flourished especially, and there I met William of Champeaux, my teacher, a man most distinguished in his science both by reputation and by intrinsic skill. I remained with him for some time, at first well liked of him; but later I brought him great grief, because I undertook to refute certain of his opinions, frequently attacking him in disputation. And now and then in these debates I was judged to be the winner. To those of my fellow students who were placed at the top of the class, this seemed all the more insufferable because of my youth and the brief duration of my studies.

Out of this sprang the beginning of my misfortunes, which have followed me even to the present day; the more widely my fame was spread abroad, the more bitter was the envy that was kindled against me. Presuming on my gifts far beyond what my youth might warrant, and despite my tender years, I aspired toward the leadership of a school. Beyond that I made preparations for the very place in which I would undertake this task, namely, none other than the castle of Melun which at that time was a royal seat. My teacher himself had some foreknowledge of this, and tried to separate my school as far as possible from his own. Working in secret, he sought in every way he could before I left his following to ruin the school I had planned and the place I had chosen for it. Since he had many rivals in this area, however, some of whom had influence with other great men of the land, I relied on their aid to achieve the fulfillment of my wish. I could solicit their support because of his unconcealed envy. From this small beginning of my school, my fame in the art of dialectics began to spread abroad; and little by little the reputation of those who had been my fellow students as well as of the teacher himself grew dim and just about died out altogether. Thus it came about that, still more confident in myself, I moved my school as soon as I could to the castle of Corbeil close to Paris. I knew I would be given more frequent chance there for my assaults in our battles in debate.

Not long thereafter I suffered a grievous illness precipitated by my uncommon zest for study. This illness forced me to go home to my native province, and thus for some years it was as if I had been cut off from France. And yet, for that very reason, I was sought out all the more eagerly by those whose hearts were troubled by the lore of dialectics. But after a few years had passed, and I was whole again from my sickness, I learned that my teacher, that same William Archdeacon of Paris, had changed his former garb and joined an order of the regular clergy. This he had done, or so men said, in order that he might be deemed more deeply religious, and so might be elevated to a loftier rank in the prelacy, a thing which occurred very soon, for he was made bishop of Chalons. Nevertheless, the garb he had donned by reason of his conversion did nothing to keep him away either from the city of Paris or from his coveted study of philosophy. And in the very monastery where he had shut himself up for the sake of religion he immediately began teaching again as he had been doing before.

I returned to him, for I was eager to learn more rhetoric from his lips; and in the course of our many arguments on various matters, I compelled him by forceful reasoning to alter his earlier opinion on the subject of the universals and, finally, to abandon it altogether. . . . It happened that when William had first revised and then finally abandoned his views on this subject, his lecturing sank into such a state of negligent reasoning that it could hardly be called lecturing on the science of dialectics at all. It was as if all his science had been confined to this one question about the nature of universals.

Thus it came about that my teaching won such strength and authority that even those who had clung most tenaciously to my former master before, and most bitterly attacked my doctrines, now flocked to my school. The very man who had succeeded to my master's chair in the Paris school offered me his post, in order that he might put himself and the others there under my tutelage; and this occurred in the very place where his master and mine had formerly reigned. And when, in a short time, my master saw me directing the study of dialectics there, it is not easy to find words to tell with what envy he was consumed or with what pain he was tormented. He found it impossible to bear the anguish of what he felt to be his wrongs, and he shrewdly attacked me that he might get rid of me. And because there was nothing in my conduct which would allow him to confront me openly, he tried to steal away the school by launching the vilest calumnies against him who had yielded his post to me, and by putting in his place a certain rival of mine. I returned to Melun, and set up my school there as before. The more openly his envy pursued me, the greater was the authority it conferred upon me. . . .

Not long afterward, when William became aware of the fact that almost all his students had grave doubts about his religion, and were whispering among themselves about his conversion, deeming that he had by no means abandoned this world, he withdrew himself and his brotherhood, together with his students, to a certain estate a great distance from the city. I immediately returned from Melun to Paris, hoping for peace from him in the future. But since, as I have

The Chastised Self

said, he had caused my place to be occupied by a rival of mine, I established my school outside the city of Mont St. Genevieve. Thus I was as one laying siege against the one who had taken possession of my post. No sooner had my master heard of this than he boldly and hastily returned to the city, bringing back as many students as he could. After he returned, however, he lost nearly all of his followers, and was compelled to give up the direction of the school. Not long afterward, apparently giving up all claims to worldly fame, he was converted to the monastic life. Following the return of our master to the city, the debates which my scholars waged both with him and with his pupils, and the successes which fortune gave to us, and above all to me, in these wars, you have long since learned of through your own experience.

While these things were happening, it became necessary for me again to return to my old home, because of my dear mother, Lucia; after the conversion of my father, Berengarius, to the monastic life, she decided to do the same thing. When all this had been completed, I returned to France primarily to study theology; by now William was active in the episcopate of Chalons. It was here that Anselm of Laon built his reputation for greatness.

I sought out this venerable man, whose fame rested more on long-established custom than on a powerful talent or intellect. If any one came to him in doubt about an issue, he went away with more doubt. He was wonderful in the eyes of these who only listened to him, but those who asked him questions came to think little of him. He had a miraculous flow of words, but they were contemptible in meaning and quite void of sense. When he kindled a fire, he filled his house with smoke but produced no flames. He was like a tree which seemed noble to those who viewed its leaves from afar; but to those who came nearer for a closer examination, it disclosed its barrenness. . . . It was not long before I made this discovery. . . . I went to his lectures less and less often, a practice which bothered many of Anselm's followers who regarded it as a sign of contempt for so distinguished a teacher. Secretly they sought to influence him against me, and by their vile insinuations made me hated of him. . . .

Now this venerable man was deeply smitten with envy, and, as I have already mentioned, was incited by the insinuations of various persons to persecute me for my lecturing on the Scriptures. He was no less bitter than my former master, William, who had opposed my work in philosophy. At that time there were two men in this old man's school who were understood to excel above the others: Alberic of Rheims and Lotulphe the Lombard. . . . Chiefly at their suggestion, the venerable coward had the impudence to forbid me to continue the work of preparing glosses in his school. The reason he gave was that the errors I might make would be charged to him. When his scholars heard about this, they were filled with complete indignation at such an undisguised manifestation of spite. The more obvious their enmity became, the more it contributed to my honor. His persecution did nothing except to make me more famous.

His Affair with Heloise

And so, after a few days I returned to Paris, and there for several years I peacefully directed the school which formerly had been destined for me, yes, even offered to me, but from which I had been driven out. At the very outset of my work there, I set about completing the glosses on Ezekiel which I had begun at Laon. These proved so satisfactory to all who read them that they came to regard me as adept in lecturing on theology as I had proved myself to be in the field of philosophy. Thus my school increased notably in size by reason of my lectures on subjects in both of these fields, and the amount of financial profit as well as glory which it brought me cannot be concealed from you, for the matter was widely publicized. But prosperity always puffs up the foolish, and worldly comfort enervates the soul, rendering it an easy prey to carnal temptations. Thus I, who by this time had come to regard myself as the only philosopher remaining in the whole world, and had ceased to fear any further disturbance of my peace, began to loosen the rein on my desires, although prior to this time I had always lived in complete continence. . . . For it is well known, I think, that philosophers and those who have devoted their lives to arousing the love of sacred study have been strong above all else in the beauty of chastity.

Thus it happened that while I was completely absorbed in pride and sensuality, divine grace, the cure for both diseases, was forced upon me, even though I would have chosen to shun it. First I was punished for my sensuality, and then for my pride. For my sensuality, I lost the organs by which I practiced it; for my pride, engendered in me by my knowledge of letters—as the Apostle said: "Knowledge puffeth itself up"—I knew the humiliation of seeing the very book in which I most treasured burned. And now it is my desire that you should know the stories of these two happenings. . . . Because I had always detested the foulness of prostitutes, because I had diligently kept myself from all excesses and from association with the women of noble birth who attended the school, because I knew so little of the common talk of ordinary people, perverse and flattering fate provided the occasion for casting me down from the heights of my own exaltation. . . .

There dwelt in Paris a certain young girl named Heloise, the niece of a canon named Fulbert. Her uncle's love for her was equalled only by his desire that she should have the best education which he could possibly procure for her. A beautiful woman, she stood out above all the rest because of her abundant knowledge of letters. This virtue is rare among women, and for that very reason it doubly graced her, and made her the choicest maiden in the entire kingdom. I carefully considered all those qualities by which lovers are attracted, and decided to unite myself to this young girl in the bonds of love. It seemed to me that this could be accomplished very easily. So distinguished was my name, along with the advantages of my youth and comeliness, that any woman I might favour with my love was not likely to reject me. Then, too, I believed that I could win the maiden's consent all the more easily by reason of her eager knowledge of letters. So, even if we were parted, we might be together in thought with the aid of written messages. Perhaps we could also write more boldly than we could speak; thus at all times we could live in joyous intimacy.

And so, utterly aflame with my passion for this maiden, I sought to discover means whereby I might talk with her daily, in order to win her consent. For this purpose I persuaded the girl's uncle, aided by some of his friends, to take me into his household—he lived near my school—in return for a small payment. My pretext for this was that the care of my own household was a serious handicap to my studies, and likewise burdened me with an expense far greater than I could afford. Now, he was an avaricious man, and was most desirous that his niece's study of letters should go forward. For these two reasons, I easily won his consent, for he was fairly eager for my money, and at the same time believed that his niece would vastly benefit by my teaching. More than this, by his own earnest entreaties he complied with my designs even more so than I had hoped for, thus opening the way for my love. He entrusted her completely to my guidance, begging me to give her instruction whenever I was free from the duties of my school, day or night, and to punish her sternly if I should ever find her negligent of her tasks. In all this the man's simplicity was nothing short of astounding to me; I should not have been more smitten with wonder if he had entrusted a tender lamb to the care of a ravenous wolf. When he had given her into my charge, not simply to be taught but even to be disciplined, he had given free scope to my desires, offering me every opportunity, even ones I had not sought, to bend her to my will with threats and blows if I failed to do so with caresses. However, there were two factors which may have served to allay any suspicions on his part: his love for his niece, and my former reputation for continence.

Should I say more? We were united first in the dwelling that sheltered our love, and then in the hearts that burned with it. Under the pretext of study we spent our hours in the happiness of love, and learning held out to us the secret opportunities that our passion craved. Our speech was more of love than of the books which lay open before us; our kisses far outnumbered our reasoned words. Our hands sought less the book than each other's bosoms; love drew our eyes together far more than the lesson drew them to the pages of our text. In order that there might be no suspicion, there were, indeed, sometimes blows, but love gave them, not anger; they were not the marks of wrath, but of a tenderness surpassing the most fragrant balm of sweetness. What followed? No degree in love's progress was left unexplored by our passion, and if love itself could imagine any wonder as yet unknown, we discovered it. Our inexperience in such delights made us all the more ardent in our pursuit of them, so that our thirst for one another was still unquenched.

As this passionate rapture absorbed me more and more, I devoted less time to philosophy and to the work of the school. Indeed it became loathsome to me to go to the school or to linger there; the work became very burdensome, since my nights were vigils of love and my days were given to study. My lecturing became utterly careless and lukewarm; I did nothing because of inspiration, but everything merely as a matter of habit. I had become nothing more than a reciter of my former discoveries; and though I still wrote poems, they dealt with love, not with the secrets of philosophy. Of these songs you yourself are aware; many of them have become well known and have been sung in many lands, I think primarily by those who delighted in the things of this world. And the sorrow, groans, and lamentations of my students when they perceived this preoccupation and chaos of my mind are difficult to overestimate.

A thing so obvious could deceive only a few, no one, I think, except the one whom it disgraced the most, the girl's uncle, Fulbert. The truth was hinted at often enough and by many persons, but he could not believe it. This was partly because of his boundless love for his niece, and partly because of my previous adherence to continence. . . . But no matter how slow a matter may be in disclosing itself, it is sure to come into the open eventually. . . . So, after the lapse of several months, it happened. Oh, how great was the uncle's grief when he learned the truth, and how bitter was the sorrow of the lovers when we were forced to part! With what shame was I overwhelmed, with what contrition smitten because of the blow which had fallen on the one I loved, and what a tempest of misery burst over her by reason of my disgrace! Each grieved most, not for himself, but for the other. Each sought relief not for his own sufferings but for those of the one he loved. Our bodily separations served only to link our souls closer together; the plentitude of love which was denied to us inflamed us more than ever. . . .

It was not long after this that Heloise found that she was pregnant. She wrote this to me in great exultation, at the same time asking me to consider what ought to be done. Accordingly, on a night when her uncle was absent, we carried out the plan we had decided on in advance, and I took her secretly away from her uncle's house, sending her without delay to my own country. She remained there with my sister until she gave birth to a son, whom she named Astrolabe. Meanwhile her uncle, after his return, was almost mad with grief; only one who had then seen him could rightly guess the burning agony of his sorrow and the bitterness of his shame. What steps to take against me, or what snares to set for me, he did not know. If he should kill me or do me some bodily harm, he feared that his beloved niece might be made to suffer for it among my family. He had no power to seize me and imprison me somewhere against my will, though I have no doubt he would have done so quickly enough had he been able to or dared. But I had taken measures to guard against any such attempt.

Finally, however, in pity for his deep grief, and bitterly blaming myself for the suffering which my love had brought upon him through the baseness of the deception I had practiced, I went to him, asked his forgiveness, and promised to make any amends that he himself might request. I pointed out that what had

The Chastised Self

happened could not seem incredible to any one who had ever felt the power of love, or who remembered how, from the very beginning of the human race, women had provoked even the noblest men to utter ruin. And in order to make amends beyond his highest wish, I offered to marry her whom I had seduced, provided only that the matter could be kept secret, so that I might suffer no loss of reputation. To this he gladly assented, pledging his own faith and that of his family, even sealing the pact with kisses—all this that he might the more easily betray me.

I returned to my own country, and brought back my mistress, that I might make her my wife. However, she violently disapproved of this, believing it to be dangerous, and thinking that it would bring disgrace upon me. She swore that her uncle would never be appeased by such satisfaction as this, as, indeed, afterwards proved only too true. She asked how she could ever be proud of me if she should make me shameful, and should shame herself along with me. What penalties, she said, would the world rightly demand of her if she should rob it of so shining a light! What curses would follow such a loss to the Church, what tears among the philosophers would result from such a marriage! How unfitting, how lamentable it would be for me, whom nature had made for the whole world, to devote myself to one woman solely, and to subject myself to such humiliation! She strongly refused a marriage which she felt would be ignominious and burdensome to me in every way.

Then, turning from the consideration of such hindrances to the study of philosophy, Heloise made me consider the conditions of honorable wedlock. What possible concord could there be between scholars and domestics, between authors and cradles, between books or tablets and distaffs, between the stylus or the pen and the spindle? What man, intent on his religious or philosophical meditations, can possibly endure the whining of children, the lullabies of the nurse seeking to quiet them, or the noisy confusion of family life? Who can endure the continual untidiness of children? The rich, you may reply, can do this, because they have palaces or houses containing many rooms, and because their wealth takes no thought of expense and protects them from daily worries. But to this the answer is that the condition of philosophers is by no means that of the wealthy, nor can those whose minds are occupied with riches and worldly cares find time for religious or philosophical study. For this reason the renowned philosophers of old utterly despised the world, fleeing from its perils rather than reluctantly giving them up, and denied themselves all its delights in order that they might repose in the embraces of philosophy alone. . . .

Now, she added, if laymen and pagans, bound by no profession of religion, lived after this fashion, what ought you, a cleric and a canon, to do in order not to prefer base obscenities to your sacred duties . . . ? If you care nothing for your privileges as a cleric, at least uphold your dignity as a philosopher. If you scorn the reverence due to God, let regard for your reputation temper your shamelessness. Remember that Socrates was chained to a wife, and by a filthy accident paid for this blot on philosophy in order that others might be made more cautious by his example. . . . Her final argument was that it would be dangerous for me to take her back to Paris, and that it would be far sweeter for her to be called my mistress than to be known as my wife. This would also be more honorable for me. In this case, she said, love alone would hold me to her, and the strength of the marriage chain would not constrain us. Even if we should by chance be parted from time to time, the joy of our meetings would be all the sweeter by reason of its rarity. But when she found that she could not convince me or dissuade me from my folly by such arguments, and because she could not bear to offend me, with grievous sighs and tears she made an end of her resistance, saying: "Then there is no more left but this, that in our doom the sorrow yet to come shall be no less than the love we two have already known." Not even in this, as the whole world now knows, did she lack the spirit of prophecy.

So, after our little son was born, we left him in my sister's care, and secretly returned to Paris. A few days later, in the early morning, having kept our secret nocturnal vigil of prayer in a certain church, we were united there in the benediction of wedlock, her uncle and a few friends of his and mine being present. We left immediately by separate ways. After that we saw each other only rarely and in private, diligently trying to conceal what we had done. But her uncle and his family, seeking solace for their disgrace, began to divulge the story of our marriage, thereby violating the pledge they had given me. Heloise, for her part, denounced her own kin and swore that they were speaking the most absolute lies. Her uncle, aroused to anger, threatened to punish her. As soon as I heard this, I sent her to a convent of nuns at Argenteuil, not far from Paris, where she herself had been brought up and educated as a young girl. I had them prepare the garments of a nun, which could be worn in the convent, except for the veil, and these I asked her to put on.

When her uncle and his family heard of this, they were convinced that I had tricked them, ridding myself of Heloise forever by forcing her to become a nun. Violently incensed, they laid a plot against me, and one night, while, unsuspecting, I lay asleep in a secret room in my lodgings, they broke in with the help of one of my servants whom they had bribed. There they took vengeance on me with a most cruel and shameful punishment, such as astounded the whole world, for they cut off those parts of my body with which I had done that which was the cause of their sorrow. This done, they fled, but two of them were captured, and suffered the loss of their eyes and their genital organs. . . .

When morning came the whole city was assembled in front of my dwelling. It is difficult, even impossible, for words of mine to describe their amazement, the lamentations they uttered, the uproar with which they harassed me, or the grief with which they increased my own suffering. The clergy, chiefly, and above all my scholars, tortured me with their intolerable lamentations and outcries, so that I suffered more intensely from their compassion than from the pain of my wound. In truth I felt the disgrace more than the hurt to my body, and was more afflicted with shame than with pain. My incessant thought was of the reputation in which I had delighted, now destroyed, yes, even swiftly blotted out by an evil happening. I saw, too, how justly God had punished me in that very part of my body from which I had sinned. I perceived that there was indeed justice in my betrayal by him whom I had myself already betrayed; and then I thought how eagerly my rivals would seize upon this manifestation of justice, how this disgrace would bring bitter and enduring grief to my family and my friends, and how the tale of this amazing outrage would spread to the ends of the earth.

What path lay open to me thereafter? How could I ever again hold up my head among men, when every finger should be pointed at me in scorn, every tongue speak my blistering shame, and when I should be a monstrous spectacle to all eyes? I was overwhelmed when I recalled that according to the letter of the law, God holds eunuchs in such abomination that men thus maimed are forbidden (along with lepers and the filthy) to enter a church. . . .

I must confess that in my misery it was the overwhelming sense of my disgrace rather than any ardor for conversion to the religious life that drove me to seek the seclusion of the monastic cloister. Heloise had already taken the veil and entered a convent. Thus it was that we both put on the sacred garb, I in the abbey of St. Denis, and she in the convent of Argenteuil. . . . For my part, scarcely had I recovered from my wound when the clergy sought me in great numbers, ceaselessly requesting both my abbot and me that now since I was done with learning for the sake of money or reputation, I should engage in it for the pure love of God. . . . It was their plea that, since I had already worked on behalf of the rich, I should now devote myself to the teaching of the poor. I would perceive that the hand of God had touched me when I had devoted my life to the study of letters free from the snares of the flesh, away from the tumultuous life of this world. Then, in truth, I would become a philosopher less of this world than of God.

Additional Tribulations

And so I stayed in that place, my body indeed hidden away, but my fame spreading throughout the whole world, until its echo reverberated mightily. My former rivals, seeing that they themselves were not powerless to do me harm, stirred up against me certain new apostles in whom the world put great faith. One of these, Norbert of Premontre, took pride in his position as canon of a regular order. The other, Bernard of Clairvaux, made it his boast that he had revived the true monastic life. These two ran everywhere preaching and shamelessly slandering me in every way they could. In time they succeeded in bringing scorn upon me from many of those of authority among both the clergy and the laity. They broadcast such sinister reports of my faith and life that even my best friends were turned against me, and those who still retained some of their former regard for me had to disguise it in every possible way because of their fear of these two men.

God is my witness that whenever I learned of the convening of a new assemblage of the clergy, I believed that it was done for the express purpose of my condemnation. Stunned by this fear like one smitten with a thunderbolt, I daily expected to be dragged before their councils or assemblies as a heretic or one guilty of impiety. Though I seem to compare a flea with a lion, or an ant with an elephant, in very truth my rivals persecuted me no less bitterly than the heretics of old hounded St. Athanasius. Often, God knows, I sank so deep in despair that I was ready to leave the world of Christendom and go forth among the heathen, paying them a stipulated tribute in order that I might live a Christian life quietly among the enemies of Christ. It seemed to me that such people might indeed be kindly disposed toward me, particularly as they would doubtless suspect me of being a poor Christian, imputing my flight to some crime I had committed, and would therefore believe that I might perhaps be won over to their form of worship.

While I was thus afflicted with so great perturbation of the spirit, and when the only way of escape seemed to be for me to seek refuge with Christ among the enemies of Christ, an opportunity came whereby I thought I could temporarily avoid the plots of my enemies. But it turned out that I fell among Christians and monks who were far more savage than heathens and even more evil. It happened this way. There was in lesser Brittany, in the bishopric of Vannes, a certain abbey of St. Gildas at Ruits which had just lost its shepherd through death. To this abbey I was selected by the brothers there; and with the approval of the prince of that land, I easily secured permission to accept the post from my own abbot and brothers. Thus did the hatred of the French drive me westward, even as that of the Romans drove Jerome toward the East. Never, God knows, would I have agreed to this thing had it not been for my longing for any possible means of escape from the sufferings which I had born so constantly.

The land was barbarous and its speech was foreign to me. As for the monks, their vile and untameable way of life was notorious almost everywhere. The people of the region, too, were uncivilized and lawless. Thus, like one who in terror of the sword that threatens him dashes headlong over a precipice, and to shun one death for a moment rushes to another, I knowingly sought this new danger in order to escape from the former one. And there amid the dreadful roar of the waves of the sea, where the land's end left me no further refuge in flight, I repeated over and over again in my prayers: "From the end of the earth will I cry unto Thee, when my heart is overwhelmed."

No one, I am sure, could fail to understand how persistently that undisciplined body of monks, the direction of which I had thus undertaken, tortured my heart day and night, or how constantly I was compelled to think of the danger alike to my body and to my soul. I was sure that if I should try to force them to live according to the principles they had themselves professed, I would not survive. And yet, if I did not do this to the utmost of my ability, I saw that my damnation was assured. Moreover, a certain lord who was exceedingly powerful in that region had earlier brought the abbey under his control, taking advantage of the state of disorder within the monastery to seize all the lands adjacent to it for his own use. And he levied heavier taxes on the monks than those which were extorted from the Jews themselves.

The monks pressed me to supply them with their daily necessities, but they held no property in common which I might administer in their behalf, and each one, with such resources as he possessed, supported himself and his concubines, as well as his sons and daughters. They took delight in harassing me on this matter, and they stole and carried off whatever they could lay their hands on, so that my failure to maintain order might make me either give up trying to enforce discipline or else abandon my post altogether. Since the entire region was equally savage, lawless and disorganized, there was not a single man to whom I could turn for aid, for the habits of all alike were foreign to me. Outside the monastery the lord and his henchmen hounded me ceaselessly, and within its walls the brethren were forever plotting against me, so that it seemed as if the Apostle had none other but me in mind when he said: "There were fightings without, and fears within."

I considered and lamented the uselessness and the wretchedness of my existence, how fruitless my life now was, both to myself and to others; how of old I had been of some service to the clerics whom I had now abandoned for the sake of these monks, so that I was no longer able to be of use to either; how incapable I had proved myself in everything I had undertaken or attempted, so that above all others I deserved the reproach, "This man began to build, and was not able to finish." My despair grew deeper still when I compared the evils I had left behind with those to which I had come, for my former sufferings now seemed as nothing to me. Often I groaned: "Justly has this sorrow come upon me because I deserted the Paraclete, which is to say the Consoler, and thrust myself into sure desolation; seeking to shun threats I fled to a certain peril."

The thing which tormented me most was the fact that, having abandoned my oratory, I could make no suitable provision for the celebration there of the divine office; the extreme poverty of the place would scarcely provide the necessities of one man. But the true Paraclete Himself brought me real consolation in the midst of my sorrow, and made all due provision for His own oratory. For it happened that in some manner or other, claiming it as having formerly legally belonged to his monastery, my abbot of St. Denis got possession of the abbey of Argenteuil, the place about which I have already spoken, where Heloise, now my sister in Christ rather than my wife, had taken the veil. From this abbey he expelled all the nuns who had dwelt there by force, even Heloise, who in the meantime had become the prioress. I perceived that this was an opportunity presented by God himself to me where I could make new provision for my oratory. Thus, returning there, I asked her to come to the oratory, along with some others from the convent who had stayed with her.

On their arrival I released the oratory to them, together with its belongings, and, through the approval and assistance of the bishop of the district, Pope Innocent II, promulgated a decree confirming my gift to them and their successors in perpetuity. This refuge of divine mercy which they served so devotedly soon brought them consolation, even though at first their life there was one of privation and, for a time, of utter destitution. But the place proved itself a true Paraclete to them, making all those who lived nearby feel pity and kindliness for the sisterhood. I think they prospered more through gifts in a single year than I should have done if I had stayed there a hundred years. It is certainly true that the weakness of women makes their needs and sufferings appeal strongly to people's feelings, just as it makes their virtue all the more pleasing to God and man. And God granted such favor in the eyes of all to her who was now my sister, and who was in authority over the rest, that the bishops loved her as a daughter, the abbots as a sister, and the laity as a mother. All alike marvelled at her religious zeal, her good judgment, and the sweetness of her incomparable patience in all things. The less often she allowed herself to be seen, shutting herself up in her cell to devote herself to sacred meditations and prayers, the more eagerly did those who dwelt without demand her presence and the spiritual guidance of her words. . . .

And now, most dear brother in Christ and comrade closest to me in the intimacy of speech, it should suffice for your sorrows and the hardships you have endured that I have written this story of my own misfortunes, amid which I have toiled almost from the cradle. For just as I said in the beginning of this letter, you too shall come to regard your tribulation as nothing, or at any rate as little, in comparison with mine; thus you shall bear it more lightly to the measure that you regard it as slight. Always take comfort in the saying of Our Lord, when he predicted for his followers in their encounters with the followers of the devil: "If they have persecuted me, they will also persecute you. If the world hate you, you know that it hated me before it hated you. If you were of the world, the world would love his own." And the apostle says: "All who live godly in Christ Jesus shall suffer persecution." Elsewhere he says: "I do not seek to please men. For if I yet pleased men, I would not be the servant of Christ." And the Psalmist says: "They who have been pleasing to men have been confounded, for God has despised them.". . . .

Inspired by those records and examples, we should endure our persecutions with greater steadfastness, especially the ones that cause us bitter hurt. We should not doubt that even if they are not according to our deserts, at least they serve to purify our souls. And since all things are done in accordance with the divine ordering, let every one of true faith console himself in all his afflictions with the thought that the great goodness of God permits nothing to be done without reason, and brings to a good end whatever may seem to happen wrongfully. Therefore, all men rightly say, "Thy will be done." And to all lovers of God is the consolation in the word of the Apostle when he says: "We know that all things work together for good to them that love God." The wise man of old had this in mind when he said in his Proverbs: "No evil shall come upon the just." By this he clearly shows that whoever grows wrathful against his sufferings for any reason has departed from the way of the righteous. His attitude shows that he doubts that these things have happened to him by divine dispensation. Unrighteous also are those who yield to their own purpose rather than to God's, and with hidden desires resist the spirit which echoes in the words, "Thy will be done," they give priority to their own will over that of the will of God. Farewell.

Suggestions for Further Reading

Etienne Gilson, *Heloise and Abelard*, translated by L. K. Shook (Ann Arbor, Mich.: University of Michigan Press, 1960).

Johan Huizinga, *Men and Ideas* (London: Eyre and Spottiswoode, 1960), pp. 178-195.

J. T. Muckle, "Letter of Heloise on Religious Life and Abelard's First Reply," *Mediaeval Studies*, Vol. XVII (1955), pp. 240-281.

Albert V. Murray, *Abelard and St. Bernard: A Study of Twelfth Century Modernism* (New York: Barnes and Noble, 1967).

Luis de Carvajal

The Memoirs and Last Testament

Those cruel beasts grabbed me
with great force and took me to the
cold and dark prison. I said nothing
except, "O Lord, reveal the truth."

Luis de Carvajal's personal documents (memoirs, last testament, and letters) are the only extant writings by a Jew in Mexico during the Spanish colonial period. Born in Spain in 1567, he was burned at the stake in Mexico City on December 8, 1596. He had been found guilty by the Inquisition of observing Jewish religious practices.

The relationship of the de Carvajal family to Judaism had been ambiguous. Luis' father was a full Jew, while his mother was Jewish on her maternal side only. His uncle, a famous Spanish admiral, had renounced Judaism. This same uncle was largely responsible for the family's immigration to the New World. When he was awarded the governorship of a principality extending from Tampico in modern Mexico to San Antonio, Texas, he persuaded Luis' father to accompany him by promising that Luis would be his successor as governor of the area.

The family arrived in the new world in 1580, and it was probably then that Luis' father encouraged him to practice Judaism. His uncle disinherited him when he suspected that his nephew was no longer a Christian. In 1589 Luis was arrested after his eldest sister confessed, under torture, that members of the family were practicing Jews. In 1590 he was released. During this year in prison he had a series of visions which gained for him the name Joseph Lumbroso, the Enlightened.

Luis de Carvajal wrote his memoirs in January of 1595, less than a month before he was re-arrested and imprisoned. His re-arrest and final conviction were

The Chastised Self

based on the testimony of Manual de Lucena, a friend who succumbed to the threats of the inquisitor and implicated Luis as a practicing Jew. Luis was imprisoned in February and, after an abortive suicide attempt, remained in prison until his execution. He was burned with eight other Jews, including his mother and three of his sisters. His memoirs were found shortly after his second imprisonment by members of the Inquisition who hoped, but in vain, that they would contain information implicating other practicing Jews.

Luis de Carvajal's memoirs disclose not only the physical torment but also the moral anguish of a Jewish family forced to choose between Christianity and martyrdom. This moral anguish was especially acute when loyalty to members of one's own family was at stake. Thus his sister's testimony was the basis for the first arrest of his mother and himself. And, though he had given up his personal safety because he feared for the safety of his mother and sisters, he nonetheless attempted to escape arrest himself rather than defend his mother against arrest.

(The parallels between these instances of moral anguish and those described by Elie Weisel in a following selection will be readily apparent. The two selections differ most markedly, however, in their disclosures of the motives which lay behind the denial of one's faith. For de Carvajal, such denials were prompted by the concern for personal survival. For Weisel, the denial was prompted by the refusal to acknowledge a God who was himself guilty of gross immorality.)

Memoirs

In the Name of the
Almighty Lord of
the Hosts
In Mexico, New Spain

The Lord brought me safely to Mexico, where I received the blessing of my loving mother and saw my orphaned sisters. They were protected by the Lord and settled in the houses of their husbands. Instead of wearing torn skirts, they were covered with velvets, gold jewels, and fine silks. In these homes also were sheltered the other widows and orphans [of our family]. Glorified be His name forever and ever.

A year later, because of the great expense of the weddings and the many people in the household to be supported, my brothers-in-law were poor, although they never wasted [money] themselves. My elder brother and I wished, as was right, to support our mother and sisters; but being very poor and without

From Luis de Carvajal, *The Enlightened: The Writings of Luis de Carvajal, El Mozo*, translated and edited by Seymour B. Liebman (Coral Gables, Fla.: University of Miami Press, 1967).

resources, we were filled with anguish. Although we appeared to be well dressed, our needs were great. Meanwhile, our brothers-in-law moved to Taxco with their families. I was in such need that I went to serve a merchant as his clerk, to do the writing in order to have a piece of bread to eat. This poverty was soon remedied by the mercy of God. . . .

A few days later my brother and I (we loved each other in the Lord as water and earth love one another) returned to Mexico while our mother and sisters remained in the homes of her sons-in-law in Taxco. Baltasar, my elder brother, had for a long time an ardent desire to be circumcised during the time of the solemn Pascua del Pan Cenceño. One day, moved by the Lord, we went together to the house of a barber and rented a blade from him. My elder brother took it in his hands and while we both knelt on the ground, he cut his prepuce and made a big wound. We both offered the sacrament together to God, praising Him and calling upon Him and David, His servant. Although no blood had dripped while we prayed, Baltasar felt blood gushing from the wound as soon as we finished.

We therefore left the house of an uncle [another Jew] of ours, where my brother had circumcised himself, and went to a house we rented in a lonely spot on the outskirts of the city, for we were afraid of what our poor, narrow-minded uncle might say. He came after us to bring us back to his house. Upon his seeing some bloodstained cloths, we were so frightened and filled with such anguish that we tried to explain the matter away by telling him that Baltasar had disciplined himself. A sister of the uncle, whom the Lord knew and loved, learned about the circumcision and spoke to me with pitying words. She complained because we had gone somewhere else in our need.

The house where we were sheltered was so bare that we could not find anything to staunch the blood. Not knowing what to do, I applied salt and wine, which only increased the pain and difficulties of the poor sick man without stopping the flow of blood. When I went to a neighbor's house to borrow some salt saying that it was for a wounded man, I found myself in a dilemma, for the neighbor wanted to perform a good deed for the love of God by himself putting salt on the wound. Realizing our danger, we went to the house of a man living near by [another Jew], who was fearful of God, and to him we told our predicament. As the sick man was still bleeding he [this Jew] took us [in] with loving kindness. At his house, the blood soon ceased flowing with the help of God. However, since the wound was large and had not been treated by a doctor, the patient endured terrible pains before it healed. The pains were merits in expiation of Baltasar's past sins. . . .

After the Lord in His immense mercy provided for the needs of the soul, He then provided for corporal needs. In one year, without our having any money or ways of getting it, or even imagining how it would happen, the Lord gave us a fortune that exceeded seven thousand pesos; blessed be He forever who provides for the hungry ones. Finding ourselves in this position, we both decided to leave with the first fleet to sail for Italy, where we could best serve the Lord. However, we considered it regrettable to leave our other elder brother [Gaspar], a narrow-minded Dominican friar who was already a preacher and teacher in his Order.

With a strong and loving hope we went to see him in his monastery, which was near the Inquisition prison. He was a teacher of novices at that time. We intended to try to show him the truth of the Lord and of His holy law. After the three of us had sat in his cell and conversed for a while, I said in a casual manner, "I think that I heard somebody say that when Moses held the Tablets of the Law God wrote on them His holy Commandments." To this the friar answered, "Yes, it was as you heard it said." Then he took a sacred Bible which he had among his books and looked for the chapter in Exodus. He gave it to me and I said, "Blessed be the Lord; so this is the law that should be guarded." Thereupon the unfortunate friar arose and spoke a great blasphemy, saying that it was good to read it but not to observe it. He added that, even if that had been the law of God once, it was old and outdated.

For confirmation of this, he gave a frivolous analogy: that of a king who wore a cape, which he gave away to his page after it was old. Let it be noted here that all three of us were seated facing the window of the cell which opened onto an orchard and through which we could see the sky and the sun, already declining, with its brilliant rays. My other brother, younger than the friar and older than me, then asked, "This mantle of the sky and this brilliant sun that the Lord created, has it changed and has it aged?" The friar answered negatively and Baltasar continued: "So, even less will the incorruptible and holy law of God and His words be changed, and this we have heard from your own preachers. Even in the Gospel it is told that your Crucified One said, 'Do not think that I came here to annul the laws of the prophets or their holy and truthful prophecies!'" He said that it was easier for the sky or the earth to be missing than a jot or tittle of this holy law.

At this the sad blind man was silent. Realizing that we had convinced him, he said, "Let's not speak about this any more, blessed be the Lord who took me out from among you." Both of us replied, "Glorified be our Lord and God who did not leave us in blindness and perdition like this wretched man." The friar said, "Mine is a better fortune." I concluded with *Non fecit taliter omni nationi,* etc.[1] As the poor blind one could not deny or contradict the truth that was being shown to him, he was stopped.

Then my two elder brothers listened to my suggestion that both study for a few days and that afterward we meet again, but the friar did not accept the proposal. . . . He argued that his law forbade him to inquire and to increase his knowledge. The unfortunate ones think that if they cover their eyes

---

[1] "Non fecit taliter omni nationi" (Ps. 147:20, Vulg.); "He hath not dealt so with any nation; . . ." (JPS).

so as not to see the light they will not fall into the lakes of hell. No wonder the holy Isaiah said of these [unfortunate ones] that they were not even capable of admitting, "All this that I believe and do is a lie." Thus their sin keeps them blind.

Since the fleet was to leave soon, we stated our preparations. However, for the benefit of us all, the Infinite Mercy and Divine Wisdom decreed that, about this time, the Inquisition should take prisoner one of my sisters, a widow [Isabel], who was accused by a heretic [Felipe Núñez], one of our own nation [a Jew], to whom she had tried to teach the divine truths a year earlier. Seeing this, in fear we decided to flee and desired to take our mother and sisters with us. This was not considered safe by some friends of ours who were fearful of the Lord. So my brother and I decided to flee by ourselves, although it was hard to leave our beloved mother and sisters in danger and alone.

I am not able to describe the sad weeping of all at this parting, for it was more than my words can express. . . . When we remembered how we had left the widows and orphans, we cried and wailed bitterly during our journey. When we reached the port [Veracruz] and were about to go aboard ship, having already taken passage, [we found] these memories were so strong that we changed our minds and decided that I should go back and see what was happening and that Baltasar should wait for my news of developments. Two or three days after my return, I went to see my mother during the night, for I dared not visit her or be with her during the day. When we were about to sit at the table for supper, the constable and his assistants from the Inquisition knocked on the door. Having opened it, they placed guards on the stairs and doors and went to take my mother prisoner. Although deeply shaken by this blow from such a cruel enemy, my mother accepted her fate with humility; and crying for her sufferings but praising the Lord for them, she was taken by these accursed ministers, torturers of our lives, to a dark prison.

My mother's two unmarried daughters who were with her [Mariana and Anica], seeing that their mother was being taken from them, let forth with such painful and sad wailings that even the worst enemies would be moved to pity. They held onto their mother, shouting, "Where are you taking her?" What the grief-stricken mother must have felt is left to the imagination of the reader. After they took her away, they arrested me, finding me behind the door where, for fear of those cruel tyrants, I had hidden myself. Those cruel beasts grabbed me with great force and took me to the cold and dark prison. I said nothing except, "O Lord, reveal the truth."

The next day, in order to let my mother know that I had been taken prisoner also, one of my unmarried sisters put some of my shirts between my mother's undergarments and sent them to her, because this was a prison where no man or letter ever came in from the outside. My mother understood immediately, to her twofold anguish. The same night that we were taken captive my elder brother had come back to Mexico and sent a young brother [Miguel]

The Chastised Self

to call for me. He received the sad news that we had already been taken prisoners. . . . Seeing that half his family had been imprisoned, Baltasar was advised to escape the anger of the Inquisition. However, he remained and confined himself to a voluntary prison or room, from which he did not take one step out for a whole year until he saw what the Lord had in store for his relatives. He shut himself in with the sacred Bible and other holy books which the Lord provided him. The constant reading of these was his only exercise. . . .

While my mother and I were in prison and in the hands of such cruel beasts, fear made us hide and deny our true beliefs and we did not confess publicly to being keepers of the sacred law of the Lord. For our difficulties and trials have reached such extremes that those who profess [the law] and confess are burned alive by these heretics with great cruelties. For this reason our fears made us deny it [our belief].

In order to investigate our denials, one Friday they called my mother to the audience chamber just as they had done so many other times. Through a small hole that my companion and I had dug in the door to our cell with the help of two lamb bones, I watched her being taken in and out. Seeing that she still denied the charges, those tyrants decided to subject her to torture. Thus they led the gentle lamb to the torture chamber, preceded by the wicked judges, the warden, and the guard. The executioner was already in the torture chamber, completely covered from head to foot with a white shroud and hood. They ordered her to undress and directed that the gentle lamb lay down her pure body on the torture rack. Then they tied her arms and legs to it. As they turned the cruel cords in the iron rings, they tightened the flesh, making her cry out with agonizing wails that everyone heard. I knelt in my cell, for this was the most bitter and anguished day of all that I had ever endured. But I did not lack the divine comfort emanating from the hand of the Lord, blessed be His name forever.

In the midst of all this affliction, He permitted me to fall asleep for a while on the ground near the door. On other days I could fall asleep only for a few moments. As soon as I fell asleep, I saw the Lord sending to me a man of my own creed who was noted for the virtue of patience. He carried in his hands a big and beautiful sweet potato which he showed to me, saying, "Look—what a lovely and beautiful fruit this is." To this I replied, "Yes, indeed." He let me smell it, and, praising the Lord who creates all, he said, "Verily, it smells good." Then he divided it in two and told me, "It smells even better now." The meaning of my dream was revealed to me. [He told me:] "Before your mother was imprisoned and broken down with torture, she was good, for she was a fragrant fruit before the Lord. But now that she is torn by torments, she exudes the aroma of fortitude before the Lord." With this I awoke and was greatly consoled; the Lord be exalted and glorified, He who comforts the afflicted. . . .

When my mother, my sisters, and I came out of prison [February, 1590], our elder brother [Baltasar], seeing the outcome, decided to start on his way.

Luis de Caravajal   121

But the Lord first performed no small miracle before he [my brother] left the house that he had used as a hideaway. In this house that had been a voluntary prison lived an Israelite friend who had the key to the door and who used to buy the food and come in and out.

About that time a constable who knew the Israelite well came to that neighborhood, calling out . . . the name of a man who was living in sin with a woman and for whom the Inquisition was looking. The constable had heard that this man was hidden in the house next to the one where my brother was. Not finding him there, the constable thought that he might have jumped the wall into the next house. He therefore asked the Israelite friend to open the door for him, because he wanted to look for the fugitive there. The Israelite swore and swore that no one was there and tried to dissuade him from coming into the house, but he did not succeed. However, the friend found time to warn my elder brother to hide under the staircase in the house. The constable went into the house and looked all over. When they were about to leave (notice God's miracles and how He protects those whom He favors), the constable passed the staircase under which my brother was hidden; as he did so, one of his subordinates said to him, "Sir, let us look under the staircase." The constable answered, "Leave it alone; no one would hide there." And so they left, giving my brother enough time to slip out from under the stairs and hide in one of the rooms which had already been searched.

No sooner were they outside, however, than the constable changed his mind and said, "All right, let us search under the stairs." They went back to look, but the one whom the Lord protected had already escaped. The constable left satisfied, and my brother remained free by the will of the Almighty, be He forever praised. . . .

I had spent four years of anguish and affliction in prison, but I always enjoyed many benefactions of the Highest, whose divine majesty granted me favors wherever I went. It was nothing short of miraculous that even my enemies [Christians] were moved to give me of their possessions—money, hens, cheese, corn, and other things—with which I returned loaded to the house of my captivity, where my mother and sisters still lived. I found shelter and food in every convent where I went, but I never forgot the law and commandments of my Lord. I did not accept their food but said that I had already eaten. Many times I left the company and table of the execrated and went to eat my bread among the animals, preferring to eat among horses, cleanly, than to eat impure food at the tables of my enemies.

Two months after my first departure I returned to my mother and my sisters, still with the fear in my heart that perhaps I was free but that they [the inquisitors] might be looking for me in order to apprehend me. Because of this, I did not dare to go to my mother's house until I was sure that all was well. Therefore, I first went to the house of my elder sister [Catalina] who lived with her husband and child and asked if there were any news. I learned from her that

The Chastised Self

after I had left a man had come looking for me. He said that he was a servant of the chief constable of the Inquisition. This had frightened my mother and my sisters very much. I considered carefully what had to be done, whether to hide or not. The Lord gave me the courage to go to my mother's house. I found out that this was God's test, so that I might always keep in mind His mercies and might value my freedom more.

I had collected over eight hundred and fifty pesos in charity from the hands of the Gentile barbarians, whom the Lord of Israel may enlighten and bring to His holy knowledge, in order that He may be praised and served by all. . . . Most of them donated all this charity of their own free will, and you could see that the Lord was with me. By that time my mother and I heard again that my brother-in-law who had escaped safely, as I have already noted, had obtained the decree of rehabilitation and freedom with the mercy of the Almighty. We received this news at a moment when it served as heavenly medicine for my mother. The joy of it brought her back from an illness which had almost caused her death. The provisions [of the release] and our freedom came aboard the first fleet that arrived in New Spain in September, 1594, just in time, after the Lord had permitted me to raise the necessary money. . . .

The decree of freedom for my mother, my sisters and me had arrived with the fleet that entered the port of New Spain [Veracruz] in September, 1594. Because the Lord has always led us along the path of His chosen servants, one Thursday afternoon, the sixth day of October of the same year, and four days before the decree arrived in the city, He ordered that an Inquisition guard should come to summon them [my mother and sisters]. They considered themselves in the worst situation imaginable and wept as if they were already imprisoned and in the hands of the cruel enemy. God, the Lord, wanted them only to be interrogated by the inquisitors about something they had declared concerning Jacob Lumbroso, my younger brother, and his being familiar with and an observer of the holy law of the Almighty. The inquisitors planned to burn Miguel [Jacob Lumbroso] in effigy. After the interrogation they were sent home. They celebrated this new mercy of His with hymns and songs to the Lord. Four days later, on the tenth of October, the decree of freedom reached us in Mexico. This was the greatest of the favors and benefactions that any sinful pilgrim people ever received from the Lord. So great was our joy at this that even strangers praised the Lord with us, seeing us so happy. . . .

The Lord ordered that the penitence cloaks should not be taken off until God sent a rich neighbor who lent us the 850 pesos. I repaid him immediately 420 pesos from the money I had collected from charity. The neighbor was willing to wait eight months for the rest. And so, on Monday, October 24, our penitence cloaks were taken off through the intercession of the Almighty. God performed a great miracle for me that day. At the very moment I went [to the Inquisition hall] to doff the sanbenito, a heretic of the same lineage as ours came to accuse a brother of his [Manuel Gómez Navarro] and Manuel de Lucena for trying to lead him along the path and knowledge of the Lord. This had happened while I was staying at the house of Lucena in Pachuca, where I had gone to gather charity money. Eight days after the accusation the above-named were apprehended by the Inquisition. Even though the accuser . . . had mentioned that I was staying at the time in Lucena's house they did not seize me, because the Lord protected me, may He be blessed and praised. Amen.

The road along which the Lord guides His servants is filled with His mercies and only with the soft blows of fears. The Lord permitted that eight days later, the following Monday, we should have one of the worst scares that we had ever had, from which the Lord freed us through His infinite mercy in two hours. I do not write of how [we were freed] or what [we were freed from] because I am still in the lands of captivity. We are on the verge of being saved, with the help and favor of the almighty and powerful God of Israel, from one of the greatest and most dangerous captivities which people of our nation have suffered. Here, by the singular goodness of our Lord, my family and I have lived in no less danger than Daniel lived in the lions' den. The Lord closed their mouths as He will close the cruel mouths which, if the Lord did not prevent it, would tear us to pieces.

For all of this I humble my heart before Him, and I glorify His holy name. I confess that He is good and the greatest and that His mercy is eternal for us and for all of Israel. *Amen.*

Testament of Luis de Carvajal

In Which He Said He Wishes to Die

Highest and Almighty God of heaven and earth, whose will none of the things Thou hast created can resist, and without whose will men, fowl, beasts, and animals could not live on earth: If Thy will did not provide and maintain order in the elements, heaven would be confounded and all things would lose their course and natural movements. The earth would tremble, the peaks and great hills would fall, the waters of the sea would cover the earth, and no living thing would be maintained. Thou, by Thine infinite kindness and mercy, dost order and sustain all, not because it is necessary to Thee but for the general benefit and profit of mankind. And because Thou bestowest so much kindness and infinite mercy upon all [men], I, the poorest and most miserable of all, beg and implore in charity that Thou, in the impending moments of my death, which I wish to welcome in honor of Thy holy name and genuine law, mayest not forsake me. Accept in Thy mercy this poor life that Thou gavest me, not looking at my innumerable sins and this immortal soul, which Thou didst create in Thine image for eternal life. I beg Thee to forgive and receive it when it leaves this mortal body. Putting in order my testament, my final and ultimate will. . . . I write and sign the religious truths in which I believe and which I reaffirm [before I] die in Thy presence. . . .

I again swear, in the name of the Almighty, to live and die for His faith. May it please Him, so that, imitating the zeal of Hananiah, Azariah, Mishael, and Matathias, I shall joyfully give away my soul for the faith of the Holy Testament for which they died—*Et siomnes obediant*, etc.—and for the holy truths that are as clear as our Lord Himself spoke them in the canticle He taught to Moses: *Audite coeli*, etc. . . . So I desire, and it is my wish to die for His holy faith and true law. I hope for strength from the Lord. I do not trust myself, since I am only flesh and of frail nature; and just as I have placed a mother and five sisters in danger for this faith, I would give away a thousand, if I had them, for the faith of each of His holy Commandments.

In testimony of which I wrote and signed this my will, and I conclude with this final answer (maintaining and reaffirming my faith) to the charges against me [by the Inquisition prosecutor]. My Lord, look upon me with grace, so that it may be known and seen in this kingdom and upon all the earth that Thou art our God and that Thine almighty and holy name, Adonai, is invoked with truth in Israel and among Israel's descendants. I commit this soul that Thou gavest me to Thy holy hands, promising with Thy help not to change my faith till death nor after it.

I end happily the narrative of my present life, having lively faith in Thy divine hope of saving me through Thine infinite mercy and of resurrecting me, when Thy holy will is accomplished, together with our fathers Abraham, Isaac, and Jacob and his faithful sons, for whose holy love I beg Thee humbly to confirm this and not to forsake me. May it please Thee to send the angel Michael, our prince, to defend and help me with his holy and angelic host, and to aid me to persevere in, and die for, Thy holy faith, delivering me from the hands and temptations of the enemy. O Lord have mercy on the glory of Thy name, Thy law, and Thy people, and the world which Thou Thyself didst create; fill it [the world] with Thy light and the truthful knowledge of Thy name, so that heaven and earth will be filled with Thy glory and praise, amen, amen. Dated in Purgatory, the fifth month of the year five thousand three hundred and fifty-seven of our creation.

Inquisitor's Note

Testament of Joseph Lumbroso, and the final answer he gives, thus definitely concluding his case.

Suggestions for Further Reading

Rabbi Ben Zion Bokser, *From the World of the Cabbalah: The Philosophy of Rabbi Judah Loew of Prague* (New York: Philosophical Library, 1954).

David Corcos, "The Jews of Morocco Under the Marinides," *The Jewish Quarterly Review*, Vol. 55, No. 1-2 (July, October 1964), pp. 53-81, 137-150.

Simon Ginzburg, *The Life and Works of Moses Hayyim Luzzato* (Philadelphia: The Dropsie College for Hebrew and Cognate Learning, 1931).

Glückel of Hameln, *The Memoirs of Glückel of Hameln*, translated by Marvin Lowenthal (New York: Harper and Brothers, 1932).

Joseph Gumbiner, "The Indian Jews of Mexico," *American Judaism*, Vol. 5 (January 1956), pp. 11-14.

Morris A. Gutstein, *The Story of the Jews in Newport: Two and a Half Centuries of Judaism, 1658-1808* (New York: Bloch Publishing Company, 1953).

Rabbi David Ben Chaim Ha-Kohen, "Kaddish for a Christian (Marrano) Father: A Response," *Judaism*, Vol. 2, No. 4 (Fall 1962), pp. 364-366.

Rudolf Kayser, *The Life and Time of Jehudah Halevi*, translated by Frank Gaynor (New York: Philosophical Library, 1949).

Henry Charles Lea, *The Inquisition in the Spanish Dependencies* (New York: The Macmillan Company, 1922).

Seymour B. Liebman, "Hernando Alonso: The First Jew on the North American Continent," *Journal of Inter-American Studies*, Vol. 5 (1963), pp. 291-296.

_____, "The Long Night of the Inquisition," *Jewish Quarterly*, London, Vol. 13 (Summer 1965), pp. 28-33.

_____, "Mexican Mestizo Jews," *American Jewish Archives*, Vol. 19 (November, 1967), pp. 144-174.

David de Sola Pool and Tamar de Sola Pool, *An Old Faith in the New World: Portrait of Shearith Israel, 1654-1954* (New York: Columbia University Press, 1955).

Cecil Roth, *A History of the Marranos* (New York and Philadelphia: Jewish Publication Society and World, 1959).

Joseph Sarachek, *Don Isaac Abravanel* (New York: Bloch Publishing Company, 1938).

Sholom A. Singer, "The Expulsion of the Jews from England in 1290," *The Jewish Quarterly Review*, Vol. 55, No. 2 (October 1964), pp. 117-136.

Jeanne Marie Guyon

Autobiography

O God, who are the sovereign
felicity, if at present I deserve
your hatred, and if in the future
I am a vessel prepared for perdition,
there remains to me at least this
consolation of having known you, of
having loved you, of having sought
you, of having followed you.

Jeanne Marie Guyon, one of the early leaders of the Quietist movement in Catholicism, was born in Montargis, France, in 1648. After an unsettled childhood in which she was shunted back and forth between convent and home, she was married at the age of 16 to 38-year-old Jacques Guyon. Twelve years later her husband died, leaving her with three children. Five years after his death she went to Switzerland to participate in the religious instruction of Huguenots who had recently been reconciled to the Catholic Church. This religious activity launched her on a course of travel, meditation, preaching, and writing that continued unabated until her imprisonment in 1698.

In these years of religious activity, Madame Guyon became the object of persistent and widespread rumors that she was guilty of improper relations with her spiritual director and traveling companion, Fr. Francois La Combe. She charged that the rumors were completely unfounded, but when La Combe at length avoided her company because of the rumors, she pursued him from Switzerland to Italy and finally to Paris. In 1687 he was imprisoned in Paris for his alleged relations with her, and in 1688 she too was arrested. Through the offices of Madame de Maintenon, mistress of Louis XIV, she was released and introduced into the royal circle. Her favor at court lasted until 1693, when her teachings aroused opposition from many within the church hierarchy.

Madame Guyon's teaching developed out of her 12 years of marriage to Jacques Guyon. Apparently the victim of mistreatment by her mother-in-law and husband, she discovered the psychological advantages of suffering indignities in silence. This passivity proved fundamental to her religious views. Basic to her Quietist perspective was an emphasis on the passivity of the soul, the suppression of human effort so that God might act unhampered. In answer to the question "What must the soul do to be faithful to God?" she replied, "Nothing, and less than nothing. It must simply suffer itself to be possessed, acted upon, and moved without resistance."

This renunciation of human effort implies an indifference even to eternal salvation. Contrasting her views with the more traditional forms of mysticism, she rejected the notion that the true mystic enjoys certain divine "consolations"—in the form of ecstasies and illuminations—to compensate him for the earthly privileges he has abandoned. In her view the true mystic abandons even the divine consolations, renouncing the traditional "way of light" for the "way of darkness." Thus mystical visions, revelations, and ecstasies hinder the process of losing oneself in God. Charging that the majority of Catholic saints have chosen the less austere path of the "way of light," Madame Guyon advocated a higher mystical path which, precisely because it renounces temporary consolations, enables the soul to experience a total mystical death which is simultaneously an uninterrupted ecstasy. This notion that one renounce the quest for eternal salvation and thereby exceed the saints in holiness was judged especially pernicious by religious authorities.

In 1694 Madame Guyon asked to be cleared of unofficial charges of doctrinal deviance, and the following year a conference was convened to determine the orthodoxy of her views. Francois Fenelon, Archbishop of Cambrai, defended her against charges leveled by Jacques Bossuet, Bishop of Meaux. Madame Guyon and Fenelon lost their case, and she was immediately arrested and imprisoned. Her quietistic views were condemned by papal decree in 1699. She was released from prison in 1703 after renouncing her views and continued to write until her death in 1717. But her spirit had been effectively broken through censorship and imprisonment, and this last period in her life was indeed one in which she experienced the absence of divine consolation. She compared herself to the crucified Christ in her profound sense of having been abandoned by her Father in heaven.

Autobiography

The Crosses of Married Life

We subsequently came to Paris, where my vanity increased. Nothing was spared to bring me out. I paraded a vain beauty; I thirsted to exhibit myself and

From *Autobiography of Madame Guyon*, 2 vols., translated by Thomas Taylor Allen (London: Kegan Paul, 1897). Selection from Vol. I.

The Chastised Self

to flaunt my pride. I wished to make myself loved without loving anybody. I was sought for by many persons who seemed good matches for me; but you, O my God, who would not consent to my ruin, did not permit things to succeed. My father discovered difficulties that you yourself made spring up for my salvation. For if I had married those persons, I should have been extremely exposed, and my vanity would have had an opportunity for displaying itself. There was a person who had sought me in marriage for some years, whom my father for family reasons had always refused. His manners were a little distasteful to my vanity, yet the fear they had I should leave the country, and the great wealth of this gentleman, led my father, in spite of all his own objections and those of my mother, to accept him for me. It was done without my being told, on the vigil of St. Francis de Sales, 28th January, 1664, and they even made me sign the articles of marriage without telling me what they were. Although I was well pleased to be married, because I imagined thereby I should have full liberty, and that I should be delivered from the ill-treatment of my mother, which doubtless I brought on myself by want of docility, you, however, O my God, had quite other views, and the state in which I found myself afterwards frustrated my hopes, as I shall hereafter tell. Although I was well pleased to be married, I nevertheless continued all the time of my engagement, and even long after my marriage, in extreme confusion. It came from two causes. The first was that natural modesty I never lost. I was very reserved with men. The other was my vanity; for though the husband provided for me was above what I merited, I did not believe him such, and the style of those who had previously sought me appeared to be very different. Their rank dazzled me, and, as in all things I consulted only my vanity, all that did not flatter this was insupportable to me. This vanity, however, was useful to me, for it prevented me falling into those irregularities which cause the ruin of families. I would not have been willing to do any external act that would have exposed me to blame, and I always guarded so well the exterior, that they could not blame my conduct; for as I was modest at church, and I never went out without my mother, and the reputation of the house was great, I passed for good. I did not see my betrothed till two or three days before the marriage. I caused Masses to be said all the time I was engaged, to know your will, O my God; for I desired to do it at least in that. Oh, goodness of my God, to suffer me at that time, and to permit me to pray with as much boldness as if I had been one of your friends!—I who treated you as if your greatest enemy!

The joy at this marriage was universal in our town, and in this rejoicing I was the only person sad. I could neither laugh like the others, nor even eat, so oppressed was my heart. I knew not the cause of my sadness; but, my God, it was as if a presentiment you were giving me of what should befall me. Hardly was I married when the recollection of my desire to be a nun came to overwhelm me. All those who came to compliment me the day after my marriage could not help rallying me because I wept bitterly, and I said to them, "Alas! I had once so desired to be a nun; why am I then now married? and by what fatality is this happened to me?" I was no sooner at home with my new husband than I clearly saw it would be for me a house of sorrow. I was obliged to change my conduct, for their manner of living was very different from that in my father's house. My mother-in-law, who had been long time a widow, thought only of saving, while in my father's house we lived in an exceedingly noble manner. Everything was showy and everything on a liberal scale, and all my husband and my mother-in-law called extravagance, and I called respectability, was observed there. I was very much surprised at this change, and the more so as my vanity would rather have increased than cut down expenditure. I was more than fifteen years—in my sixteenth year—when I was married. My astonishment greatly increased when I saw I must give up what I had with so much trouble acquired. At my father's house we had to live with much refinement, learn to speak correctly. All I said was there applauded and made much of. Here I was not listened to, except to be contradicted and to be blamed. If I spoke well, they said it was to read them a lesson. If any one came and a subject was under discussion, while my father used to make me speak, here, if I wished to express my opinion, they said it was to dispute, and they ignominiously silenced me, and from morning to night they chided me. They led my husband to do the same, and he was only too well disposed for it. I should have a difficulty in writing these sorts of things to you, which cannot be done without wounding charity, if you had not forbidden me to omit anything, and if you had not absolutely commanded me to explain everything, and give all particulars. One thing I ask you, before going further, which is, not to regard things from the side of the creature, for this would make persons appear more faulty than they were; for my mother-in-law was virtuous, and my husband was religious and had no vice. But we must regard all things in God, who permitted these things for my salvation, and because he would not destroy me. I had, besides, so much pride that if a different conduct had been observed with me, I would have been upheld in that, and I should not, perhaps, have turned to God, as I did eventually, through the wretchedness to which I was reduced by crosses.

To return to my subject, I will say that my mother-in-law conceived such a hostility to me, that in order to annoy me she made me do the most humiliating things; for her temper was so extraordinary, from not having conquered it in her youth, that she could not live with any one. There was another cause also that, from not praying, and only repeating vocal prayers, she did not see these sorts of defects, or else, while seeing them, from not gathering strength by prayer, she was unable to rid herself of them; and it was a pity, for she had merit and cleverness. I was thus made the victim of her tempers. Her whole occupation was to continually thwart me, and she inspired her son with the same sentiments. They insisted that persons far below me should take precedence, in order to annoy me. My mother, who was very sensitive on the point of honour, could not endure this, and when she learned it from others—for I never said anything of it—she found fault with me, thinking I did it from not knowing how to maintain my rank, that I had no spirit, and a thousand other things of this kind. I dared not tell her how I was situated, but I was dying of vexation, and what increased it still more was the recollection of the persons who had sought me in marriage, the difference of their temper and their manner of acting, the love and esteem they had for me, and their gentleness and politeness: this was very hard for me to bear. My mother-in-law incessantly spoke to me disparagingly of my father and my mother, and I never went to see them but I had to endure this disagreeable talk on my return. On the other hand, my mother complained of me that I did not see her often enough. She said I did not love her, that I attached myself too much to my husband; thus I had much to suffer from all sides. What increased still more my crosses was that my mother related to my mother-in-law the troubles I had given her in my childhood, so that the moment I spoke, they reproached me with this, and told me I was a wicked character. My husband wished me to remain all day in the room of my mother-in-law, without being allowed to go to my apartment: I had not therefore a moment for seclusion or breathing a little. She spoke disparagingly of me to every one, hoping thereby to diminish the esteem and affection each had for me, so that she put insults upon me in the presence of the best society. . . .

My crosses redoubled each day, and what rendered them more painful was that my mother-in-law was not content with the sharp words she said to me in public and private, but for the smallest things she would continue in a temper for a fortnight at a time. I passed a part of my life in lamentations when I could be alone, and my grief became each day more bitter. I sometimes was carried away when I saw maids who were my servants, and who owed me submission, treating me so ill. Nevertheless, I did what I could to conquer my temper—a thing that has cost me not a little. Such deadly blows diminished my natural vivacity to that degree that I became gentle. The greater part of the time I was like a lamb that is being shorn. I prayed our Lord to help me, and he was my resource. As my age was so different from theirs—for my husband was twenty-two years my senior—I saw there was no chance of changing their temper; it was strengthened with their age. I caused Masses to be said in order that you might give me the grace, O my God, to adapt myself to it. It was what I incessantly asked of you. As I saw all I said offended them, and even things at which others would have felt themselves obliged, I knew not what to do. One day, beside myself with grief—I had only been six months married—I took a knife when I was alone to cut off my tongue, in order to be no longer obliged to speak to persons who made me speak only to have matter for getting into a passion. I would have performed this mad operation, if you had not suddenly stopped me, O my God, and if you had not made me see my folly. I prayed you continually, I even communicated and had Masses said that I might become dumb, such a child was I still. I have had large experience of crosses, but I have never found any more difficult to bear than that of an unrelaxing contrariety, and while one does what one can to satisfy persons, in place of succeeding, to offend by the very things that ought to oblige them, and being still compelled to be with them from morning to evening, not daring to leave them for a moment; for I have found great crosses overwhelm and even deaden anger, but as for continual contrariety, it irritates and wakes up a certain bitterness, it produces so strange an effect, that one must practise the most extreme violence on one's self not to fly into a passion.

Such was my married life rather that of a slave than of a free person. To increase my disgrace, it was discovered, four months after my marriage, that my husband was gouty. This disease, which doubtless has sanctified him, caused me many real crosses both without and within. That year he twice had the gout six weeks at a time, and it again seized him shortly after, much more severely. At last he became so indisposed that he did not leave his room, nor often even his bed, which he ordinarily kept many months. I watched him with great care, and, though I was very young, I did not fail in my duty. I even did it to excess. But, alas! all that did not win me their friendship. I had not even the consolation of knowing if they were pleased with what I did; never did they exhibit the least sign of it. I deprived myself of all even the most innocent diversions to remain near my husband, and I did what I thought might please him. Sometimes he tolerated me, and I thought myself very happy. At other times I was insupportable. My own friends used to say that I was indeed of a nice age to be nurse to a sick man; that it was a disgraceful thing not to make use of my talents. I answered them that, as I had a husband, I ought to share his troubles as well as his wealth. I did not let any one know I was suffering, and, as my face appeared content, they would have thought me very happy with my husband, if he had not sometimes, in the presence of people, let bitter words to me escape him. Besides, my mother could hardly suffer the assiduity I exhibited to my husband, assuring me I was thereby securing unhappiness for myself, and in the end he would exact as a duty what I was doing as virtue; instead of pitying me, she often found fault with me. It is true that, to look at things humanly, it was a folly to make a slave of myself in this way for persons who had no gratitude for it; but, O my God, how different were my thoughts from those of all these persons! and how different was that which appeared to them on the outside from that which was within! My husband had this foible, that when any one said anything against me, he was at once angered, and his natural violence at once took fire. It was God's mode of leading me; for my husband was reasonable and loved me. When I was ill he was inconsolable, even to a degree I cannot tell; and yet he did not cease to get into passions with me. I believe that, but for his mother and that maid of whom I have spoken, I should have been very happy with him; for as to hastiness, there is hardly a man who has not plenty of it, and it is the duty of a reasonable woman to put up with it quietly without increasing it by sharp answers. You made use of all these things, O my God, for my salvation. Through your goodness you have so managed things that I have

The Chastised Self

afterwards seen this course was absolutely necessary for me, in order to make me die to my vain and haughty natural character. I should not have had the strength to destroy it myself, if you had not worked for it by an altogether wise dispensation of your providence. I urgently asked patience from you, O my God. Nevertheless, I often had outbursts, and my quick and hasty natural character often betrayed the resolutions I had taken to hold my tongue. You permitted it, doubtless, O my God, in order that my self-love should not nourish itself on my patience; for an outburst of a moment caused me many months of humiliation, reproach, and sorrow. It was a matter for new crosses. . . .

My husband's ailment became every day more obstinate and he himself had a presentiment of death. His mind was made up for it, for the languishing life he led became every day more burdensome to him. To his other ailments was added a disgust for all kinds of nourishment, so great that he did not even take the things necessary for life. The little he took, there was no one but I had the courage to force on him. The doctors advised him to go to the country for change of air. The first few days he was there he appeared to be better, when suddenly he was seized by a colic and continued fever. I was well prepared for anything it might please Providence to ordain; for I saw some time back he could hardly live longer. His patience increased with his illness, and his illness was very crucifying for me; yet the good use he made of it softened all my troubles. I was extremely pained that my mother-in-law kept me away from his bedside as much as she could, and influenced him against me. I much feared he might die in this feeling, and it afflicted me extremely. I seized a moment, when my mother-in-law was not there, and approaching his bed, I knelt down and said to him, that if I had done anything which had displeased him, I asked his pardon. I begged him to believe it was not voluntarily. He appeared much touched, and as if he had recovered from a profound stupor, he said to me—what he had never said before—"It is I who ask your pardon. I did not deserve you." From this time not only had he no longer a dislike to see me, but he gave me advice as to what I should do after his death, in order not to be dependent on the persons on whom I am at present. He was eight days very resigned and patient; although, owing to the gangrene which increased, they cut him up with a lancet, I sent to Paris to fetch the best surgeon, but he was dead when he arrived.

It would be impossible to die with more Christian dispositions or courage than he did, after having received all the Sacraments in an edifying manner. I was not there when he died, for he had made me withdraw, not through hostility, but through tenderness, and he was more than twenty hours unconscious at the last. I believe, O my God, that you delayed his death only for my sake, for he was entirely eaten up with gangrene, the entrails and stomach quite black, while he yet lived. You willed he should die on the eve of Magdalen's Day, in order to make me see I must be wholly yours. Every year on the Magdalen's Day I used to renew the contract I had made with you, my Lord, and I found myself free to renew it for good. I was at once enlightened that there was much mystery therein. It was the morning of the 21st of July, 1676, he died. The evening, when alone in my room in full daylight, I perceived a warm shade pass near me. The next day I went into my closet, where was the image of my dear and divine Spouse, Jesus Christ. I renewed my marriage, and I added to it a vow of chastity for a time, with a promise to make it perpetual if M. Bertot permitted me. After that a great interior joy seized me, which was the more novel to me as for a long time I had been in bitterness. It seemed to me our Lord wished to grant me some favor. Immediately I had a very great interior certainty that at the instant our Lord delivered my husband from purgatory. I have never since doubted it for a moment; although I have tried to be diffident. Some years after, Mother Granger appeared to me in a dream, and said to me: "Rest assured that our Lord, for the love he bears you, has delivered your husband from purgatory on the Magdalen's Day. He, however, entered heaven on the day of St. James, the 25th, which was his *fete*." This surprised me, but I have since learned that there are two kinds of purgatory, one where they suffer the pain of the senses, and the other where they suffer only the privation of God; that there are persons who pass through the latter without passing through the former, others who pass through the former and go afterwards into the latter. A great servant of God revealed after her death to many of her intimates that she was three days deprived of the vision of God without any pain of the senses.

As soon as I learned my husband had expired, I said to you, "O my God, you have broken my bonds. I will offer to you a sacrifice of praise." After that I remained in a very great silence, exterior and interior; silence, however, dry and without support. I could neither weep nor speak. My mother-in-law said very beautiful things, at which every one was edified, and they were scandalized at my silence, which was put down to want of resignation. A monk told me that every one admired the beautiful behavior of my mother-in-law; that as for me, they did not hear me say anything—that I must offer my loss to God. But it was impossible for me to say a single word, whatever effort I made. I was, besides, much prostrated, for although I had recently given birth to my daughter, I nevertheless watched my husband without leaving his room the twenty-four nights he was ill. I was more than a year in recovering from the fatigue of that. The prostration of body and the prostration of my spirit, the dryness and stupidity I was in, made me unable to speak. I, however, for some moments was in admiration at your goodness, O my God, which had set me free exactly on the day I had taken you for Spouse. I saw that crosses would not be wanting to me since my mother-in-law had survived my husband; and I could not understand your conduct, O my God, which, while setting me free, had yet more strongly bound me by giving me two children immediately before the death of my husband. This surprised me extremely, my God, that you set me at liberty only by making me captive. I have since learned that you had by your wisdom provided for me a means of being afterwards the plaything of your providence. . . .

The Chastised Self

Suggestions for Further Reading

Michael De La Bedoyere, *The Archbishop and the Lady: The Story of Fenelon and Madame Guyon* (London: Collins, 1956).

Francois de Salignac de La Mothe Fenelon, *Christian Perfection*, edited by Charles F. Whiston, translated by Mildred Whitney Stillman (New York: Harper, 1947).

_____, *Fenelon's Letters to Men and Women*, selected by Derek Stanford (London: Peter Owen Limited, 1957).

Ronald A. Knox, *Enthusiasm* (Oxford: Clarendon Press, 1951).

Miguel de Molinos, *Golden Thoughts from the Spiritual Guide of Molinos, the Quietist* (New York: White, Stokes, Allen, 1883).

Thomas Cogswell Upham, *Life, Religious Opinions and Experience of Madame de La Mothe Guyon* (London: S. Low, Son and Company, 1859).

Cotton Mather

Diary

*I cried to the Lord, that he would
support me under all the reproaches
which are cast upon me; and refresh
me with the Divine consolations of a
name written in heaven and precious
among the heavenly angels.*

The most celebrated (if not the most typical) Puritan in our history, Cotton Mather was born in 1663 and died in 1728. His career was diversified and influential. His father, Increase Mather, was president of Harvard College. For a time Cotton Mather taught at Harvard, though he was unable to ascend to its presidency. (Instead, he encouraged Elihu Yale to found a new college, Yale, in Connecticut.) Mather was also a very active Congregational minister, a noted preacher, and the author of a number of books. His writings indicate that he regarded his ancestral background and strong religious inclinations as tokens that he had been destined for great work in spiritually strengthening the settlements of the first colonists.

Mather's life was one of turmoil. His strong attachment to his father led him to defend a religious stance which many of his contemporaries saw as outmoded. Believing he was divinely selected to effect the fulfillment of the work of the first colonists, Mather nevertheless clung to the belief that Massachusetts was purest at the time of its earliest implantation. Thus any deviation from the culture and religion implicit in the colonial origins, according to Mather, must be watched with suspicion and dread. His wish to restore the past led Mather to feel personal defeat on a number of occasions. In 1698, for example, Mather watched as a rival church—the Brattle Street Church—was founded in Boston on the basis of relaxing membership qualifications. Despite Mather's objections, the new church prospered. Three years later, in 1701,

Mather watched as his father was forced to give up the presidency of Harvard. This was not only a further blow to the prestige of the Mathers, but a blow to their ideological ambitions as well. And, on another front, Mather's lifelong interest in tracking the manifestations of the supernatural—his innate mystical tendencies—contributed to the impact created by the outbreak of witchcraft, a phenomenon which Mather was concerned to counteract.

The Mathers kept diaries for generations. Increase Mather wrote a biography of his father Richard from autobiographical notes that Richard had left. Cotton, in turn, wrote a biography of Increase from materials that the father had kept in his diary. After Cotton's death, Samuel Mather, Cotton's son, wrote his father's biography from autobiographical documents that Cotton had prepared. Cotton Mather's diary was thus intended deliberately as a report to his son. The personal document was to serve posterity as both inspiration and edification.

The selection from Cotton Mather's *Diary* which is included here records a few of his impressions of events which transpired during the course of the year 1700. Though very much abbreviated, the document reflects Mather's attitudes toward both his father and his son, his understanding of his own vocation, and an interpretation of his ultimate significance. The author designed his autobiography to reveal a person of profound intellect and saintly piety.

Dairy of Cotton Mather

1700

The compassion of heaven this day consummates the thirty-seventh year of my age. I am not fond of keeping my birthday lest I fall into a superstition, and though I find some examples indeed for keeping such a day, yet some of them were not the most encouraging.

However, I did this day particularly address the Lord with praises for the favors of the year past, and with prayers for the pardon of the sins in that year, and for preserving, supplying, and supporting mercy in the year to come.

And the Wednesday following I set apart for prayer with fasting to obtain with larger supplications the pardon and the mercy which I had been seeking two days before. On this day likewise I visited a meeting of the faithful to whom I preached a sermon on those words (Luke 13:8), Lord, let it alone this year also.

I must with some sadness of reflection observe that my devotions of late have had such a drowsiness upon them as to make me fear lest some afflictions be near me, to rouse me out of my drowsy frame.

And, behold, my fear comes to pass.

From Cotton Mather, *Diary of Cotton Mather*, Vol. I, 1681-1709 (New York: Frederick Ungar, 1957). (Some minor editing has been done.)

For on Friday this week, my only and lovely son, a son given to me in answer to many prayers among the people of God, and a son of much observation and expectation, was taken with convulsion-fits. The Lord now not only called me but also helped me to resign my son unto him. Nevertheless, that I might more effectually conform to the dispensations of heaven, when I saw an angel of death with a drawn sword thus over my family, I thought it my duty to take myself to more than ordinary supplications. Wherefore, although I have already kept one day of prayer with fasting this week, yet on Saturday I kept another. I then heartily and cheerfully gave away my son to the Lord Jesus Christ, professing, that if the child may not be a servant of his, I was far from desiring the life of it; but if the child might serve him exceedingly, I cried to him to speak for it the word by which it might live. The convulsions of the child followed it this day until a seventh fit had sorely shaken it. This caused me in my study three times to turn to the prayer-hearing Lord, with this as the special errand of the addresses (besides what I did in other addresses), "Father, if it may be, let the cup (the funeral cup for this my son) pass from me; yet not my will, but thine be done." Towards the evening, the convulsions left the child.

25d. 12m. Lords-day. If I had not a very earthly heart, how much might I live in heaven while on earth! Such are the concerns of my ministry that this afternoon, between one o'clock and seven, I address heaven with prayers no less than ten several times. First, there is my secret prayer in my study, relating to the Church of God, and the Coming and Kingdom of Christ, and the great Sabbatises, for which I set apart some time every Lord's-day-noon. Then there is my secret prayer before my public labor and relating to it. Then there is my prayer before the sermon in the congregation. There follow at the baptism two prayers. Another prayer is made with the church who stay to receive the accounts of them that are candidates for our communion. Family-prayer with repetition is performed when I come home. And secret prayer. And in visiting two sick persons, two prayers more are called for.

I am at this time assaulted with some very particular temptations. I, and yet not I, but the grace of God which was with me, have newly done a service of some consequence to all our churches by publishing *A Warning to the Flocks against Wolves in Sheep's Clothing.* The devices of Satan whereby the welfare of our churches is exceedingly threatened, are, I hope, effectually and eternally defeated by this little book, and the Holy Lord Jesus Christ is glorified. Satan being exceedingly enraged at what I have done, stirs up a wonderful storm of clamor and slander against me, from a numerous crew in this town, which (it is astonishing!) are not able to bear the detection of the folly they discovered in following one of the imposters, and the remarkable story of whom I have laid before the churches. And the venom of that malignant company, who have lately built a new church in Boston, disposes them to add to the storm of my present persecution; for it may be, never had any men more of that character of grievous revolters to be walking with slanders, than too many of that poor people have.

When I heard the defaming of many, I thought it my duty to humble myself before the Lord with extraordinary supplications. I endeavored it, on

6d. lm. (March) Wednesday. On this day I laid before the Lord the reproaches which I suffered from abundance of impious people, for the sake of my faithfulness to his churches and interests.

I acknowledged myself to be viler before him than any of my causeless and cruel adversaries could make me when they reviled me. And I gave exceeding thanks to him for his preserving me from the unhappiness of being made obnoxious to their malice by any real blemish, whereof if they could get the least notice, how wonderfully would they aggravate it!

I bewailed my many miscarriages for which the terrible justice of God might righteously and easily make me loathsome among all his people. And among the rest, I confessed and bewailed whatever injuries I may have done to the esteem of other men.

I cried to the Lord, that he would support me under all the reproaches which are cast upon me; and refresh me with the Divine consolations of a name written in heaven and precious among the heavenly angels; and prevent my falling into any errors of impatience, by which the devil might gain any of his designs upon me; and assist me to learn all those Holy Lessons, that I should fetch out of the exercises now upon me.

I then did humbly commit my name into the hands of the Lord Jesus Christ cheerfully declaring, that if he had no occasion for my name, I have none for it myself; and that if it were for his honor for my name to be reproached, I did freely resign it. But I besought the Lord, that for the sake of the reproaches which my Lord Jesus Christ underwent for me, I might be delivered from all reproaches that might be disadvantage to me in my glorifying of his name, which to do is, indeed, all my salvation and all my desire. . . .

Another thing, which brought me on my knees this day before the Lord is that my lovely and only son is again the last night arrested with convulsions, and the life of the infant is exceedingly in danger.

This morning, the child received almost a miraculous deliverance from choking by a pin, which he sucked out of the silver nipple of his bottle, though we did not know how it came there.

And when I was this day (his fits being this day more violently than ever again returned upon him) resigning the child to the Lord, a strange thing was said to me from heaven: my son shall yet live, and after this my faith was tried by the child's falling into more convulsions; but the Lord sent help from heaven against them. . . .

Cotton Mather

I now cast myself prostrate on my study-floor, with my sinful mouth in the dust before the Lord. I adored the free-grace that had been displayed, in granting such precious and matchless opportunities of glorifying the Lord Jesus Christ to me, that am on many accounts the vilest person in all New England. I bewailed the sins which have attended me, especially vain-glory, in making use of my opportunities. But with tears and strong cries, I declared to the Lord that he knew I had no desire, no delight, no study comparable to that of glorifying my Lord Jesus Christ; I have chosen it as my very heaven and my all. I earnestly besought him that this desire, which his own spirit had produced in me, might not be defeated, and that I might not be rejected from serving him in such ways as I had already served him. It was now told me from heaven that the Lord will yet make a great use of me, and that I shall have greater opportunities to glorify my Lord Jesus Christ than ever I had.

16d. lm. Saturday. This day I also set apart for the exercises of a secret fast before the Lord, on the same occasions that procured my being the last week so engaged.

In the close of the day, after black dejections and sore discouragements, I cried to the Lord, that before I broke off, he would give me some token of his accepting me. I did with bitter anguish of soul confess to the Lord, that if I should not be left to all sort of sin and misery and confusion, and be made the astonishment of all the churches, and be thrown in the most horrible torments of hell after all, it would be a very glorious and marvelous display of sovereign grace! But how much more would the sovereignty of divine grace be magnified if such a wretch as I am, one all over vile, should be employed in eminent services for the Lord Jesus Christ! Nevertheless, his Holy Spirit had inclined me to make choice of this as all my salvation and all my desire. And now my weeping soul was again assured from heaven that it shall not be denied to me.

Behold, how the Lord is mercifully confuting my fears of being unserviceable. . . .

I was many ways tired and spent and faint, especially with torturing pains in my head, which have diverse days molested me, (such as I have so often found pre-praeludious to my doing some special service for my Lord Jesus Christ, that I cannot but have particular thoughts about the origin of them). I was this day to preach Boston-lecture, but I was so extremely feeble, that I could not see how I should get comfortably through it. . . .

On my knees in my study, before my going abroad, I had a strange particular faith of this matter. And now, when I came to my public services, I felt a wonderful force from heaven strengthening, and assisting, and enlarging me. I cannot express the heavenly efficacy that I felt irradiating me and inspiring a powerful vigor into my ministrations. The vast assembly which were come together saw that the Lord was truly with me.

Now, O my soul, feed, feed upon these experiences!

The Chastised Self

10d. 2m My little and lovely and only son is visited with a return of convulsions which greatly threaten his life. Diverse convulsions do this day particularly shake our hopes of the child's continuance with us. But as I was in the afternoon with distress crying to the Lord for the child, it was told me from heaven that the child should yet live.

13d. 2m Saturday. . . . This town and land has in it many people that are full of enmity to the interests of the Lord Jesus Christ; and if he were on earth again, as once he was, he would be persecuted with wonderful malignity from vast numbers of people that now go by the name of Christians. By my faithfulness to the interests of the Lord Jesus Christ, and of holiness, and of that holy evangelical Church-state, which he would have to be mentioned, I cannot but expose myself to a deal of raging and railing malignity. Well, if now I find myself hated by them that hate the Lord Jesus Christ, or that hate what is loved by the Lord Jesus Christ; and if the reproaches of them that would reproach him fall upon me, I will triumph in all such conformity to him as being indeed good to me, and in these my sufferings, as being really my honors; and my spirit will gloriously rejoice in God my Saviour.

When I was thus thinking, it was powerfully set home upon my heart that I have in this disposition an infallible symptom that my Lord Jesus Christ will before long fetch me away to heavenly glory, and that He will glorify me with himself world without end.

Memorandum. The convulsions upon my little son after some respite, now return upon him. There seems very much danger in the case. But in my prayers before the Lord on this occasion, I am assured from heaven that the child shall outlive the danger.

21d. 2m Lord's-day. . . .

Memorandum. The terrible convulsions which threaten the life of my little and lovely son do now grow to that extremity as to render his cure little short of desperate; all means and hopes do fail. But when I am carrying and resigning the child to the Lord, I have it strangely assured me from heaven, that the child shall recover. The good angel of the Lord has told me so!

11d. 3m [May] Saturday. This day I am with affliction of soul through fasting, at prayer in secret before the Lord.

The blessing of heaven on my family, and especially my little son, who is visited with some return of his illness, I this day obtained.

The blessing of heaven on my ministry especially my composures going to the press, and my sermon, at the next election, I this day also obtained.

I obtained likewise an assurance from heaven, that something shall befall the disorderly society of innovators (now causing much temptation and iniquity in the place) that shall confirm these churches in the right ways of the Lord.

Finally, prostrate on my study-floor, in the evening, I obtained assurance of the Lord, that the Spirit of my Lord Jesus Christ will yet marvelously fill me, and I shall be employed in eminent services for his glorious name. . . .

16d. 4m. Lord's-day. I am going to relate one of the most astonishing things that ever befell me, in all the time of my pilgrimage.

A particular faith has been unaccountably produced in my father's heart and in my own, that God will carry him to England, and there give him a short but great opportunity to glorify the Lord Jesus Christ before his entrance into the heavenly kingdom.

There appears no possibility of my father's going there to obtain a charter for our college. This matter, having been for several years at the very point of being carried in the General Assembly, has strangely miscarried whenever it was about to come to birth. It is now again before the Assembly, in circumstances, in which, if it did not succeed, it is never likely to be revived and resumed. Many times, when I have been lately spreading the case before the Lord, with a faith triumphantly exercised on his power and wisdom and goodness, I have had renewed to my amazement my assurances that my father shall yet glorify the Lord Jesus Christ in England.

But the matter in the Assembly being likely now to come to nothing, I was this day in extreme distress of spirit concerning it. My flesh indeed would be on all accounts imaginable against my father's removal from me; it will doubtless plunge me into ten thousand inconveniences. But my faith on the other side, having been so supernaturally raised for it, the thoughts of that's being wholly disappointed, were insupportable.

After I had finished all the other duties of the day, I did in my distress cast myself prostrate on my study-floor before the Lord. There I acknowledge my own manifold and horrible sinfulness, and my worthiness by reason of that sinfulness to be put off with delusions, and have a serpent given to me, when I asked and looked for the Holy Spirit. Nevertheless, I, that am dust and ashes and worthy to be made so by fire from heaven, craved leave to plead with heaven concerning the matter of the particular faith which had been wrought in my mind, as I thought, by the Lord's own holy operation. I pleaded that my Lord Jesus Christ had invested me with his own glorious righteousness, and was now making intercession for me in the Holy of Holies; and because of his interest there, I might approach to the most High God with humble boldness as to a prayer-hearing Lord. I spread before him the consequences of things and the present posture and aspect of them; and having told the Lord that I had always taken a particular faith, to be a work of heaven on the minds of the faithful. But if it should prove a deceit, in that remarkable instance, which was now the cause

The Chastised Self

of my agony, I should be cast into a most wonderful confusion. I then begged of the Lord, that if my particular faith about my father's voyage to England were not a delusion, he would please to renew it upon me.

All this while, my heart had the coldness of a stone upon it, and the straitness that is to be expected from the bare exercise of reason. But now all of a sudden, I felt an inexpressible force to fall on my mind: an afflatus that cannot be described in words; none knows it, but he that has it. If an angel from heaven had spoken it articulately to me, the communication would not have been more powerful and perceptible. It was told me that the Lord Jesus Christ loved my father and loved me, and that he took delight in us, as in two of his faithful servants; and that he had not permitted us to be deceived in our particular faith; but that my father should be carried into England, and there glorify the Lord Jesus Christ, before his passing into glory; and that there shall be illustrious revenues of praise to the Lord Jesus Christ, from our particular faith about this concern; and that I shall also live to see it; and that a sentence of death shall be written on the effect and success of our particular faith; but the Lord Jesus Christ, who raises the dead, and is the Resurrection and Life, shall give a new life to it; he will do it, he will do it!

Having left a flood of tears on my study-floor, fetched from me by these rays from the invisible world, I rose and went to my chair. There I took up my Bible, and the first place that I opened, was at Acts 27:23,24,25. "There stood by me the angel of God, whose I am, and whom I serve: saying, Fear not, thou must be brought before Caesar: I believe God, that it shall be even as it was told me." A new flood of tears immediately gushed from my flowing eyes; and I broke out into these expressions: "What! Shall my father yet appear before Caesar? Has an angel from heaven told me so? And must I believe what has been told me? Well then, it shall be so; it shall be so!"

And now what shall I say? When the affair of my father's agency after this came to a turning point in the court, it strangely miscarried: All came to nothing! Some of our Tories had so wrought upon the Governor, that though he had first moved this matter and had given us also both directions and promises about it, yet he now (not without base unhandsomeness) deserted it. The Lt. Governor, who had formerly been for it, now (not without great ebulitions of unaccountable prejudice, and ingratitude) appeared with all the little tricks imaginable to confound it. It had, for all this, been carried, had not some of the Council been inconveniently called off and absent. But now the whole affair of the college was left to the management of the E. of Bellomont. So that all expectation of a voyage for my father to England on any such occasion is utterly at an end.

What shall I make of this wonderful matter? Wait! Wait!

There have been several customs in my life, which upon reflection I find, I have not inserted, either at the time when I first of all took them up, nor at any other time. And yet it may be a little instructive to my son, if I leave some hint concerning some of them, which I may do as well in this place, perhaps, as in another, and bring in here a small collection of Paralipomena under the head of "Methods of pressing after piety."

From my youth it has been my frequent, my daily practice, to make occasional reflections, or from occasions which I have seen in occurrences before me, to raise thoughts of piety, and these mostly by finding similitudes to assist and excite such thoughts in those occurrences.

These occasional reflections do not only serve me very commonly, to carry on useful conferences, made savory with some little sort of wit, when I am in company; but they are also a delightful entertainment to me when I am alone.

But at length, I saw I had one opportunity every day for such occasional reflections, as it might not be amiss for me to oblige myself rarely to let pass me without them.

I was once emptying the cistern of nature, and making water at the wall. At the same time, there came a dog, who did so too, before me. Thought I, "What mean and vile things are the children of men in this mortal state! How much do our natural necessities abase us and place us in some regard, on the same level with the very dogs!"

My thought proceeded. "Yet I will be a more noble creature; and at the very time when my natural necessities debase me into the condition of the beast, my spirit shall (I say, at that very time!) rise and soar, and fly up towards the employment of the angel."

Accordingly, I resolved, that it should be my ordinary practice, whenever I stop to answer the one or other necessity of nature, to make it an opportunity of shaping in my mind, some holy, noble, divine thought; usually, by way of occasional reflection on some sensible object which I either then have before me, or have lately had so: a thought that may leave upon my spirit some further tincture of piety!

And I have done according to this resolution!

Suggestions for Further Reading

Otho T. Beall and R. H. Shyrock, *Cotton Mather: First Significant Figure in American Medicine* (Baltimore: John Hopkins Press, 1954).

Ralph P. Boas and Louise S. Boas, *Cotton Mather; Keeper of the Puritan Conscience* (Hamden, Conn.: Shoe String Press, 1964).

Thomas James Holmes, *Cotton Mather: A Bibliography of his Works* (Cambridge, Mass.: Harvard University Press, 1940).

D. Levin, "The Hazing of Cotton Mather: the Creation of a Biographical Personality," *New England Quarterly,* Vol. XXXVI (1963), pp. 147-171.

Kenneth B. Murdock, *Selections from Cotton Mather* (New York: Hafner, 1961).

Daniel B. Shea, Jr., *Spiritual Autobiography in Early America* (Princeton, N.J.: Princeton University Press, 1968). Especially pp. 152-181 on the Mathers and pp. 270-276, a bibliographical essay.

Barrett Wendell, *Cotton Mather, the Puritan Priest* with Introduction by Alan Heimert (New York: Harcourt, Brace and World, 1963).

Elie Wiesel

Night

What does Your greatness mean,
Lord of the Universe, in the face
of all this weakness, this
decomposition, and this decay? Why
do You still trouble their sick
minds, their crippled bodies?

Elie Wiesel (b. 1928) is an author and a playwright. Born in Hungary, he was deported while still a young boy to the Nazi concentration camps, first to Auschwitz and then to Buchenwald. In the latter camp Wiesel's father, mother, and sister were executed. Wiesel himself survived and was rescued at the end of the war by Allied troops. He found his way to Paris, where he began his career as a writer, first as a journalist. He followed the journalist's profession in both Israel and the United States, and then began concentrating more on novels and plays. He now lives in New York City.

His chief works are *Dawn, The Town beyond the Wall, The Jews of Silence, Legends of Our Time, The Gates of the Forest,* and *Night.* In addition to their literary worth, these works have served as a means of expressing, interpreting, and remembering the holocaust—the genocidal massacre of Jews during the era of World War II. The novel *The Gates of the Forest* questions whether there can be any hope when outward circumstances lead to despair. *Night,* an autobiographical account, treats the Auschwitz experience directly. All of the writings are concerned with the possibilities of maintaining Jewish identity in a world for which the Messiah is already too late.

The selection which follows recalls the decisive events in the life of a young boy who witnessed the destruction of his family during the war and who is suffering under the anticipation of his own execution in the concentration camp. The reader is never able to forget that the boy is Elie Wiesel

The Chastised Self

himself—called by one scholar "the greatest Jewish witness to the holocaust." On the matter of eloquence Wiesel himself wrote in 1968 that "no testimony seems of any value to me unless the witness identifies himself with the subject." Extending the same point a bit further, he said, "To be a Jew is often to wait for someone who doesn't come, and, if need be, to become that very person."

Night

The summer was coming to an end. The Jewish year was nearly over.

On the eve of Rosh Hashanah, the last day of that accursed year, the whole camp was electric with the tension which was in all our hearts. In spite of everything, this day was different from any other. The last day of the year. The word "last" rang very strangely. What if it were indeed the last day?

They gave us our evening meal, a very thick soup, but no one touched it. We wanted to wait until after prayers. At the place of assembly, surrounded by the electrified barbed wire, thousands of silent Jews gathered, their faces stricken.

Night was falling. Other prisoners continued to crowd in, from every block, able suddenly to conquer time and space and submit both to their will.

"What are You, my God," I thought angrily, "compared to this afflicted crowd, proclaiming to You their faith, their anger, their revolt? What does Your greatness mean, Lord of the Universe, in the face of all this weakness, this decomposition, and this decay? Why do You still trouble their sick minds, their crippled bodies?"

Ten thousand men had come to attend the solemn service, heads of the blocks, Kapos, functionaries of death.

"Bless the Eternal. . . . "

The voice of the officiant had just made itself heard. I thought at first it was the wind.

"Blessed be the Name of the Eternal!"

Thousands of voices repeated the benediction; thousands of men prostrated themselves like trees before a tempest.

"Blessed be the Name of the Eternal!"

Why, but why should I bless Him? In every fibre I rebelled. Because He had had thousands of children burned in His pits? Because He kept six crematories working night and day, on Sundays and feast days? Because in His great might He had created Auschwitz, Birkenau, Buna, and so many factories of death? How could I say to Him: "Blessed art Thou, Eternal, Master of the

From *Night* by Elie Wiesel. © Les Editions de Minuit, 1958. English translation © MacGibbon and Kee, 1960. Reprinted by permission of Hill and Wang, Inc., and MacGibbon and Kee.

Universe, Who chose us from among the races to be tortured day and night, to see our fathers, our mothers, our brothers, end in the crematory? Praised be Thy Holy Name, Thou Who hast chosen us to be butchered on Thine altar?"

I heard the voice of the officiant rising up, powerful yet at the same time broken, amid the tears, the sobs, the sighs of the whole congregation:

"All the earth and the Universe are God's!"

He kept stopping every moment, as though he did not have the strength to find the meaning beneath the words. The melody choked in his throat.

And I, mystic that I had been, I thought:

"Yes, man is very strong, greater than God. When You were deceived by Adam and Eve, You drove them out of Paradise. When Noah's generation displeased You, You brought down the Flood. When Sodom no longer found favor in Your eyes, You made the sky rain down fire and sulphur. But these men here, whom You have betrayed, who You have allowed to be tortured, butchered, gassed, burned, what do they do? They pray before You! They praise Your name!"

"All creation bears witness to the greatness of God!"

Once, New Year's Day had dominated my life. I knew that my sins grieved the Eternal; I implored his forgiveness. Once, I had believed profoundly that upon one solitary deed of mine, one solitary prayer, depended the salvation of the world.

This day I had ceased to plead. I was no longer capable of lamentation. On the contrary, I felt very strong. I was the accuser, God the accused. My eyes were open and I was alone—terribly alone in a world without God and without man. Without love or mercy. I had ceased to be anything but ashes, yet I felt myself to be stronger than the Almighty, to whom my life had been tied for so long. I stood amid that praying congregation, observing it like a stranger.

The service ended with the Kaddish. Everyone recited the Kaddish over his parents, over his children, over his brothers, and over himself.

We stayed for a long time at the assembly place. No one dared to drag himself away from this mirage. Then it was time to go to bed and slowly the prisoners made their way over to their blocks. I heard people wishing one another a Happy New Year!

I ran off to look for my father. And at the same time I was afraid of having to wish him a Happy New Year when I no longer believed in it.

He was standing near the wall, bowed down, his shoulders sagging as though beneath a heavy burden. I went up to him, took his hand and kissed it. A tear fell upon it. Whose was that tear? Mine? His? I said nothing. Nor did he. We had never understood one another so clearly.

The sound of the bell jolted us back to reality. We must go to bed. We came back from far away. I raised my eyes to look at my father's face leaning over mine, to try to discover a smile or something resembling one upon the aged, dried-up countenance. Nothing. Not the shadow of an expression. Beaten.

Yom Kippur. The Day of Atonement.

Should we fast? The question was hotly debated. To fast would mean a surer, swifter death. We fasted here the whole year round. The whole year was Yom Kippur. But others said that we should fast simply because it was dangerous to do so. We should show God that even here, in this enclosed hell, we were capable of singing His praises.

I did not fast, mainly to please my father, who had forbidden me to do so. But further, there was no longer any reason why I should fast. I no longer accepted God's silence. As I swallowed my bowl of soup, I saw in the gesture an act of rebellion and protest against Him.

And I nibbled my crust of bread.

In the depths of my heart, I felt a great void.

Akiba Drumer left us, a victim of the selection. Lately, he had wandered among us, his eyes glazed, telling everyone of his weakness: "I can't go on. . . . It's all over. . . ." It was impossible to raise his morale. He didn't listen to what we told him. He could only repeat that all was over for him, that he could no longer keep up the struggle, that he had no strength left, nor faith. Suddenly his eyes would become blank, nothing but two open wounds, two pits of terror.

He was not the only one to lose his faith during those selection days. I knew a rabbi from a little town in Poland, a bent old man, whose lips were always trembling. He used to pray all the time, in the block, in the yard, in the ranks. He would recite whole pages of the Talmud from memory, argue with himself, ask himself questions and answer himself. And one day he said to me: "It's the end. God is no longer with us."

And, as though he had repented of having spoken such words, so clipped, so cold, he added in faint voice:

"I know. One has no right to say things like that. I know. Man is too small, too humble and inconsiderable to seek to understand the mysterious ways of God. But what can I do? I'm not a sage, one of the elect, nor a saint. I'm just an ordinary creature of flesh and blood. I've got eyes, too, and I can see what they're doing here. Where is the divine Mercy? Where is God? How can I believe, how could anyone believe, in this merciful God?"

Poor Akiba Drumer, if he could have gone on believing in God, if he could have seen a proof of God in this Calvary, he would not have been taken by the selection. But as soon as he felt the first cracks forming in his faith, he had lost his reason for struggling and had begun to die.

When the selection came, he was condemned in advance, offering his own neck to the executioner. All he asked of us was:

"In three days I shall no longer be here . . . . Say the Kaddish for me."

We promised him. In three days' time, when we saw the smoke rising from the chimney, we would think of him. Ten of us would gather together and hold a special service. All his friends would say the Kaddish.

Then he went off toward the hospital, his step steadier, not looking back. An ambulance was waiting to take him to Birkenau.

These were terrible days. We received more blows than food; we were crushed with work. And three days after he had gone we forgot to say the Kaddish. . . .

Two days after my operation, there was a rumor going round the camp that the front had suddenly drawn nearer. The Red Army, they said, was advancing on Buna; it was only a matter of hours now.

We were already accustomed to rumors of this kind. It was not the first time a false prophet had foretold to us peace-on-earth, negotiations-with-the-Red-Cross-for-our release, or other false rumors. . . . And often we believed them. It was an injection of morphine.

But this time these prophecies seemed more solid. During these last few nights, we had heard the guns in the distance.

My neighbor, the faceless one, said:

"Don't let yourself be fooled with illusions. Hitler has made it very clear that he will annihilate all the Jews before the clock strikes twelve, before they can hear the last stroke."

I burst out:

"What does it matter to you? Do we have to regard Hitler as a prophet?"

His glazed, faded eyes looked at me. At last he said in a weary voice:

"I've got more faith in Hitler than in anyone else. He's the only one who's kept his promises, all his promises, to the Jewish people."

At four o'clock on the afternoon of the same day, as usual the bell summoned all the heads of the block to go and report.

They came back shattered. They could only just open their lips enough to say the word: evacuation. The camp was to be emptied, and we were to be sent farther back. Where to? To somewhere right in the depths of Germany, to other camps; there was no shortage of them.

"When?"

"Tomorrow evening."

"Perhaps the Russians will arrive first."

"Perhaps."

We knew perfectly well that they would not.

The camp had become a hive. People ran about, shouting at one another. In all the blocks, preparations for the journey were going on. I had forgotten about my bad foot. A doctor came into the room and announced:

"Tomorrow, immediately after nightfall, the camp will set out. Block after block. Patients will stay in the infirmary. They will not be evacuated."

This news made us think. Were the SS going to leave hundreds of prisoners to strut about in the hospital blocks, waiting for their liberators? Were they going to let the Jews hear the twelfth stroke sound? Obviously not.

The Chastised Self

"All the invalids will be summarily killed," said the faceless one. "And sent to the crematory in a final batch."

"The camp is certain to be mined," said another. "The moment the evacuation's over, it'll blow up."

As for me, I was not thinking about death, but I did not want to be separated from my father. We had already suffered so much, borne so much together; this was not the time to be separated.

I ran outside to look for him. The snow was thick, and the windows of the blocks were veiled with frost. One shoe in my hand, because it would not go onto my right foot, I ran on, feeling neither pain nor cold.

"What shall we do?"

My father did not answer.

"What shall we do, father?"

He was lost in thought. The choice was in our hands. For once we could decide our fate for ourselves. We could both stay in the hospital, where I could, thanks to my doctor, get him entered as a patient or a nurse. Or else we could follow the others.

"Well, what shall we do, father?"

He was silent.

"Let's be evacuated with the others," I said to him.

He did not answer. He looked at my foot.

"Do you think you can walk?"

"Yes, I think so."

"Let's hope that we shan't regret it, Eliezer."

I learned after the war the fate of those who had stayed behind in the hospital. They were quite simply liberated by the Russians two days after the evacuation. . . .

In the morning, the face of the camp had changed. Prisoners appeared in strange outfits: it was like a masquerade. Everyone had put on several garments, one on top of the other, in order to keep out the cold. Poor mountebanks, wider than they were tall, more dead than alive; poor clowns, their ghostlike faces emerging from piles of prison clothes. Buffoons!

I tried to find a shoe that was too large. In vain. I tore up a blanket and wrapped my wounded foot in it. Then I went wandering through the camp, looking for a little more bread and a few potatoes.

Some said we were being taken to Czechoslovakia. No, to Gros-Rosen. No, to Gleiwitz. No, to. . . .

Two o'clock in the afternoon. The snow was still coming down thickly.

The time was passing quickly now. Dusk had fallen. The day was disappearing in a monochrome of gray.

The head of the block suddenly remembered that he had forgotten to clean out the block. He ordered four prisoners to wash the wooden floor. . . . An hour before leaving the camp! Why? For whom?

"For the liberating army," he cried. "So that they'll realize there were men living here and not pigs."

Were we men then? The block was cleaned from top to bottom, washed in every corner.

At six o'clock the bell rang. The death knell. The burial. The procession was about to begin its march.

"Form up! Quickly!"

In a few moments we were all in rows, by blocks. Night had fallen. Everything was in order, according to the prearranged plan.

The searchlights came on. Hundreds of armed SS men rose up out of the darkness, accompanied by sheepdogs. The snow never ceased.

The gates of the camp opened. It seemed that an even darker night was waiting for us on the other side.

The first blocks began to march. We waited. We had to wait for the departure of the fifty-six blocks who came before us. It was very cold. In my pocket I had two pieces of bread. With how much pleasure could I have eaten them! But I was not allowed to. Not yet.

Our turn was coming: Block 53. . . Block 55. . . .

Block 57, forward march!

It snowed relentlessly.

An icy wind blew in violent gusts. But we marched without faltering.

The SS made us increase our pace. "Faster, you swine, you filthy sons of bitches!" Why not? The movement warmed us up a little. The blood flowed more easily in our veins. One felt oneself reviving. . . .

"Faster, you filthy sons of bitches!" We were no longer marching; we were running. Like automatons. The SS were running too, their weapons in their hands. We looked as though we were fleeing before them.

Pitch darkness. Every now and then, an explosion in the night. They had orders to fire on any who could not keep up. Their fingers on the triggers, they did not deprive themselves of this pleasure. If one of us stopped for a second, a sharp shot finished off another filthy son of a bitch.

I was putting one foot in front of the other mechanically. I was dragging with me this skeletal body which weighed so much. If only I could have got rid of it! In spite of my efforts not to think about it, I could feel myself as two entities—my body and me. I hated it.

I repeated to myself: "Don't think. Don't stop. Run."

Near me, men were collapsing in the dirty snow. Shots.

At my side marched a young Polish lad called Zalman. He had been working in the electrical warehouse at Buna. They had laughed at him because he was always praying or meditating on some problem of the Talmud. It was his way of escaping from reality, of not feeling the blows. . . .

The Chastised Self

He was suddenly seized with cramp in the stomach. "I've got a stomach ache," he whispered to me. He could not go on. He had to stop for a moment. I begged him:

"Wait a bit, Zalman. We shall all be stopping soon. We're not going to run like this till the end of the world."

But as he ran he began to undo his buttons, crying:

"I can't go on any longer. My stomach's bursting. . . . "

"Make an effort, Zalman. . . . Try. . . . "

"I can't . . . . " he groaned.

His trousers lowered, he let himself sink down.

That is the last picture I have of him. I do not think it can have been the SS who finished him, because no one had noticed. He must have been trampled to death beneath the feet of the thousands of men who followed us.

I quickly forgot him. I began to think of myself again. Because of my painful foot, a shudder went through me at each step. "A few more yards," I thought. "A few more yards, and that will be the end. I shall fall. A spurt of red flame. A shot." Death wrapped itself around me till I was stifled. It stuck to me. I felt that I could touch it. The idea of dying, of no longer being, began to fascinate me. Not to exist any longer. Not to feel the horrible pains in my foot. Not to feel anything, neither weariness, nor cold, nor anything. To break the ranks, to let oneself slide to the edge of the road. . . .

My father's presence was the only thing that stopped me. . . . He was running at my side, out of breath, at the end of his strength, at his wit's end. I had no right to let myself die. What would he do without me? I was his only support. . . .

An endless road. Letting oneself be pushed by the mob; letting oneself be dragged along by a blind destiny. When the SS became tired, they were changed. But no one changed us. Our limbs numb with cold despite the running, our throats parched, famished, breathless, on we went.

We were masters of nature, masters of the world. We had forgotten everything—death, fatigue, our natural needs. Stronger than cold or hunger, stronger than the shots and the desire to die, condemned and wandering, mere numbers, we were the only men on earth.

At last, the morning star appeared in the gray sky. A trail of indeterminate light showed on the horizon. We were exhausted. We were without strength, without illusions.

The commandant announced that we had already covered forty-two miles since we left. It was a long time since we had passed beyond the limits of fatigue. Our legs were moving mechanically, in spite of us, without us.

We went through a deserted village. Not a living soul. Not the bark of a dog. Houses with gaping windows. A few slipped out of the ranks to try and hide in some deserted building.

Elie Wiesel 153

Still one hour's marching more, and at last came the order to rest. . . .

I do not know how long I slept. A few moments or an hour. When I woke up, a frozen hand was patting my cheeks. I forced myself to open my eyes. It was my father.

How old he had grown since the night before! His body was completely twisted, shriveled up into itself. His eyes were petrified, his lips withered, decayed. Everything about him bore witness to extreme exhaustion. His voice was damp with tears and snow. . . .

"Don't be afraid, son. Sleep—you can sleep, I'll look after you myself."

"No, you first, father. Go to sleep."

He refused. I lay down and tried to force myself to sleep, to doze a little, but in vain. God knows, what I would not have given for a few moments of sleep. But, deep down, I felt that to sleep would mean to die. And something within me revolted against this death. All round me death was moving in, silently, without violence. It would seize upon some sleeping being, enter into him, and consume him bit by bit. Next to me there was someone trying to wake up his neighbor, his brother, perhaps, or a friend. In vain. Discouraged in the attempt, the man lay down in his turn, next to the corpse, and slept too. Who was there to wake him up? Stretching out an arm, I touched him:

"Wake up. You mustn't sleep here. . . . "

He half opened his eyes.

"No advice," he said in a faint voice. "I'm tired. Leave me alone. Leave me."

My father, too, was gently dozing. I could not see his eyes. His cap had fallen over his face.

"Wake up," I whispered in his ear.

He started up. He sat up and looked round him, bewildered, stupefied—a bereaved stare. He stared all round him in a circle as though he had suddenly decided to draw up an inventory of his universe, to find out exactly where he was, in what place, and why. Then he smiled.

I shall always remember that smile. From which world did it come?

The snow continued to fall in thick flakes over the corpses.

The door of the shed opened. An old man appeared, his moustache covered with frost, his lips blue with cold. It was Rabbi Eliahou, the rabbi of a small Polish community. He was a very good man, well loved by everyone in the camp, even by the Kapos and the heads of the blocks. Despite the trials and privations, his face still shone with his inner purity. He was the only rabbi who was always addressed as "Rabbi" at Buna. He was like one of the old prophets, always in the midst of his people to comfort them. And, strangely, his words of comfort never provoked rebellion; they really brought peace.

He came into the shed and his eyes, brighter than ever, seemed to be looking for someone:

The Chastised Self

"Perhaps someone has seen my son somewhere?"

He had lost his son in the crowd. He had looked in vain among the dying. Then he had scratched up the snow to find his corpse. Without result.

For three years they had stuck together. Always near each other, for suffering, for blows, for the ration of bread, for prayer. Three years, from camp to camp, from selection to selection. And now—when the end seemed near—fate had separated them. Finding himself near me, Rabbi Eliahou whispered:

"It happened on the road. We lost sight of one another during the journey. I had stayed a little to the rear of the column. I hadn't any strength left for running. And my son didn't notice. That's all I know. Where has he disappeared? Where can I find him? Perhaps you've seen him somewhere?"

"No, Rabbi Eliahou, I haven't seen him."

He left then as he had come: like a wind-swept shadow.

He had already passed through the door when I suddenly remembered seeing his son running by my side. I had forgotten that, and I didn't tell Rabbi Eliahou!

Then I remembered something else: his son had seen him losing ground, limping, staggering back to the rear of the column. He had seen him. And he had continued to run on in front, letting the distance between them grow greater.

A terrible thought loomed up in my mind: he had wanted to get rid of his father! He had felt that his father was growing weak, he had believed that the end was near and had sought this separation in order to get rid of the burden, to free himself from an encumbrance which could lessen his own chances of survival.

I had done well to forget that. And I was glad that Rabbi Eliahou should continue to look for his beloved son.

And, in spite of myself, a prayer rose in my heart, to that God in whom I no longer believed.

My God, Lord of the Universe, give me strength never to do what Rabbi Eliahou's son has done.

Shouts rose outside in the yard, where darkness had fallen. The SS ordered the ranks to form up.

The march began again. The dead stayed in the yard under the snow, like faithful guards assassinated, without burial. No one had said the prayer for the dead over them. Sons abandoned their fathers' remains without a tear. . . .

At the gate of the camp, SS officers were waiting for us. They counted us. Then we were directed to the assembly place. Orders were given us through loudspeakers:

"Form fives!" "Form groups of a hundred!" "Five paces forward!"

I held onto my father's hand—the old, familiar fear: not to lose him.

Right next to us the high chimney of the crematory oven rose up. It no longer made any impression on us. It scarcely attracted our attention.

An established inmate of Buchenwald told us that we should have a shower and then we could go into the blocks. The idea of having a hot bath fascinated me. My father was silent. He was breathing heavily beside me.

"Father," I said. "Only another moment more. Soon we can lie down—in a bed. You can rest. . . ."

He did not answer. I was so exhausted myself that his silence left me indifferent. My only wish was to take a bath as quickly as possible and lie down in a bed.

But it was not easy to reach the showers. Hundreds of prisoners were crowding there. The guards were unable to keep any order. They struck out right and left with no apparent result. Others, without the strength to push or even to stand up, had sat down in the snow. My father wanted to do the same. He groaned.

"I can't go on. . . . This is the end. . . . I'm going to die here. . . ."

He dragged me toward a hillock of snow from which emerged human shapes and ragged pieces of blanket.

"Leave me," he said to me. "I can't go on. . . . Have mercy on me. . . . I'll wait here until we can get into the baths. . . . You can come and find me."

I could have wept with rage. Having lived through so much, suffered so much, could I leave my father to die now? Now, when we could have a good hot bath and lie down?

"Father!" I screamed. "Father! Get up from here! Immediately! You're killing yourself. . . . "

I seized him by the arm. He continued to groan.

"Don't shout, son. . . . Take pity on your old father. . . . Leave me to rest here. . . . Just for a bit, I'm so tired . . . at the end of my strength. . . . "

He had become like a child, weak, timid, vulnerable.

"Father," I said. "You can't stay here."

I showed him the corpses all around him; they too had wanted to rest here.

"I can see them, son. I can see them all right. Let them sleep. It's so long since they closed their eyes. . . . They are exhausted . . . . "

His voice was tender.

I yelled against the wind:

"They'll never wake again! Never! Don't you understand?"

For a long time this argument went on. I felt that I was not arguing with him, but with death itself, with the death that he had already chosen.

The sirens began to wail. An alert. The lights went out throughout the camp. The guards drove us toward the blocks. In a flash, there was no one left on the assembly place. We were only too glad not to have had to stay outside longer in the icy wind. We let ourselves sink down onto the planks. The beds were in several tiers. The cauldrons of soup at the entrance attracted no one. To sleep, that was all that mattered.

It was daytime when I awoke. And then I remembered that I had a father. Since the alert, I had followed the crowd without troubling about him. I had known that he was at the end, on the brink of death, and yet I had abandoned him.

I went to look for him.

But at the same moment this thought came into my mind: "Don't let me find him! If only I could get rid of this dead weight, so that I could use all my strength to struggle for my own survival, and only worry about myself." Immediately I felt ashamed of myself, ashamed forever.

I walked for hours without finding him. Then I came to the block where they were giving out black "coffee". The men were lining up and fighting.

A plaintive, beseeching voice caught me in the spine:

"Eliezer . . . my son . . . bring me . . . a drop of coffee. . . ."

I ran to him.

"Father! I've been looking for you for so long. . . . Where were you? Did you sleep?. . . . How do you feel?"

He was burning with fever. Like a wild beast, I cleared a way for myself to the coffee cauldron. I managed to carry back a cupful. I had a sip. The rest was for him. I can't forget the light of thankfulness in his eyes while he gulped it down—an animal gratitude. With those few gulps of hot water, I probably brought him more satisfaction than I had done during my whole childhood.

He was lying on a plank, livid, his lips pale and dried up, shaken by tremors. I could not stay by him for long. Orders had been given to clear the place for cleaning. Only the sick could stay.

We stayed outside for five hours. Soup was given out. As soon as we were allowed to go back to the blocks, I ran to my father.

"Have you had anything to eat?"

"No."

"Why not?"

"They didn't give us anything . . . they said that if we were ill we should die soon anyway and it would be a pity to waste the food. I can't go on any more. . . ."

I gave him what was left of my soup. But it was with a heavy heart. I felt that I was giving it up to him against my will. No better than Rabbi Eliahou's son had I withstood the test.

He grew weaker day by day, his gaze veiled, his face the color of dead leaves. On the third day after our arrival at Buchenwald, everyone had to go to the showers. Even the sick, who had to go through last.

On the way back from the baths, he had to wait outside for a long time. They had not yet finished cleaning the blocks.

Seeing my father in the distance, I ran to meet him. He went by me like a ghost, passed me without stopping, without looking at me. I called to him. He did not come back. I ran after him:

Elie Wiesel

"Father, where are you running to?"

He looked at me for a moment, and his gaze was distant, visionary; it was the face of someone else. A moment only and on he ran again. . . .

When I came back from the bread distribution, I found my father weeping like a child:

"Son, they keep hitting me!"

"Who?"

I thought he was delirious.

"Him, the Frenchman . . . and the Pole . . . they were hitting me."

Another wound to the heart, another hate, another reason for living lost.

"Eliezer . . . Eliezer . . . tell them not to hit me . . . . I haven't done anything. . . . Why do they keep hitting me?"

I began to abuse his neighbors. They laughed at me. I promised them bread, soup. They laughed. Then they got angry; they could not stand my father any longer, they said, because he was now unable to drag himself outside to relieve himself.

The following day he complained that they had taken his ration of bread.

"While you were asleep?"

"No. I wasn't asleep. They jumped on top of me. They snatched my bread . . . and they hit me . . . again. . . . I can't stand any more, son . . . a drop of water. . . . "

I knew that he must not drink. But he pleaded with me for so long that I gave in. Water was the worst poison he could have but what else could I do for him? With water, without water, it would all be over soon anyway. . . .

"You, at least, have some mercy on me. . . ."

Have mercy on him! I, his only son!

A week went by like this.

"This is your father, isn't it?" asked the head of the block.

"Yes."

"He's very ill."

"The doctor won't do anything for him."

"The doctor *can't* do anything for him, now. And neither can you."

He put his great hairy hand on my shoulder and added:

"Listen to me, boy. Don't forget that you're in a concentration camp. Here, every man has to fight for himself and not think of anyone else. Even of his father. Here, there are no fathers, no brothers, no friends. Everyone lives and dies for himself alone. I'll give you a sound piece of advice—don't give your ration of bread and soup to your old father. There's nothing you can do for him. And you're killing yourself. Instead, you ought to be having his ration."

I listened to him without interrupting. He was right, I thought in the most secret region of my heart, but I dared not admit it. It's too late to save your old father, I said to myself. You ought to be having two rations of bread, two rations of soup. . . .

The Chastised Self

Only a fraction of a second, but I felt guilty. I ran to find a little soup to give my father. But he did not want it. All he wanted was water.

"Don't drink water . . . have some soup. . . . "

"I'm burning . . . why are you being so unkind to me, my son? Some water. . . . "

I brought him some water. Then I left the block for roll call. But I turned around and came back again. I lay down on the top bunk. Invalids were allowed to stay in the block. So I would be an invalid myself. I would not leave my father.

There was silence all round now, broken only by groans. In front of the block, the SS were giving orders. An officer passed by the beds. My father begged me:

"My son, some water . . . . I'm burning . . . . My stomach. . . . "

"Quiet, over there!" yelled the officer.

"Eliezer," went on my father, "some water. . . . "

The officer came up to him and shouted at him to be quiet. But my father did not hear him. He went on calling me. The officer dealt him a violent blow on the head with his truncheon.

I did not move. I was afraid. My body was afraid of also receiving a blow.

Then my father made a rattling noise and it was my name: "Eliezer."

I could see that he was still breathing—spasmodically.

I did not move.

When I got down after roll call, I could see his lips trembling as he murmured something. Bending over him, I stayed gazing at him for over an hour, engraving into myself the picture of his blood-stained face, his shattered skull.

Then I had to go to bed. I climbed into my bunk, above my father, who was still alive. It was January 28, 1945.

I awoke on January 29 at dawn. In my father's place lay another invalid. They must have taken him away before dawn and carried him to the crematory. He may still have been breathing.

There were no prayers at his grave. No candles were lit to his memory. His last word was my name. A summons, to which I did not respond.

I did not weep, and it pained me that I could not weep. But I had no more tears. And, in the depths of my being, in the recess of my weakened conscience, could I have searched it, I might perhaps have found something like—free at last!

Suggestions for Further Reading

Elie Wiesel, *The Accident*, translated by Anne Borchardt (New York: Hill and Wang, 1962).

_____, "Appointment with Hate," *Commentary*, XXXIV (December 1962), pp. 470-476.

_____, *Dawn*, translated by Frances Frenaye (New York: Hill and Wang, 1961).

_____, "The Death of My Father," *Jubilee*, VIII (November 1960), pp. 21-27.

_____, "From Exile to Exile," *Nation*, 202 (April 26, 1966), pp. 494-495.

_____, *The Gates of the Forest*, translated by Frances Frenaye (New York: Holt, Rinehart and Winston, 1966).

_____, "Jewish Values in the Post-Holocaust Future: A Symposium," *Judaism: A Quarterly Review*, 16, No. 3 (Summer 1967), pp. 281-283.

_____, *The Jews of Silence: A Personal Report on Soviet Jewry*, translated by Neal Kozodov (New York: Holt, Rinehart and Winston, 1966).

_____, "Madmen of Sighet. Story," *Commentary*, XLV (May 1968), pp. 38-41.

_____, *Night*, translated by Stella Rodway (New York: Hill and Wang, 1964).

_____, *The Town Beyond the Wall*, translated by Stephen Becker (New York: Holt, Rinehart and Winston, 1967).

The Chastised Self

Part Three

The Fraternal Self

Benjamin Franklin

The Autobiography

His discourses were chiefly either
polemic arguments or explications of
the peculiar doctrines of our sect,
and were all to me very dry, unin-
teresting, and unedifying; since not
a single moral principle was incul-
cated or enforced, their aim seeming
to be rather to make us Presbyterians
than good citizens.

Benjamin Franklin, the highly versatile scientist, civic leader, and statesman, was born in Boston in 1706, the youngest of Josiah and Abiah Franklin's ten children. At the age of 12 he was apprenticed to his elder brother, a printer, but at 17 he slipped out of Boston and sailed to New York and then to Philadelphia. After a year and a half in London, he returned to Philadelphia in 1726 and for the next six years consolidated his position as a printer and city father. In 1746 he became internationally famous through his electrical experiments. Immanuel Kant celebrated him as "a new Prometheus who had stolen fire from heaven." Two years later Franklin entered political affairs directly when he organized the state militia.

Concerning Franklin's religious life, he was raised by his parents in the tradition of New England Congregationalism. In Philadelphia he was affiliated with the Presbyterian Church, at that time regarded as nearly identical with Congregationalism. His attendance at church was sporadic until he became embroiled in a controversy involving a new assistant clergyman, the Rev. Samuel Hemphill. After Hemphill was brought to trial for heresy and suspended, Franklin and his wife switched their allegiance to the Anglican Church, though there is no record of his formally becoming a member. In any event, Franklin's church attendance does not accurately reflect his religiosity. As a friend once wrote him: "I know nothing that would promote the cause of [religion] so much as Dr. Franklin's adding the performance of its rituals to that inward devotion of his heart and his truly virtuous conduct."

Essentially, Franklin's religious perspective centered on the problem of creating order out of chaos. In affirming his belief in the goodness, wisdom, and power of God, he asserts that "this religion will be a powerful regulator of our actions." Franklin's own personal struggle against moral chaos was an enduring one. It was especially acute in 1730, the year he devised the exercise in morality described in the following selection, for that same year he fathered an illegitimate child. But it was also evident in his later life when, for example, he took a more than casual interest in a notorious secret society, the Order of Saint Francis, whose members allegedly took part in black masses and sexual excesses.

Franklin's struggle against moral chaos paralleled his concern for political order. While Goethe, recoiling from a civilized milieu which sapped his spiritual strength, championed the return to nature, Franklin concerned himself with the problem of "cultivating the earth," of replacing untamed nature with a culture based on moral and rational control. This concern is clearly expressed in the following selection in the episode involving the Indians. In a similar way, his scientific investigations, especially his work on electricity, were directed toward taming the cosmos. As Carl van Doren suggests, Franklin "had hit upon a secret which enabled him, and other men, to catch and tame lightning, so dread that it was still mythological. . . . Secular as he was, he had often a vision, not unlike religion's, of an enormous universe of order and law which sometime might be understood." Thus the problem of creating order from chaos, perhaps the fundamental problem of a rising young nation, was mirrored in Franklin's own religious conviction.

Autobiography

Providential Beginnings

I have ever had a pleasure in obtaining any little anecdotes of my ancestors. You [he is writing to his son] may remember the inquiries I made among the remains of my relations when you were with me in England, and the journey I undertook for that purpose. Imagining it may be equally agreeable to you to learn the circumstances of *my* life, many of which you are unacquainted with, and expecting the enjoyment of a few weeks' uninterrupted leisure, I sit down to write them. Besides, there are some other inducements that excite me to this undertaking. From the poverty and obscurity in which I was born and in which I passed my earliest years, I have raised myself to a state of affluence and

From Benjamin Franklin, *The Autobiography of Benjamin Franklin* (New York: A. L. Burt, 1912).

The Fraternal Self

some degree of celebrity in the world. As constant good fortune has accompanied me even to an advanced period of life, my posterity will perhaps be desirous of learning the means which I employed, and which, thanks to Providence, so well succeeded with me. They may also deem them fit to be imitated, should any of them find themselves in similar circumstances.

This good fortune, when I reflect on it (which is frequently the case), has induced me sometimes to say that if it were left to my choice I should have no objection to go over the same life from its beginning to the end; requesting only the advantage authors have of correcting in a second edition the faults of the first. So would I also wish to change some incidents of it for others more favorable. Notwithstanding, if this condition was denied I should still accept the offer recommencing the same life. But as this repetition is not to be expected, that which resembles most living one's life over again seems to be to recall all the circumstances of it, and, to render this remembrance more durable, to record them in writing.

In thus employing myself, I shall yield to the inclination, so natural to old men, of talking of themselves and their own actions; and I shall indulge it without being tiresome to those who, from respect to my age, might conceive themselves obliged to listen to me, since they will be always free to read me or not. And lastly (I may as well confess it, as the denial of it would be believed by nobody), I shall, perhaps, not a little gratify my own vanity. Indeed, I never heard or saw the introductory words, "Without vanity I may say," etc., but some vain thing immediately followed. Most people dislike vanity in others, whatever share they have of it themselves; but I give it fair quarter wherever I meet with it, being persuaded that it is often productive of good to the possessor and to others who are within his sphere of action; and therefore, in many cases, it would not be altogether absurd if a man were to thank God for the *vanity* among the other comforts of life.

And now I speak of thanking God, I desire with all humility to acknowledge that I attribute the mentioned happiness of my past life to his divine providence, which led me to the means I used and gave the success. My belief of this induces me to *hope*, though I must not *presume*, that the same goodness will still be exercised toward me in continuing that happiness or enabling me to bear a fatal reverse, which I may experience as others have done; the complexion of my future fortune being known to Him only in whose power it is to bless us, even in our afflictions. . . .

My elder brothers were all put apprentices to different trades. I was put to the grammar school at eight years of age, my father intending to devote me as the tithe of his sons to the service of the Church. My early readiness in learning to read, which must have been very early, as I do not remember when I could not read, and the opinion of all his friends that I should certainly make a good scholar, encouraged him in this purpose of his. My uncle Benjamin, too, approved of it, and proposed to give me his shorthand volumes of sermons to set up with if I would learn his short-hand. I continued, however, at the grammar school rather less than a year, though in that time I had risen gradually from the middle of the class of that year to be at the head of the same class, and was removed into the next class, whence I was to be placed in the third at the end of the year.

But my father, burdened with a numerous family, was unable, without inconvenience, to support the expense of a college education. Considering, moreover, as he said to one of his friends in my presence, the little encouragement that line of life afforded to those educated for it, he gave up his first intentions, [and] took me from the grammar school. . . . At ten years old I was taken to help my father in his business, which was that of a tallow-chandler and soap-boiler; a business to which he was not bred, but had assumed on his arrival in New England, because he found that his dyeing trade, being in little request, would not maintain his family. Accordingly I was employed in cutting wicks for the candles, filling the molds for cast candles, attending the shop, going on errands, etc. . . .

I continued thus employed in my father's business for two years, that is, till I was twelve years old, and my brother John, who was bred to that business, having left my father, married and set up for himself at Rhode Island, there was every appearance that I was destined to supply his place and become a tallow-chandler. But my dislike to the trade continuing, my father had apprehensions that if he did not put me to one more agreeable I should break loose and go to sea, as my brother Josiah had done, to his great vexation. . . . From my infancy I was passionately fond of reading, and all the money that came into my hands was laid out in the purchasing of books. . . . This bookish inclination at length determined my father to make me a printer, although he had already one son, James, in that profession. In 1717 my brother James returned from England, with a press and letters, to set up his business in Boston. I liked it much better than that of my father, but still had a hankering for the sea. To prevent the apprehended effect of such an inclination, my father was impatient to have me bound to my brother. I stood out some time, but at last was persuaded and signed the indenture when I was yet but twelve years old. I was to serve an apprenticeship till I was twenty-one years of age, only I was to be allowed journeyman's wages during the last year. In a little time I made a great progress in the business and became a useful hand to my brother. . . .

When about sixteen years of age I happened to meet with a book, written by one Tryon, recommending a vegetable diet. I determined to go into it. My brother being yet unmarried did not keep house, but boarded himself and his apprentices in another family. My refusing to eat flesh occasioned an inconvenience, and I was frequently chid for my singularity. I made myself acquainted with Tryon's manner of preparing some of his dishes, such as boiling potatoes or rice, making hasty-pudding and a few others, and then proposed to my brother that if he would give me weekly half the money he paid for my board, I would board myself. He instantly agreed to it, and I presently found that I could save half what he paid me. This was an additional fund for buying of books; but I had another advantage in it. My brother and the rest going from the printing-house to their meals, I remained there alone, and dispatching presently my light repast (which was often no more than a biscuit or a slice of bread, a handful of raisins or a tart from the pastry-cook's, and a glass of water), had the rest of the time till their return for study; in which I made the greater progress from that greater clearness of head and quick apprehension which generally attend temperance in eating and drinking. . . .

At length, a fresh difference arising between my brother and me, I took upon me to assert my freedom, presuming that he would not venture to produce the new indentures. It was not fair in me to take this advantage, and this I therefore reckon one of the first *errata* of my life; but the unfairness of it weighed little with me when under the impressions of resentment for the blows his passion too often urged him to bestow upon me. Though he was otherwise not an ill-natured man; perhaps I was too saucy and provoking. . . .

The inclination I had had for the sea was by this time done away, or I might now have gratified it. But having another profession and conceiving myself a pretty good workman, I offered my services to a printer [in New York], old Mr. William Bradford, who had been the first printer in Pennsylvania, but had removed thence in consequence of a quarrel with the governor, George Keith. He could give me no employment, having little to do and hands enough already; but he said, "My son at Philadelphia has lately lost his principal hand, Aquila Rose, by death; if you go thither I believe he may employ you." Philadelphia was one hundred miles further. I set out, however, in a boat for Amboy, leaving my chest and things to follow me round by sea. . . .

I [shall be] the more particular in this description . . . of my first entry into that city, that you may in your mind compare such unlikely beginnings with the figure I have since made there. I was in my working dress, my best clothes coming round by sea. I was dirty, from my being so long in the boat. My pockets were stuffed out with shirts and stockings, and I knew no one nor where to look for lodging. Fatigued with walking, rowing, and the want of sleep, I was very hungry; and my whole stock of cash consisted in a single dollar, and about a shilling in copper coin, which I gave to the boatmen for my passage. At first they refused it, on account of my having rowed; but I insisted on their taking it. Man is sometimes more generous when he has little money than when he has plenty; perhaps to prevent his being thought to have but little.

I walked toward the top of the street, gazing about till near Market Street, when I met a boy with bread. I had often made a meal of dry bread, and inquiring where he had bought it, I went immediately to the baker's he directed me to. I asked for biscuits, meaning such as we had at Boston; that sort, it seems, was not made at Philadelphia. I then asked for a three-penny loaf and was told they had none. Not knowing the different prices nor the names of the different sorts of bread, I told him to give me threepenny worth of any sort. He gave me accordingly three great puffy rolls. I was surprised at the quantity, but took it, and having no room in my pockets, walked off with a roll under each arm and eating the other. Thus I went up Market Street as far as Fourth Street, passing by the door of Mr. Read, my future wife's father; when she, standing at the door, saw me, and thought I made, as I certainly did, a most awkward, ridiculous appearance. . . .

A Scheme for Moral Perfection

Before I enter upon my public appearance in business, it may be well to let you know the then state of my mind with regard to my principles and morals, that you may see how far these influenced the future events of my life. My parents had early given me religious impressions and brought me through my childhood piously in the Dissenting way. But I was scarce fifteen, when, after doubting by turns several points as I found them disputed in the different books I read, I began to doubt of the Revelation itself. Some books against deism fell into my hands; they were said to be the substance of the sermons which had been preached at Boyle's Lectures. It happened that they wrought an effect on me quite contrary to what was intended by them. For the arguments of the deists, which were quoted to be refuted, appeared to me much stronger than the refutations; in short, I soon became a thorough deist. My arguments perverted some others, particularly Collins and Ralph, but each of these having wronged me greatly without the least compunction, and recollecting Keith's conduct toward me (who was another freethinker) and my own toward Vernon and Miss Read, which at times gave me great trouble, I began to suspect that this doctrine, though it might be true, was not very useful. . . .

I grew convinced that *truth, sincerity*, and *integrity*, in dealings between man and man, were of the utmost importance to the felicity of life; and I formed written resolution, which still remain in my journal book, to practice them ever while I lived. Revelation had indeed no weight with me as such; but I entertained an opinion that though certain actions might not be bad *because* they were forbidden by it, or good *because* it commanded them, yet probably these actions might be forbidden *because* they were bad for us, or commanded *because* they were beneficial to us in their own natures, all the circumstances of things considered. And this persuasion, with the kind hand of Providence, or some guardian angel, or accidental favorable circumstances and situations, or all together, preserved me, through this dangerous time of youth and the hazardous situations I was sometimes in among strangers, remote from the eye and advice of my father, free from any *willful* gross immorality or injustice that might have been expected from my want of religion. I say *willful*, because the instances I have mentioned had something of *necessity* in them, from my youth, inexperience, and the knavery of others. I had therefore a tolerable character to begin in the world with. I valued it properly and determined to preserve it. . . .

I had been religiously educated as a Presbyterian; but though some of the dogmas of that persuasion, such as *the eternal decrees of God, election, reprobation, etc.,* appeared to me very unintelligible, others doubtful, and I early absented myself from the public assemblies of the sect, Sunday being my studying day, I never was without some religious principles. I never doubted, for instance, the existence of a Deity—that he made the world and governed it by his providence—that the most acceptable service of God was the doing good to man—that our souls are immortal—and that all crimes will be punished and virtue rewarded, either here or hereafter. These I esteemed the essentials of every religion; and being to be found in all the religions we had in our country, I respected them all, though with different degrees of respect, as I found them more or less mixed with other articles which, without any tendency to inspire, promote, or confirm morality, served principally to divide us and make us unfriendly to one another. This respect to all, with an opinion that the worst had some good effects, induced me to avoid all discourse that might tend to lessen the good opinion another might have of his own religion; and as our province increased in people and new places of worship were continually wanted and generally erected by voluntary contribution, my mite for such purpose, whatever might be the sect, was never refused.

Though I seldom attended any public worship, I had still an opinion of its propriety and of its utility when rightly conducted, and I regularly paid my annual subscription for the support of the only Presbyterian minister or meeting we had in Philadelphia. He used to visit me sometimes as a friend and admonish me to attend his administrations, and I was now and then prevailed on to do so, once for five Sundays successively. Had he been in my opinion a good preacher, perhaps I might have continued, notwithstanding the occasion I had for Sunday's leisure in my course of study; but his discourses were chiefly either polemic arguments or explications of the peculiar doctrines of our sect, and were all to me very dry, uninteresting, and unedifying; since not a single moral principle was inculcated or enforced, their aim seeming to be rather to make us *Presbyterians* than *good citizens.*

At length he took for his text that verse of the fourth chapter to the Philippians: "*Finally, brethren, whatsoever things are true, honest, JUST, PURE, LOVELY, OR OF GOOD REPORT, IF THERE BE ANY VIRTUE, or any praise, think on these things.*" And I imagined in a sermon on such a text, we could not miss of having some morality. But he confined himself to five points only, as meant by the apostle: 1. Keeping holy the Sabbath day. 2. Being diligent in reading the holy Scriptures. 3. Attending duly the public worship. 4. Partaking of the Sacrament. 5. Paying due respect to God's ministers. These might be all good things; but as they were not the kind of good things that I expected from the text, I despaired of ever meeting with them from any other, was disgusted, and attended his preaching no more. I had some years before composed a little liturgy or form of prayer for my own private use (in 1728), entitled "Articles of Belief and Acts of Religion." I returned to the use of this and went no more to the public assemblies. My conduct might be blamable, but I leave it without attempting further to excuse it; my present purpose being to relate facts and not to make apologies for them.

It was about this time I conceived the bold and arduous project of arriving at *moral perfection*. I wished to live without committing any fault at any time, and to conquer all that either natural inclination, custom, or company might lead me into. As I knew, or thought I knew, what was right and wrong, I did not see why I might not *always* do the one and avoid the other. But I soon found I had undertaken a task of more difficulty than I had imagined. While my attention was taken up and care employed in guarding against one fault, I was often surprised by another; habit took the advantage of inattention; inclination was sometimes too strong for reason. I concluded at length that the mere speculative conviction that it was our interest to be completely virtuous was not sufficient to prevent our slipping, and that the contrary habits must be broken and good ones acquired and established before we can have any dependence on a steady, uniform rectitude of conduct. For this purpose I therefore tried the following method.

In the various enumerations of the *moral virtues* I had met with in my reading, I found the catalogue more or less numerous, as different writers included more or fewer ideas under the same name. *Temperance*, for example, was by some confined to eating and drinking; while by others it was extended to mean the moderating every other pleasure, appetite, inclination, or passion, bodily or mentally, even to our avarice and ambition. I proposed to myself, for the sake of clearness, to use rather more names, with fewer ideas annexed to each, than a few names with more ideas; and I included under thirteen names of virtues all that at that time occurred to me as necessary or desirable, and annexed to each a short precept which fully expressed the extent I gave to its meaning.

The names of *virtues*, with their precepts, were

1. *Temperance—Eat not to dullness; drink not to elevation.*

2. *Silence—Speak not but what may benefit others or yourself; avoid trifling conversation.*

3. *Order—Let all your things have their places; let each part of your business have its time.*

4. *Resolution—Resolve to perform what you ought; perform without fail what you resolve.*

5. *Frugality—Make no expense but to do good to others or yourself; that is, waste nothing.*

The Fraternal Self

6. *Industry—Lose no time; be always employed in something useful; cut off all unnecessary actions.*

7. *Sincerity—Use no hurtful deceit; think innocently and justly; and, if you speak, speak accordingly.*

8. *Justice—Wrong none by doing injuries or omitting the benefits that are your duty.*

9. *Moderation—Avoid extremes; forbear resenting injuries, so much as you think they deserve.*

10. *Cleanliness—Tolerate no uncleanliness in body, clothes, or habitation.*

11. *Tranquility—Be not disturbed at trifles or at accidents common or unavoidable.*

12. *Chastity. . . .*

13. *Humility—Imitate Jesus and Socrates.*

My intention being to acquire the habitude of all these virtues, I judged it would be well not to distract my attention by attempting the whole at once, but to fix it on *one* of them at a time; and when I should be master of that, then to proceed to another; and so on till I should have gone through the thirteen. And as the previous acquisition of some might facilitate the acquisition of certain others, I arranged them with the view as they stand above.

I made a little book, in which I allotted a page for each of the virtues. I ruled each page with red ink, so as to have seven columns, one for each day of the week, marking each column with a letter for the day. I crossed these columns with thirteen red lines, marking the beginning of each line with the first letter of one of the virtues; on which line, and in its proper column, I might mark, by a little black spot, every fault I found upon examination to have been committed respecting that virtue upon that day.

I determined to give a week's strict attention to each of the virtues successively. Thus in the first week my great guard was to avoid every day the least offense against *temperance*; leaving other virtues to their ordinary chance, only marking every evening the faults of the day. Thus if in the first week I could keep my first line, marked Tem., clear of spots, I supposed the habit of that virtue so much strengthened and its opposite weakened that I might venture extending my attention to include the next, and for the following week keep both lines clear of spots. Proceeding thus to the last, I could get through a course complete in thirteen weeks and four courses in a year. And like him who, having a garden to weed, does not attempt to eradicate all the bad herbs at once, which would exceed his reach and his strength, but works on one of the beds at a time, and having accomplished the first proceeds to the second, so I should have, I hoped, the encouraging pleasure of seeing on my pages the progress made in virtue, by clearing successively my lines of their spots; till in the end, by a number of courses, I should be happy in viewing a clean book after a thirteen weeks' daily examination. . . .

I entered upon the execution of this plan for self-examination and continued it with occasional intermissions for some time. I was surprised to find myself so much fuller of faults than I had imagined; but I had the satisfaction of seeing them diminish. To avoid the trouble of renewing now and then my little book, which, by scraping out the marks on the paper of old faults to make room for new ones in a new course, became full of holes, I transferred my tables and precepts to the ivory leaves of a memorandum book, on which the lines were drawn with red ink, that made a durable stain; and on those lines I marked my faults with a black-lead pencil, which marks I could easily wipe out with a wet sponge. After awhile I went through one course only in a year, and afterward only one in several years, till at length I omitted them entirely, being employed in voyages and business abroad with a multiplicity of affairs that interfered; but I always carried my little book with me. . . .

It may be well my posterity should be informed that to this little artifice, with the blessing of God, their ancestor owed the constant felicity of his life down to his seventy-ninth year, in which this is written. What reverses may attend the remainder is in the hand of Providence; but if they arrive, the reflection on past happiness enjoyed ought to help his bearing them with more resignation. To *temperance* he ascribes his long-continued health and what is still left to him of a good constitution; to *industry* and *frugality* the early easiness of his circumstances and acquisition of his fortune, with all that knowledge that enabled him to be a useful citizen and obtained for him some degree of reputation among the learned; to *sincerity* and *justice* the confidence of his country and the honorable employs it conferred upon him; and to the joint influence of the whole mass of the virtues, even in the imperfect state he was able to acquire them, all that evenness of temper and that cheerfulness in conversation which makes his company still sought for and agreeable even to his young acquaintance. I hope, therefore, that some of my descendants may follow the example and reap the benefit.

It will be remarked that though my scheme was not wholly without religion, there was in it no mark of any of the distinguishing tenets of any particular sect. I had purposely avoided them; for being fully persuaded of the utility and excellency of my method, and that it might be serviceable to people in all religions, and intending some time or other to publish it, I would not have anything in it that should prejudice any one, of any sect, against it. . . .

My list of virtues contained at first but twelve; but a Quaker friend having kindly informed me that I was generally thought proud, that my pride showed itself frequently in conversation, that I was not content with being in the right when discussing any point but was overbearing and rather insolent, of which he convinced me by mentioning several instances, I determined to endeavor to cure myself, if I could, of this vice or folly among the rest; and I added *humility* to

The Fraternal Self

my list, giving an extensive meaning to the word. . . . In reality there is, perhaps, no one of our natural passions so hard to subdue as *pride*. Disguise it, struggle with it, stifle it, mortify it as much as one pleases, it is still alive and will every now and then peep out and show itself; you will see it, perhaps often in this history. For even if I could conceive that I had completely overcome it, I should probably be *proud* of my *humility*.

My business was now constantly augmenting and my circumstances growing daily easier, my newspaper having become very profitable, as being for a time almost the only one in this and the neighboring provinces. I experienced, too, the truth of the observation that *"after getting the first hundred pounds it is more easy to get the second"*; money itself being of a prolific nature. . . .

Cultivators of the Earth

The year following, a treaty being to be held with the Indians at Carlisle, the governor sent a message to the House proposing that they should nominate some of their members, to be joined with some members of Council, as commissioners, for that purpose. The House named the Speaker (Mr. Norris) and myself, and being commissioned we went to Carlisle and met the Indians accordingly.

As these people are extremely apt to get drunk, and when so are very quarrelsome and disorderly, we strictly forbade the selling any liquor to them; and when they complained of this restriction, we told them that if they would continue sober during the treaty we would give them plenty of rum when the business was over. They promised this, and they kept their promise, because they could get no rum; and the treaty was conducted very orderly and concluded to mutual satisfaction. They then claimed and received the rum; this was in the afternoon. They were near one hundred men, women, and children, and were lodged in temporary cabins, built in the form of a square, just without the town. In the evening, hearing a great noise among them, the commissioners walked to see what was the matter. We found they had made a great bonfire in the middle of the square; they were all drunk, men and women, quarreling and fighting. Their dark-colored bodies, half-naked, seen only by the gloomy light of the bonfire, running after and beating one another with fire-brands, accompanied by their horrid yellings, formed a scene the most resembling our ideas of hell that could well be imagined! There was no appeasing the tumult, and we retired to our lodging. At midnight a number of them came thundering at our door, demanding more rum, of which we took no notice.

The next day, sensible they had misbehaved in giving us that disturbance, they sent three of their old counselors to make their apology. The orator acknowledged the fault, but laid it upon the rum; and then endeavored to excuse the rum by saying: "The Great Spirit, who made all things, made everything for some use; and whatever use he designed anything for, that use it should always be put it. Now, when he made rum, he said, '*Let this be for the Indians to get drunk with*'; and it must be so." And, indeed, if it be the design of Providence to extirpate these savages in order to make room for the cultivators of the earth, it seems not impossible that rum may be the appointed means. It has already annihilated all the tribes who formerly inhabited the sea-coast.

Suggestions for Further Reading

Alfred Owen Aldridge, *Benjamin Franklin and Nature's God* (Durham, N.C.: Duke University Press, 1967).

———, "Benjamin Franklin and Philosophical Necessity," *Modern Language Quarterly*, XII (September 1951), pp. 292-309.

———, *Benjamin Franklin, Philosopher and Man* (Philadelphia: Lippincott, 1965).

Carl L. Becker, *Benjamin Franklin* (Ithaca, N.Y.: Cornell University Press, 1946).

Bruce William Cabell, *Benjamin Franklin Self-Revealed*, 2 vols, 2nd revised edition (New York: C.P. Putnam and Sons, 1923).

I. Bernard Cohen, *Benjamin Franklin: His Contributions to the American Tradition* (Indianapolis: Bobbs Merrill, 1953).

William S. Hanna, *Benjamin Franklin and Pennsylvania Politics* (Stanford, Calif.: Stanford University Press, 1964).

David Levin, editor, *The Puritan in the Enlightenment: Franklin and Edwards*, (Chicago: Rand McNally, 1963).

———, "The Autobiography of Benjamin Franklin: The Experimenter in Life and Acts," *Yale Review*, LIII (Winter 1964), pp. 258-275.

F.L. Lucas, *The Art of Living: Four Eighteenth-Century Minds: Hume, Horace Walpole, Burke, Benjamin Franklin* (New York: Macmillan, 1960).

Philips Russell, *Benjamin Franklin, the First Civilized American* (New York: Brentano's, 1926).

H.W. Schneider, "The Significance of Benjamin Franklin's Moral Philosophy," *Studies in the History of Ideas*, Vol. 2 (New York: Columbia University Press, 1925), pp. 293-312.

Carl Van Doren, *Benjamin Franklin* (New York: The Viking Press, 1945).

Mohandas K. Gandhi

The Story of My Experiments with Truth

To see the universal and all-pervading
Spirit of Truth face to face one must
be able to love the meanest of
creation as oneself.

Mohandas Gandhi, the Indian political and spiritual leader, was born in 1869 in Porbandar, a tiny state in western India. His father and grandfather both served as prime ministers of Porbandar. Gandhi was the fourth child of his father's fourth marriage and was himself married at the age of 13 to Kasturbai Nakanji, the 13-year-old daughter of a Porbandar merchant. This child marriage was understandably stormy, and Gandhi therefore welcomed the opportunity at the age of 17 to leave his wife and infant child in order to study law in England. He remained in England for nearly three years, returning to India the day following his admittance to the bar.

On his return to India he practiced law with little success for somewhat less than two years. Then in 1892 a business firm of Porbandar Muslims offered to send him to South Africa for a year to handle the firm's legal problems there. He arrived in South Africa in 1893 and shortly thereafter was the victim of an act of racial prejudice. This experience marked the beginning of his lifelong career of civil disobedience. He was traveling by train to Pretoria, the capital of Transvaal, when a white passenger objected to the presence of a "colored" man in the first class coach. He was ordered to the third class coaches, and when he refused he was ejected from the train. He spent the night in the Maritzburg station, and, as Louis Fischer puts it, "That frigid night at Maritzburg the germ of social protest was born." In the course of the next 20 years in South Africa, he led the Indians' protest against discriminatory legislation designed to frustrate their numerical and economic growth. At the conclusion of these 20 years, in 1914, the British government under General Jan Smuts had made sufficient modifications in its proposed Indian legislation to warrant Gandhi's return to India.

The most significant breakthrough of the campaign in South Africa was Gandhi's employment of Satyagraha, or nonviolent civil disobedience, as a means of applying political pressure on the British government. This same nonviolent form of civil disobedience was his basic political strategy in India, where, from 1919 until his assassination in 1948, he fought for Indian home rule and against the partitioning of India and Pakistan. But Satyagraha—"truth force" or "love force"—was not simply a political strategy. As "a method of recognizing and mobilizing the forces of truth and peace in the oppressor as well as in the oppressed" (Erik H. Erikson), Satyagraha appealed to and sought the release of spiritual tendencies— purity of motive, peacefulness, and honesty—that remain untapped in typical political conflicts.

On the practical level, therefore, the employment of Satyagraha was limited to those situations in which the release of these spiritual tendencies was a distinct possibility. As a portion of the following selection illustrates, Gandhi experienced his greatest frustration when the situation, due to its volatile character, forced him to resist the employment of his "truth force" for fear of unleashing counter forces of uncontrollable violence. As he said on another but similar occasion, "I felt helpless" and "I have never put up with helplessness in all my life." Thus, situations of unmitigatable evil rendered Satyagraha virtually impotent. On the other hand, given reasonably favorable circumstances, Gandhi did not shrink from civil disobedience of a militant nature. In acknowledging his spiritual affinities with Indian anarchists, he clearly implied that he was in fact capable of greater self-abandonment than they were: "I am myself an anarchist, but of another type. Their anarchism is a sign of fear." Struggling to attain a disregard of self which creates immunity to fear, he was deeply conscious of the fact that Satyagraha was as much a matter of saintliness as of political stratagem.

We find in Gandhi, therefore, the remarkable convergence of the religious and political man. As Fischer says, "the important fact is that in politics Gandhi always cleaved to religious and moral considerations, and as a saint he never thought his place was in a cave or cloister but rather in the popular struggle for right and rights." Erikson further points out that if Gandhi was a saint, he "was no troubadour saint, but a tough activist." But perhaps Gandhi's own appraisal of his vocational identity is most illuminating. Noting that "Men say I am a saint losing myself in politics," he countered, "The fact is that I am a politician trying my hardest to be a saint." In the selection which follows, Gandhi enlarges on this sense of vocational identity where to be a "political man" is the professional "given," while achieving "saintliness" is an enduring struggle.

Experiments with Truth

It is not my purpose to attempt a real autobiography. I simply want to tell the story of my numerous experiments with truth, and as my life consists of nothing but those experiments, it is true that the story will take the shape of an autobiography. But I shall not mind, if every page of it speaks only of my experiments. I believe, or at any rate flatter myself with the belief, that a connected account of all these experiments will not be without benefit to the reader. My experiments in the political field are now known, not only to India, but to a certain extent to the 'civilized' world. For me, they have not much value; and the title of 'Mahatma' that they have won for me has, therefore, even less. Often the title has deeply pained me; and there is not a moment I can recall when it may be said to have tickled me. But I should certainly like to narrate my experiments in the spiritual field which are known only to myself, and from which I have derived such power as I possess for working in the political field. If the experiments are really spiritual, then there can be no room for self-praise. They can only add to my humility. The more I reflect and look back on the past, the more vividly do I feel my limitations.

What I want to achieve,—what I have been striving and pining to achieve these thirty years,—is self-realization, to see God face to face, to attain Moksha.[1] I live and move and have my being in pursuit of this goal. All that I do by way of speaking and writing, and all my ventures in the political field, are directed to this same end. But as I have all along believed that what is possible for one is possible for all, my experiments have not been conducted in the closet, but in the open; and I do not think that this fact detracts from their spiritual value. There are some things which are known only to oneself and one's Maker. These are clearly incommunicable. The experiments I am about to relate are not such. But they are spiritual, or rather moral; for the essence of religion is morality. . . .

If I had only to discuss academic principles, I should clearly not attempt an autobiography. But my purpose being to give an account of various practical applications of these principles, I have given the chapters I propose to write the title of *The Story of My Experiments with Truth*. These will of course include experiments with non-violence, celibacy and other principles of conduct believed to be distinct from truth. But for me, truth is the sovereign principle, which includes numerous other principles. This truth is not only truthfulness in word, but truthfulness in thought also, and not only the relative truth of our conception, but the Absolute Truth, the Eternal Principle, that is God. There are innumerable definitions of God, because His manifestations are innumerable.

From *Gandhi's Autobiography: The Story of My Experiments with Truth* (Washington, D.C.: Public Affairs Press, 1960). Reprinted by permission.

[1] Lit. freedom from birth and death. The nearest English equivalent is salvation.

They overwhelm me with wonder and awe and for a moment stun me. But I worship God as Truth only. I have not yet found Him, but I am seeking after Him. I am prepared to sacrifice the things dearest to me in pursuit of this quest. Even if the sacrifice demanded be my very life, I hope I may be prepared to give it. But as long as I have not realized this Absolute Truth, so long must I hold by the relative truth as I have conceived it. That relative truth must, meanwhile, be my beacon, my shield and buckler. Though this path is strait and narrow and sharp as the razor's edge, for me it has been the quickest and easiest. Even my Himalayan[2] blunders have seemed trifling to me because I have kept strictly to this path. For the path has saved me from coming to grief, and I have gone forward according to my light. Often in my progress I have had faint glimpses of the Absolute Truth, God, and daily the conviction is growing upon me that He alone is real and all else is unreal. Let those, who wish, realize how the conviction has grown upon me; let them share my experiments and share also my conviction if they can. The further conviction has been growing upon me that whatever is possible for me is possible even for a child, and I have sound reasons for saying so. The instruments for the quest of truth are as simple as they are difficult. They may appear quite impossible to an arrogant person, and quite possible to an innocent child. The seeker after truth should be humbler than the dust. The world crushes the dust under its feet, but the seeker after truth should so humble himself that even the dust could crush him. Only then, and not till then, will he have a glimpse of truth. The dialogue between Vasishtha and Vishvamitra makes this abundantly clear. Christianity and Islam also amply bear it out.

If anything that I write in these pages should strike the reader as being touched with pride, then he must take it that there is something wrong with my quest, and that my glimpses are no more than mirage. Let hundreds like me perish, but let truth prevail. Let us not reduce the standard of truth even by a hair's breadth for judging erring mortals like myself.

I hope and pray that no one will regard the advice interspersed in the following chapters as authoritative. The experiments narrated should be regarded as illustrations, in the light of which every one may carry on his own experiments according to his own inclinations and capacity. I trust that to this limited extent the illustrations will be really helpful; because I am not going either to conceal or understate any ugly things that must be told. I hope to acquaint the reader fully with all my faults and errors. My purpose is to describe experiments in the science of Satyagraha, not to say how good I am. In judging myself I shall try to be as harsh as truth, as I want others also to be. Measuring myself by that standard I must exclaim with Surdas:

---

[2] Gandhi here means his large, colossal blunders.

Where is there a wretch
So wicked and loathsome as I?
I have forsaken my Maker,
So faithless have I been.

For it is an unbroken torture to me that I am still so far from Him, who, as I fully know, governs every breath of my life, and whose offspring I am. I know that it is evil passions within that keep me so far from Him, and yet I cannot get away from them.

But I must close. I can only take up the actual story in the next chapter. . . .

Marriage to Kasturbai

Much as I wish that I had not to write this chapter, I know that I shall have to swallow many such bitter draughts in the course of this narrative. And I cannot do otherwise, if I claim to be a worshipper of Truth. It is my painful duty to have to record here my marriage at the age of thirteen. As I see the youngsters of the same age about me who are under my care, and think of my own marriage, I am inclined to pity myself and to congratulate them on having escaped my lot. I can see no moral argument in support of such a preposterously early marriage.

Let the reader make no mistake. I was married, not betrothed. For in Kathiawad there are two distinct rites,—betrothal and marriage. Betrothal is a preliminary promise on the part of the parents of the boy and girl to join them in marriage, and it is not inviolable. The death of the boy entails no widowhood on the girl. It is an agreement purely between the parents, and the children have no concern with it. Often they are not even informed of it. It appears that I was betrothed thrice, though without my knowledge. I was told that two girls chosen for me had died in turn, and therefore I infer that I was betrothed three times. I have a faint recollection, however, that the third betrothal took place in my seventh year. But I do not recollect having been informed about it. In the present chapter I am talking about my marriage, of which I have the clearest recollection.

It will be remembered that we were three brothers. The first was already married. The elders decided to marry my second brother, who was two or three years my senior, a cousin, possibly a year older, and me, all at the same time. In doing so there was no thought of our welfare, much less our wishes. It was purely a question of their own convenience and economy. . . .

Little did I dream then that one day I should severely criticize my father for having married me as a child. Everything on that day seemed to me right and proper and pleasing. There was also my own eagerness to get married. And as everything that my father did then struck me as beyond reproach, the recollection of those things is fresh in my memory. I can picture to myself, even today, how we sat on our wedding dais, how we performed the *Saptapadi*,[3] how we, the newly wedded husband and wife, put the sweet *Kansar*[4] into each other's mouth, and how we began to live together. And oh! that first night. Two innocent children all unwittingly hurled themselves into the ocean of life. My brother's wife had thoroughly coached me about my behaviour on the first night. I do not know who had coached my wife. I have never asked her about it, nor am I inclined to do so now. The reader may be sure that we were too nervous to face each other. We were certainly too shy. How was I to talk to her, and what was I to say? The coaching could not carry me far. But no coaching is really necessary in such matters. The impressions of the former birth are potent enough to make all coaching superfluous. We gradually began to know each other, and to speak freely together. We were the same age. But I took no time in assuming the authority of a husband. . . .

About the time of my marriage, little pamphlets costing a pice, or a pie (I now forget how much), used to be issued, in which conjugal love, thrift, child marriages, and other such subjects were discussed. Whenever I came across any of these, I used to go through them from cover to cover, and it was a habit with me to forget what I did not like, and to carry out in practice whatever I liked. Lifelong faithfulness to the wife, inculcated in these booklets as the duty of the husband, remained permanently imprinted on my heart. Furthermore, the passion for truth was innate in me, and to be false to her was therefore out of the question. And then there was very little chance of my being faithless at that tender age.

But the lesson of faithfulness had also an untoward effect. 'If I should be pledged to be faithful to my wife, she also should be pledged to be faithful to me,' I said to myself. The thought made me a jealous husband. Her duty was easily converted into my right to exact faithfulness from her, and if it had to be exacted, I should be watchfully tenacious of the right. I had absolutely no reason to suspect my wife's fidelity, but jealousy does not wait for reasons. I must needs be forever on the look-out regarding her movements, and therefore she could not go anywhere without my permission. This sowed the seeds of a bitter quarrel between us. The restraint was virtually a sort of imprisonment. And Kasturbai was not the girl to brook any such thing. She made it a point to go out whenever and wherever she liked. More restraint on my part resulted in more liberty being taken by her, and in my getting more and more cross. Refusal to speak to one another thus became the order of the day with us, married

---

[3] *Saptapadi* are seven steps a Hindu bride and bridegroom walk together, making at the same time promises of mutual fidelity and devotion, after which the marriage becomes irrevocable.
[4] *Kansar* is a preparation of wheat which the pair partake of together after the completion of the ceremony.

children. I think it was quite innocent of Kasturbai to have taken those liberties with my restrictions. How could a guileless girl brook any restraint on going to the temple or on going on visits to friends? If I had the right to impose restrictions on her, had not she also a similar right? All this is clear to me today. But at that time I had to make good my authority as a husband!

Let not the reader think, however, that ours was a life of unrelieved bitterness. For my severities were all based on love. I wanted to *make* my wife an ideal wife. My ambition was to *make* her live a pure life, learn what I learnt, and identify her life and thought with mine.

I do not know whether Kasturbai had any such ambition. She was illiterate. By nature she was simple, independent, persevering and, with me at least, reticent. She was not impatient of her ignorance and I do not recollect my studies having ever spurred her to go in for a similar adventure. I fancy, therefore, that my ambition was all one-sided. My passion was entirely centred on one woman, and I wanted it to be reciprocated. But even if there were no reciprocity, it could not be all unrelieved misery because there was active love on one side at least.

I must say I was passionately fond of her. Even at school I used to think of her, and the thought of nightfall and our subsequent meeting was ever haunting me. Separation was unbearable. I used to keep her awake till late in the night with my idle talk. If with this devouring passion there had not been in me a burning attachment to duty, I should either have fallen a prey to disease and premature death, or have sunk into a burdensome existence. . . .

His Father's Death

The time of which I am now speaking is my sixteenth year. My father, as we have seen, was bed-ridden, suffering from a fistula. My mother, an old servant of the house, and I were his principal attendants. I had the duties of a nurse, which mainly consisted in dressing the wound, giving my father his medicine, and compounding drugs whenever they had to be made up at home. Every night I massaged his legs and retired only when he asked me to do so or after he had fallen asleep. I loved to do this service. I do not remember ever having neglected it. All the time at my disposal, after the performance of the daily duties, was divided between school and attending on my father. I would only go out for an evening walk either when he permitted me or when he was feeling well.

This was also the time when my wife was expecting a baby,—a circumstance which, as I can see today meant a double shame for me. For one thing I did not restrain myself, as I should have done, whilst I was yet a student. And secondly, this carnal lust got the better of what I regarded as my duty to study, and of what was even a greater duty, my devotion to my parents, Shravan having been my ideal since childhood. Every night whilst my hands were busy massaging my father's legs, my mind was hovering about the bed-room,—and that too at a time when religion, medical science and commonsense alike forbade sexual intercourse. I was always glad to be relieved from my duty, and went straight to the bed-room after doing obeisance to my father.

At the same time my father was getting worse every day. Ayurvedic physicians had tried all their ointments, Hakims their plasters, and local quacks their nostrums. An English surgeon had also used his skill. . . . He despaired of living any longer. He was getting weaker and weaker, until at last he had to be asked to perform the necessary functions in bed. But up to the last he refused to do anything of the kind, always insisting on going through the strain of leaving his bed. The Vaishnavite rules about external cleanliness are so inexorable. . . .

The dreadful night came. My uncle was then in Rajkot. I have a faint recollection that he came to Rajkot having had news that my father was getting worse. The brothers were deeply attached to each other. My uncle would sit near my father's bed the whole day, and would insist on sleeping by his bed-side after sending us all to sleep. No one had dreamt that this was to be the fateful night. The danger of course was there.

It was 10-30 or 11 p.m. I was giving the massage. My uncle offered to relieve me. I was glad and went straight to the bed-room. My wife, poor thing, was fast asleep. But how could she sleep when I was there? I woke her up. In five or six minutes, however, the servant knocked at the door. I started with alarm. 'Get up,' he said, 'Father is very ill.' I knew of course that he was very ill, and so I guessed what 'very ill' meant at that moment. I sprang out of bed.

'What is the matter? Do tell me!'

'Father is no more.'

So all was over! I had but to wring my hands. I felt deeply ashamed and miserable. I ran to my father's room. I saw that, if animal passion had not blinded me, I should have been spared the torture of separation from my father during his last moments. I should have been massaging him, and he would have died in my arms. But now it was my uncle who had had this privilege. He was so deeply devoted to his elder brother that he had earned the honour of doing him the last services! My father had forebodings of the coming event. He had made a sign for pen and paper, and written: 'Prepare for the last rites.' He had then snapped the amulet off his arm and also his gold necklace of *tulasi*-beads and flung them aside. A moment after this he was no more.

The shame, to which I have referred in a foregoing chapter, was this shame of my carnal desire even at the critical hour of my father's death, which demanded wakeful service. It is a blot I have never been able to efface or forget, and I have always thought that, although my devotion to my parents knew no bounds and I would have given up anything for it, yet it was weighed and found unpardonably wanting because my mind was at the same moment in the grip of lust. I have therefore always regarded myself as a lustful, though a faithful, husband. It took me long to get free from the shackles of lust, and I had to pass through many ordeals before I could overcome it.

The Fraternal Self

Before I close this chapter of my double shame, I may mention that the poor mite that was born to my wife scarcely breathed for more than three or four days. Nothing else could be expected. Let all those who are married be warned by my example. . . .

Reflections on His Marriage

A variety of incidents in my life have conspired to bring me in close contact with people of many creeds and many communities, and my experience with all of them warrants the statement that I have known no distinction between relatives and strangers, countrymen and foreigners, white and coloured, Hindus and Indians of other faiths, whether Musalmans, Parsis, Christians or Jews. I may say that my heart has been incapable of making any such distinctions. I cannot claim this as a special virtue, as it is in my very nature, rather than a result of any effort on my part, whereas in the case of *ahimsa* (non-violence), *brahmacharya* (celibacy), *aparigraha* (non-possession) and other cardinal virtues, I am fully conscious of a continuous striving for their cultivation.

When I was practising in Durban, my office clerks often stayed with me, and there were among them Hindus and Christians, or to describe them by their provinces, Gujaratis and Tamilians. I do not recollect having ever regarded them as anything but my kith and kin. I treated them as members of my family, and had unpleasantness with my wife if ever she stood in the way of my treating them as such. One of the clerks was a Christian, born of Panchama parents.[5]

The house was built after the Western model and the rooms rightly had no outlets for dirty water. Each room had therefore chamber-pots. Rather than have these cleaned by a servant or a sweeper, my wife or I attended to them. The clerks who made themselves completely at home would naturally clean their own pots, but the Christian clerk was a newcomer, and it was our duty to attend to his bedroom. My wife managed the pots of the others, but to clean those used by one who had been a Panchama seemed to her to be the limit, and we fell out. She could not bear the pots being cleaned by me, neither did she like doing it herself. Even today I can recall the picture of her chiding me, her eyes red with anger, and pearl drops streaming down her cheeks, as she descended the ladder, pot in hand. But I was a cruelly kind husband. I regarded myself as her teacher, and so harassed her out of my blind love for her.

I was far from being satisfied by her merely carrying the pot. I would have her do it cheerfully. So I said, raising my voice: 'I will not stand this nonsense in my house.'

The words pierced her like an arrow.

---

[5] That is, his parents were outcastes, and he had converted to Christianity in order to avoid the indignities of his caste.

She shouted back: 'Keep your house to yourself and let me go.' I forgot myself and the spring of compassion dried up in me. I caught her by the hand, dragged the helpless woman to the gate, which was just opposite the ladder, and proceeded to open it with the intention of pushing her out. The tears were running down her cheeks in torrents, and she cried: 'Have you no sense of shame? Must you so far forget yourself? Where am I to go? I have no parents or relatives here to harbour me. Being your wife, you think I must put up with your cuffs and kicks? For Heaven's sake behave yourself, and shut the gate. Let us not be found making scenes like this!'

I put on a brave face, but was really ashamed and shut the gate. If my wife could not leave me, neither could I leave her. We have had numerous bickerings, but the end has always been peace between us. The wife, with her matchless powers of endurance, has always been the victor.

Today I am in a position to narrate the incident with some detachment, as it belongs to a period out of which I have fortunately emerged. I am no longer a blind, infatuated husband, I am no more my wife's teacher. Kasturbai can, if she will, be as unpleasant to me today, as I used to be to her before. We are tried friends, the one no longer regarding the other as the object of lust. She has been a faithful nurse throughout my illnesses, serving without any thought of reward.

The incident in question occurred in 1898, when I had no conception of *brahmacharya*. It was a time when I thought that the wife was the object of her husband's lust, born to do her husband's behest, rather than a helpmate, a comrade and a partner in the husband's joys and sorrows.

It was in the year 1900 that these ideas underwent a radical transformation, and in 1906 they took concrete shape. But of this I propose to speak in its proper place. Suffice it to say that with the gradual disappearance in me of the carnal appetite, my domestic life became and is becoming more and more peaceful, sweet and happy.

Let no one conclude from this narrative of a sacred recollection that we are by any means an ideal couple, or that there is a complete identity of ideals between us. Kasturbai herself does not perhaps know whether she has any ideals independently of me. It is likely that many of my doings have not her approval even today. We never discuss them, I see no good in discussing them. For she was educated neither by her parents nor by me at the time when I ought to have done it. But she is blessed with one great quality to a very considerable degree, a quality which most Hindu wives possess in some measure. And it is this; willingly or unwillingly, consciously or unconsciously, she has considered herself blessed in following in my footsteps, and has never stood in the way of my endeavour to lead a life of restraint. Though, therefore, there is a wide difference between us intellectually, I have always had the feeling that ours is a life of contentment, happiness and progress. . . .

The Vow of Celibacy

We now reach the stage in this story when I began seriously to think of taking the *brahmacharya* vow. I had been wedded to a monogamous ideal ever since my marriage, faithfulness to my wife being part of the love of truth. But it was in South Africa that I came to realize the importance of observing *brahmacharya* even with respect to my wife. I cannot definitely say what circumstance or what book it was, that set my thoughts in that direction, but I have a recollection that the predominant factor was the influence of Raychandbhai, of whom I have already written. I can still recall a conversation that I had with him. On one occasion I spoke to him in high praise of Mrs. Gladstone's devotion to her husband. I had read somewhere that Mrs. Gladstone insisted on preparing tea for Mr. Gladstone even in the House of Commons, and that this had become a rule in the life of this illustrious couple, whose actions were governed by regularity. I spoke of this to the poet, and incidentally eulogized conjugal love. 'Which of the two do you prize more', asked Raychandbhai, 'the love of Mrs. Gladstone for her husband as his wife, or her devoted service irrespective of her relation to Mr. Gladstone? Supposing she had been his sister, or his devoted servant, and ministered to him with the same attention, what would you have said? Do we not have instances of such devoted sisters or servants? Supposing you had found the same loving devotion in a male servant, would you have been pleased in the same way as in Mrs. Gladstone's case? Just examine the viewpoint suggested by me.'

Raychandbhai was himself married. I have an impression that at the moment his words sounded harsh, but they gripped me irresistibly. The devotion of a servant was, I felt, a thousand times more praiseworthy than that of a wife to her husband. There was nothing surprising in the wife's devotion to her husband, as there was an indissoluble bond between them. The devotion was perfectly natural. But it required a special effort to cultivate equal devotion between master and servant. The poet's point of view began gradually to grow upon me.

What then, I asked myself, should be my relation with my wife? Did my faithfulness consist in making my wife the instrument of my lust? So long as I was the slave of lust, my faithfulness was worth nothing. To be fair to my wife, I must say that she was never the temptress. It was therefore the easiest thing for me to take the vow of *brahmacharya*, if only I willed it. It was my weak will or lustful attachment that was the obstacle.

Even after my conscience had been roused in the matter, I failed twice. I failed because the motive that actuated the effort was none the highest. My main object was to escape having more children. Whilst in England I had read something about contraceptives. I have already referred to Dr. Allinson's birth control propaganda in the chapter on Vegetarianism. If it had some temporary effect on me, Mr. Hill's opposition to those methods and his advocacy of internal effort as opposed to outward means, in a word, of self-control, had a far greater effect, which in due time came to be abiding. Seeing, therefore, that I did not desire more children I began to strive after self-control. There was endless difficulty in the task. We began to sleep in separate beds. I decided to retire to bed only after the day's work had left me completely exhausted. All these efforts did not seem to bear much fruit, but when I look back upon the past, I feel that the final resolution was the cumulative effect of those unsuccessful strivings.

The final resolution could only be made as late as 1906. Satyagraha had not then been started. I had not the least notion of its coming. I was practising in Johannesburg at the time of the Zulu 'Rebellion' in Natal, which came soon after the Boer War. I felt that I must offer my services to the Natal Government on that occasion. The offer was accepted, as we shall see in another chapter. But the work set me furiously thinking in the direction of self-control, and according to my wont I discussed my thoughts with my co-workers. It became my conviction that procreation and the consequent care of children were inconsistent with public service. I had to break up my household at Johannesburg to be able to serve during the 'Rebellion'. Within one month of offering my services, I had to give up the house I had so carefully furnished. I took my wife and children to Phoenix and led the Indian ambulance corps attached to the Natal forces. During the difficult marches that had then to be performed, the idea flashed upon me that if I wanted to devote myself to the service of the community in this manner, I must relinquish the desire for children and wealth and live the life of a *vanaprastha*—of one retired from household cares.

The 'Rebellion' did not occupy me for more than six weeks, but this brief period proved to be a very important epoch in my life. The importance of vows grew upon me more clearly than ever before. I realized that a vow, far from closing the door to real freedom, opened it. Up to this time I had not met with success because the will had been lacking, because I had had no faith in myself, no faith in the grace of God, and therefore, my mind had been tossed on the boisterous sea of doubt. I realized that in refusing to take a vow man was drawn into temptation, and that to be bound by a vow was like a passage from libertinism to a real monogamous marriage. 'I believe in effort, I do not want to bind myself with vows,' is the mentality of weakness and betrays a subtle desire for the thing to be avoided. Or where can be the difficulty in making a final decision? I vow to flee from the serpent which I know will bite me, I do not simply make an effort to flee from him. I know that mere effort may mean certain death. Mere effort means ignorance of the certain fact that the serpent is bound to kill me. The fact, therefore, that I could rest content with an effort only, means that I have not yet clearly realized the necessity of definite action. 'But supposing my views are changed in the future, how can I bind myself by a vow?' Such a doubt often deters us. But that doubt also betrays a lack of clear

The Fraternal Self

perception that a particular thing must be renounced. That is why Nishkulanand has sung:

'Renunciation without aversion is not lasting.'

Where therefore the desire is gone, a vow of renunciation is the natural and inevitable fruit.

After full discussion and mature deliberation I took the vow in 1906. I had not shared my thoughts with my wife until then, but only consulted her at the time of taking the vow. She had no objection. But I had great difficulty in making the final resolve. I had not the necessary strength. How was I to control my passions? The elimination of carnal relationship with one's wife seemed then a strange thing. But I launched forth with faith in the sustaining power of God.

As I look back upon the twenty years of the vow, I am filled with pleasure and wonderment. The more or less successful practice of self-control had been going on since 1901. But the freedom and joy that came to me after taking the vow had never been experienced before 1906. Before the vow I had been open to being overcome by temptation at any moment. Now the vow was a sure shield against temptation. The great potentiality of *brahmacharya* daily became more and more patent to me. The vow was taken when I was in Phoenix. As soon as I was free from ambulance work, I went to Phoenix, whence I had to return to Johannesburg. In about a month of my returning there, the foundation of Satyagraha was laid. As though unknown to me, the *brahmacharya* vow had been preparing me for it. Satyagraha had not been a preconceived plan. It came on spontaneously, without my having willed it. But I could see that all my previous steps had led up to that goal. I had cut down my heavy household expenses at Johannesburg and gone to Phoenix to take, as it were, the *brahmacharya* vow.

The knowledge that a perfect observance of *brahmacharya* means realization of *brahman*, I did not owe to a study of the Shastras. It slowly grew upon me with experience. The shastraic texts on the subject I read only later in life. Every day of the vow has taken me nearer the knowledge that in *brahmacharya* lies the protection of the body, the mind and the soul. For *brahmacharya* was now no process of hard penance, it was a matter of consolation and joy. Every day revealed a fresh beauty in it.

But if it was a matter of ever-increasing joy, let no one believe that it was an easy thing for me. Even when I am past fifty-six years, I realize how hard a thing it is. Every day I realize more and more that it is like walking on the sword's edge and I see every moment the necessity for eternal vigilance. . . .

Brahmacharya means control of the senses in thought, word and deed. Every day I have been realizing more and more the necessity for restraints of the kind I have detailed above. There is no limit to the possibilities of renunciation, even as there is none to those of *brahmacharya*. Such *brahmacharya* is impossible of attainment by limited effort. For many it must remain only as an ideal. An aspirant after *brahmacharya* will always be conscious of his shortcomings, will seek out the passions lingering in the innermost recesses of his heart and will incessantly strive to get rid of them. So long as thought is not under complete control of the will, *brahmacharya* in its fulness is absent. Involuntary thought is an affection of the mind, and curbing of thought, therefore, means curbing of the mind which is even more difficult to curb than the wind. Nevertheless the existence of God within makes even control of the mind possible. Let no one think that it is impossible because it is difficult. It is the highest goal, and it is no wonder that the highest effort should be necessary to attain it. . . .

But it was after coming to India that I realized that such *brahmacharya* was impossible to attain by mere human effort. Until then I had been labouring under the delusion that fruit diet alone would enable me to eradicate all passions, and I had flattered myself with the belief that I had nothing more to do.

But I must not anticipate the chapter of my struggles. Meanwhile let me make it clear that those who desire to observe *bramacharya* with a view to realizing God need not despair, provided their faith in God is equal to their confidence in their own effort. The sense-objects turn away from an abstemious soul, leaving the relish behind. The relish also disappears with the realization of the Highest.[6] Therefore His name and His grace are the last resources of the aspirant after *moksha*. This truth came to me only after my return to India.

Satyagraha as a Political Force

Events were so shaping themselves in Johannesburg as to make this self-purification on my part a preliminary as it were to Satyagraha. I can now see that all the principal events of my life, culminating in the vow of *brahmacharya*, were secretly preparing me for it. The principle called Satyagraha came into being before that name was invented. Indeed when it was born, I myself could not say what it was. In Gujarati also we used the English phrase 'passive resistance' to describe it. When in a meeting of Europeans I found that the term 'passive resistance' was too narrowly construed, that it was supposed to be a weapon of the weak, that it could be characterized by hatred, and that it could finally manifest itself as violence, I had to demur to all these statements and explain the real nature of the Indian movement. It was clear that a new word must be coined by the Indians to designate their struggle.

[6] The *Bhagavad Gita*, 2-59.

The Fraternal Self

But I could not for the life of me find out a new name, and therefore offered a nominal prize through *Indian Opinion* to the reader who made the best suggestion on the subject. As a result Maganlal Gandhi coined the word 'Sadagraha' (Sat=truth, Agraha=firmness) and won the prize. But in order to make it clearer I changed the word to 'Satyagraha' which has since become current in Gujarati as a designation for the struggle. . . .

Almost immediately after the Ahmedabad meeting I went to Nadiad.[7] It was here that I first used the expression 'Himalayan miscalculation' which obtained such a wide currency afterwards. Even at Ahmedabad I had begun to have a dim perception of my mistake. But when I reached Nadiad and saw the actual state of things there and heard reports about a large number of people from Kheda district having been arrested, it suddenly dawned upon me that I had committed a grave error in calling upon the people in Kheda district and elsewhere to launch upon civil disobedience prematurely, as it now seemed to me. I was addressing a public meeting. My confession brought down upon me no small amount of ridicule. But I have never regretted having made that confession. For I have always held that it is only when one sees one's own mistakes with a convex lens, and does just the reverse in the case of others, that one is able to arrive at a just relative estimate of the two. I further believe that a scrupulous and conscientious observance of this rule is necessary for one who wants to be a Satyagrahi.

Let us now see what the Himalayan miscalculation was. Before one can be fit for the practice of civil disobedience one must have rendered a willing and respectful obedience to the state laws. For the most part we obey such laws out of fear of the penalty for their breach, and this holds good particularly in respect of such laws as do not involve a moral principle. For instance, an honest, respectable man will not suddenly take to stealing, whether there is a law against stealing or not, but this very man will not feel any remorse for failure to observe the rule about carrying head-lights on bicycles after dark. Indeed it is doubtful whether he would even accept advice kindly about being more careful in this respect. But he would observe any obligatory rule of this kind, if only to escape the inconvenience of facing a prosecution for a breach of the rule. Such compliance is not, however, the willing and spontaneous obedience that is required of a Satyagrahi. A Satyagrahi obeys the laws of society intelligently and of his own free will, because he considers it to be his sacred duty to do so. It is only when a person has thus obeyed the laws of society scrupulously that he is in a position to judge as to which particular rules are good and just and which unjust and iniquitous. Only then does the right accrue to him of the civil disobedience of certain laws in well-defined circumstances. My error lay in my failure to observe this necessary limitation. I had called on the people to launch

[7] In April 1919, the Satyagraha movement had itself resorted to acts of violence in resistance to British rule.

upon civil disobedience before they had thus qualified themselves for it, and this mistake seemed to me of Himalayan magnitude. As soon as I entered the Kheda district, all the old recollections of the Kheda Satyagraha struggle came back to me, and I wondered how I could have failed to perceive what was so obvious. I realized that before a people could be fit for offering civil disobedience, they should thoroughly understand its deeper implications. That being so, before re-starting civil disobedience on a mass scale, it would be necessary to create a band of well-tried, pure-hearted volunteers who thoroughly understood the strict conditions of Satyagraha. They could explain these to the people, and by sleepless vigilance keep them on the right path.

With these thoughts filling my mind I reached Bombay, raised a corps of Satyagrahi volunteers through the Satyagraha Sabha there, and with their help commenced the work of educating the people with regard to the meaning and inner significance of Satyagraha. This was principally done by issuing leaflets of an educative character bearing on the subject.

But whilst this work was going on, I could see that it was a difficult task to interest the people in the peaceful side of Satyagraha. The volunteers too failed to enlist themselves in large numbers. Nor did all those who actually enlisted take anything like a regular systematic training, and as the days passed by, the number of fresh recruits began gradually to dwindle instead of to grow. I realized that the progress of the training in civil disobedience was not going to be as rapid as I had at first expected.

Thus, whilst this movement for the preservation of non-violence was making steady though slow progress on the one hand, Government's policy of lawless repression was in full career on the other, and was manifesting itself in the Punjab in all its nakedness. Leaders were put under arrest, martial law, which in other words meant no law, was proclaimed, special tribunals were set up. These tribunals were not courts of justice but instruments for carrying out the arbitrary will of an autocrat. Sentences were passed unwarranted by evidence and in flagrant violation of justice. In Amritsar innocent men and women were made to crawl like worms on their bellies. Before this outrage the Jalianwala Bagh tragedy paled into insignificance in my eyes, though it was this massacre principally that attracted the attention of the people of India and of the world.

I was pressed to proceed to the Punjab immediately in disregard of consequences. I wrote and also telegraphed to the Viceroy asking permission to go there, but in vain. If I proceeded without the necessary permission, I should not be allowed to cross the boundary of the Punjab, but left to find what satisfaction I could from civil disobedience. I was thus confronted by a serious dilemma. As things stood, to break the order against my entry into the Punjab could, it seemed to me, hardly be classed as civil disobedience, for I did not see around me the kind of peaceful atmosphere that I wanted, and the unbridled repression in the Punjab had further served to aggravate and deepen the feeling of resentment. For me, therefore, to offer civil disobedience at such a time, even if it were possible, would have been like fanning the flame. I therefore decided not to proceed to the Punjab in spite of the suggestion of friends. It was a bitter pill for me to swallow. Tales of rank injustice and oppression came pouring in daily from the Punjab, but all I could do was to sit helplessly by and gnash my teeth. . . .

Farewell

The time has now come to bring these chapters to a close.

My life from this point onward has been so public that there is hardly anything about it that people do not know. Moreover, since 1921 I have worked in such close association with the Congress leaders that I can hardly describe any episode in my life since then without referring to my relations with them. . . . A reference to my relations with the leaders would therefore be unavoidable, if I set about describing my experiments further. And this I may not do, at any rate for the present, if only from a sense of propriety. Lastly, my conclusions from my current experiments can hardly as yet be regarded as decisive. It therefore seems to me to be my plain duty to close this narrative here. In fact my pen instinctively refuses to proceed further.

It is not without a wrench that I have to take leave of the reader. I set high value on my experiments. I do not know whether I have been able to do justice to them. I can only say that I have spared no pains to give a faithful narrative. To describe truth, as it has appeared to me, and in the exact manner in which I have arrived at it, has been my ceaseless effort. The exercise has given me ineffable mental peace, because, it has been my fond hope that it might bring faith in Truth and Ahimsa to waverers.[8]

My uniform experience has convinced me that there is no other God than Truth. And if every page of these chapters does not proclaim to the reader that the only means for the realization of Truth is Ahimsa, I shall deem all my labour in writing these chapters to have been in vain. And, even though my efforts in this behalf may prove fruitless, let the readers know that the vehicle, not the great principle, is at fault. After all, however sincere my strivings after Ahimsa may have been, they have still been imperfect and inadequate. The little fleeting glimpses, therefore, that I have been able to have of Truth can hardly convey an idea of the indescribable lustre of Truth, a million times more intense than that of the sun we daily see with our eyes. In fact what I have caught is only the faintest glimmer of that mighty effulgence. But this much I can say with assurance, as a result of all my experiments, that a perfect vision of Truth can only follow a complete realization of Ahimsa.

[8]Himsa is the destruction of life. Thus Ahimsa means affirmation of life, compassion, non-violence.

To see the universal and all-pervading Spirit of Truth face to face one must be able to love the meanest of creation as oneself. And a man who aspires after that cannot afford to keep out of any field of life. That is why my devotion to Truth has drawn me into the field of politics; and I can say without the slightest hesitation, and yet in all humility, that those who say that religion has nothing to do with politics do not know what religion means.

Identification with everything that lives is impossible without self-purification; without self-purification the observance of the law of Ahimsa must remain an empty dream; God can never be realized by one who is not pure of heart. Self-purification therefore must mean purification in all the walks of life. And purification being highly infectious, purification of oneself necessarily leads to the purification of one's surroundings.

But the path of self-purification is hard and steep. To attain to perfect purity one has to become absolutely passion-free in thought, speech and action; to rise above the opposing currents of love and hatred, attachment and repulsion. I know that I have not in me as yet that triple purity in spite of constant ceaseless striving for it. That is why the world's praise fails to move me, indeed it very often stings me. To conquer the subtle passions seems to me to be harder far than the physical conquest of the world by the force of arms. Ever since my return to India I have had experiences of the dormant passions lying hidden within me. The knowledge of them has made me feel humiliated though not defeated. The experiences and experiments have sustained me and given me great joy. But I know that I have still before me a difficult path to traverse. I must reduce myself to zero. So long as a man does not of his own free will put himself last among his fellow creatures, there is no salvation for him. Ahimsa is the farthest limit of humility.

In bidding farewell to the reader, for the time being at any rate, I ask him to join with me in prayer to the God of Truth that He may grant me the boon of Ahimsa in mind, word and deed.

Suggestions for Further Reading

Dhirendra Mohan Datta, *The Philosophy of Mahatma Gandhi* (Madison, Wis.: University of Wisconsin Press, 1953).

Erik H. Erikson, "Gandhi's Autobiography: The Leader as a Child," *American Scholar*, Vol. 35 (Autumn, 1966), pp. 632-646.

_____, *Gandhi's Truth: On The Origin of Militant Nonviolence* (New York: W.W. Norton, 1969).

_____, "On the Nature of Psycho-Historical Evidence: In Search of Gandhi," *Daedalus*, Vol. 97, No. 3 (Summer 1968), pp. 695-730.

Louis Fischer, *The Life of Mahatma Gandhi* (New York: Harper and Brothers, 1950).

Mohandas K. Gandhi, *Essential Gandhi*, edited by Louis Fischer (New York: Random House, 1962).

————, *Satyagraha in South Africa*, translated by Valji Govindji Desai (Stanford, California: Academic Reprints, 1954).

————, *Ethical Religion* (Madras: S. Ganesan, 1922).

Richard Bartlett Gregg, *The Power of Nonviolence*, 2nd revised edition, foreword by Martin Luther King, Jr. (Nyack, N.Y.: Fellowship Publications, 1959).

Arne Naess, *Gandhi and the Nuclear Age* (Totowa, N.J.: Bedminster Press, 1965).

B.R. Nanda, *Mahatma Gandhi: A Biography* (Boston: Beacon Press, 1958).

Sushila Nayyar, *Kasturbai, Wife of Gandhi* (Wallingford, Pa.: Pendle Hill, 1948).

Jawaharlal Nehru, *Freedom from Fear: Reflections on the Personality and Teachings of Gandhi*, selected and edited by T.K. Mahadevan (New Delhi: Gandhi Smarak Nidhi, 1960).

Susanne Hoeber Rudolph, "Self-Control and Political Potency: Gandhi's Asceticism," *American Scholar*, Vol. 35 (Winter 1965), pp. 75-97.

E. Victor Wolfenstein, *Revolutionary Personality: Lenin, Trotsky, Gandhi* (Princeton, N.J.: Princeton University Press, 1967).

Black Elk Speaks

*And a Voice said: "Behold, they have
given you the center of the nation's
hoop to make it live."*

Black Elk, a holy man of the Oglala Sioux Indians, was first met by
John G. Neihardt, poet laureate of Nebraska and recorder of Black Elk's story,
in 1930. Neihardt had come to the Indian reservation near Pine Ridge, South
Dakota, to get an account of the Indian massacre which was associated with a
great messianic dream in the mid-1880's. Black Elk had lived through that
experience. Neihardt sought him out to get a sensitive first-hand report of the
massacre, intending to draw upon it in writing *The Song of the Messiah*, the final
narrative poem in his *Cycle of the West*.

Neihardt knew of Black Elk, who had been described as a "kind of a
preacher," but was not fully prepared for the documentary which Black Elk was
to supply. Through a series of meetings with the Indian holy man, Neihardt
learned about the massacre, but he learned more importantly about a vision
which had come to Black Elk early in his youth. In Neihardt's presence Black
Elk told his personal story, describing the vision and then explaining the fate of
his tribe at the hands of the white man in light of the story and vision.

The vision secures Black Elk's place in an ancestral tradition and illustrates
how tribal power and authority are transmitted through that tradition. The
vision was used to prepare Black Elk for the imminent battles against the white
men and was meant to assure him that his tribe's position at the center of the
cosmos implied the eventual fulfillment of their destiny. The language of the
vision is richly symbolic of religious themes which have also appeared in many
other cultures: the idea of the center, the sacred tree, the convenantal basis of
the tribe or nation, the dependence of cultic life and social order upon a
transcendent archetypal order, and many more. Through all of it, Black Elk's

The Fraternal Self

individual calling is disposed, as it were, by the people with whom he is identified. Their fate and his obligations become synonymous.

The dream comes to an unhappy end when the tribe is devastated in a battle with the white men. Black Elk, sensing the effects of "butchering" recognized that "it was all over." "A people's dream died there . . . a beautiful dream." Because of the fact that the life of the group is drawn from the cosmic order, Black Elk adds, "There is no center any longer, and the sacred tree is dead." However, as far as Black Elk was concerned, though the dream was over the vision had not completely died. He felt it incumbent upon his role in the tribe that his story and the vision be disclosed to Neihardt. Then, asking that he be returned to the holy mountain where he stood just prior to the original reception of the vision, he begged of the ancestral Spirit that what "little root of the sacred tree still lives" might be strengthened, to nourish his people and to lead them back to the earth's center.

Black Elk Speaks

The Great Vision

What happened after that until the summer I was nine years old is not a story. There were winters and summers, and they were good; for the Wasichus had made their iron road along the Platte and traveled there. This had cut the bison herd in two, but those that stayed in our country with us were more than could be counted, and we wandered without trouble in our land. . . .

It was the summer when I was nine years old, and our people were moving slowly towards the Rocky Mountains. We camped one evening in a valley beside a little creek just before it ran into the Greasy Grass,[1] and there was a man by the name of Man Hip who liked me and asked me to eat with him in his tepee.

While I was eating, a voice came and said: "It is time; now they are calling you." The voice was so loud and clear that I believed it, and I thought I would just go where it wanted me to go. So I got right up and started. As I came out of the tepee, both my thighs began to hurt me, and suddenly it was like waking from a dream, and there wasn't any voice. So I went back into the tepee, but I didn't want to eat. Man Hip looked at me in a strange way and asked me what was wrong. I told him that my legs were hurting me.

The next morning the camp moved again, and I was riding with some boys. We stopped to get a drink from a creek, and when I got off my horse, my legs crumpled under me and I could not walk. So the boys helped me up and put me on my horse; and when we camped again that evening, I was sick. The next day

[1] The Little Big Horn River.

the camp moved on to where the different bands of our people were coming together, and I rode in a pony drag, for I was very sick. Both my legs and both my arms were swollen badly and my face was all puffed up.

When we had camped again, I was lying in our tepee and my mother and father were sitting beside me. I could see out through the opening, and there two men were coming from the clouds, head-first like arrows slanting down, and I knew they were the same that I had seen before. Each now carried a long spear, and from the points of these a jagged lightning flashed. They came clear down to the ground this time and stood a little way off and looked at me and said: "Hurry! Come! Your Grandfathers are calling you!"

Then they turned and left the ground like arrows slanting upward from the bow. When I got up to follow, my legs did not hurt me any more and I was very light. I went outside the tepee, and yonder where the men with flaming spears were going, a little cloud was coming very fast. It came and stooped and took me and turned back to where it came from, flying fast. And when I looked down I could see my mother and my father yonder, and I felt sorry to be leaving them.

Then there was nothing but the air and the swiftness of the little cloud that bore me and those two men still leading up to where white clouds were piled like mountains on a wide blue plain, and in them thunder beings lived and leaped and flashed.

Now suddenly there was nothing but a world of cloud, and we three were there alone in the middle of a great white plain with snowy hills and mountains staring at us; and it was very still; but there were whispers.

Then the two men spoke together and they said: "Behold him, the being with four legs!"

I looked and saw a bay horse standing there, and he began to speak: "Behold me!" he said, "My life-history you shall see." Then he wheeled about to where the sun goes down, and said: "Behold them! Their history you shall know."

I looked, and there were twelve black horses yonder all abreast with necklaces of bison hoofs, and they were beautiful, but I was frightened, because their manes were lightning and there was thunder in their nostrils.

Then the bay horse wheeled to where the great white giant lives (the north) and said: "Behold!" And yonder there were twelve white horses all abreast. Their manes were flowing like a blizzard wind and from their noses came a roaring, and all about them white geese soared and circled.

Then the bay wheeled round to where the sun shines continually (the east) and bade me look; and there twelve sorrel horses, with necklaces of elk's teeth, stood abreast with eyes that glimmered like the day-break start and manes of morning light.

Then the bay wheeled once again to look upon the place where you are always facing (the south), and yonder stood twelve buckskins all abreast with horns upon their heads and manes that lived and grew like trees and grasses.

The Fraternal Self

And when I had seen all these, the bay horse said: "Your Grandfathers are having a council. These shall take you; so have courage."

Then all the horses went into formation, four abreast—the blacks, the whites, the sorrels, and the buckskins—and stood behind the bay, who turned now to the west and neighed; and yonder suddenly the sky was terrible with a storm of plunging horses in all colors that shook the world with thunder, neighing back.

Now turning to the north the bay horse whinnied, and yonder all the sky roared with a mighty wind of running horses in all colors, neighing back.

And when he whinnied to the east, there too the sky was filled with glowing clouds of manes and tails of horses in all colors singing back. Then to the south he called, and it was crowded with many colored, happy horses, nickering.

Then the bay horse spoke to me again and said: "See how your horses all coming dancing!" I looked, and there were horses, horses everywhere—a whole skyful of horses dancing round me.

"Make haste!" the bay horse said; and we walked together side by side, while the blacks, the whites, the sorrels, and the bucksins followed, marching four by four.

I looked about me once again, and suddenly the dancing horses without number changed into animals of every kind and into all the fowls that are, and these fled back to the four quarters of the world from whence the horses came, and vanished.

Then as we walked, there was a heaped up cloud ahead that changed into a tepee, and a rainbow was the open door of it; and through the door I saw six old men sitting in a row.

The two men with the spears now stood beside me, one on either hand, and the horses took their places in their quarters, looking inward four by four. And the oldest of the Grandfathers spoke with a kind voice and said: "Come right in and do not fear." And as he spoke, all the horses of the four quarters neighed to cheer me. So I went in and stood before the six, and they looked older than men can ever be—old like hills, like stars.

The oldest spoke again: "Your Grandfathers all over the world are having a council, and they have called you here to teach you." His voice was very kind, but I shook all over with fear now, for I knew that these were not old men, but the Powers of the World. And the first was the Power of the West; the second, of the North; the third, of the East, the fourth, of the South; the fifth, of the Sky; the sixth, of the Earth. I knew this, and was afraid, until the first Grandfather spoke again: "Behold them yonder where the sun goes down, the thunder beings! You shall see, and have from them my power; and they shall take you to the high and lonely center of the earth that you may see; even to the place where the sun continually shines, they shall take you there to understand."

Black Elk

And as he spoke of understanding, I looked up and saw the rainbow leap with flames of many colors over me.

Now there was a wooden cup in his hand and it was full of water and in the water was the sky.

"Take this," he said. "It is the power to make live, and it is yours."

Now he had a bow in his hands. "Take this," he said. "It is the power to destroy, and it is yours."

Then he pointed to himself and said: "Look close at him who is your spirit now, for you are his body and his name is Eagle Wing Stretches."

And saying this, he got up very tall and started running toward where the sun goes down; and suddenly he was a black horse that stopped and turned and looked at me, and the horse was very poor and sick; his ribs stood out.

Then the second Grandfather, he of the North, arose with a herb of power in his hand, and said: "Take this and hurry." I took and held it toward the black horse yonder. He fattened and was happy and came prancing to his place again and was the first Grandfather sitting there.

The second Grandfather, he of the North, spoke again: "Take courage, younger brother," he said; "on earth a nation you shall make live, for yours shall be the power of the white giant's wing, the cleansing wind." Then he got up very tall and started running toward the north; and when he turned toward me, it was a white goose wheeling. I looked about me now, and the horses in the west were thunders and the horses of the north were geese. And the second Grandfather sang two songs that were like this:

> *They are appearing, may you behold!*
> *They are appearing, may you behold!*
> *The thunder nation is appearing, behold!*

> *They are appearing, may you behold!*
> *They are appearing, may you behold!*
> *The white geese nation is appearing, behold!*

And now it was the third Grandfather who spoke, he of where the sun shines continually. "Take courage, younger brother," he said, "for across the earth they shall take you!" Then he pointed to where the daybreak star was shining, and beneath the star two men were flying. "From them you shall have power," he said, "from them who have awakened all the beings of the earth with roots and legs and wings." And as he said this, he held in his hand a peace pipe which had a spotted eagle outstretched upon the stem; and this eagle seemed alive, for it was poised there, fluttering, and its eyes were looking at me. "With this pipe," the Grandfather said, "you shall walk upon the earth, and whatever sickens there you shall make well." Then he pointed to a man who was bright

The Fraternal Self

red all over, the color of good and of plenty, and as he pointed the red man lay down and rolled and changed into a bison that got up and galloped toward the sorrel horses of the east, and they too turned to bison, fat and many.

And now the fourth Grandfather spoke, he of the place where you are always facing (the south), whence comes the power to grow. "Younger brother," he said, "with the powers of the four quarters you shall walk, a relative. Behold the living center of a nation I shall give you, and with it many you shall save." And I saw that he was holding in his hand a bright red stick that was alive, and as I looked it sprouted at the top and sent forth branches, and on the branches many leaves came out and murmured and in the leaves the birds began to sing. And then for just a little while I thought I saw beneath it in the shade the circled villages of people and every living thing with roots or legs or wings, and all were happy. "It shall stand in the center of the nation's circle," said the Grandfather, "a cane to walk with and a people's heart; and by your powers you shall make it blossom."

Then when he had been still a little while to hear the birds sing, he spoke again: "Behold the earth!" So I looked down and saw it lying yonder like a hoop of peoples, and in the center bloomed the holy stick that was a tree, and where it stood there crossed two roads, a red one and a black. "From where the giant lives (the north) to where you always face (the south) the red road goes, the road of good," the Grandfather said, "and on it shall your nation walk. The black road goes from where the thunder beings live (the west) to where the sun continually shines (the east), a fearful road, a road of troubles and of war. On this also you shall walk, and from it you shall have the power to destroy a people's foes. In four ascents you shall walk the earth with power."

I think he meant that I should see four generations, counting me, and now I am seeing the third.

Then he rose very tall and started running toward the south, and was an elk; and as he stood among the buckskins yonder, they too were elks.

Now the fifth Grandfather spoke, the oldest of them all, the Spirit of the Sky. "My boy," he said, "I have sent for you and you have come. My power you shall see!" He stretched his arms and turned into a spotted eagle hovering. "Behold," he said, "all the wings of the air shall come to you, and they and the winds and the stars shall be like relatives. You shall go across the earth with my power." Then the eagle soared above my head and fluttered there; and suddenly the sky was full of friendly wings all coming toward me.

Now I knew the sixth Grandfather was about to speak, he who was the Spirit of the Earth, and I saw that he was very old, but more as men are old. His hair was long and white, his face was all in wrinkles and his eyes were deep and dim. I stared at him, for it seemed I knew him somehow; and as I stared, he slowly changed, for he was growing backwards into youth, and when he had become a boy, I knew that he was myself with all the years that would be mine at last. When he was old again, he said: "My boy, have courage, for my power shall be yours, and you shall need it, for your nation on the earth will have great troubles. Come."

He rose and tottered out through the rainbow door, and as I followed I was riding on the bay horse who had talked to me at first and led me to that place.

Then the bay horse stopped and faced the black horses of the west, and a voice said: "They have given you the cup of water to make live the greening day, and also the bow and arrow to destroy." The bay neighed, and the twelve black horses came and stood behind me, four abreast.

The bay faced the sorrels of the east, and I saw that they had morning stars upon their foreheads and they were very bright. And the voice said: "They have given you the sacred pipe and the power that is peace, and the good red day." The bay neighed, and the twelve sorrels stood behind me, four abreast.

My horse now faced the buckskins of the south, and a voice said: "They have given you the sacred stick and your nation's hoop, and the yellow day; and in the center of the hoop you shall set the stick and make it grow into a shielding tree, and bloom." The bay neighed, and the twelve buckskins came and stood behind me, four abreast.

Then I knew that there were riders on all the horses there behind me, and a voice said: "Now you shall walk the black road with these; and as you walk, all the nations that have roots or legs or wings shall fear you."

I entered the village, riding, with the four horse troops behind me—the blacks, the whites, the sorrels, and the buckskins; and the place was filled with moaning and with mourning for the dead. The wind was blowing from the south like fever, and when I looked around I saw that in nearly every tepee the women and the children and the men lay dying with the dead.

So I rode around the circle of the village, looking in upon the sick and dead, and I felt like crying as I rode. But when I looked behind me, all the women and the children and the men were getting up and coming forth with happy faces.

And a Voice said: "Behold, they have given you the center of the nation's hoop to make it live."

So I rode to the center of the village, with the horse troops in their quarters round about me, and there the people gathered. And the Voice said: "Give them now the flowering stick that they may flourish, and the sacred pipe that they may know the power that is peace, and the wing of the white giant that they may have endurance and face all winds with courage."

So I took the bright red stick and at the center of the nation's hoop I thrust it in the earth. As it touched the earth it leaped mightily in my hand and was a waga chun, the rustling tree,[2] very tall and full of leafy branches and of all

2The cottonwood.

birds singing. And beneath it all the animals were mingling with the people like relatives and making happy cries. The women raised their tremolo of joy, and the men shouted all together: "Here we shall raise our children and be as little chickens under the mother sheo's[3] wing."

Then I heard the white wind blowing gently through the tree and singing there, and from the east the sacred pipe came flying on its eagle wings, and stopped before me there beneath the tree, spreading deep peace around it.

Then the daybreak star was rising, and a Voice said: "It shall be a relative to them; and who shall see it, shall see much more, for thence comes wisdom; and those who do not see it shall be dark." And all the people raised their faces to the east, and the star's light fell upon them, and all the dogs barked loudly and the horses whinnied.

Then when the many little voices ceased, the great Voice said: "Behold the circle of the nation's hoop, for it is holy, being endless, and thus all powers shall be one power in the people without end. Now they shall break camp and go forth upon the red road, and your Grandfathers shall walk with them." So the people broke camp and took the good road with the white wing on their faces. . . .

And as we went the Voice behind me said: "Behold a good nation walking in a sacred manner in a good land!"

Then I looked up and saw that there were four ascents ahead, and these were generations I should know. Now we were on the first ascent, and all the land was green. And as the long line climbed, all the old men and women raised their hands, palms forward, to the far sky yonder and began to croon a song together, and the sky ahead was filled with clouds of baby faces.

When we came to the end of the first ascent we camped in the sacred circle as before, and in the center stood the holy tree, and still the land about us was all green.

Then we started on the second ascent, marching as before, and still the land was green, but it was getting steeper. And as I looked ahead, the people changed into elks and bison and all four-footed beings and even into fowls, all walking in a sacred manner on the good red road together. And I myself was a spotted eagle soaring over them. But just before we stopped to camp at the end of that ascent, all the marching animals grew restless and afraid that they were not what they had been, and began sending forth voices of trouble, calling to their chiefs. And when they camped at the end of that ascent, I looked down and saw that leaves were falling from the holy tree.

And the Voice said: "Behold your nation, and remember what your Six Grandfathers gave you, for thenceforth your people walk in difficulties."

Then the people broke camp again, and saw the black road before them towards where the sun goes down, and black clouds coming yonder; and they

[3]Prairie hen.

did not want to go but could not stay. And as they walked the third ascent, all the animals and fowls that were the people ran here and there, for each one seemed to have his own little vision that he followed and his own rules; and all over the universe I could hear the winds at war like wild beasts fighting.[4]

And when we reached the summit of the third ascent and camped, the nation's hoop was broken like a ring of smoke that spreads and scatters and the holy tree seemed dying and all its birds were gone. And when I looked ahead I saw that the fourth ascent would be terrible.

Then when the people were getting ready to begin the fourth ascent, the Voice spoke like someone weeping, and it said: "Look there upon your nation." And when I looked down, the people were all changed back to human, and they were thin, their faces sharp, for they were starving. Their ponies were only hide and bones, and the holy tree was gone.

And as I looked and wept, I saw that there stood on the north side of the starving camp a sacred man who was painted red all over his body, and he held a spear as he walked into the center of the people, and there he lay down and rolled. And when he got up, it was a fat bison standing there, and where the bison stood a sacred herb sprang up right where the tree had been in the center of the nation's hoop. The herb grew and bore four blossoms on a single stem while I was looking—a blue,[5] a white, a scarlet, and a yellow—and the bright rays of these flashed to the heavens.

I know now what this meant, that the bison were the gift of a good spirit and were our strength, but we should lose them, and from the same good spirit we must find another strength. For the people all seemed better when the herb had grown and bloomed, and the horses raised their tails and neighed and pranced around, and I could see a light breeze going from the north among the people like a ghost; and suddenly the flowering tree was there again at the center of the nation's hoop where the four-rayed herb had blossomed.

I was still the spotted eagle floating, and I could see that I was already in the fourth ascent and the people were camping yonder at the top of the third long rise. It was dark and terrible about me, for all the winds of the world were fighting. It was like rapid gun-fire and like whirling smoke, and like women and children wailing and like horses screaming all over the world.

I could see my people yonder running about, setting the smoke-flap poles and fastening down their tepees against the wind, for the storm cloud was coming on them very fast and black, and there were frightened swallows without number fleeing before the cloud.

---

[4]At this point Black Elk remarked: "I think we are near that place now, and I am afraid something very bad is going to happen all over the world." He cannot read and knows nothing of world affairs.

[5]Blue as well as black may be used to represent the power of the west.

Then a song of power came to me and I sang it there in the midst of that terrible place where I was. It went like this:

> *A good nation I will make live.*
> *This the nation above has said.*
> *They have given me the power to make over.*

And when I had sung this, a Voice said: "To the four quarters you shall run for help, and nothing shall be strong before you. Behold him!"

Now I was on my bay horse again, because the horse is of the earth, and it was there my power would be used. And as I obeyed the Voice and looked, there was a horse all skin and bones yonder in the west, a faded brownish black. And a Voice there said: "Take this and make him over"; and it was the four-rayed herb that I was holding in my hand. So I rode above the poor horse in a circle, and as I did this I could hear the people yonder calling for spirit power, "A-hey! a-hey! a-hey! a-hey!" Then the poor horse neighed and rolled and got up, and he was a big, shiny, black stallion with dapples all over him and his mane about him like a cloud. He was the chief of all the horses; and when he snorted, it was a flash of lightning and his eyes were like the sunset star. He dashed to the west and neighed, and the west was filled with a dust of hoofs, and horses without number, shiny black, came plunging from the dust. Then he dashed toward the north and neighed, and to the east and to the south, and the dust clouds answered, giving forth their plunging horses without number—whites and sorrels and buckskins, fat, shiny, rejoicing in their fleetness and their strength. It was beautiful, but it was also terrible.

Then they all stopped short, rearing, and were standing in a great hoop about their black chief at the center, and were still. And as they stood, four virgins, more beautiful than women of the earth can be, came through the circle, dressed in scarlet, one from each of the four quarters, and stood about the great black stallion in their places; and one held the wooden cup of water, and one the white wing, and one the pipe, and one the nation's hoop. All the universe was silent, listening; and then the great black stallion raised his voice and sang. . . . His voice was not loud, but it went all over the universe and filled it. There was nothing that did not hear, and it was more beautiful than anything can be. It was so beautiful that nothing anywhere could keep from dancing. The virgins danced, and all the circled horses. The leaves on the trees, the grasses on the hills and in the valleys, the waters in the creeks and in the rivers and the lakes, the four-legged and the two-legged and the wings of the air—all danced together to the music of the stallion's song.

And when I looked down upon my people yonder, the cloud passed over, blessing them with friendly rain, and stood in the east with a flaming rainbow over it.

Then all the horses went singing back to their places beyond the summit of the fourth ascent, and all things sang along with them as they walked.

And a Voice said: "All over the universe they have finished a day of happiness." And looking down I saw that the whole wide circle of the day was beautiful and green, with all fruits growing and all things kind and happy.

Then a Voice said: "Behold this day, for it is yours to make. Now you shall stand upon the center of the earth to see, for there they are taking you."

I was still on my bay horse, and once more I felt the riders of the west, the north, the east, the south, behind me in formation, as before, and we were going east. I looked ahead and saw the mountains there with rocks and forests on them, and from the mountains flashed all colors upward to the heavens. Then I was standing on the highest mountain of them all, and round about beneath me was the whole hoop of the world.[6] And while I stood there I saw more than I can tell and I understood more than I saw; for I was seeing in a sacred manner the shapes of all things in the spirit, and the shape of all shapes as they must live together like one being. And I saw that the sacred hoop of my people was one of many hoops that made one circle, wide as daylight and as starlight, and in the center grew one mighty flowering tree to shelter all the children of one mother and one father. And I saw that it was holy.

Then as I stood there, two men were coming from the east, head first like arrows flying, and between them rose the day-break star. They came and gave a herb to me and said: "With this on earth you shall undertake anything and do it." It was the day-break-star herb, the herb of understanding, and they told me to drop it on the earth. I saw it falling far, and when it struck the earth it rooted and grew and flowered, four blossoms on one stem, a blue, a white, a scarlet, and a yellow; and the rays from these streamed upward to the heavens so that all creatures saw it and in no place was there darkness.

Then the Voice said: "Your Six Grandfathers—now you shall go back to them."

I had not noticed how I was dressed until now, and I saw that I was painted red all over, and my joints were painted black, with white stripes between the joints. My bay had lightning stripes all over him, and his mane was cloud. And when I breathed, my breath was lightning.

Now two men were leading me, head first like arrows slanting upward—the two that brought me from the earth. And as I followed on the bay, they turned into four flocks of geese that flew in circles, one above each quarter, sending forth a sacred voice as they flew: Br-r-r-p, br-r-r-p, br-r-r-p, br-r-r-p!

Then I saw ahead the rainbow flaming above the tepee of the Six Grandfathers, built and roofed with cloud and sewed with thongs of lightning;

---

[6] Black Elk said the mountain he stood upon in his vision was Harney Peak in the Black Hills. "But anywhere is the center of the world," he added.

and underneath it were all the wings of the air and under them the animals and men. All these were rejoicing, and thunder was like happy laughter.

As I rode in through the rainbow door, there were cheering voices from all over the universe, and I saw the Six Grandfathers sitting in a row, with their arms held toward me and their hands, palms out; and behind them in the cloud were faces thronging, without number, of the people yet to be.

"He has triumphed!" cried the six together, making thunder. And as I passed before them there, each gave again the gift that he had given me before—the cup of water and the bow and arrows, the power to make live and to destroy; the white wing of cleansing and the healing herb; the sacred pipe; the flowering stick. And each one spoke in turn from west to south, explaining what he gave as he had done before, and as each one spoke he melted down into the earth and rose again; and as each did this, I felt nearer to the earth.

Then the oldest of them all said: "Grandson, all over the universe you have seen. Now you shall go back with power to the place from whence you came. . . ."

When I went through the door, the face of the day of earth was appearing with the day-break star upon its forehead; and the sun leaped up and looked upon me, and I was going forth alone. . . .

I was all alone on a broad plain now with my feet upon the earth, alone but for the spotted eagle guarding me. I could see my people's village far ahead, and I walked very fast, for I was homesick now. Then I saw my own tepee, and inside I saw my mother and my father bending over a sick boy that was myself. And as I entered the tepee, someone was saying: "The boy is coming to; you had better give him some water."

Then I was sitting up; and I was sad because my mother and my father didn't seem to know I had been so far away. . . .

After a Battle: The Vanquished Dream

After the soldiers marched away, Red Crow and I started back toward Pine Ridge together, and I took the little baby that I told you about. Red Crow had one too.

We were going back to Pine Ridge, because we thought there was peace back home; but it was not so. While we were gone, there was a fight around the Agency, and our people had all gone away. They had gone away so fast that they left all the tepees standing.

It was nearly dark when we passed north of Pine Ridge where the hospital is now, and some soldiers shot at us, but did not hit us. We rode into the camp, and it was all empty. We were very hungry because we had not eaten anything since early morning, so we peeped into the tepees until we saw where there was a pot with papa (dried meat) cooked in it. We sat down in there and began to eat. While we were doing this, the soldiers shot at the tepee, and a bullet struck right between Red Crow and me. It threw dust in the soup, but we kept right on eating until we had our fill. Then we took the babies and got on our horses and rode away. If that bullet had only killed me, then I could have died with papa in my mouth.

The people had fled down Clay Creek, and we followed their trail. It was dark now, and late in the night we came to where they were camped without any tepees. They were just sitting by little fires, and the snow was beginning to blow. We rode in among them and I heard my mother's voice. She was singing a death song for me, because she felt sure I had died over there. She was so glad to see me that she cried and cried.

Women who had milk fed the little babies that Red Crow and I brought with us.

I think nobody but the little children slept any that night. The snow blew and we had no tepees.

When it was getting light, a war party went out and I went along; but this time I took a gun with me. When I started out the day before to Wounded Knee, I took only my sacred bow, which was not made to shoot with; because I was a little in doubt about the Wanekia religion at that time, and I did not really want to kill anybody because of it.

But I did not feel like that any more. After what I had seen over there, I wanted revenge; I wanted to kill.

We crossed White Clay Creek and followed it up, keeping on the west side. Soon we could hear many guns going off. So we struck west, following a ridge to where the fight was. It was close to the Mission, and there are many bullets in the Mission yet.

From this ridge we could see that the Lakotas were on both sides of the creek and were shooting at soldiers who were coming down the creek. As we looked down, we saw a little ravine, and across this was a big hill. We crossed and rode up the hillside.

They were fighting right there, and a Lakota cried to me: "Black Elk, this is the kind of a day in which to do something great!" I answered: "How!"[7]

Then I got off my horse and rubbed earth on myself, to show the Powers that I was nothing without their help. Then I took my rifle, got on my horse and galloped up to the top of the hill. Right below me the soldiers were shooting, and my people called out to me not to go down there; that there were some good shots among the soldiers and I should get killed for nothing.

But I remembered my great vision, the part where the geese of the north appeared. I depended upon their power. Stretching out my arms with my gun in the right hand, like a goose soaring when it flies low to turn in a change of weather, I made the sound the geese make—br-r-r-p, br-r-r-p, br-r-r-p; and, doing this, I charged. The soldiers saw, and began shooting fast at me. I kept right on

[7]Signifying assent.

with my buckskin running, shot in their faces when I was near, then swung wide and rode back up the hill.

All this time the bullets were buzzing around me and I was not touched. I was not even afraid. It was like being in a dream about shooting. But just as I had reached the very top of the hill, suddenly it was like waking up, and I was afraid. I dropped my arms and quit making the goose cry. Just as I did this, I felt something strike my belt as though some one had hit me there with the back of an ax. I nearly fell out of my saddle, but I managed to hold on, and rode over the hill.

An old man by the name of Protector was there, and he ran up and held me, for now I was falling off my horse. I will show you where the bullet struck me sidewise across the belly here (showing a long deep scar on the abdomen). My insides were coming out. Protector tore up a blanket in strips and bound it around me so that my insides would stay in. By now I was crazy to kill, and I said to Protector: "Help me on my horse! Let me go over there. It is a good day to die, so I will go over there!" But Protector said: "No, young nephew! You must not die to-day. That would be foolish. Your people need you. There may be a better day to die." He lifted me into my saddle and led my horse away down hill. Then I began to feel very sick.

By now it looked as though the soldiers would be wiped out, and the Lakotas were fighting harder; but I heard that, after I left, the black Wasichu soldiers came, and the Lakotas had to retreat.

There were many of our children in the Mission, and the sisters and priests were taking care of them. I heard there were sisters and priests right in the battle helping wounded people and praying.

There was a man by the name of Little Soldier who took charge of me and brought me to where our people were camped. While we were over at the Mission Fight, they had fled to the O-ona-gazhee[8] and were camped on top of it where the women and children would be safe from soldiers. Old Hollow Horn was there. He was a very powerful bear medicine man, and he came over to heal my wound. In three days I could walk, but I kept a piece of blanket tied around my belly.

It was now nearly the middle of the Moon of Frost in the Tepee (January). We heard that soldiers were on Smoky Earth River and were coming to attack us in the O-ona-gazhee. They were near Black Feather's place. So a party of about sixty of us started on the war-path to find them. My mother tried to keep me at home, because, although I could walk and ride a horse, my wound was not all healed yet. But I would not stay; for, after what I had seen at Wounded Knee, I wanted a chance to kill soldiers.

---

[8]Sheltering place, an elevated plateau in the Badlands, with precipitous sides, and inaccessible save by one narrow neck of land easily defended.

Black Elk   207

We rode down Grass Creek to Smoky Earth, and crossed riding down stream. Soon from the top of a little hill we saw wagons and cavalry guarding them. The soldiers were making a corral of their wagons and getting ready to fight. We got off our horses and went behind some hills to a little knoll, where we crept up to look at the camp. Some soldiers were bringing harnessed horses down to a little creek to water, and I said to the others: "If you will stay here and shoot at the soldiers, I will charge over there and get some good horses." They knew of my power, so they did this, and I charged on my buckskin while the others kept shooting. I got seven of the horses; but when I started back with these, all the soldiers saw me and began shooting. They killed two of my horses, but I brought five back safe and was not hit. When I was out of range, I caught up a fine baldfaced bay and turned my buckskin loose. Then I drove the others back to our party.

By now more cavalry were coming up the river, a big bunch of them, and there was some hard fighting for a while, because there were not enough of us. We were fighting and retreating, and all at once I saw Red Willow on foot running. He called to me: "Cousin, my horse is killed!" So I caught up a soldier's horse that was dragging a rope and brought it to Red Willow while the soldiers were shooting fast at me. Just then, for a little while, I was a wanekia[9] myself. In this fight Long Bear and another man, whose name I have forgotten, were badly wounded; but we saved them and carried them along with us. The soldiers did not follow us far into the Badlands, and when it was night we rode back with our wounded to the O-ona-gazhee.

We wanted a much bigger war-party so that we could meet the soldiers and get revenge. But this was hard, because the people were not all of the same mind, and they were hungry and cold. We had a meeting there, and were all ready to go out with more warriors, when Afraid-of-His-Horses came over from Pine Ridge to make peace with Red Cloud, who was with us there.

Our party wanted to go out and fight anyway, but Red Cloud made a speech to us something like this: "Brothers, this is a very hard winter. The women and children are starving and freezing. If this were summer, I would say to keep on fighting to the end. But we cannot do this. We must think of the women and children and that it is very bad for them. So we must make peace, and I will see that nobody is hurt by the soldiers."

The people agreed to this, for it was true. So we broke camp next day and went down from the O-ona-gazhee to Pine Ridge, and many, many Lakotas were already there. Also, there were many, many soldiers. They stood in two lines with their guns held in front of them as we went through to where we camped.

And so it was all over.

I did not know then how much was ended. When I look back now from this high hill of my old age, I can still see the butchered women and children

[9]A "make-live" savior.

lying heaped and scattered all along the crooked gulch as plain as when I saw them with eyes still young. And I can see that something else died there in the bloody mud, and was buried in the blizzard. A people's dream died there. It was a beautiful dream.

And I, to whom so great a vision was given in my youth,—you see me now a pitiful old man who has done nothing, for the nation's hoop is broken and scattered. There is no center any longer, and the sacred tree is dead.

Suggestions for Further Reading

George Crook, *General George Crook: His Autobiography*, edited by Martin F. Schmitt (Norman, Okla.: University of Oklahoma Press, 1946).

Carlos B. Embry, *America's Concentration Camps* (New York: David McKay, 1956).

Peter Farb, *Man's Rise to Civilization as Shown By the Indians of North America From Primeval Times to the Coming of the Industrial State* (New York: E. P. Dutton, 1968).

Erma Fergusson, *Dancing Gods: Indian Ceremonials of New Mexico and Arizona* (Albuquerque, New Mexico: University of New Mexico Press, 1931).

Lee Eldridge Huddleston, *Origins of the American Indians: European Concepts 1492-1729* (Austin, Tex.: University of Texas Press, 1967).

Nancy Oestreich Lurie, *Mountain Wolf Woman, Sister of Crashing Thunder: The Autobiography of a Winnebago Indian* (Ann Arbor, Mich.: University of Michigan Press, 1961).

Margaret Mead, *The Changing Culture of an Indian Tribe* (New York: Columbia University Press, 1932).

James Mooney, *The Ghost-Dance Religion and the Sioux Outbreak of 1890* (Chicago: University of Chicago Press, 1965).

Georgiana C. Nammack, *Fraud, Politics, and the Dispossession of the Indians* (Norman, Okla.: University of Oklahoma Press, 1969).

Paul Radin, *The Autobiography of a Winnebago Indian* (New York: Dover Publications, 1963).

———, *The Road of Life and Death: A Ritual Drama of the American Indians* (New York: Pantheon Books [Bollingen Series] , 1945).

Leo W. Simmons, editor, *Sun Chief: The Autobiography of a Hopi Indian* (New Haven: Yale University Press, 1942).

Laura Thompson, *Culture in Crisis: A Study of the Hopi Indians* (New York: Harper and Brothers, 1950).

Ruth M. Underhill, *Papago Indian Religion* (New York: Columbia University Press, 1946).

Dale Van Every, *Disinherited: The Lost Birthright of the American Indian* (New York: William Morrow, 1966).

Mary C. Wheelwright, *Hail Chant and Water Chant* (Santa Fe, N. Mex: Museum of Navajo Ceremonial Art, 1946).

_____, *The Myth and Prayers of the Great Star Chant and the Myth of Coyote Chant* (Santa Fe, N. Mex.: Museum of Navajo Ceremonial Art, 1956).

Dietrich Bonhoeffer

Letters and Papers from Prison

*And I regard my sitting here . . . as
my own part in the fate of Germany.*

Dietrich Bonhoeffer was born the son of a prominent physician in 1906 in Breslau, Germany. He showed an early proficiency for theological studies, and in 1930 published his first book, *Sanctorum Communio*, which was finished in 1927, when he was only 21. In 1930 he journeyed to America to become Sloane Fellow at Union Theological Seminary. Then, within a year, Bonhoeffer went back to Germany to work as a pastor of the Evangelical church. During this period of his life he also wrote a variety of books and taught at theological schools.

On January 30, 1933, Adolf Hitler became Chancellor of Germany. On February 1, 1933—two days later—Bonhoeffer spoke over the radio to the German people, warning them against the dangers inherent in accepting a leader by virtue of the alleged supremacy of his person. The radio broadcast was cut off before Bonhoeffer had finished, but it signaled the beginning of his open resistance to the Nazi movement. From this time on he was involved in political and ecclesiastical conflicts. He rejected the alliance between the church and Hitler's party. He produced a theological treatise which refuted Hitler's "Aryan Clause," the rule which forbade those of Jewish origin to hold office in state or church. Then, in that same year, he left Germany to minister to German congregations in London. In explaining this action to Karl Barth, Bonhoeffer wrote, "If one is going to discover quite definite reasons for such decisions after the event, one of the strongest, I believe, was that I simply did not any longer feel up to the questions and demands which came to me." His stay in England was reasonably short. From 1934 to 1939 he helped form resistance movements in Germany and wrote a number of tracts for the *Times*. Then in 1939 two professors at Union Seminary, Reinhold Niebuhr and Paul Lehmann, succeeded in bringing Bonhoeffer back to New York City for safety. But Bonhoeffer's identification with the German problem and the German people was so great that he felt compelled to return to his homeland after only a few months in America. Back in Germany his books and tracts were forbidden, and many of them were destroyed. He was not allowed to speak in public assemblies, but his work in the German resistance movement continued.

In 1942, by prearrangement, Bonhoeffer met A. K. A. Bell, Bishop of Chichester, England, in Stockholm. Carrying official proposals for a peace treaty, Bonhoeffer revealed the plan by which Hitler would be overthrown. As history records it, the plan became known and was interrupted by the authorities, and Bonhoeffer was arrested and imprisoned on April 5, 1943. On April 9, 1945, he was hanged in the concentration camp in Flassenburg.

Since his death, readers and scholars have puzzled over the suggestions in the prison papers regarding the future of religion in Western culture. These papers are responsible for introducing the idea of "a world come of age" into contemporary conversation. They also outline many attitudes which have since been accepted by the religiously inclined. According to this reading, Bonhoeffer's own experiences convinced him that the survival of Christianity in the modern age could not be assumed. Indeed, as Bonhoeffer saw it, men would find the idea almost inconceivable that human affairs imply the reality of God or depend upon that reality for their explanation.

The account that follows is full of irony. Bonhoeffer announced that the "world had come of age" during the time when the world was at war. He rendered his description of the God in the midst of life as he himself awaited death. He illustrated his contention that the religious man is not the "peculiarly" religious but the truly human by reference to the singular model of "the man for others." These are some of the ideas which have allowed his martyrdom, by symbolizing the end of an old era, to serve as a rite of initiation to the new secular age for many who have come to identify with him.

Letters and Papers from Prison

November 20th 1943. If I should still be here over Christmas, don't worry about me. I should not really be frightened about it. A Christian can keep Christmas even in prison, more easily than family occasions, anyhow. My special thanks for getting permission to visit me. I am not expecting any complications this time. I didn't dare ask you to do anything about it. I only hope it will come off this time. But you know that even if it is refused at the last moment, there is still the joy of thinking that you have tried, and it will only serve to make us more angry with certain people for the time being (I sometimes think I don't get nearly angry enough over the whole business). So if it comes to that, let us swallow even that bitter pill, for after all we have been gradually getting used to such things in the past few months. I'm so glad I saw you just when I was arrested, and I shall never forget it.

Just one more point—about my daily routine. I get up at the same time as you do, and my day lasts till eight in the evening. I wear out my trousers sitting down while you wear out your soles running about. I read the *Voelkischer Beobachter* and the *Reich*, and I've got to know some *very* nice people. Every day they take me for half an hour's solitary exercise, and in the afternoon they are giving me treatment for my rheumatism—I must say, they are very gentle with me, but it doesn't seem to do me much good. Once a week I get the most wonderful food parcels from you. Many thanks for them, and also for the cigars and cigarettes you sent me when you were away. I only hope you get your will—are you often hungry? That would be too awful for words. There is nothing I miss here, except all of you. I wish you and I could play the G minor sonata and sing some Schütz together, and you could read to me Psalms 70 and 47. They were the best you ever did!

My cell is being spring cleaned. During the operations I am able to give the cleaner something to eat. One of them was sentenced to death the other day—that was a shock for me. In seven and a half months there is plenty to see, and especially one notices trivial acts of folly. I think a lengthy confinement is demoralising for the bulk of the prisoners. I have been thinking out an alternative penal system, the principle of which is that everybody should be punished in the sphere in which his crime was committed: e.g. for absence without leave, the cancelling of all leave; for unlawful wearing of medals, longer service at the front; for robbing other soldiers, the temporary wearing of a label saying that the man is a thief; for black-marketing, the reduction of rations, etc. Why is it that the Old Testament never punishes a man by depriving him of his liberty? . . .

November 23rd 1943. Last night's raid wasn't exactly pleasant. I was thinking of you all the time. At such moments prison life is no joke. I do hope you will be going back to S. again. It surprised me last night to see how nervous some of the soldiers who have come straight from the front line were while the alarm was on.

November 24th 1943. After yesterday's raid I think it is only right that I should let you know what arrangements I have made in case of my death. . . . I hope you will read this with your usual absence of sentimentality.

Dietrich Bonhoeffer   213

Friday, November 26th 1943. So it really came off! True it was all too brief, but that does not matter. Even an hour or two wouldn't be enough. After we have been cut off from the world here for so long, we become so receptive that even a few minutes gives us food for thought for a long time after. I shall often think of how the four people who are my nearest and dearest were here with me. When I got back to my cell afterwards I paced up and down for a whole hour, while my dinner lay waiting for me on the table until it got quite cold, and in the end it made me laugh when I caught myself saying from time to time, "How wonderful it was!" I never like calling anything "indescribable," for it is a word you hardly ever need use if you take the trouble to express yourself clearly, but at the moment that's just what this morning seems to be. Karl's cigar is on the table before me, and that's something really indescribable!. . . And they are my favourite Wolf cigars from Hamburg, which I used to love so in better times. And beside me on a box there is the Advent wreath, and your gigantic eggs on the shelf, which will provide my breakfast for several days to come. . . .

November 29th 1943. This Monday is quite unique. Usually on a Monday morning the shouting and swearing in the corridors is at its worst, but after the experiences of last week even the noisiest ones have become subdued, a change one cannot help noticing! Now something which will particularly interest you. During these heavy air raids, and especially the last one, the windows were blown out by the land mine, and bottles and medical supplies from the shelves and cupboards fell to the ground. All this time I lay in complete darkness on the floor, with little hope of coming through it all safely. Now here's the point—it led me back to prayer and to the Bible just like a child. More of that later when I see you. In more than one respect my confinement is acting like a wholesome though drastic cure. But I can only tell you the details when we meet again. . . .

In the last month or two I have learnt as never before how much comfort and help I get from others. . . . We often want to do everything ourselves, but that is a mark of false pride. Even what we owe to others belongs to ourselves, and is a part of our own lives. And when we want to calculate just how much we have learnt ourselves and how much we owe to others, it is not only un-Christian, but useless. What we are in ourselves, and what we owe to others makes us a complete whole. I wanted to tell you this because I've only just found it out, though not really for the first time, for we have realised it implicitly all through the years of our *via communis*. . . .

December 15th 1943. . . . I often feel as though the best part of my life was already past, and that all I have to do now is to finish my *Ethics*. Yet you know, when I feel like this there comes over me an incomparable longing not to quit this life without leaving some traces behind me, a wish that seems more redolent of the Old Testament than of the New. . . . If only I could see you as a free man before you leave! But if it is now their intention to keep me here over

Christmas, I shall face it my own way like a Christmas in the front line, so you needn't worry about that. Great battles are easier to fight and less wearing than daily skirmishes.

December 22nd 1943. They seem to have made up their minds that I am not to be with you for Christmas, though nobody dares to tell me so. . . . I do want you to realise that I believe my attitude towards my case ought to be one of faith, whereas I am letting it become too much a matter of calculation and foresight. I am not really bothered about whether I shall be home for Christmas, for that is only a childish question. I am sure I could renounce that, if only I could do so in faith, knowing that it is inevitable. I can bear all things in faith (I hope so, anyhow), even my condemnation, and even the other consequences I fear (see Psalm 18.29): but anxious calculation wears one down. Don't worry if something worse befalls me [removal to a concentration camp] . Several of the other brethren have already been through that. But this shilly-shallying, this continual consultation without action, this refusal to face up to risks is positively dangerous. I must be able to know for certain that I am in the hands of God, and not in men's. Then everything can be easy, even the severest privations. There is no question of my being "understandably impatient," as people are probably saying of me: what matters is that I should face everything in faith. . . .

You ought to know that I have not for a moment regretted coming home in 1939. I knew quite well what I was about, and acted with a clear conscience. I have no desire to cross out of my life anything that has happened since, either in the world at large, or to me personally (Sigurdshof, East Prussia, Ettal, my illness, and all the help you gave me then, the time in Berlin, and my present confinement). And I regard my sitting here (do you remember how I prophesied last March what the coming year would bring?) as my own part in the fate of Germany. I look back on the past without any self-reproach, and accept the present in the same spirit. But I don't want to be unsettled by the machinations of men. We can only live in faith and assurance, you out there at the front, and I in my cell.—I have just come across this in the *Imitation of Christ: Custodi deligenter cellam tuam, et custodiet te* ("Look after your cell, and it will look after you"). May God keep the light of faith burning in our souls. . . .

Christmas Day. . . . Once more all my marvellous Christmas presents are arranged on the edge of the tipped-up bed, and in front of me are the pictures which I enjoy so much. The memory of your visit gives me food for thought all the time. It was something I really couldn't do without. My longing to have someone to talk to is far worse than physical hunger. . . . They have tried to do everything possible here to give me a pleasant Christmas, but I was glad to be alone again. I often wonder how I shall adapt myself to company again after this. You remember how I often used to retire to my room after some great

Dietrich Bonhoeffer

celebration. I'm afraid I must have grown even worse, for despite all my privations I have come to love solitude. I enjoy a talk with one or two others, but I simply loathe any larger gathering, and anything in the nature of chatter or gossip I just cannot stand. . . .

January 23rd 1944. Since you left for the front on Jan. 9th my thoughts about you have taken a new shape. . . . That Sunday it was a wrench for me as well as for you, though in a different way. It is a strange feeling to see a friend whose life has been bound up so intimately with your own for so many years going out to meet an unknown future which you can do practically nothing about. It makes you feel so utterly helpless. There are however, it seems to me, two sides to this helplessness. It brings both anxiety and relief. For so long as we are able to influence another's life, we can't help wondering whether what we are doing for him is really for his best. But when every opportunity of intervening in his life is cut off at a blow, you cannot help feeling that however anxious you may be about him, his life has now been placed in better and more powerful hands than your own. Our greatest task during these coming weeks, and maybe months, will be to trust in these hands. Whatever weakness, self-reproach and guilt we contribute to these events, in the events themselves is God. If we survive all this we shall be able to see quite clearly that all has turned out for the best. The idea that we could have avoided many of life's difficulties if we had taken things more quietly is one that cannot be taken seriously for a moment. As I look back on your past I am sure that everything has turned out for the best, and so we have every reason to hope that what is happening at the present can only be for the best too. To renounce a full life and all its joys in order to escape pain is neither Christian nor human. . . .

The news of the Nettune landing has just come in. Are you anywhere thereabouts? When things like this happen I see how hard it is for me to take things calmly: I can only do so at the cost of repeated effort. . . . Is there not a kind of self-possession which proudly grinds its teeth, but is quite different from a dour, rigid, lifeless and unthinking submission to the inevitable? I am sure we honour God more if we gratefully accept the life he gives us with all its blessings, loving it and drinking it to the full, grieving deeply and sincerely when we have belittled or thrown away any of the precious things of life. . . .

January 23rd 1944. . . . What will happen to Rome? I can't bear to think of its being destroyed. What a good thing we saw it in peacetime. . . .

I have had to take a new line with the companion of my daily walks. Although he has done his best to ingratiate himself with me, he said something about the Jews the other day, which made me more off-handed and cool to him than I have ever been to anyone before, and I have also seen to it that he has been deprived of certain little comforts. Now he feels himself obliged to go round whimpering for a

The Fraternal Self

while, but I haven't a scrap of pity for him. He is really a sorry figure, but certainly not poor Lazarus! ...

February 21st 1944. ... I am sorry to have to tell you that it does not look as though I shall be out of here before Easter now.

... I am wondering whether my excessive scrupulousness, which you often used to shake your head about with amusement (I am thinking of our travels!) is not really the other side of bourgeois existence. I mean, is it not a part of our faithlessness which hides below the surface all the time we are secure, but comes to the top in times of insecurity in the form of "dread" (I don't mean cowardice, which is something quite different: dread can be manifested in rash daring just as much as in cowardice), dread in the face of straightforward, simple duty, dread in having to make vital decisions. I have often wondered when it is that the moment comes for us to throw up the sponge and abandon our resistance to fate. Resistance and submission are both equally necessary at different times. Don Quixote is the symbol of resistance carried on to the point of folly, and similarly Michael Kohlhaas insisted on his rights until it became his own undoing. In both cases resistance in the end defeats its own object, and vanishes into illusion and fantasy. Sancho Panza is the type of complacent and sly accommodation to things as they are. I am sure we must rise to the great responsibilities which are peculiarly our own, and yet at the same time fulfil the commonplace tasks of daily life. We must sally forth to defy fate—I think the neuter gender of *Schicksal* (fate) is significant—with just as much resolution as we submit to it when the time comes. One can only speak of providence on the other side of this dialectical process. God encounters us not only as a Thou, but also disguised as an It; so in the last resort my question is how we are to find the Thou in this It (i.e. fate). In other words, how does fate become providence? It is impossible therefore to define the boundary between resistance and submission in the abstract. Faith demands this elasticity of behaviour. Only so can we stand our ground in each situation as it comes along, and turn it to gain. ...

March 19th 1944. With the news of the heavy fighting in your neighbourhood you are hardly ever out of my thoughts. Every word I read in the Bible and hymns I apply to you. You ... must be feeling very homesick during these dangerous days, and every letter will only make it worse. But surely, it is the mark of a grown-up man, as compared with a callow youth, that he finds his centre of gravity wherever he happens to be at the moment, and however much he longs for the object of his desire, it cannot prevent him from staying at his post and doing his duty? The adolescent is never quite "all there": if he were, he wouldn't be an adolescent, but a dullard. There is a wholeness about the fully grown man which makes him concentrate on the present moment. He may have unsatisfied desires, but he always keeps them out of sight, and manages to

Dietrich Bonhoeffer

217

master them some way or other. And the more need he has of self-mastery, the more confidence he will inspire among his comrades, especially the younger ones, who are still on the road he has already travelled. Clinging too much to our desires easily prevents us from being what we ought to be and can be. Desires repeatedly mastered for the sake of present duty make us, conversely, all the richer. To be without desire is a mark of poverty. At the moment I am surrounded by people who cling to their desires, so much so that they haven't any interest for others: they give up listening, and are incapable of loving their neighbour. I think we should live even in this place as though we had no desires and no future to hope for, and just be our true selves. It is remarkable what an influence one acquires in this way over other men. They come and confide in us, and let us speak to them. I am writing to you about this because I think there is a lot for you to do too just now, and later on you will be glad to think that you have done your best. When we know that a friend is in danger, we somehow want to be assured that he is being his true self. We can have a full life even when we haven't got everything we want—that is what I am really trying to say. Forgive me for troubling you with my thoughts, but thinking is my chief amusement here. I'm sure you'll understand. I ought to add, by the way, that I am more convinced than ever that it won't be long before *our* wishes are fulfilled, and there's no need for *us* to resign ourselves to the worst.

. . . I am going through another spell of finding it difficult to read the Bible. I never know quite what to make of it. I don't feel guilty at all about it, and I know it won't be long before I return to it again with renewed zest. Is it just a psychological process? I am almost inclined to think so. Do you remember how we often used to find it like that when we were together? True, there is always a danger of indolence, but it would be wrong to get fussed about it. Far better to trust that after wobbling a bit the compass will come to rest in the right direction. Don't you agree? . . . It's almost a year since we spent those last days working together. . . . I wish I knew what the future has in store for us. I wonder if we shall be together again, perhaps in some work—or must we be content with the past? . . .

April 30th 1944.. . . How good it would be if we could go through this time together, standing side by side. But it is probably best for us to face it alone. I am so sorry I can't help you at all, except by thinking of you as I read the Bible every morning and evening, and often during the day. You really must not worry about me, for I'm getting on uncommonly well, and you would be astonished if you came to see me. They keep on telling me that I am "radiating so much peace around me," and that I am "always so cheerful." Very flattering, no doubt, but I'm afraid I don't always feel like that myself. You would be surprised and perhaps disturbed if you knew how my ideas on theology are taking shape. This is where I miss you most of all, for there is no one else who could help me so much to clarify my own mind. The thing that keeps coming

The Fraternal Self

back to me is, what *is* Christianity, and indeed what *is* Christ, for us to-day? The time when men could be told everything by means of words, whether theological or simply pious, is over, and so is the time of inwardness and conscience, which is to say the time of religion as such. We are proceeding towards a time of no religion at all: men as they are now simply cannot be religious any more. Even those who honestly describe themselves as "religious" do not in the least act up to it, and so when they say "religious" they evidently mean something quite different. Our whole nineteen-hundred-year-old Christian preaching and theology rests upon the "religious premise" of man. What we call Christianity has always been a pattern—perhaps a true pattern—of religion. But if one day it becomes apparent that this *a priori* "premise" simply does not exist, but was a historical and temporary form of human self-expression, i.e. if we reach the stage of being radically without religion—and I think this is more or less the case already, else how is it, for instance, that this war, unlike any of those before it, is not calling forth any "religious" reaction?—what does that mean for "Christianity"?

It means that the linchpin is removed from the whole structure of our Christianity to date, and the only people left for us to light on in the way of "religion" are a few "last survivals of the age of chivalry," or else one or two who are intellectually dishonest. Would they be the chosen few? Is it on this dubious group and none other that we are to pounce, in fervour, pique, or indignation, in order to sell them the goods we have to offer? Are we to fall upon one or two unhappy people in their weakest moment and force upon them a sort of religious coercion?

If we do not want to do this, if we had finally to put down the western pattern of Christianity as a mere preliminary stage to doing without religion altogether, what situation would result for us, for the Church? How can Christ become the Lord even of those with no religion? If religion is no more than the garment of Christianity—and even that garment has had very different aspects at different periods—then what is a religionless Christianity? Barth, who is the only one to have started on this line of thought, has still not proceeded to its logical conclusion, but has arrived at a positivism of revelation which has nevertheless remained essentially a restoration. For the religionless working man, or indeed, man generally, nothing that makes any real difference is gained by that. The questions needing answers would surely be: What is the significance of a Church (church, parish, preaching, Christian life) in a religionless world? How do we speak of God without religion, i.e. without the temporally-influenced presuppositions of metaphysics, inwardness, and so on? How do we speak (but perhaps we are no longer capable of speaking of such things as we used to) in secular fashion of God? In what way are we in a religionless and secular sense Christians, in what way are we the *Ekklesia*, "those who are called forth," not conceiving of ourselves religiously as specially favoured, but as wholly belonging to the world? Then Christ is no longer an object of religion, but something quite different, indeed and in truth the Lord of the world. Yet what does that signify?

Dietrich Bonhoeffer

What is the place of worship and prayer in an entire absence of religion? Does the secret discipline, or, as the case may be, the distinction (which you have met with me before) between penultimate and ultimate, at this point acquire fresh importance? I must break off for to-day, so that the letter can be posted straight away. In two days I will write to you further on the subject. I hope you have a rough idea of what I'm getting at, and that it does not bore you. Good-bye for the present. It isn't easy to keep writing without any echo from you. You must excuse me if that makes it rather a monologue!

I find after all I can carry on writing.—The Pauline question whether circumcision is a condition of justification is to-day, I consider, the question whether religion is a condition of salvation. Freedom from circumcision is at the same time freedom from religion. I often ask myself why a Christian instinct frequently draws me more to the religionless than to the religious, by which I mean not with any intention of evangelising them, but rather, I might almost say, in "brotherhood." While I often shrink with religious people from speaking of God by name—because that Name somehow seems to me here not to ring true, and I strike myself as rather dishonest (it is especially bad when others start talking in religious jargon: then I dry up almost completely and feel somehow oppressed and ill at ease)—with people who have no religion I am able on occasion to speak of God quite openly and as it were naturally. Religious people speak of God when human perception is (often just from laziness) at an end, or human resources fail: it is in fact always the *Deus ex machina* they call to their aid, either for the so-called solving of insoluble problems or as support in human failure—always, that is to say, helping out human weakness or on the borders of human existence. Of necessity, that can only go on until men can, by their own strength, push those borders a little further, so that God becomes superfluous as a *Deus ex machina*. I have come to be doubtful even about talking of "borders of human existence." Is even death to-day, since men are scarcely afraid of it anymore, and sin, which they scarcely understand any more, still a genuine borderline? It always seems to me that in talking thus we are only seeking frantically to make room for God. I should like to speak of God not on the borders of life but at its centre, not in weakness but in strength, not, therefore, in man's suffering and death but in his life and prosperity. On the borders it seems to me better to hold our peace and leave the problem unsolved. Belief in the Resurrection is not the solution of the problem of death. The "beyond" of God is not the beyond of our perceptive faculties. Epistemological theory has nothing to do with the transcendence of God. God is the "beyond" in the midst of our life. The Church stands not where human powers give out, on the borders, but in the centre of the village. That is the way it is in the Old Testament, and in this sense we still read the New Testament far too little on the basis of the Old. The outward aspect of this religionless Christianity, the form it takes, is something to which I am giving much thought, and I shall be writing to you about it again soon. It may be that on us in particular, midway between East and West, there will fall an important responsibility.

It would be grand to have a line from you on all this; indeed it would mean more to me than you can imagine, I'm sure. I suggest you should look at Proverbs 22.11, 12. There's something that will bar the way against any kind of pious escapism. . . .

May 20th 1944. There is always a danger of intense love destroying what I might call the "polyphony" of life. What I mean is that God requires that we should love him eternally with our whole hearts, yet not so as to compromise or diminish our earthly affections, but as a kind of *cantus firmus* to which the other melodies of life provide the counterpoint. Earthly affection is one of these contrapuntal themes, a theme which enjoys an autonomy of its own. Even the Bible can find room for the Song of Songs, and one could hardly have a more passionate and sensual love than is there portrayed (see 7.6). It is a good thing that that book is included in the Bible as a protest against those who believe that Christianity stands for the restraint of passion (is there any example of such restraint anywhere in the Old Testament?). Where the ground bass is firm and clear, there is nothing to stop the counterpoint from being developed to the utmost of its limits. Both ground bass and counterpoint are "without confusion and yet distinct," in the words of the Chalcedonian formula, like Christ in his divine and human natures. Perhaps the importance of polyphony in music lies in the fact that it is a musical reflection of this Christological truth, and that it is therefore an essential element in the Christian life. All this occurred to me after you were here. Can you see what I'm driving at? I wanted to tell you that we must have a good, clear *cantus firmus*. Without it there can be no full or perfect sound, but with it the counterpoint has a firm support and cannot get out of tune or fade out, yet is always a perfect whole in its own right. Only a polyphony of this kind can give life a wholeness, and at the same time assure us that nothing can go wrong so long as the *cantus firmus* is kept going. Perhaps your leave and the separation which lies ahead will be easier for you to bear. Please do not fear or hate separation if it should come, with all its attendant perils, but pin your faith on the *cantus firmus.*—I don't know if I have made myself clear, but one speaks so seldom of such things. . . .

May 30th 1944 Evening. I am sitting upstairs by myself. All is quiet in the house: outside a few birds are still singing, and I can even hear the cuckoo in the distance. I find these long, warm evenings rather trying—it's the second time I have had to live through them here. I long to be outside, and if I weren't such a rational person, I might do something foolish. I wonder if we have become too rational? When you have deliberately suppressed every desire for so long, it burns you up inside, or else you get so bottled up that one day there is a terrific explosion. The only alternative is the achievement of complete selflessness. I know better than anyone else that that has not happened to me. I expect you will say it's wrong to suppress one's desires, and you will be quite right. . . . So I seek diversion in thinking and writing letters . . . and curb my desires as a measure of self-protection. I know it sounds paradoxical, but it would be more selfless if I had no fear of my desires, but could give them free rein—but that would be very difficult. Just now I happened to hear Solveig's song on the wireless up in the guardroom. It quite got hold of me. To wait loyally a whole lifetime—that is triumphing over the hostility of space, that is, separation, and of time, that is, the past. Don't you agree that loyalty like this is the only road to happiness, and that disloyalty is the source of unhappiness? Well, I'm off to bed now, in case we get another disturbed night. Good night. . . .

June 30th 1944. Let me carry on a bit with the theological reflections I started on a little while ago. I began by saying that God is being increasingly edged out of the world, now that it has come of age. Knowledge and life are thought to be perfectly possible without him. Ever since Kant, he has been relegated to the realm beyond experience.

Theology has endeavoured to produce an apologetic to meet this development, engaging in futile rear-guard actions against Darwinism, etc. At other times it has accommodated itself to this development by restricting God to the so-called last questions as a kind of *Deus ex machina*. God thus became the answer to life's problems, the solution of its distresses and conflicts. As a result, if anyone had no such difficulties, if he refused to identify himself in sympathy with those who had, it was no good trying to win him for God. The only way of getting at him was to show that he had all these problems, needs and conflicts without being aware of it or owning up to it. Existentialist philosophy and psychotherapy have both been pretty clever at this sort of thing. It is then possible to talk to a man about God, and methodism can celebrate its triumph. If however it does not come off, if a man won't see that his happiness is really damnation, his health sickness, his vigour and vitality despair; if he won't call them what they really are, the theologian is at his wits' end. He must be a hardened sinner of a particularly vicious type. If not, he is a case of bourgeois complacency, and the one is as far from salvation as the other.

You see, this is the attitude I am contending against. When Jesus blessed sinners, they were real sinners, but Jesus did not make every man a sinner first. He called them out of their sin, not into their sin. Of course encounter with Jesus meant the reversal of all human values. So it was in the conversion of St. Paul, though in his case the knowledge of sin preceded his encounter with Jesus. Of course Jesus took to himself the dregs of human society, harlots, and publicans, but never them alone, for he sought to take to himself man as such. Never did Jesus throw any doubt on a man's health, vigour or fortune, regarded in themselves, or look upon them as evil fruits. Else why did he heal the sick and restore strength to the weak? Jesus claims for himself and the kingdom of God the whole of human life in all its manifestations.

Of course I would be interrupted just now! Let me briefly summarise what I am concerned about: it is, how can we reclaim for Christ a world which has come of age? . . .

July 8th 1944. . . .When God was driven out of the world, and from the public side of human life, an attempt was made to retain him at least in the sphere of the "personal," the "inner life," the private life. And since every man still has a private sphere, it was thought that he was most vulnerable at this point. The secrets known by a man's valet, that is, to put it crudely, the area of his intimate life—from prayer to his sexual life—have become the hunting ground of modern psychotherapists. In this way they resemble, though quite involuntarily, the dirtiest gutter journalists. Think of the newspapers which specialise in bringing to light the most intimate details about prominent people. They practise social, financial and political blackmail on their victims: the psychotherapists practise religious blackmail. Forgive me, but I cannot say less about them.

From the sociological point of view this is a revolution from below, a revolt of inferiority. Just as the vulgar mentality is never satisfied until it has seen some highly placed personage in his bathing attire, or in other compromising situations, so it is here. There is a kind of malicious satisfaction in knowing that everyone has his weaknesses and nakednesses. In my contacts with the outcasts of society, its pariahs, I have often noticed how mistrust is the dominant motive in their judgements of other people. Every act of a person of high repute, be it never so altruistic, is suspected from the outset. Incidentally, I find such outcasts in all ranks of society. In a flower garden they grub around for the dung on which the flowers grow. The less responsible a man's life, the more easily he falls a victim to this attitude.

This irresponsibility and absence of bonds has its counterpart among the clergy in what I should call the "priestly" snuffing around in the sins of men in order to catch them out. It is as though a beautiful house could only be known after a cobweb had been found in the furthermost corner of the cellar, or as though a good play could only be appreciated after one had seen how the actors behave off-stage. It is the same kind of thing you find in the novels of the last fifty years, which think they have only depicted their characters properly when they have described them in bed, or in films where it is thought necessary to include undressing scenes. What is clothed, veiled, pure and chaste is considered to be deceitful, disguised and impure, and in fact only shows the impurity of the writers themselves. Mistrust and suspicion as the basic attitude of men is characteristic of the revolt of inferiority.

From the theological point of view the error is twofold. First, it is thought that a man can be addressed as a sinner only after his weaknesses and meannesses have been spied out. Second, it is thought that man's essential nature consists of his inmost and most intimate background, and that is defined as his "interior life"; and it is in these secret human places that God is now to have his domain!

On the first point it must be said that man is certainly a sinner, but by no means mean or common. To put the matter in the most banal way, are Goethe or Napoleon sinners because they were not always faithful husbands? It is not the sins of weakness, but the sins of strength, which matter here. It is not in the least necessary to spy out things. The Bible never does so. (Sins of strength: in the genius, *hybris*, in the peasant, the breaking of the order of life—is the Decalogue a peasant ethic?—in the bourgeois, fear of free responsibility. Is this correct?)

On the second point it must be said that the Bible does not recognise our distinction of outer and inner. And why should it? It is always concerned with *anthropos teleios*, the *whole* man, even where, as in the Sermon on the Mount, the decalogue is pressed home to refer to inward disposition. It is quite unbiblical to suppose that a "good intention" is enough. What matters is the whole good. The discovery of inwardness, so-called, derives from the Renaissance, from Petrarch perhaps. The "heart" in the biblical sense is not the inward life, but the whole man in relation to God. The view that man lives just as much from outwards to inwards as from inwards to outwards is poles apart from the view that his essential nature is to be understood from his intimate background.

This is why I am so anxious that God should not be relegated to some last secret place, but that we should frankly recognise that the world and men have come of age, that we should not speak ill of man in his worldliness, but confront him with God at his strongest point, that we should give up all our clerical subterfuges, and our regarding of psychotherapy and existentialism as precursors of God. The importunity of these people is far too unaristocratic for the Word of God to ally itself with them. The Word of God is far removed from this revolt of mistrust, this revolt from below. But it reigns.

It's high time I said something concrete on the worldly interpretation of the terminology of the Bible, but it's too hot! . . .

July 21st 1944. During the last year or so I have come to appreciate the "worldliness" of Christianity as never before. The Christian is not a *homo religiosus*, but a man, pure and simple, just as Jesus was a man, compared with John the Baptist anyhow. I don't mean the shallow this-worldliness of the enlightened, of the busy, the comfortable or the lascivious. It's something much more profound than that, something in which the knowledge of death and resurrection is ever present. I believe Luther lived a this-worldly life in this sense. I remember talking to a young French pastor at A. thirteen years ago. We were discussing what our real purpose was in life. He said he would like to become a saint. I think it is quite likely he did become one. At the time I was very much

The Fraternal Self

impressed, though I disagreed with him, and said I should prefer to have faith, or words to that effect. For a long time I did not realise how far we were apart. I thought I could acquire faith by trying to live a holy life, or something like it. It was in this phase that I wrote *The Cost of Discipleship*. To-day I can see the dangers of this book, though I am prepared to stand by what I wrote.

Later I discovered and am still discovering up to this very moment that it is only by living completely in this world that one learns to believe. One must abandon every attempt to make something of oneself, whether it be a saint, a converted sinner, a churchman (the priestly type, so-called!), a righteous man or an unrighteous one, a sick man or a healthy one. This is what I mean by worldliness—taking life in one's stride, with all its duties and problems, its successes and failures, its experiences and helplessness. It is in such a life that we throw ourselves utterly into the arms of God and participate in his sufferings in the world and watch with Christ in Gethsemane. That is faith, that is *metanoia*, and that is what makes a man and a Christian (cf. Jeremiah 45). How can success make us arrogant or failure lead us astray, when we participate in the sufferings of God by living in this world?

I think you get my meaning, though I put it so briefly. I am glad I have been able to learn it, and I know I could only have done so along the road I have travelled. So I am grateful and content with the past and the present. Perhaps you are surprised at the personal tone of this letter, but if for once I want to talk like this, to whom else should I say it? May God in his mercy lead us through these times. But above all may he lead us to himself!

I was delighted to hear from you, and glad you aren't finding it too hot. There must still be many letters from me on the way. Did we travel more or less along that way in 1936?

Good-bye. Take care of yourself and don't lose hope that we shall all meet again soon! . . .

July 28th 1944. . . . To turn to a different point, not only action, but also suffering is a way to freedom. The deliverance consists in placing our cause unreservedly in the hands of God. Whether our deeds are wrought in faith or not depends on our realisation that suffering is the extension of action and the perfection of freedom. That, to my mind, is very important and very comforting.

I am getting on all right, and there's nothing to report about the family either. Hans is definitely down with diphtheria, but there seems to be good hope for him. Good-bye, and keep up your spirits as we are doing. And don't forget—we *shall* meet again soon! . . .

August 23rd 1944. Please don't ever get anxious or worried about me, but don't forget to pray for me—I'm sure you don't! I am so sure of God's guiding hand, and I hope I shall never lose that certainty. You must never doubt that I am travelling my appointed road with gratitude and cheerfulness. My past life is replete with God's goodness, and my sins are covered by the forgiving love of Christ crucified. I am thankful for all those who have crossed my path, and all I wish is never to cause them sorrow, and that they like me will always be thankful for the forgiveness and mercy of God and sure of it. Please don't for a moment get upset by all this, but let it rejoice your heart. But I did want to say this for once, and I could not think of anyone else who would take it in the right spirit.

Did you get the poem on freedom? I'm afraid it was very unpolished, but it's a subject about which I feel deeply.

I am now working on the chapter about "Taking Stock of Christianity." I'm afraid I can't work unless I smoke pretty hard, though I have many sources of supply, thank goodness, so I manage all right. I am often shocked at the things I am saying, especially in the first part, which is mainly critical. I shall be glad when I get to the more positive part. But the whole subject has never been properly thrashed out, so it sounds very undigested. However, it can't be printed at present anyhow, and it will doubtless improve with waiting. I find it hard going having to write everything by hand, and I can scarcely read what I have written. Amusingly enough, I am obliged to use German handwriting, and then there are all the corrections. Perhaps I shall be able to make a fair copy. . . .

I do so hope you will have quiet time both in body and mind. May God take care of you, and all of us, and grant us the joy of meeting again soon! I am praying for you every day!

Your true and grateful friend,

D.

Suggestions for Further Reading

Eberhard Bethge, "Dietrich Bonhoeffer: An Account of His Life," *The Plough*, III, 2 (1955), pp. 35-42.

_____, *Preface to Bonhoeffer: The Man and Two of His Shorter Writings* (Philadelphia: Fortress Press, 1965).

Eugene B. Borowitz, "Bonhoeffer's World Comes of Age," *Judaism*, XIV (1965), pp. 81-87. Review article.

Gerhard Ebeling, *Word and Faith* (Philadelphia: Fortress Press, 1963). Especially chapters IV and IX.

John D. Godsey, *The Theology of Dietrich Bonhoeffer* (Philadelphia: Westminster Press, 1960).

_____, "Theology from a Prison Cell," *The Drew Gateway*, XXVII, 3 (1957), pp. 139-54.

William Kuhns, *In Pursuit of Dietrich Bonhoeffer* (London: Burns and Oates, 1968).

S.B. Leibholz, "Dietrich Bonhoeffer: A Glimpse into Our Childhood," *Union Seminary Quarterly Review*, XX (1965), pp. 319-331.

John Macquarrie, *Twentieth Century Religious Thought* (New York: Harper and Row, 1963). Chapter XX, "A German Theologian: Dietrich Bonhoeffer."

Jürgen Moltmann and Jürgen Weissbach, *Two Studies in the Theology of Bonhoeffer*, translated by Reginald H. Fuller and Elsie Fuller (New York: Charles Scribner's Sons, 1967).

Reinhold Niebuhr, "The Death of a Martyr," *Christianity and Crisis*, V, 11 (June 1945), pp. 6-7.

Ronald Gregor Smith, *The New Man* (New York: Harper and Brothers, 1956).

_____, editor, *World Come of Age: A Symposium on Dietrich Bonhoeffer* (London: Collins, 1967).

P. Vorkink, editor, *Bonhoeffer in a World Come of Age* (Philadelphia: Fortress Press, 1968).

Wolf-Dieter Zimmermann and Ronald Gregor Smith, editors, *I Knew Dietrich Bonhoeffer*, translated by Käthe Gregor Smith (New York: Harper, 1966).

Malcolm X

Autobiography

*Despite the artificially created
separation and distance
between us, we still remained
very close in our feelings
toward each other.*

Malcolm X, influential leader of the Organization for Afro-American Unity, was born in Omaha, Nebraska, on May 19, 1925, and was killed by assassins' bullets on February 21, 1965. His father, Earl Little, a free-lance Christian preacher, was killed while working for Marcus Garvey's Universal Negro Improvement Association (a back-to-Africa movement) when Malcolm was six years old. His mother, Louise Little, whose father was a white man, was left husbandless with eight children at the age of 34 and shortly thereafter was committed to an asylum. Malcolm and his brothers and sisters spent their childhood moving from foster home to foster home, all of the time suffering the indignities of the black minority in America.

Malcolm's personal history can be said to fall into four periods. His early and adolescent years were spent in black ghettos in Omaha, Milwaukee, and Lansing, Michigan. During his middle teens he moved to Boston to live with an older sister and her family. This second portion of his life is marked by his participation in the "hustling society" both in Boston and Harlem. Writing about himself, Malcolm said, "There I was . . . in Harlem's streets among all the rest of the hustlers. I couldn't sell reefers; the dope squad detectives were too familiar with me. I was a true hustler—uneducated, unskilled at anything honorable, and I considered myself nervy and cunning enough to live by my wits, exploiting any prey that presented itself. I would risk about anything." Hustlers, he said, "inevitably move into more and more, worse and worse, illegality and immorality." Malcolm followed suit. Eventually he was caught by the police, convicted, and sent for several years to state prisons in Massachusetts. The prison provided the context for the next phase in Malcolm's life. Here, learning how to read, he came in contact with a number of books which acquainted him with the exploitation of black people by the white majority throughout world history. Also, while in prison Malcolm established contact and carried on dutiful correspondence with Elijah Muhammad, the chief figure in the Black Muslim movement in America. Consequently on his release from prison he became an assistant to Muhammad, testifying to a religious conversion which impelled him to work for the reclamation of black people's identity as well as their release from religious and economic enslavement to whites. The fourth period in his life begins with his censure by Elijah Muhammad and includes his efforts to transcend the sectarian character of the Black Muslim movement, his richly symbolic journey to Mecca, and his assassination (allegedly by Black Muslim opponents).

It is the mark of "the fraternal self" to see his own religious pilgrimage in terms of the aspirations of a particular group of people. In assuming the struggle of black people as his own, Malcolm X sought to achieve a corporate sense of integrity. Putting forth an ideological scheme and a political stance which might enable his people to honor and implement their own freedom, Malcolm X was responsible for the fusion, in the lives of his followers, of racial consciousness and religious identity.

Autobiography

The Early Years

When my mother was pregnant with me, she told me later, a party of hooded Ku Klux Klan riders galloped up to our home in Omaha, Nebraska, one night. Surrounding the house, brandishing their shotguns and rifles, they shouted for my father to come out. My mother went to the front door and opened it. Standing where they could see her pregnant condition, she told them that she was alone with her three small children, and that my father was away, preaching, in Milwaukee. The Klansmen shouted threats and warnings at her that we had better get out of town because "the good Christian white people" were not going to stand for my father's "spreading trouble" among the "good" Negroes of Omaha with the "back to Africa" preachings of Marcus Garvey.

My father, the Reverend Earl Little, was a Baptist minister, a dedicated organizer for Marcus Aurelius Garvey's U.N.I.A. (Universal Negro Improvement Association). With the help of such disciples as my father, Garvey, from his headquarters in New York City's Harlem, was raising the banner of black-race purity and exhorting the Negro masses to return to their ancestral African

From Malcolm X, *The Autobiography of Malcolm X*, assisted by Alex Haley (New York: Grove Press, 1966). Reprinted by permission of Grove Press, Inc. Copyrights ©1964 by Alex Haley and Malcolm X. Copyright © 1965 by Alex Haley and Betty Shabazz.

homeland—a cause which had made Garvey the most controversial black man on earth.

Still shouting threats, the Klansmen finally spurred their horses and galloped around the house, shattering every window pane with their gun butts. Then they rode off into the night, their torches flaring, as suddenly as they had come.

My father was enraged when he returned. He decided to wait until I was born—which would be soon—and then the family would move. I am not sure why he made this decision, for he was not a frightened Negro, as most then were, and many still are today. My father was a big, six-foot-four, very black man. He had only one eye. How he had lost the other one I have never known. He was from Reynolds, Georgia, where he had left school after the third or maybe fourth grade. He believed, as did Marcus Garvey, that freedom, independence and self-respect could never be achieved by the Negro in America, and that therefore the Negro should leave America to the white man and return to his African land of origin. Among the reasons my father had decided to risk and dedicate his life to help disseminate this philosophy among his people was that he had seen four of his six brothers die by violence, three of them killed by white men, including one by lynching. What my father could not know then was that of the remaining three, including himself, only one, my Uncle Jim, would die in bed, of natural causes. Northern white police were later to shoot my Uncle Oscar. And my father was finally himself to die by the white man's hands.

It has always been my belief that I, too, will die by violence. I have done all that I can to be prepared.

I was my father's seventh child. He had three children by a previous marriage—Ella, Earl, and Mary, who lived in Boston. He had met and married my mother in Philadelphia, where their first child, my oldest full brother, Wilfred, was born. They moved from Philadelphia to Omaha, where Hilda and then Philbert were born.

I was next in line. My mother was twenty-eight when I was born on May 19, 1925, in an Omaha hospital. Then we moved to Milwaukee, where Reginald was born. From infancy, he had some kind of hernia condition which was to handicap him physically for the rest of his life.

Louise Little, my mother, who was born in Grenada, in the British West Indies, looked like a white woman. Her father *was* white. She had straight black hair, and her accent did not sound like a Negro's. Of this white father of hers, I know nothing except her shame about it. I remember hearing her say she was glad that she had never seen him. It was, of course, because of him that I got my reddish-brown "mariny" color of skin, and my hair of the same color. I was the lightest child in our family. (Out in the world later on, in Boston and New York, I was among the millions of Negroes who were insane enough to feel that it was some kind of status symbol to be light-complexioned—that one was actually fortunate to be born thus. But, still later, I learned to hate every drop of that white rapist's blood that is in me.)

Our family stayed only briefly in Milwaukee, for my father wanted to find a place where he could raise our own food and perhaps build a business. The teaching of Marcus Garvey stressed becoming independent of the white man. We went next, for some reason, to Lansing, Michigan. My father bought a house and soon, as had been his pattern, he was doing free-lance Christian preaching in local Negro Baptist churches, and during the week he was roaming about spreading word of Marcus Garvey.

He had begun to lay away savings for the store he had always wanted to own when, as always, some stupid local Uncle Tom Negroes began to funnel stories about his revolutionary beliefs to the local white people. This time, the get-out-of-town threats came from a local hate society called The Black Legion. They wore black robes instead of white. Soon, nearly everywhere my father went, Black Legionnaires were reviling him as an "uppity nigger" for wanting to own a store, for living outside the Lansing Negro district, for spreading unrest and dissension among "the good niggers."

As in Omaha, my mother was pregnant again, this time with my youngest sister. Shortly after Yvonne was born came the nightmare night in 1929, my earliest vivid memory. I remember being suddenly snatched awake into a frightening confusion of pistol shots and shouting and smoke and flames. My father had shouted and shot at the two white men who had set the fire and were running away. Our home was burning down around us. We were lunging and bumping and tumbling all over each other trying to escape. My mother, with the baby in her arms, just made it into the yard before the house crashed in, showering sparks. I remember we were outside in the night in our underwear, crying and yelling our heads off. The white police and firemen came and stood around watching as the house burned down to the ground.

My father prevailed on some friends to clothe and house us temporarily; then he moved us into another house on the outskirts of East Lansing. In those days Negroes weren't allowed after dark in East Lansing proper. There's where Michigan State University is located; I related all of this to an audience of students when I spoke there in January, 1963 (and had the first reunion in a long while with my younger brother, Robert, who was there doing postgraduate studies in psychology). I told them how East Lansing harassed us so much that we had to move again, this time two miles out of town into the country. This was where my father built for us with his own hands a four-room house. This is where I really begin to remember things—this home where I started to grow up.

After the fire, I remember that my father was called in and questioned about a permit for the pistol with which he had shot at the white men who set the fire. I remember that the police were always dropping by our house, shoving things around, "just checking" or "looking for a gun." The pistol they were looking for—which they never found, and for which they wouldn't issue a permit—was sewed up inside a pillow. My father's .22 rifle and his shotgun, though, were right out in the open; everyone had them for hunting birds and rabbits and other game.

homelife
friction filled

After that, my memories are of the friction between my father and mother. They seemed to be nearly always at odds. Sometimes my father would beat her. It might have had something to do with the fact that my mother had a pretty good education. Where she got it I don't know. But an educated woman, I suppose, can't resist the temptation to correct an uneducated man. Every now and then, when she put those smooth words on him, he would grab her.

My father was also belligerent toward all of the children, except me. The older ones he would beat almost savagely if they broke any of his rules—and he had so many rules it was hard to know them all. Nearly all my whippings came from my mother. I've thought a lot about why. I actually believe that as anti-white as my father was, he was subconsciously so afflicted with the white man's brainwashing of Negroes that he inclined to favor the light ones, and I was his lightest child. Most Negro parents in those days would almost instinctively treat any lighter children better than they did the darker ones. It came directly from the slavery tradition that the "mulatto," because he was visibly nearer to white, was therefore "better."

My two other images of my father are both outside the home. One was his role as a Baptist preacher. He never pastored in any regular church of his own; he was always a "visiting preacher." I remember especially his favorite sermon: "That little *black* train is a-comin' . . . an' you better get all your business right!" I guess this also fit his association with the back-to-Africa movement, with Marcus Garvey's "Black Train Homeward." My brother Philbert, the one just older than me, loved church, but it confused and amazed me. I would sit goggle-eyed at my father jumping and shouting as he preached, with the congregation jumping and shouting behind him, their souls and bodies devoted to singing and praying. Even at that young age, I just couldn't believe in the Christian concept of Jesus as someone divine. And no religious person, until I was a man in my twenties—and then in prison—could tell me anything. I had very little respect for most people who represented religion. . . .

The day was to come when our family was so poor that we would eat the hole out of a doughnut; but at that time we were much better off than most town Negroes. The reason was we raised much of our own food out there in the country where we were. We were much better off than the town Negroes who would shout, as my father preached, for the pie-in-the-sky and their heaven in the hereafter while the white man had his here on earth.

I knew that the collections my father got for his preaching were mainly what fed and clothed us, and he also did other odd jobs, but still the image of him that made me proudest was his crusading and militant campaigning with the words of Marcus Garvey. As young as I was then, I knew from what I overheard that my father was saying something that made him a "tough" man. I remember an old lady, grinning and saying to my father, "You're scaring these white folks to death!"

faith

232

One of the reasons I've always felt that my father favored me was that to the best of my remembrance, it was only me that he sometimes took with him to the Garvey U.N.I.A. meetings which he held quietly in different people's homes. There were never more than a few people at any one time—twenty at most. But that was a lot, packed into someone's living room. I noticed how differently they all acted, although sometimes they were the same people who jumped and shouted in church. But in these meetings both they and my father were more intense, more intelligent and down to earth. It made me feel the same way.

I can remember hearing of "Adam driven out of the garden into the caves of Europe," "Africa for the Africans," "Ethiopians, Awake!" And my father would talk about how it would not be much longer before Africa would be completely run by Negroes—"by black men," was the phrase he always used. "No one knows when the hour of Africa's redemption cometh. It is in the wind. It is coming. One day, like a storm, it will be here."

I remember seeing the big, shiny photographs of Marcus Garvey that were passed from hand to hand. My father had a big envelope of them that he always took to these meetings. The pictures showed what seemed to me millions of Negroes thronged in parade behind Garvey riding in a fine car, a big black man dressed in a dazzling uniform with gold braid on it, and he was wearing a thrilling hat with tall plumes. I remember hearing that he had black followers not only in the United States but all around the world, and I remember how the meetings always closed with my father saying, several times, and the people chanting after him, "Up, you mighty race, you can accomplish what you will!"

I have never understood why, after hearing as much as I did of these kinds of things, I somehow never thought, then, of the black people in Africa. My image of Africa, at that time, was of naked savages, cannibals, monkeys and tigers and steaming jungles. . . .

One afternoon in 1931 when Wilfred, Hilda, Philbert, and I came home, my mother and father were having one of their arguments. There had lately been a lot of tension around the house because of Black Legion threats. Anyway, my father had taken one of the rabbits which we were raising, and ordered my mother to cook it. We raised rabbits, but sold them to whites. My father had taken a rabbit from the rabbit pen. He had pulled off the rabbit's head. He was so strong, he needed no knife to behead chickens or rabbits. With one twist of his big black hands he simply twisted off the head and threw the bleeding-necked thing back at my mother's feet.

My mother was crying. She started to skin the rabbit, preparatory to cooking it. But my father was so angry he slammed on out of the front door and started walking up the road toward town.

It was then that my mother had this vision. She had always been a strange woman in this sense, and had always had a strong intuition of things about to happen. And most of her children are the same way, I think. When something is about to happen, I can feel something, sense something. I never have known something to happen that has caught me completely off guard—except once. And that was when, years later, I discovered facts I couldn't believe about a man who, up until that discovery, I would gladly have given my life for.

My father was well up the road when my mother ran screaming out onto the porch. *"Early! Early!"* She screamed his name. She clutched up her apron in one hand, and ran down across the yard and into the road. My father turned around. He saw her. For some reason, considering how angry he had been when he left, he waved at her. But he kept on going.

She told me later, my mother did, that she had a vision of my father's end. All the rest of the afternoon, she was not herself, crying and nervous and upset. She finished cooking the rabbit and put the whole thing in the warmer part of the black stove. When my father was not back home by our bedtime, my mother hugged and clutched us, and we felt strange, not knowing what to do, because she had never acted like that.

I remember waking up to the sound of my mother's screaming again. When I scrambled out, I saw the police in the living room; they were trying to calm her down. She had snatched on her clothes to go with them. And all of us children who were staring knew without anyone having to say it that something terrible had happened to our father.

My mother was taken by the police to the hospital, and to a room where a sheet was over my father in a bed, and she wouldn't look, she was afraid to look. Probably it was wise that she didn't. My father's skull, on one side, was crushed in, I was told later. Negroes in Lansing have always whispered that he was attacked, and then laid across some tracks for a streetcar to run over him. His body was cut almost in half.

He lived two and a half hours in that condition. Negroes then were stronger than they are now, especially Georgia Negroes. Negroes born in Georgia had to be strong simply to survive.

It was morning when we children at home got the word that he was dead. I was six. I can remember a vague commotion, the house filled up with people crying, saying bitterly that the white Black Legion had finally gotten him. My mother was hysterical. In the bedroom, women were holding smelling salts under her nose. She was still hysterical at the funeral.

I don't have a very clear memory of the funeral, either. Oddly, the main thing I remember is that it wasn't in a church, and that surprised me, since my father was a preacher, and I had been where he preached people's funerals in churches. But his was in a funeral home.

And I remember that during the service a big black fly came down and landed on my father's face, and Wilfred sprang up from his chair and he shooed the fly away, and he came groping back to his chair—there were folding chairs for us to sit on—and the tears were streaming down his face. When we went by the casket, I remember that I thought that it looked as if my father's strong black face had been dusted with flour, and I wished they hadn't put on such a lot of it.

Back in the big four-room house, there were many visitors for another week or so. They were good friends of the family, such as the Lyons from Mason, twelve miles away, and the Walkers, McGuires, Liscoes, the Greens, Randolphs, and the Turners, and others from Lansing, and a lot of people from other towns, whom I had seen at the Garvey meetings.

We children adjusted more easily than our mother did. We couldn't see, as clearly as she did, the trials that lay ahead. As the visitors tapered off, she became very concerned about collecting the two insurance policies that my father had always been proud he carried. He had always said that families should be protected in case of death. One policy apparently paid off without any problem—the smaller one. I don't know the amount of it. I would imagine it was not more than a thousand dollars, and maybe half of that.

But after that money came, and my mother had paid out a lot of it for the funeral and expenses, she began going into town and returning very upset. The company that had issued the bigger policy was balking at paying off. They were claiming that my father had committed suicide. Visitors came again, and there was bitter talk about white people: how could my father bash himself in the head, then get down across the streetcar tracks to be run over?

So there we were. My mother was thirty-four years old now, with no husband, no provider or protector to take care of her eight children. But some kind of a family routine got going again. And for as long as the first insurance money lasted, we did all right. . . .

Then, about in late 1934, I would guess, something began to happen. [9 yrs old.] Some kind of psychological deterioration hit our family circle and began to eat away our pride. Perhaps it was the constant tangible evidence that we were destitute. We had known other families who had gone on relief. We had known without anyone in our home ever expressing it that we had felt prouder not to be at the depot where the free food was passed out. And, now, we were among them. At school, the "on relief" finger suddenly was pointed at us, too, and sometimes it was said aloud.

It seemed that everything to eat in our house was stamped Not To Be Sold. All Welfare food bore this stamp to keep the recipients from selling it. It's a wonder we didn't come to think of Not To Be Sold as a brand name.

Sometimes, instead of going home from school, I walked the two miles up the road into Lansing. I began drifting from store to store, hanging around outside where things like apples were displayed in boxes and barrels and baskets, and I would watch my chance and steal me a treat. You know what a treat was to me? Anything!

Or I began to drop in about dinnertime at the home of some family that we knew. I knew that they knew exactly why I was there, but they never embarrassed me by letting on. They would invite me to stay for supper, and I would stuff myself.

Meanwhile, the state Welfare people kept after my mother. By now, she didn't make it any secret that she hated them, and didn't want them in her house. But they exerted their right to come, and I have many, many times reflected upon how, talking to us children, they began to plant the seeds of division in our minds. They would ask such things as who was smarter than the other. And they would ask me why I was "so different."

I think they felt that getting children into foster homes was a legitimate part of their function, and the result would be less troublesome, however they went about it.

And when my mother fought them, they went after her—first, through me. I was the first target. I stole; that implied that I wasn't being taken care of by my mother.

All of us were mischievous at some time or another, I more so than any of the rest. Philbert and I kept a battle going. And this was just one of a dozen things that kept building up the pressure on my mother.

I'm not sure just how or when the idea was first dropped by the Welfare workers that our mother was losing her mind.

But I can distinctly remember hearing "crazy" applied to her by them when they learned that the Negro farmer who was in the next house down the road from us had offered to give us some butchered pork—a whole pig, maybe even two of them—and she had refused. We all heard them call my mother "crazy" to her face for refusing good meat. It meant nothing to them even when she explained that we had never eaten pork, that it was against her religion as a Seventh Day Adventist.

They were as vicious as vultures. They had no feelings, understanding, compassion, or respect for my mother. They told us, "She's crazy for refusing food." Right then was when our home, our unity, began to disintegrate. We were having a hard time, and I wasn't helping. But we could have made it, we could have stayed together. As bad as I was, as much trouble and worry as I caused my mother, I loved her. . .

My mother remained in the same hospital at Kalamazoo for about twenty-six years. Later, when I was still growing up in Michigan, I would go to visit her every so often. Nothing that I can imagine could have moved me so deeply as seeing her pitiful state. In 1963, we got my mother out of the hospital, and she now lives there in Lansing with Philbert and his family.

It was so much worse than if it had been a physical sickness, for which a cause might be known, medicine given, a cure effected. Every time I visited her, when finally they led her—a case, a number—back inside from where we had been sitting together, I felt worse.

My last visit, when I knew I would never come to see her again—there—was in 1952. I was twenty-seven. My brother Philbert had told me that on his last visit, she had recognized him somewhat. "In spots," he said.

~10 yrs old. mother institutionally complete breakdown P.2). she stayed in hosp for 26 yrs.

The Fraternal Self

But she didn't recognize me at all.

She stared at me. She didn't know who I was.

Her mind, when I tried to talk, to reach her, was somewhere else. I asked, "Mama, do you know what day it is?"

She said, staring, "All the people have gone."

I can't describe how I felt. The woman who had brought me into the world, and nursed me, and advised me, and chastised me, and loved me, didn't know me. It was as if I was trying to walk up the side of a hill of feathers. I looked at her. I listened to her "talk." But there was nothing I could do.

I truly believe that if ever a state social agency destroyed a family, it destroyed ours. We wanted and tried to stay together. Our home didn't have to be destroyed. But the Welfare, the courts, and their doctor, gave us the one-two-three punch. And ours was not the only case of this kind.

I knew I wouldn't be back to see my mother again because it could make me a very vicious and dangerous person—knowing how they had looked at us as numbers and as a case in their book, not as human beings. And knowing that my mother in there was a statistic that didn't have to be, that existed because of a society's failure, hypocrisy, greed, and lack of mercy and compassion. Hence I have no mercy or compassion in me for a society that will crush people, and then penalize them for not being able to stand up under the weight.

I have rarely talked to anyone about my mother, for I believe that I am capable of killing a person, without hesitation, who happened to make the wrong kind of remark about my mother. So I purposely don't make any opening for some fool to step into.

Back then when our family was destroyed, in 1937, Wilfred and Hilda were old enough so that the state let them stay on their own in the big four-room house that my father had built. Philbert was placed with another family in Lansing, a Mrs. Hackett, while Reginald and Wesley went to live with a family called Williams, who were friends of my mother's. And Yvonne and Robert went to live with a West Indian family named McGuire.

Separated though we were, all of us maintained fairly close touch around Lansing—in school and out—whenever we could get together. Despite the artificially created separation and distance between us, we still remained very close in our feelings toward each other. . . .

Later, the Event Which Led to Imprisonment

Setting up what I wanted to be the perfect operation, I thought about pulling the white girls into it for two reasons. One was that I realized we'd be too limited relying only upon places where Rudy worked as a waiter. He didn't get to work in too many places; it wouldn't be very long before we ran out of sources. And when other places had to be found and cased in the rich, white residential areas, Negroes hanging around would stick out like sore thumbs, but these white girls could get invited into the right places.

I disliked the idea of having too many people involved, all at the same time. But with Shorty and Sophia's sister so close now, and Sophia and me as though we had been together for fifty years, and Rudy as eager and cool as he was, nobody would be apt to spill, everybody would be under the same risk; we would be like a family unit.

I never doubted that Sophia would go along. Sophia would do anything I said. And her sister would do anything that Sophia said. They both went for it. Sophia's husband was away on one of his trips to the coast when I told her and her sister.

Most burglars, I knew, were caught not on the job, but trying to dispose of the loot. Finding the fence we used was a rare piece of luck. We agreed upon the plan for operations. The fence didn't work with us directly. He had a representative, an ex-con, who dealt with me, and no one else in my gang. Aside from his regular business, he owned around Boston several garages and small warehouses. The arrangement was that before a job, I would alert the representative, and give him a general idea of what we expected to get, and he'd tell me at which garage or warehouse we should make the drop. After we had made our drop, the representative would examine the stolen articles. He would remove all identifying marks from everything. Then he would call the fence, who would come and make a personal appraisal. The next day the representative would meet me at a prearranged place and would make the payment for what we had stolen—in cash.

One thing I remember. This fence always sent your money in crisp, brand-new bills. He was smart. Somehow that had a very definite psychological effect upon all of us, after we had pulled a job, walking around with that crisp green money in our pockets. He may have had other reasons.

We needed a base of operations—not in Roxbury. The girls rented an apartment in Harvard Square. Unlike Negroes, these white girls could go shopping for the locale and physical situation we wanted. It was on the ground floor, where, moving late at night, all of us could come and go without attracting notice.

(In any organization, someone must be the boss. If it's even just one person, you've got to be the boss of yourself.)

At our gang's first meeting in the apartment, we discussed how we were going to work. The girls would get into houses to case them by ringing bells and saying they were saleswomen, poll-takers, college girls making a survey, or anything else suitable. Once in the houses, they would get around as much as they could without attracting attention. Then, back, they would report what special valuables they had seen, and where. They would draw the layout for Shorty, Rudy, and me. We agreed that the girls would actually burglarize only in special cases where there would be some advantage. But generally the three men would go, two of us to do the job while the third kept watch in the getaway car, with the motor running.

The Fraternal Self

Talking to them, laying down the plans, I had deliberately sat on a bed away from them. All of a sudden, I pulled out my gun, shook out all five bullets, and then let them see me put back only one bullet. I twirled the cylinder, and put the muzzle to my head.

"Now, I'm going to see how much guts all of you have," I said.

I grinned at them. All of their mouths had flapped open. I pulled the trigger—we all heard it *click*.

"I'm going to do it again, now."

They begged me to stop. I could see in Shorty's and Rudy's eyes some idea of rushing me.

We all heard the hammer *click* on another empty cylinder.

The women were in hysterics. Rudy and Shorty were begging, *"Man . . . Red[1] . . . cut it out man! . . . Freeze!"* I pulled the trigger once more.

"I'm doing this, showing you I'm not afraid to die." I told them. "Never cross a man not afraid to die . . . now, let's get to work!"

I never had one moment's trouble with any of them after that. Sophia acted awed, her sister all but called me "Mr. Red." Shorty and Rudy were never again quite the same with me. Neither of them ever mentioned it. They thought I was crazy. They were afraid of me.

We pulled the first job that night—the place of the old man who hired Rudy to sprinkle him with talcum powder. A cleaner job couldn't have been asked for. Everything went like clockwork. The fence was full of praise; he proved he meant it with his crisp, new money. The old man later told Rudy how a small army of detectives had been there—and they decided that the job had the earmarks of some gang which had been operating around Boston for about a year.

We quickly got it down to a science. The girls would scout and case in wealthy neighborhoods. The burglary would be pulled; sometimes it took no more than ten minutes. Shorty and I did most of the actual burglary. Rudy generally had the getaway car.

If the people weren't at home, we'd use a passkey on a common door lock. On a patent lock, we'd use a jimmy, as it's called, or a lockpick. Or, sometimes, we would enter by windows from a fire-escape, or a roof. Gullible women often took the girls all over their houses, just to hear them exclaiming over the finery. With the help of the girls' drawings and a finger-beam searchlight, we went straight to the things we wanted.

Sometimes the victims were in their beds asleep. That may sound very daring. Actually, it was almost easy. The first thing we had to do when people were in the house was to wait, very still, and pick up the sounds of breathing. Snorers we loved; they made it real easy. In stockinged feet, we'd go right into the bedrooms. Moving swiftly, like shadows, we would lift clothes, watches, wallets, handbags, and jewelry boxes.

[1] "Red" is Malcolm's nickname, designating his light complexion.

The Christmas season was Santa Claus for us; people had expensive presents lying all over their houses. And they had taken more cash than usual out of their banks. Sometimes, working earlier than we usually did, we even worked houses that we hadn't cased. If the shades were drawn full, and no lights were on, and there was no answer when one of the girls rang the bell, we would take the chance and go in.

I can give you a very good tip if you want to keep burglars out of your house. A light on for the burglar to see is the very best single means of protection. One of the ideal things is to leave a bathroom light on all night. The bathroom is one place where somebody could be, for any length of time, at any time of the night, and he would be likely to hear the slightest strange sound. The burglar, knowing this, won't try to enter. It's also the cheapest possible protection. The kilowatts are a lot cheaper than your valuables.

We became efficient. The fence sometimes relayed tips as to where we could find good loot. It was in this way that for one period, one of our best periods, I remember, we specialized in Oriental rugs. I have always suspected that the fence himself sold the rugs to the people we stole them from. But, anyway, you wouldn't imagine the value of those things. I remember one small one that brought us a thousand dollars. There's no telling what the fence got for it. Every burglar knew that fences robbed the burglars worse than the burglars had robbed the victims.

Our only close brush with the law came once when we were making our getaway, three of us in the front seat of the car, and the back seat loaded with stuff. Suddenly we saw a police car round the corner, coming toward us, and it went on past us. They were just cruising. But then in the rear-view mirror, we saw them make a U-turn, and we knew they were going to flash us to stop. They had spotted us, in passing, as Negroes, and they knew that Negroes had no business in the area at that hour.

It was a close situation. There was a lot of robbery going on; we weren't the only gang working, we knew, not by any means. But I knew that the white man is rare who will ever consider that a Negro can outsmart him. Before their light began flashing, I told Rudy to stop. I did what I'd done once before—got out and flagged them, walking toward them. When they stopped, I was at their car. I asked them, bumbling my words like a confused Negro, if they could tell me how to get to a Roxbury address. They told me, and we, and they, went on about our respective businesses.

We were going along fine. We'd make a good pile and then lay low awhile, living it up. Shorty still played with his band, Rudy never missed attending his sensitive old man, or the table-waiting at his exclusive parties, and the girls maintained their routine home schedules.

Sometimes, I still took the girls out to places where Shorty played, and to other places, spending money as though it were going out of style, the girls dressed in jewelry and furs they had selected from our hauls. No one knew our hustle, but it was clear that we were doing fine. And sometimes, the girls would come over and we'd meet them either at Shorty's in Roxbury or in our Harvard Square place, and just smoke reefers, and play music. It's a shame to tell on a man, but Shorty was so obsessed with the white girl that even if the lights were out, he would pull up the shade to be able to see that white flesh by the street lamp from outside . . . .

I had put a stolen watch into a jewelry shop to replace a broken crystal. It was about two days later, when I went to pick up the watch, that things fell apart.

As I have said, a gun was as much a part of my dress as a necktie. I had my gun in a shoulder holster, under my coat.

The loser of the watch, the person from whom it had been stolen by us, I later found, had described the repair that it needed. It was a very expensive watch, that's why I had kept it for myself. And all of the jewelers in Boston had been alerted.

The Jew waited until I had paid him before he laid the watch on the counter. He gave his signal—and this other fellow suddenly appeared, from the back, walking toward me.

One hand was in his pocket. I knew he was a cop.

He said, quietly, "Step into the back."

Just as I started back there, an innocent Negro walked into the shop. I remember later hearing that he had just that day gotten out of the military. The detective, thinking he was with me, turned to him.

There I was, wearing my gun, and the detective talking to that Negro with his back to me. Today I believe that Allah was with me even then. I didn't try to shoot him. And that saved my life.

I remember that his name was Detective Slack.

I raised my arm, and motioned to him, "Here, take my gun."

I saw his face when he took it. He was shocked. Because of the sudden appearance of the other Negro, he had never thought about a gun. It really moved him that I hadn't tried to kill him.

Then, holding my gun in his hand, he signaled. And out from where they had been concealed walked two other detectives. They'd had me covered. One false move, I'd have been dead.

I was going to have a long time in prison to think about that.

If I hadn't been arrested right when I was, I could have been dead another way. Sophia's husband's friend had told her husband about me. And the husband had arrived that morning, and had gone to the apartment with a gun, looking for me. He was at the apartment just about when they took me to the precinct.

The detectives grilled me. They didn't beat me. They didn't even put a finger on me. And I knew it was because I hadn't tried to kill the detective.

Malcolm X   241

They got my address from some papers they found on me. The girls soon were picked up. Shorty was pulled right off the bandstand that night. The girls also implicated Rudy. To this day, I have always marveled at how Rudy, somehow, got the word, and I know he must have caught the first thing smoking out of Boston, and he got away. They never got him.

I have thought a thousand times, I guess, about how I so narrowly escaped death twice that day. That's why I believe that everything is written.

The cops found the apartment loaded with evidence—fur coats, some jewelry, other small stuff—plus the tools of our trade. A jimmy, a lockpick, glass cutters, screwdrivers, pencil-beam flashlights, false keys . . . and my small arsenal of guns.

The girls got low bail. They were still white—burglars or not. Their worst crime was their involvement with Negroes. But Shorty and I had bail set at $10,000 each, which they knew we were nowhere near able to raise.

The social workers worked on us. White women in league with Negroes was their main obsession. The girls weren't so-called "tramps," or "trash," they were well-to-do upper-middle-class whites. That bothered the social workers and the forces of the law more than anything else.

How, where, when, had I met them? Did we sleep together? Nobody wanted to know anything at all about the robberies. All they could see was that we had taken the white man's women.

I just looked at the social workers: "Now, what do *you* think?"

Even the court clerks and the bailiffs: "Nice white girls . . . goddam niggers—" it was the same even from our court-appointed lawyers as we sat down, under guard, at a table, as our hearing assembled. Before the judge entered, I said to one lawyer, "We seem to be getting sentenced because of those girls." He got red from the neck up and shuffled his papers: "You had no business with white girls!"

Later, when I had learned the full truth about the white man, I reflected many times that the average burglary sentence for a first offender, as we all were, was about two years. But we weren't going to get the average—not for *our* crime.

I want to say before I go on that I have never previously told anyone my sordid past in detail. I haven't done it now to sound as though I might be proud of how bad, how evil, I was.

But people are always speculating—why am I as I am? To understand that of any person, his whole life, from birth, must be reviewed. All of our experiences fuse into our personality. Everything that ever happened to us is an ingredient.

Today, when everything that I do has an urgency, I would not spend one hour in the preparation of a book which had the ambition to perhaps titillate some readers. But I am spending many hours because the full story is the best way that I know to have it seen, and understood, that I had sunk to the very bottom of the American white man's society when—soon now, in prison—I found Allah and the religion of Islam and it completely transformed my life. . . .

Conversion to Black Muslim Ideology

All of them urged me to "accept the teachings of The Honorable Elijah Muhammad." Reginald explained that pork was not eaten by those who worshiped in the religion of Islam, and not smoking cigarettes was a rule of the followers of The Honorable Elijah Muhammad, because they did not take injurious things such as narcotics, tobacco, or liquor into their bodies. Over and over, I read, and heard, "The key to a Muslim is submission, the attunement of one toward Allah."

And what they termed "the true knowledge of the black man" that was possessed by the followers of The Honorable Elijah Muhammad was given shape for me in their lengthy letters, sometimes containing printed literature.

"The true knowledge," reconstructed much more briefly than I received it, was that history had been "whitened" in the white man's history books, and that the black man had been "brainwashed for hundreds of years." Original Man was black, in the continent called Africa where the human race had emerged on the planet Earth.

The black man, original man, built great empires and civilizations and cultures while the white man was still living on all fours in caves. "The devil white man," down through history, out of his devilish nature, had pillaged, murdered, raped, and exploited every race of man not white.

Human history's greatest crime was the traffic in black flesh when the devil white man went into Africa and murdered and kidnapped to bring to the West in chains, in slave ships, millions of black men, women, and children, who were worked and beaten and tortured as slaves.

The devil white man cut these black people off from all knowledge of their own kind, and cut them off from any knowledge of their own language, religion, and past culture, until the black man in America was the earth's only race of people who had absolutely no knowledge of his true identity.

In one generation, the black slave women in America had been raped by the slavemaster white man until there had begun to emerge a homemade, handmade, brainwashed race that was no longer even of its true color, that no longer even knew its true family names. The slavemaster forced his family name upon this rape-mixed race, which the slavemaster began to call "the Negro."

This "Negro" was taught of his native Africa that it was peopled by heathen, black savages, swinging like monkeys from trees. This "Negro" accepted this along with every other teaching of the slavemaster that was designed to make him accept and obey and worship the white man.

And where the religion of every other people on earth taught its believers of a God with whom they could identify, a God who at least looked like one of their own kind, the slavemaster injected his Christian religion into this "Negro." This "Negro" was taught to worship an alien God having the same blond hair, pale skin, and blue eyes as the slavemaster.

This religion taught the "Negro" that black was a curse. It taught him to hate everything black, including himself. It taught him everything white was good, to be admired, respected, and loved. It brainwashed this "Negro" to think he was superior if his complexion showed more of the white pollution of the slavemaster. This white man's Christian religion further deceived and brainwashed this "Negro" to always turn the other cheek, and grin, and scrape, and bow, and be humble, and to sing, and to pray, and to take whatever was dished out by the devilish white man; and to look for his pie in the sky, and for his heaven in the hereafter, while right here on earth the slavemaster white man enjoyed *his* heaven.

Many a time, I have looked back, trying to assess, just for myself, my first reactions to all this. Every instinct of the ghetto jungle streets, every hustling fox and criminal wolf instinct in me, which would have scoffed at and rejected anything else, was struck numb. It was as though all of that life merely was back there, without any remaining effect, or influence. I remember how, some time later, reading the Bible in the Norfolk Prison Colony library, I came upon, then I read, over and over, how Paul on the road to Damascus, upon hearing the voice of Christ, was so smitten that he was knocked off his horse, in a daze. I do not now, and I did not then, liken myself to Paul. But I do understand his experience.

I have since learned—helping me to understand what then began to happen within me—that the truth can be quickly received, or received at all, only by the sinner who knows and admits that he is guilty of having sinned much. Stated another way: only guilt admitted accepts truth. The Bible again: the one people whom Jesus could not help were the Pharisees; they didn't feel they needed any help.

The very enormity of my previous life's guilt prepared me to accept the truth.

In early 1953, I left the furniture store. I earned a little better weekly pay check working at the Gar Wood factory in Detroit. Where big garbage truck bodies were made, I cleaned up behind the welders each time they finished another truck body.

Mr. Muhammad was saying at his dining table by this time that one of his worst needs was more young men willing to work as hard as they would have to in order to bear the responsibilities of his ministers. He was saying that the teachings should be spreading further than they had, and temples needed to be established in other cities.

The Fraternal Self

It simply had never occurred to me that *I* might be a minister. I had never felt remotely qualified to directly represent Mr. Muhammad. If someone had asked me about becoming a minister, I would have been astonished, and told them I was happy and willing to serve Mr. Muhammad in the lowliest capacity.

I don't know if Mr. Muhammad suggested it or if our Temple One Minister Lemuel Hassan on his own decision encouraged me to address our assembled brothers and sisters. I know that I testified to what Mr. Muhammad's teachings had done for me: "If I told you the life I have lived, you would find it hard to believe me. . . . When I say something about the white man, I am not talking about someone I don't know. . . ."

Soon after that, Minister Lemuel Hassan urged me to address the brothers and sisters with an extemporaneous lecture. I was uncertain, and hesitant—but at least I had debated in prison, and I tried my best. (Of course, I can't remember exactly what I said, but I do know that in my beginning efforts my favorite subject was Christianity and the horrors of slavery, where I felt well-equipped from so much reading in prison.)

"My brothers and sisters, our white slavemaster's Christian religion has taught us black people here in the wilderness of North America that we will sprout wings when we die and fly up into the sky where God will have for us a special place called heaven. This is white man's Christian religion used to brainwash us black people! We have *accepted* it! We have *embraced* it! We have *believed* it! We have *practiced* it! And while we are doing all of that, for himself, this blue-eyed devil has *twisted* his Christianity, to keep his *foot* on our backs . . . to keep our eyes fixed on the pie in the sky and heaven in the hereafter . . . while *he* enjoys *his* heaven right *here* . . . on *this earth* . . . in *this life.*"

Today when thousands of Muslims and others have been audiences out before me, when audiences of millions have been beyond radio and television microphones, I'm sure I rarely feel as much electricity as was then generated in me by the upturned faces of those seventy-five or a hundred Muslims, plus other curious visitors, sitting there in our storefront temple with the squealing of pigs filtering in from the slaughterhouse just outside.

In the summer of 1953—all praise is due to Allah—I was named Detroit Temple Number One's Assistant Minister.

Every day after work, I walked, "fishing" for potential converts in the Detroit black ghetto. I saw the African features of my black brothers and sisters whom the devilish white man had brainwashed. I saw the hair as mine had been for years, conked by cooking it with lye until it lay limp, looking straight like the white man's hair. Time and again Mr. Muhammad's teachings were rebuffed and even ridiculed. . . . "Aw, man, get out of my face, you niggers are crazy!" My head would reel sometimes, with mingled anger and pity for my poor blind black brothers. I couldn't wait for the next time our Minister Lemuel Hassan would let me speak:

"We didn't land on Plymouth Rock, my brothers and sisters—Plymouth Rock landed on *us!*" . . . "Give *all* you can to help Messenger Elijah Muhammad's independence program for the black man! . . . This white man always has controlled us black people by keeping us running to him begging, 'Please, lawdy, please, Mr. White Man, boss, would you push me off another crumb down from your table that's sagging with riches. . . .'

". . . my *beautiful*, black brothers and sisters! And when we say 'black,' we mean everything not white, brothers and sisters! Because *look* at your skins! We're all black to the white man, but we're a thousand and one different colors. Turn around, *look* at each other! What shade of black African polluted by devil white man are you? You see me—well, in the streets they used to call me Detroit Red. Yes! Yes, that raping, red-headed devil was my *grandfather!* That close, yes! My *mother's* father! She didn't like to speak of it, can you blame her? She said she never laid eyes on him! She was *glad* for that! I'm *glad* for her! If I could drain away *his* blood that pollutes *my* body, and pollutes *my* complexion, I'd do it! Because I hate every drop of the rapist's blood that's in me!

"And it's not just me, it's *all* of us! During slavery, *think* of it, it was a *rare* one of our black grandmothers, our great-grandmothers and our great-great-grandmothers who escaped the white rapist slavemaster. That rapist slavemaster who emasculated the black man . . . with threats, with fear . . . until even today the black man lives with fear of the white man in his heart! Lives even today still under the heel of the white man!

"*Think* of it—think of that black slave man filled with fear and dread, hearing the screams of his wife, his mother, his daughter being *taken*—in the barn, the kitchen, in the bushes! *Think* of it, my dear brothers and sisters! *Think* of hearing wives, mothers, daughters, being *raped!* And you were too filled with *fear* of the rapist to do anything about it! And his vicious, animal attacks' offspring, this white man named things like 'mulatto' and 'quadroon' and 'octoroon' and all those other things that he has called us—you and me—when he is not calling us *'nigger'!*

"Turn around and look at each other, brothers and sisters, and *think* of this! You and me, polluted all these colors—and this devil has the arrogance and the gall to think we, his victims, should *love* him!"

I would become so choked up that sometimes I would walk in the streets until late into the night. Sometimes I would speak to no one for hours, thinking to myself about what the white man had done to our poor people here in America. . . .

Malcolm Describes His Journey to Mecca

The first letter was, of course, to my wife, Betty. I never had a moment's question that Betty, after initial amazement, would change her thinking to join

The Fraternal Self

mine. I had known a thousand reassurances that Betty's faith in me was total. I knew that she would see what I had seen—that in the land of Muhammad and the land of Abraham, I had been blessed by Allah with a new insight into the true religion of Islam, and a better understanding of America's entire racial dilemma.

After the letter to my wife, I wrote next essentially the same letter to my sister Ella. And I knew where Ella would stand. She had been saving to make the pilgrimage to Mecca herself.

I wrote to Dr. Shawarbi, whose belief in my sincerity had enabled me to get a passport to Mecca.

All through the night, I copied similar long letters for others who were very close to me. Among them was Elijah Muhammad's son Wallace Muhammad, who had expressed to me his conviction that the only possible salvation for the Nation of Islam would be its accepting and projecting a better understanding of Orthodox Islam.

And I wrote to my loyal assistants at my newly formed Muslim Mosque, Inc. in Harlem, with a note appended, asking that my letter be duplicated and distributed to the press.

I knew that when my letter became public knowledge back in America, many would be astounded—loved ones, friends, and enemies alike. And no less astounded would be millions whom I did not know—who had gained during my twelve years with Elijah Muhammad a "hate" image of Malcolm X.

Even I was myself astounded. But there was precedent in my life for this letter. My whole life had been a chronology of—*changes.*

Here is what I wrote . . . from my heart:

"Never have I witnessed such sincere hospitality and the overwhelming spirit of true brotherhood as is practiced by people of all colors and races here in this Ancient Holy Land, the home of Abraham, Muhammad, and all the other prophets of the Holy Scriptures. For the past week, I have been utterly speechless and spellbound by the graciousness I see displayed all around me by people *of all colors.*

"I have been blessed to visit the Holy City of Mecca. I have made my seven circuits around the Ka'ba, led by a young *Mutawaf* named Muhammad. I drank water from the well of Zem Zem. I ran seven times back and forth between the hills of Mt. Al-Safa and Al-Marwah. I have prayed in the ancient city of Mina, and I have prayed on Mt. Arafat.

"There were tens of thousands of pilgrims, from all over the world. They were of all colors, from blue-eyed blonds to black-skinned Africans. But we were all participating in the same ritual, displaying a spirit of unity and brotherhood that my experiences in America had led me to believe never could exist between the white and the non-white.

"America needs to understand Islam, because this is the one religion that erases from its society the race problem. Throughout my travels in the Muslim world, I have met, talked to, and even eaten with people who in America would have been considered 'white'—but the 'white'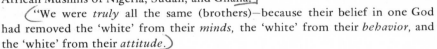attitude was removed from their minds by the religion of Islam. I have never before seen *sincere* and *true* brotherhood practiced by all colors together, irrespective of their color.

"You may be shocked by these words coming from me. But on this pilgrimage, what I have seen, and experienced, has forced me to *re-arrange* much of my thought-patterns previously held, and to *toss aside* some of my previous conclusions. This was not too difficult for me. Despite my firm convictions, I have been always a man who tries to face facts, and to accept the reality of life as new experience and new knowledge unfolds it. I have always kept an open mind, which is necessary to the flexibility that must go hand in hand with every form of intelligent search for truth.

"During the past eleven days here in the Muslim world, I have eaten from the same plate, drunk from the same glass, and slept in the same bed (or on the same rug)—while praying to the *same God*—with fellow Muslims, whose eyes were the bluest of blue, whose hair was the blondest of blond, and whose skin was the whitest of white. And in the *words* and in the *actions* and in the *deeds* of the 'white' Muslims, I felt the same sincerity that I felt among the black African Muslims of Nigeria, Sudan, and Ghana.

"We were *truly* all the same (brothers)—because their belief in one God had removed the 'white' from their *minds,* the 'white' from their *behavior,* and the 'white' from their *attitude.*

"I could see from this, that perhaps if white Americans could accept the Oneness of God, then perhaps, too, they could accept *in reality* the Oneness of Man—and cease to measure, and hinder, and harm others in terms of their 'differences' in color.

"With racism plaguing America like an incurable cancer, the so-called 'Christian' white American heart should be more receptive to a proven solution to such a destructive problem. Perhaps it could be in time to save America from imminent disaster—the same destruction brought upon Germany by racism that eventually destroyed the Germans themselves.

"Each hour here in the Holy Land enables me to have greater spiritual insights into what is happening in America between black and white. The American Negro never can be blamed for his racial animosities—he is only reacting to four hundred years of the conscious racism of the American whites. But as racism leads America up the suicide path, I do believe, from the experiences that I have had with them, that the whites of the younger generation, in the colleges and universities, will see the handwriting on the wall and many of them will turn to the *spiritual* path of *truth*—the *only* way left to America to ward off the disaster that racism inevitably must lead to.

"Never have I been so highly honored. Never have I been made to feel more humble and unworthy. Who would believe the blessings that have been heaped upon an *American Negro?* A few nights ago, a man who would be called in America a 'white' man, a United Nations diplomat, an ambassador, a companion of kings, gave me *his* hotel suite, *his* bed. By this man, His Excellency Prince Faisal, who rules this Holy Land, was made aware of my presence here in Jedda. The very next morning, Prince Faisal's son, in person, informed me that by the will and decree of his esteemed father, I was to be a State Guest.

"The Deputy Chief of Protocol himself took me before the Hajj Court. His Holiness Sheikh Muhammad Harkon himself okayed my visit to Mecca. His Holiness gave me two books on Islam, with his personal seal and autograph, and he told me that he prayed that I would be a successful preacher of Islam in America. A car, a driver, and a guide have been placed at my disposal, making it possible for me to travel about this Holy Land almost at will. The government provides air-conditioned quarters and servants in each city that I visit. Never would I have even thought of dreaming that I would ever be a recipient of such honors—honors that in America would be bestowed upon a King—not a Negro.

"All praise is due to Allah, the Lord of all the Worlds.

"Sincerely,

"El-Hajj Malik El-Shabazz
"(Malcolm X)"

After Mecca: Back in America

One of the major troubles that I was having in building the organization that I wanted—an all-black organization whose ultimate objective was to help create a society in which there could exist honest white-black brotherhood—was that my earlier public image, my old so-called "Black Muslim" image, kept blocking me. I was trying to gradually reshape that image. I was trying to turn a corner, into a new regard by the public, especially Negroes; I was no less angry than I had been, but at the same time the true brotherhood I had seen in the Holy World had influenced me to recognize that anger can blind human vision.

Every free moment I could find, I did a lot of talking to key people whom I knew around Harlem, and I made a lot of speeches, saying: "True Islam taught me that it takes all of the religious, political, economic, psychological, and racial ingredients, or characteristics, to make the Human Family and the Human Society complete.

"Since I learned the *truth* in Mecca, my dearest friends have come to include *all* kinds—some Christians, Jews, Buddhists, Hindus, agnostics, and even atheists! I have friends who are called capitalists, Socialists, and Communists! Some of my friends are moderates, conservatives, extremists—some are even Uncle Toms! My friends today are black, brown, red, yellow, and *white!*"

I said to Harlem street audiences that only when mankind would submit to the One God who created all—only then would mankind even approach the "peace" of which so much *talk* could be heard . . . but toward which so little *action* was seen.

I said that on the American racial level, we had to approach the black man's struggle against the white man's racism as a human problem, that we had to forget hypocritical politics and propaganda. I said that both races, as human beings, had the obligation, the responsibility, of helping to correct America's human problem. The well-meaning white people, I said, had to combat, actively and directly, the racism in other white people. And the black people had to build within themselves much greater awareness that along with equal rights there had to be the bearing of equal responsibilities.

I knew, better than most Negroes, how many white people truly wanted to see American racial problems solved. I knew that many whites were as frustrated as Negroes. I'll bet I got fifty letters some days from white people. The white people in meeting audiences would throng around me, asking me after I had addressed them somewhere, "What *can* a sincere white person do?"

When I say that here now, it makes me think about that little co-ed I told you about, the one who flew from her New England college down to New York and came up to me in the Nation of Islam's restaurant in Harlem, and I told her that there was "nothing" she could do. I regret that I told her that. I wish that now I knew her name, or where I could telephone her, or write to her, and tell her what I tell white people now when they present themselves as being sincere, and ask me, one way or another, the same thing she asked.

The first thing I tell them is that at least where my own particular Black Nationalist organization, the Organization of Afro-American Unity, is concerned, they can't *join* us. I have these very deep feelings that white people who want to join black organizations are really just taking the escapist way to salve their consciences. By visibly hovering near us, they are "proving" that they are "with us." But the hard truth is this *isn't* helping to solve America's racist problem. The Negroes aren't the racists. Where the really sincere white people have got to do their "proving" of themselves is not among the black *victims*, but out on the battle lines of where America's racism really *is*—and that's in their own home communities; America's racism is among their own fellow whites. That's where the sincere whites who really mean to accomplish something have got to work.

Aside from that, I mean nothing against any sincere whites when I say that as members of black organizations, generally whites' very presence subtly renders the black organization automatically less effective. Even the best white members will slow down the Negroes' discovery of what they need to do, and particularly of what they can do—for themselves, working by themselves, among their own kind, in their own communities.

I sure don't want to hurt anybody's feelings, but in fact I'll even go so far as to say that I never really trust the kind of white people who are always so anxious to hang around Negroes, or to hang around in Negro communities. I

The Fraternal Self

don't trust the kind of whites who love having Negroes always hanging around them. I don't know—this feeling may be a throwback to the years when I was hustling in Harlem and all of those red-faced, drunk whites in the afterhours clubs were always grabbing hold of some Negroes and talking about "I just want you to know you're just as good as I am—" And then they got back in their taxicabs and black limousines and went back downtown to the places where they lived and worked, where no black except servants had better get caught. But, anyway, I know that every time that whites join a black organization, you watch, pretty soon the blacks will be leaning on the whites to support it, and before you know it a black may be up front with a title, but the whites, because of their money, are the real controllers.

I tell sincere white people, "Work in conjunction with us—each of us working among our own kind." Let sincere white individuals find all other white people they can who feel as they do—and let them form their own all-white groups, to work trying to convert other white people who are thinking and acting so racist. Let sincere whites go and teach non-violence to white people!

We will completely respect our white co-workers. They will deserve every credit. We will give them every credit. We will meanwhile be working among our own kind, in our way, in black communities—showing and teaching black men in ways that only other black men can—that the black man has got to help himself. Working separately, the sincere white people and sincere black people actually will be working together.

In our mutual sincerity we might be able to show a road to the salvation of America's very soul. It can only be salvaged if human rights and dignity, in full, are extended to black men. Only such real, meaningful actions as those which are sincerely motivated from a deep sense of humanism and moral responsibility can get at the basic causes that produce the racial explosions in America today. Otherwise, the racial explosions are only going to grow worse. Certainly nothing is ever going to be solved by throwing upon me and other so-called black "extremists" and "demagogues" the blame for the racism that is in America.

Sometimes, I have dared to dream to myself that one day, history may even say that my voice—which disturbed the white man's smugness, and his arrogance, and his complacency—that my voice helped to save America from a grave, possibly even a fatal catastrophe.

Suggestions for Further Reading

James Baldwin, *Nobody Knows My Name: More Notes of a Native Son* (New York: The Dial Press, 1961).

Lerone Bennett Jr., *The Negro Mood and Other Essays* (Chicago: Johnson, 1964).

George Breitman, editor, *Malcolm X Speaks* (New York: Grove Press, 1965).

William Brink and Louis Harris, *Black and White: A Study of U.S. Racial Attitudes Today* (New York: Simon and Schuster, 1966).

H. Rap Brown, *Die Nigger Die!* (New York: The Dial Press, 1969).

Jay David, editor, *Growing Up Black* (New York: William Morrow, 1968).

Melvin Drimmer, editor, *Black History: A Reappraisal* (Garden City, N.Y.: Doubleday, 1968).

Archie Epps, editor, *The Speeches of Malcolm X at Harvard* (New York: William Morrow, 1968).

John Hope Franklin, editor, *Three Negro Classics: Up From Slavery, The Souls of Black Folk and The Autobiography of an Ex-Colored Man* (New York: Avon Books, 1965).

Eli Ginzberg and Alfred S. Eichner, *The Troublesome Presence: American Democracy and the Negro* (Glencoe, Ill.: The Free Press, 1964).

Martin Luther King, Jr., *Why We Can't Wait* (New York: Harper and Row, 1963).

William M. Kunstler, *Deep in My Heart* (New York: William Morrow, 1966).

C. Eric Lincoln, *My Face is Black* (Boston: Beacon Press, 1964).

_____, *Sounds of the Struggle: Persons and Perspectives in Civil Rights* (New York: William Morrow, 1967).

_____, *The Black Muslims in America* (Boston: Beacon Press, 1961).

Jack Mendelsohn, *The Martyrs: Sixteen Who Gave Their Lives for Racial Justice* (New York: Harper and Row, 1967).

Gilbert Osofsky, *The Burden of Race: A Documentary History of Negro-White Relations in America* (New York: Harper and Row, 1967).

Benjamin Quarles, *The Negro in the Making of America* (New York: Collier Books, 1964).

Benjamin Scott, *The Coming of the Black Man* (Boston: Beacon Press, 1969).

Robert L. Scott and Wayne Brockriede, *The Rhetoric of Black Power* (New York: Harper and Row, 1969).

Dorothy Sterling, *Tear Down the Walls* (Garden City, N.Y.: Doubleday, 1968).

Stanton L. Wormley and Lewis H. Fenderson, editors, *Many Shades of Black* (New York: William Morrow, 1969).

Richard L. Rubenstein

The Making of a Rabbi

*Had I rejected myself as a
Jew, I would have had to enthrone
the opinions of others as ultimately
decisive for my inner life. I could
not grant the world that tyranny
over me.*

Richard L. Rubenstein was born in New York City on January 8, 1924. He attended Hebrew Union College from 1942 to 1945 and received his baccalaureate degree from the University of Cincinnati in 1946. He became a rabbi in 1952 upon his graduation from Jewish Theological Seminary and earned the PhD. from Harvard University in 1960.

Since 1958 Rabbi Rubenstein has been university chaplain to Jewish students at the University of Pittsburgh and at Carnegie Institute of Technology. He has also taught at the Jewish Theological Seminary in New York City, and has been Charles E. Merrill lecturer in the humanities at the University of Pittsburgh as well as guest lecturer at the Universities of Edinburgh and Munster.

Referred to occasionally as the only authentic Jewish God-is-dead theologian, Rubenstein is engaged in an attempt to discover the meaning of Jewish existence in the present day. In the book *After Auschwitz* Rubenstein provided testimony for the final destruction of European Judaism. Since *After Auschwitz* he has been turning his attention to the historical and psychological roots of Judaism. *The Religious Imagination*, for example, consists in large part of analyses of rabbinical legends and applications of psychoanalytic theory. Both in his career and in his personal history Rubenstein has been occupied with questions of Jewish identity. The following autobiographical account illustrates how that concern brings career and personal history together.

The Making of a Rabbi

I do not know when I began to fear death. I was first aware of my fright when my grandfather died. I was seven at the time. From then on, my childhood fears centered about the fact that I would some day die.

There were times when I assured myself that science would provide a cure for death long before I became an old man. That hope was not destined to last. By my tenth year I understood that though the miracles of science promised much they would never overcome death. Even as a child, I could never entirely escape the nihilism with which I have struggled ever since. I found it impossible to believe in a providential God. I believed that when I died the whole world of my experience would disappear with me. My world would last only as long as I did. It would then disappear as if it had never been. I was convinced that I had arisen out of nothingness and was destined to return to nothingness. All things human were locked in the same fatality. In the final analysis, omnipotent nothingness was lord of all creation. Nothing in the bleak, cold, unfeeling universe was remotely concerned with human aspiration and longing. Even as a rabbi, I have never really departed from my primordial feelings about my place in the cosmos.

Long before I had read the existentialists, I regarded existence as ultimately gratuitous and absurd. I asked myself why I had come to be. I could only answer that I had been cast up in the world absurdly to no ultimate end or purpose. This was coupled with a tragic sense of life which has never left me. Oblivion was the final destiny of all creation. No matter what a man's aspirations, no matter how impressive his accomplishments, all alike were destined to be enveloped in the indifferent nothingness which was our beginning and will be our end. Even if others survived to appreciate our achievements, it mattered not at all to those in the grave, unaware alike of what they had been and what they had wrought.

I had only the most minimal Hebrew education. I attended Hebrew school at Temple Israel in Long Beach, Long Island, where I spent the better part of my childhood years. I do not recall having learned very much or having been especially interested. Hebrew school was part of the Jewish landscape in suburban Long Beach in the thirties. We came to learn how to read the Hebrew prayers so that we could fulfill the Bar Mitzvah ritual. We learned little more than that. It was very rare for anyone to continue his studies after Bar Mitzvah. I was not even to have a Bar Mitzvah.

Our home was not religiously observant. We did observe Rosh Hashanah and Yom Kippur after a fashion, but the rest of the year was devoid of any sense

From Richard L. Rubenstein, "The Making of a Rabbi," in *The Varieties of Jewish Belief*, edited by Ira Eisenstein (New York: Jewish Reconstructionist Press, 1965). Reprinted by permission.

The Fraternal Self

of the majesty of Jewish tradition. We did not keep any of the dietary laws. Ham and bacon were deliberately included in our diet. My mother came from a traditional religious background. Her parents were very religious immigrants from Lithuania. Because of her background, she was incapable of eating meat and dairy products together or of eating pork products. She regarded this as neurotic and wanted to be sure that her children were "free" of such limitations.

Perhaps if I had had a Bar Mitzvah I might never have become seriously interested in Jewish life. I might simply have taken my Jewishness for granted without experiencing the promptings toward rebellion, negation, and reconciliation which were to preoccupy me for so very long. My parents opposed my having a Bar Mitzvah. They rejected the ceremony as superficial and ostentatious. Their refusal was probably more complicated than it seemed at the time. They were both "loners" who did not have a very wide circle of friends. My father's business did not prosper during the thirties. We never quite made it as comfortable members of the Jewish middle class. However, since my mother was one of the relatively few Jewish women who had completed college in the twenties, there really was no other place for her. We had more culture than money. Mother never adjusted to a world in which money counted. It did in Jewish Long Beach. She could never accept the fact that women with far less education invariably made a bigger splash simply because their husbands were doing well. She consoled herself with her superior intellect and turned unsuccessfully toward writing and literary research. In my twelfth year we left Long Beach. We moved to the Bronx for a few months and finally settled in a brownstone apartment on Manhattan's upper East Side. I was constantly aware of the great world of luxury which surrounded us but which I could never enter. I had by this time acquired an overly exaggerated view of the value of the intellect and a deep sense of not belonging anywhere. Had my parents felt at home in the nascent Jewish suburbia of the thirties, I would have had my Bar Mitzvah and taken the normal route to a life as a prosperous Jewish doctor, lawyer, or businessman. By my twelfth year the normal routes were closed to me, though I did not know it.

My parents' refusal to consent to the Bar Mitzvah shocked our more traditional relatives and grieved my maternal grandmother. They felt that something very important was being withheld from me. I wanted a Bar Mitzvah badly. I had no understanding of why the ceremony was so important to me. I remember feeling cheated. I also recall that I was afraid I was no longer quite like the other boys I knew.

I was given a consolation prize. There was an elaborate surprise party at a Rockefeller Center restaurant. All of my cousins came, but it wasn't the same. I had wanted a Bar Mitzvah. My parents were unable to comply. I had been confirmed neither in my identity as a man nor as a Jew at the crucial turning point of adolescence. Had I lived in a community in which the rules of the game of life were relatively explicit, the identity problem would have been less urgent.

Unfortunately I was growing up in the heart of Manhattan where people hardly acknowledged their next-door neighbors.

People joke about the Bar Mitzvah boy's assertion, "Now I am a man." At least he has some confirmation of who he is at a very important turning point in his life. I had none. This was aggravated by the fact that my mother was the real authority at home. She ran things. She had far more formal education than my father, although, in retrospect, I think he knew more about what was really important. The worst blow to his ego came when he had to accept employment from my mother's brother. I suspect that he didn't feel very competent as a man, as a father, or as a breadwinner. I had been exposed neither to the male puberty rite of Judaism nor to a male model whose example might have offered me a measure of confidence in my own development.

The Bar Mitzvah episode was crucial. Unlike my parents, I could never regard religious ritual as without significance. I eventually came to regard ritual as a historically and psychologically authenticated way of dealing with the crises in the timetable of life. Insofar as religious temperaments are either "Catholic" or "Protestant," mine has been strongly "Catholic." I admire believing Orthodox Jews and Roman Catholics for the structure and order in their lives. They have had it given to them; I have had to find it within myself through great and terrible pain. Bar Mitzvah and the Passover Seder were the first rituals which impressed me. As I matured, other rituals were to become meaningful to me.

My adolescence coincided with the Hitler years and the rise of world-wide anti-Semitism. I grew up in a home milieu in which being Jewish was regarded as old fashioned, outmoded, and perhaps even a bit un-American. We did, however, know that we were Jews. We had the normal range of concern for the condition of Jews throughout the world. I found myself thrust into an era in which the Jewish question could not be ignored but in which I had only the most tenuous sort of Jewish identity. I did not know myself either as a man or as a Jew. Self-acceptance as a man and as a Jew were destined to be linked in my life.

I remember one crucial incident very clearly from my high-school days. I had been to a dance for teen-agers at the Ninety-second Street Y.M.H.A. one Saturday evening and was returning home about midnight. Suddenly I heard some drunken Irishmen screaming from across the street, "God damned dirty Jews." They weren't yelling at me, but I very foolishly told them to shut up. It was an uneven encounter. The three of them pounced on me and beat me mercilessly with their umbrellas. They left me on the sidewalk thoroughly beaten. My parents called the police, who were Irish and anti-Semitic. Those were the days when Father Coughlin and the Christian Front had a very strong influence on New York's Irish. The police were not the least concerned about the beating. They were interested in establishing the "fact" that I was potentially delinquent because I had been on the street after midnight. That evening I conceived a bitter hatred for the Irish and a distrust of the police which did not dissipate itself until long after I became a rabbi and came to understand some of the problems of Irish history which engendered their bitterness.

Perhaps the most disturbing aspect of the beating was my parents' helplessness in the face of the hostility of the police. I was more disturbed by their lack of political *savoir-faire* and their desire not to make trouble than by the beating itself. At this point Jewishness seemed even emptier and more meaningless than ever. It appeared to me as an incurable hereditary disease from which I had to liberate myself by whatever means I could muster. The personal beating was the analogue of a world-wide condition which became very real to me when I found myself directly affected by it. My first response was flight.

At the time I was a student at New York's Townsend Harris High School, a special school for bright boys. It is now defunct. Over 90 percent of the student body was Jewish in the late thirties. Moved to rid myself of a seemingly meaningless Jewish burden, I began to study theology with great avidity. I read Gibbon's accounts of the religious conflicts during the decline of the Roman Empire. I spent my afternoons in the local library studying the history and literature of a number of Christian sects. Given my background, it was not surprising that I concluded that Unitarianism was more congruent with my embryonic religious attitudes than any other Christian group. I decided to become a Unitarian.

I did not live far from Manhattan's All Soul's Unitarian Church. I made inquiries and learned that I would be welcome to attend the church's young people's group. I did not have the courage to join alone. My best friend, in spite of my feelings about the Irish, was Bob A., a fellow student at Townsend Harris of Irish background. He was as eager to rid himself of his Irish Catholic identity as I was to divest myself of my Jewish ties. We decided to join the Unitarian youth group together. Being *plus royaliste que le roi,* I became very involved in Unitarian youth activities. I very quickly decided to become a minister. Beneath my surface reasons for wanting to become a minister, there was a pathetic yearning to overcome the curse of a Jewishness I could neither understand nor accept. I was somewhat unhappy that Unitarian ministers did not wear clerical collars. Sometimes, as I sat in a bus or a subway, I envied priests and ministers their collars. I felt that nobody would mistake me for a Jew if I could only wear one.

My desire to enter the ministry reached a crisis in my last year of high school, 1940. There were a number of scholarships available to candidates for the ministry at the better colleges. I began to investigate the available scholarships. In the course of my inquiries I came to know some very helpful Unitarian ministers. One of my new friends suggested that I might stand a better chance of prospering as a Unitarian minister if I changed my name to one less obviously Jewish. He insisted that, while Unitarians were close to Reform Jews theologically, there remained some residual anti-Semitism in Unitarian churches. This made it advisable for me to choose an Anglo-Saxon name.

Richard L. Rubenstein   257

His suggestion fit in with my desire for flight. Nevertheless, at a deeper level, something in me rejected both the suggestion and my recently acquired Unitarian affiliation. There were some things that couldn't be altered. His suggestion made me understand this. I remain grateful to him to this day. Apparently there was a limit to the extent to which I could allow myself to escape the absurd destiny of having been born a Jew in a home in which Jewishness seemed to have so little meaning. When I realized that I could purchase entrance into the non-Jewish world only at the price of a fundamental self-falsification, I refused. In the archaic sensibility of mankind, few things about a man are as important as his name. In an adolescent crisis, I discovered that I could not renounce mine. I had begun my return to Jewish life. At sixteen I had learned that self-contempt was a far greater burden to bear than the hostility of others.

Unitarians very frequently stress their theological similarities to Reform Judaism. When I realized that Unitarianism involved an impossible self-rejection for me, I turned to Reform Judaism. It seemed at first glance to be a kind of Jewish Unitarianism. For some Jews, Reform has proved to be a way out of Judaism; for me it was to be the way in.

When I think of my original decision to enter the rabbinate, it seems silly and even presumptuous. Realizing the impossibility of becoming a Unitarian minister, I resolved to become a Reform rabbi. I knew almost nothing about Jewish life or literature. I could not read Hebrew. It took some effort for me to become accustomed even to the relatively attenuated Reform service I found at Temple Emanuel. I began to study Hebrew and Jewish history. I was aided by several rabbis who were extremely generous with both their time and their personal encouragement. Without their help it would have been impossible for me to enter the Hebrew Union College in Cincinnati, which I did in 1942.

I became a rabbinical student with the most minimal Jewish knowledge. I could barely read Hebrew. I could not understand the language. It was through an act of generosity and good will that I was admitted to the Hebrew Union College at all. The Judaism I had come to know was classical, anti-Zionist Reform Judaism. In spite of the fact that the bloodiest war in mankind's history was then raging, I believed in the progress and enlightenment of mankind. I regarded liberal Judaism, with its lack of ritual, myth, and religious symbolism, as the most rational and therefore the most enlightened of religions. I especially appreciated classical Reform Judaism's bitter opposition to Zionism and Jewish nationalism. Although a war was being fought in which the vast majority of Europe's Jews were slaughtered, I accepted the belief that Jews differed from their fellow citizens in religious persuasion alone. I shared Reform Judaism's optimism concerning human potentialities and its hope that the education and enlightenment of men would eventually end anti-Semitism. I was most comfortable in a deritualized Judaism in which the language of worship was the only one I understood, English. Unaware of the emotional necessities which had brought me to rabbinical training, I was largely incognizant of the power of the irrational in religion or in myself.

I can remember distinctly the objective issues which brought about my disenchantment with classical Reform and my eventual turning to a more traditional Judaism. By the fall of 1944, the facts about the Nazi death camps had become generally known. Reports of the capture of the camp at Madjdanek, Poland, with its huge piles of ownerless shoes, left an indelible impression upon me. I read about Madjdanek at about the same time I was preparing to serve as a student rabbi for the High Holy days in Tupelo, Mississippi.

The revelation of the death camps caused me to reject the whole optimistic theology of liberal religion. People weren't getting any better, nor did I believe they ever would. The evil rooted in human nature would never entirely disappear. Like the plague in Albert Camus's novel, radical evil might lie dormant for long periods but it remained forever capable of disrupting the pathetically weak fragments of reason and decency with which men have constructed their fragile civilization. My generation might add to the treasury of knowledge, but it was incapable of adding significantly to humanity's store of goodness. Each generation had to confront the choice between good and evil unaided by those who went before.

The death camps spelled the end of my optimism concerning the human condition. Though twenty years have passed, I see little reason to alter my pessimism. I regarded the camps and Nazism as far more than a sport of history. They revealed the full potentiality of the demonic as a permanent aspect of human nature. I was all the more shaken because I began to recognize that the difference between the Germans and other men was not very great. Given similar conditions of political and social stress, most of us could commit very terrible crimes. Moral nihilism had, in any event, been one of the deepest strains in my nature. I had struggled to overcome it from childhood, but the anarchic creature of infantile desire within me had never been put to death. During my years at the Hebrew Union College, it had been suppressed by the regnant liberal optimism. The discovery of the Nazi camps again demonstrated its potency to me. The polite, optimistic religion of a prosperous middle class hardly offered much hope against the deep strains of disorder I saw in the world and in myself.

The shock of the extermination camps was paralleled by the shock of realization of the degree to which both the occupied peoples and even the Allies had, to a degree, cooperated in or assented to the Nazi holocaust. I began to understand the relationship between the Christian theology of history and the deep and abiding hatred of the Jew in the Occident. When the death camps were followed by Britain's refusal to permit the entry of the survivors into Palestine, I came to understand the inadequacy of any definition of Jewish life which rested on religious confession alone. Perhaps the healthiest aspect of my understanding of the ethnic aspect of Jewish life was that I could now see myself and the

Richard L. Rubenstein

Jews of eastern Europe as united by ties of common fate and psychology. I had become and remain unimpressed with American Jewish life as a special case.

At about the same time, I became enormously impressed with the Jewish concept of *galuth* or exile. Objectively the destruction of European Jewry and the attempt to establish a new Jewish nation were both expressions of *galuth* as the abiding condition of Jewish life. Liberal Judaism had rejected the notion. Since the war liberal Jewish thinkers have re-examined *galuth* as a meaningful religious category. At the time, many Jewish religious liberals were convinced that we lived in the best of times, in spite of the recent setback, a conviction I found impossible to sustain. I especially remember the blindness with which some of the leaders opposed the establishment of the State of Israel. They insisted that Europe's Jews had an obligation to re-establish themselves and contribute to the liberalism and democracy of their native lands.

The notion of *galuth* seemed to make a great deal of sense both psychologically and existentially. Even in America, I felt that Jews would remain in *galuth* to an extent. *Galuth* had long ceased to be only a Jewish fact. Modern literature is replete with protagonists in real or psychological exile: Kafka's Joseph K., Mann's Joseph, Camus's Mersault, Sartre's Antoine Rocquentin, Melville's Ahab are a few who come to mind. Neither as a Jew nor as an intellectual would I ever entirely be "in," but then who would be? Existence is exile. We are all superfluous men, whether we know it or not. I was surprised that "old fashioned," "unenlightened," traditional Judaism was more directly on target in its description of both the Jewish and the human condition than was "liberal," "progressive," "modern" Judaism. I began to wonder whether I could in good conscience remain tied to a liberal prayer-book and system of worship which so falsified the human condition by its unwarranted optimism.

Exile expresses theologically much the same reality which underlies the concept of alienation in contemporary social science. It has remained a cornerstone of my religious and psychological perspective. At the level of Jewish-Christian relations, I progressively gave up real hope that the Jew could ever feel entirely at home in the gentile world. This may sound harsher than it is meant to be. There are countless gentiles who have experienced a similar alienation, though it does have a special quality for Jews. We are destined to be strangers and wanderers upon the earth to the end of days. Even the State of Israel cannot escape this destiny, being the Jewish nation in a gentile world. Abraham's destiny would never depart from his progeny.

I also turned to the question of *geulah* or redemption, which is the other side of the coin of exile. Classical Reform Judaism was convinced that the Messiah had already come in the form of German and American enlightenment. As one reads the social and intellectual history of the late nineteenth century, one realizes how hopelessly out of touch the Reformers were. Important social forces were preparing a northern European racial tribalism which would effectively isolate all Jews. My pessimistic reading of twentieth-century Jewish

The Fraternal Self

history made me ask the age-old Jewish question, "When will the Messiah come? When will redemption begin?" My real concern was not about a personal Messiah but about the dream of the redemptive alteration of the human condition.

I was very much drawn to the insights of the Jewish mystics on this issue. In the years following the expulsion of the Jewish community from Spain in 1492, Jewish mystics were agonized by a problem similar to the one which had seized our times. The catastrophic destruction of Spanish Jewry made the problems of exile and redemption central to them; the end of European Jewry had made exile and redemption central to me.

The insights of Rabbi Isaac Luria of Safed, Palestine (d. 1572), and his followers have been especially helpful. They saw existence itself as alienation. Even God the Creator could exist only through an act of self-alienation. In their system, the first creative act was the self-diminution, *tsimtsum,* of the absolutely simple Ground of existence into Himself, leaving thereby a space for the created world. According to Luria, the primal act of creation was one in which that which was All, and therefore no discrete limiting thing, withdrew into Himself so that both He and the created world could be limited and defined by each other. This accorded strangely with my earliest nihilism which saw nothingness as the origin and destiny of all things. I saw God as the Holy Nothingness. I had exchanged my atheistic nihilism for a mystical nihilism. To be all that there is, as God was in the beginning and will be in the end, is equivalent to being, so to speak, absolutely nothing. In the beginning, God dwelt in the womb of his own omnipotent nothingness. The first act of creation was an act of self-estrangement whereby the revealed God, in contrast to the primordial hidden ground, and the created world came into existence.

Since the world came into existence, so to speak, out of God's nothingness, all conscious existence is beset by a conflict between the desire for survival, identity, and individual self-maintenance and the yearning to return to its source in God's nothingness. Redemption is return; existence is exile. We purchase identity at the price of estrangement. We know who we are only insofar as we know who we are not. We both crave and fear redemption because its reward and its price are the same: disappearance of the individual into the Source whence he came. This mystical doctrine is not unlike Freud's secularized version of the same conflict in his late work *Beyond the Pleasure Principle.* Freud posited a lifelong conflict between our instinct for life and our yearning to return to the quiescence which preceded our existence. Freud used the metaphor of the *eros-thanatos* conflict. The mystics tended to see the very same conflict in terms of the polarities of the maintenance of the self and the return to the Source. I tended to regard both the mystics and Freud as utilizing different symbolic systems to point to a common reality.

I was particularly struck by the remark a later mystic, Rav Schneur Zalman of Ladi (d. 1813), is reputed to have made. Interrupting his prayers, he declared, "I do not want Your paradise. I do not want Your world to come. I want You and You only."

Eternal separation is external exile. The Rav of Ladi yearned ultimately to return. He also knew, insofar as it is given to any human being to know, what it was he was returning to. Shortly before his death he asked his grandson, "Do you see anything?" The boy was astonished. The Rav then said, "All I can see is the Holy Nothingness which gives life to the world."

Life is exile. Evil, pain, suffering can be ended only by ending life. The Jewish situation, like so many Jewish gestures, exaggerates what is common to all men. The Jewish people remain in exile awaiting the redeeming Messiah. The conflict with Christianity is strongest at this point. The good news of the Church is that the Messiah has come, bringing with him actual or potential redemption. There is sadness in the Jewish rejection of the Christian claim. It rests upon a tragic wisdom which asserts the inevitability of pain and evil, along with real moments of joy and fulfillment, as long as life continues. By asserting that the Messiah will come, the Jewish community was also saying of any given *actual era* that his redemption has yet to begin.

There are many Jewish speculations concerning the time of the coming of the Messiah. Isaac Bashevis Singer, the contemporary novelist, has, I believe, penetrated to the heart of the mystical meaning of the hour of the Messiah at the very end of his novel *The Family Moskat*. As Hitler's armies approach the gates of Warsaw, bringing the final destruction of European Jewry with them, one of Singer's characters affirms that the Messiah will come speedily. This affirmation of faith is greeted with astonishment, whereupon Hertz Yanovar clarifies his assertion: "Death is the Messiah. That is the real truth."

Only death perfects life and ends its problems. God can redeem only by slaying. We have nothing to hope for beyond what we are capable of creating in the time we have allotted to us. Of course, this leaves room for much doing and much creating. Nevertheless, in the final analysis all things crumble away into the nothingness which is at the beginning and end of creation.

If existence is ultimately devoid of hope and God offers us absolutely nothing, why bother with religion at all? I must confess that at a significant level I have much sympathy with the contemporary "death of God" Protestant theologians, though many of their concerns are specifically rooted in the ethos of Christianity, which has had to grapple with the meaning of the death of God involved in the crucifixion of Jesus. The question, "Why religion?" probably is meaningless. There are men and women devoid of all illusion who nevertheless regard withdrawal from the religious community as unthinkable. I am one of them. The decision to partake of the life of a community rests upon forces within the psyche which have little to do with rational argument. There is absolutely no reason for those who can do without religion to bother. At a certain tribal level, religion is inescapable in the United States. Our identities are shaped by the religious groups into which we are born. Our religions are less what we profess than what we inherit. There are Protestant, Catholic, and Jewish atheists. Jewish "death of God" theology is very different from its Christian counterpart. At the level of religious philosophy, Jewish and Christian radical theologians make similar denials. Their life styles inevitably reflect the communities they come from. Was it not Santayana who declared that there is no God but Mary is his mother? Nowhere in America can one find abstract men who are Americans without any other qualification.

Inheritance may influence personal identity. It does not necessarily compel religious commitment or affiliation. Undoubtedly the need for a community of manageable proportions to which one can belong and in which one is welcome has had a lot to do with the proliferation of churches and synagogues in middle-class America. For me, another need determined my affiliation. Like the Polish Jew in the East European *Shtedtl,* the tribesman in an African tribe untouched by "civilization," and the Spanish peasant, I cannot dispense with the institution through which I can dramatize, make meaningful, and share the decisive moments of my life. For me that institution is the synagogue; for all men it is the religious community they have inherited. Of course there is something absurd and irrational about this. I did not choose to be Jewish. It has been one of the givens of my nature, but no religious institution other than the synagogue is psychologically and culturally appropriate for my need to celebrate and share the decisive moments of existence. These moments include birth, puberty, marriage, temporary or permanent infirmity, the marking of time irretrievably past, the rearing of children, the need to express and find catharsis for feelings of guilt, the need for personal renewal, and the feeling of awe and wonder which overcomes me when I think about God's nothingness as the ultimate source and the final end.

This may be a highly subjective rationale for synagogue participation, but such subjectivity need not be solipsistic. I suspect other people find the life and liturgy of the synagogue meaningful for similar reasons. Each of the crises I have enumerated tends to be emotionally overdetermined and requires a significant context in which our emotions concerning it can be expressed, objectified, and clarified. Over the years I have come to question the adequacy of non-traditional liturgy for this purpose. The very fact that so much of liberal Jewish liturgy is in the vernacular suggests that it is in the language appropriate to the conscious level of response. There are other levels of response which require drama, grandeur, and mystery. I have found increasingly that the traditional Jewish liturgy, with the fewest possible rationalistic alterations, is the most appropriate vehicle for the expression of both my conscious and my unconscious feelings toward the crises I have enumerated. Myth and ritual are the domains in which we express and project our unconscious feelings concerning the dilemmas of existence. They are indispensable vehicles of expression in an institution in which the decisive moments of existence are to be shared and celebrated at both the conscious and unconscious levels.

Richard L. Rubenstein

263

I have not said much about the details of my spiritual development after the revelation of the death camps at Madjdanek. Much has happened of religious importance since then. I left Reform and completed my rabbinical studies at the Jewish Theological Seminary, ultimately finding academic and intellectual work more suitable to my capacities than the congregational rabbinate. Nevertheless, I prefer to conclude the recital of personal details, insofar as they are relevant to my religious development, with Madjdanek. That is as it should be. I am convinced that the problem of God and the death camps is the central problem for Jewish theology in the twentieth century. The one pre-eminent measure of the adequacy of all contemporary Jewish theologies is the seriousness with which they deal with this supreme problem of Jewish history. The fact of the death camps cannot be dismissed or swept under an intellectual rug. It will not be forgotten. On the contrary, we have yet to experience the full religious impact of the terrible happenings of World War II. The catastrophe of 1939-45 represents a psychological and religious time bomb which has yet to explode fully in the midst of Jewish religious life.

Already there are clear and unmistakable symptoms of Jewish reaction to what took place. The birth of Israel is the most obvious. Another has been the massive defection of young Jews from Jewish life in both Europe and the United States. Young Jews tend to be highly intelligent and well educated. They have learned all the lessons of contemporary skepticism. They know how terrible the price of being a Jew can be in an age of murderous technology. Many of them have said to themselves, especially in western Europe, "If being Jewish involves the threat of a future death camp for my children, I will use the respite between the explosions of anti-Semitism to marry outside the Jewish community and give my children a decent chance to escape this fate." Judaism is simply no longer worth the price of martyrdom for far more young Jews than most of us can possibly imagine. One of the results of the age of "broken symbols," as Paul Tillich has called it, is that martyrdom has gone out of fashion among Jews and has been replaced by the possibility of massive defection.

I suspect that many of us remain Jewish because we have concluded that self-contempt and self-falsification are too great a price to pay for safety. I must affirm my identity as a Jew. I have no choice. That is the kind of man I am. Nevertheless, I see no special virtue in my decision. It is simply my pathway to authenticity as a human being. There have been rewards. Self-acceptance as a Jew has made it possible for me to accept myself as a man and to learn how to live, given a decent respect for the necessities of society, in terms of my own needs and my own perspectives. Had I rejected myself as a Jew, I would have had to enthrone the opinions of others as ultimately decisive for my inner life. I could not grant the world that tyranny over me. I am prepared to do many things that society requires of me, granted their consistency with the canons of human decency, but I am not prepared to bestow upon others the right to determine how I shall think of myself or my community. By accepting myself as a Jew, I have liberated myself from the most futile and degrading of servilities, that of forever attempting to appease the irrational mythology that the Christian world has constructed of the Jew. As long as the Christian world regards a Palestinian Jew as God incarnate, it will find it excessively difficult to see Jews in terms devoid of mythic distortion. The only way I can live free of such distortion is through self-acceptance as a Jew.

I believe I have, against surprising odds, found myself insofar as this is possible. The death camps helped me to understand the religious meaning of our era. Ours is the time of the death of God. That time which Nietzsche's madman had said was too far off has come upon us. I understood the meaning of the death of God when I understood the meaning of Auschwitz and Madjdanek. The terrible fact is that the Germans set out to annihilate European Jewry and they succeeded quite well. Most of the participants in the most monstrous crime in history sleep undisturbed in comfortable and even luxurious beds in their newly prosperous fatherland. There has been no real retribution nor will there be. I doubt that there are even real pangs of conscience. On the contrary, when the *Alte Kameraden* gather together to discuss the good old days in the SS, they undoubtedly recall their murders in the same good spirit as hunters regaling each other with tales of the hunt. God really died at Auschwitz. This does not mean that God is not the beginning and will not be the end. It does mean that nothing in human choice, decision, value, or meaning can any longer have vertical reference to transcendent standards. We are alone in a silent, unfeeling cosmos. Our actions are human actions. Their entailments are human entailments. Morality and religion can no longer rest upon the conviction that divinely validated norms offer a measure against which what we do can be judged. As Jean Paul Sartre has shown in *The Flies,* if we are prepared to accept the consequences of our actions, nothing prevents us from carrying out any crime, even matricide. Though most of us will refrain from antisocial behavior, we do so because of the fear of ourselves and others rather than fear of God.

What then of Judaism? It is the way we Jews share our lives in an unfeeling and silent cosmos. It is the flickering candle we have lighted in the dark to enlighten and to warm us. Somehow it will continue for a very long time because there will always be some men who will accept and affirm what they were born to be. Ultimately, as with all things, it will pass away, for omnipotent Nothingness is Lord of All Creation.

Suggestions for Further Reading

David Bakan, *Sigmund Freud and the Jewish Mystical Tradition* (New York: Schocken Books, 1965).

Martin Buber, *Eclipse of God* (New York: Harper Torchbooks, 1957).

Richard L. Rubenstein

Arthur A. Cohen, *The Natural and the Supernatural Jew* (New York: Pantheon Books, 1962).

Emil L. Fackenheim, "On the Eclipse of God," *Commentary,* Vol. 37, No. 6 (June 1964), pp. 55-60.

_____ *Quest for Past and Future,* (Bloomington, Ind.: Indiana University Press, 1968).

Nahum N. Glatzer, editor, *The Dynamics of Emancipation: The Jew in the Modern Age,* (Boston: Beacon Press, 1965).

Nathan Glazer, *American Judaism* (Chicago: University of Chicago Press, 1957).

Robert Gordis, *The Root and the Branch: Judaism and the Free Society* (Chicago: University of Chicago Press, 1962).

Will Herberg, *Judaism and Modern Man* (New York: Farrar, Straus, and Young, 1951).

_____ *Protestant-Catholic-Jew: An Essay in American Religious Sociology,* revised edition, (Garden City, N.Y.: Anchor Books, 1960).

Max Kadushin, *The Rabbinic Mind* (New York: Blaisdell, 1965).

David Polish, *The Higher Freedom: A New Turning Point in Jewish History* (Chicago: Quadrangle Books, 1965).

Richard L. Rubenstein, *After Auschwitz: Radical Theology and Contemporary Judaism* (Indianapolis: Bobbs-Merrill, 1966).

_____ in *The Condition of Jewish Belief: A Symposium,* edited by the editors of *Commentary Magazine* (New York: Macmillan, 1966), pp. 192-201.

_____ "Did Christians Fail Israel?" *Lutheran Quarterly,* Vol. 20, No. 3 (August 1958), pp. 251-254.

_____ "The Protestant Establishment and the Jews," *Judaism: A Quarterly Journal,* Vol. 14, No. 2 (Spring 1965), pp. 131-145.

_____ *The Religious Imagination: A Study in Psychoanalysis and Jewish Theology* (Indianapolis: Bobbs-Merrill, 1968).

Gershom G. Scholem, *Major Trends in Jewish Mysticism* (New York: Schocken Books, 1961).

_____ "Religious Authority and Mysticism," *Commentary,* Vol. 38, No. 5 (November 1964), pp. 31-39.

_____ "Tradition and Commentary as Religious Categories in Judaism," *Judaism: A Quarterly Journal,* Vol. 15, No. 1 (Winter 1966), pp. 23-39.

Part Four

The Aesthetic Self

Johann Goethe

Poetry and Truth

*The God who stands in immediate
connection with nature, and owns and
loves it as his work, seemed to him
the proper God, who might be brought
into closer relationship with man.*

Johann Wolfgang Goethe, one of the great seminal thinkers in the history of the West, was born in 1749 in the town of Frankfort-on-the-Main. Destined by his father for a career in law, he attended the University of Leipsic for three years beginning in 1765. In the course of his career at Leipsic he turned his attention to poetry and drama. On his return to Frankfort at the end of three years, he was subjected to his father's interrogation regarding his professional ambitions. Eventually they reached an agreement that he would take his law degree at Strassburg. By autumn of 1770 he had passed the law examinations, and, now freed from attendance at law lectures to write his dissertation, he was again able to concentrate on poetry and drama. In 1772 he began to practice law, first in Wetzlar and then in his native town of Frankfort.

The year 1773 was a momentous one for Goethe. That year Charlotte Buff, to whom he was "attracted and enslaved," married his friend Kestner. Although Kestner had been betrothed to Miss Buff before Goethe met her, he nonetheless plunged into an extreme depression which included persistent thoughts of suicide. However, this event opened up for him a career of seemingly unlimited literary prospects. *The Sorrows of Young Werther*, a drama involving a love triangle leading to Werther's decision to take his own life, brought Goethe immediate public acclaim. In 1775 he took up residence at the court at Weimar at the invitation of Duke Karl August. His official role was that of providing dramatic entertainment at the court, but he also distinguished himself through his administrative and political acumen. He was appointed Privy Councillor in 1782.

Toward the end of his first decade in residence at the court Goethe's behavior changed radically. Initially at the center of court activities, he became increasingly solitary and ascetic. His affair with Frau von Stein (which at one point he said was "no longer a passion, but a disease") provided respite from his self-imposed isolation, but it became increasingly clear to him that he must "escape or die." Through his escape to Italy in 1786 he became acquainted with Italian art but especially with what he called the "splendid spectacle" of living nature and humanity. Some biographers have suggested that Goethe underwent a "conversion" during or after his Italian journey. If so, it was the experience of a rebirth through the recovery of his literary creativity, leading to the rejection of his earlier asceticism in a profound appreciation of the natural world.

His penetrating awareness of the spiritual potentialities of nature constituted the heart of his religious sensitivity from this time forward. Martin Buber suggests that the mature Goethe evidenced, perhaps more than any other writer, a deep appreciation of the I-Thou encounter afforded by the individual's meeting with nature. Buber exclaims: "How lovely and how legitimate the sound of the full I of Goethe! It is the I of pure intercourse with nature; nature gives herself to it and speaks unceasingly with it, revealing her mysteries to it but not betraying her mystery." In the following selection, Goethe relates his efforts to penetrate the mystery of nature. He sought in nature the spiritual harmony which transcends the contrarieties of human existence. But nature is "manifested in contradictions," it is both unreasonable and beneficent, arbitrary and providential. From the understanding that nature reveals itself in contradiction, that the God of nature is steeped in paradox, Goethe addressed himself to the "fearful principle" of the daemonic. The daemonic imagination anticipates harmony beyond contrariety and conflict. Acknowledging that the dialectical incorporation of contrarieties into a comprehensive harmony remains a prospect beyond human perception, Goethe nonetheless suggests that the heroic dimension of human existence emerges out of this anticipation. To be heroic is to endure the ultimate mystery of nature and her God.

(There were, of course, other highly significant events in Goethe's life after his return to Weimar from Italy, including his friendship with the poet Schiller, his marriage in 1806, and the completion of *Faust* in 1831, less than a year before his death. The critical event in his life, however, was his trip to Italy.)

Poetry and Truth

Family Influences

On the 28th of August, 1749, at mid-day, as the clock struck twelve, I came into the world, at Frankfort-on-the Maine. My horoscope was propitious: the sun stood in the sign of the Virgin, and had culminated for the day; Jupiter

From Johann Goethe, *The Autobiography of Goethe. Truth and Poetry: From My Own Life*, translated by John Oxenford (London: Henry G. Bohn, 1848).

and Venus looked on him with a friendly eye, and Mercury not adversely; while Saturn and Mars kept themselves indifferent; the Moon alone, just full, exerted the power of her reflection all the more, as she had then reached her planetary hour. She opposed herself, therefore, to my birth, which could not be accomplished until this hour was passed.

These good aspects, which the astrologers managed subsequently to reckon very auspicious for me, may have been the causes of my preservation; for, through the unskilfulness of the midwife, I came into the world as dead, and only after various efforts was I enabled to see the light. This event, which had put our household into sore straits, turned to the advantage of my fellow-citizens, inasmuch as my grandfather, the *Schultheiss*, John Wolfgang Textor, took occasion from it to have an *accoucheur* established, and to introduce or revive the tuition of midwives, which may have done some good to those who were born after me.

When we desire to recall what befell us in the earliest period of youth, it often happens that we confound what we have heard from others with that which we really possess from our own direct experience. Without, therefore, instituting a very close investigation into the point, which after all could lead to nothing, I am conscious that we lived in an old house, which in fact consisted of two adjoining houses, that had been opened into each other. A spiral stair-case led to rooms on different levels, and the unevenness of the stories was remedied by steps. For us children, a younger sister and myself, the favourite resort was a spacious floor below, near the door of which was a large wooden lattice that allowed us direct communication with the street and open air. A bird-cage of this sort, with which many houses were provided, was called a Frame (*Geräms*). The women sat in it to sew and knit; the cook picked her salad there; female neighbors chatted with each other, and the streets consequently in the fine season wore a southern aspect. One felt at ease while in communication with the public. We children, too, by means of these frames, were brought into contact with our neighbors, of whom three brothers Von Ochsenstein, the surviving sons of the deceased Schultheiss, living on the other side of the way, won my love and occupied and diverted themselves with me in many ways. . . .

In the interior of the house my eyes were chiefly attracted by a series of Roman Views, with which my father had ornamented an ante-room. They were engravings by some of the accomplished predecessors of Piranesi, who well understood perspective and architecture, and whose touches were clear and excellent. There I saw every day, the *Piazza del Popolo*, the *Colosseum*, the Piazza of *St. Peter's* and St. Peter's Church, within and without, the castle of *St. Angelo*, and many other places. These images impressed themselves deeply upon me, and my otherwise very laconic father was often so kind as to furnish descriptions of the objects. His partiality for the Italian language, and for every thing pertaining to Italy, was very decided. A small collection of marbles and natural curiosities, which he had brought with him thence, he often showed to

Johann Goethe

us; and he devoted a great part of his time to a description of his travels, written in Italian, the copying and correction of which he slowly and accurately completed, in several parcels, with his own hand. A lively old teacher of Italian, called Giovinazzi, was of service to him in this work. The old man moreover did not sing badly, and my mother every day must accompany him and herself upon the clavichord, and thus I speedily learned the *Solitario bosco ombroso* so as to know it by heart before I understood it.

My father was altogether of a didactic turn, and in his retirement from business liked to communicate to others what he knew or was able to do. Thus, during the first years of their marriage, he had kept my mother busily engaged in writing, playing the clavichord, and singing, by which means she had been laid under the necessity of acquiring some knowledge and a slight readiness in the Italian tongue.

Generally we passed all our leisure hours with my grandmother, in whose spacious apartment we found plenty of room for our sports. She contrived to engage us with various trifles, and to regale us with all sorts of nice morsels. But one Christmas evening, she crowned all her kind deeds, by having a puppet-show exhibited before us, and thus unfolding a new world in the old house. This unexpected drama attracted our young minds with great force; upon the Boy particularly it made a very strong impression, which continued to vibrate with a great and lasting effect. . . .

But an extraordinary event deeply disturbed the Boy's peace of mind, for the first time. On the 1st of November, 1755, the earthquake at Lisbon took place, and spread a prodigious alarm over the world, long accustomed to peace and quiet. A great and magnificent capital, which was, at the same time, a trading and mercantile city, is smitten, without warning, by a most fearful calamity. The earth trembles and totters, the sea roars up, ships dash together, houses fall in, and over them churches and towers, the royal palace is in part swallowed by the waters, the bursting land seems to vomit flames, since smoke and fire are seen everywhere amid the ruins. Sixty thousand persons, a moment before in ease and comfort, fall together, and he is to be deemed most fortunate who is no longer capable of a thought or feeling about the disaster. The flames rage on, and with them rage a troop of desperadoes, before concealed, or set at large by the event. The wretched survivors are exposed to pillage, massacre, and every outrage: and thus, on all sides, Nature asserts her boundless capriciousness.

Intimations of this event had spread over wide regions more quickly than the authentic reports: slight shocks had been felt in many places: in many springs, particularly those of a mineral nature, an unusual receding of the waters had been remarked; and so much the greater was the effect of the accounts themselves, which were rapidly circulated, at first in general terms, but finally with dreadful particulars. Hereupon, the religious were neither wanting in reflections, nor the philosophic in grounds for consolation, nor the clergy in warnings. So complicated an event arrested the attention of the world for a long

The Aesthetic Self

time; and, as additional and more detailed accounts of the extensive effects of this explosion came from every quarter, the minds already aroused by the misfortunes of strangers, began to be more and more anxious about themselves and their friends. Perhaps the demon of terror had never so speedily and powerfully diffused his terrors over the earth.

The Boy, who was compelled to put up with frequent repetitions of the whole matter, was not a little staggered. God, the Creator and Preserver of Heaven and Earth, whom the explanation of the first article of the Creed declared so wise and benignant, having given both the just and the unjust a prey to the same destruction, had not manifested Himself, by any means, in a fatherly character. In vain the young mind strove to resist these impressions. It was the more impossible, as the wise and scripture-learned could not themselves agree as to the light in which such a phenomenon should be regarded.

The next summer gave a closer opportunity of knowing directly that angry God, of whom the Old Testament records so much. A sudden hail-storm, accompanied by thunder and lightning, violently broke the new panes at the back of our house, which looked towards the west, damaged the new furniture, destroyed some valuable books and other things of worth, and was the more terrible to the children, as the whole household, quite beside themselves, dragged them into a dark passage, where, on their knees, with frightful groans and cries, they thought to conciliate the wrathful Deity. Meanwhile, my father, who was alone self-possessed, forced open and unhinged the window-frames, by which we saved much glass, but made a broader inlet for the rain that followed the hail, so that after we were finally quieted, we found ourselves in the rooms and on the stairs completely surrounded by floods and streams of water.

These events, startling as they were on the whole, did not greatly interrupt the course of instruction which my father himself had undertaken to give us children. He had passed his youth in the Cobourg Gymnasium, which stood as one of the first among German educational institutions. He had there laid a good foundation in languages, and other matters reckoned part of a learned education, had subsequently applied himself to jurisprudence at Leipzig, and had at last taken his degree at Giessen. His dissertation, *"Electa de aditione Hereditatis,"* which had been earnestly and carefully written, is yet cited by jurists with approval.

It is a pious wish of all fathers to see what they have themselves failed to attain, realized in their sons, as if in this way they could live their lives over again, and, at last, make a proper use of their early experience . . . He very soon declared, that I must study jurisprudence in Leipzig, for which he retained a strong predilection, and I was afterwards to visit some other university and take my degree. As for this second one he was indifferent which I might choose, except that he had for some reason or other a disinclination to Gottingen, to my disappointment, since it was precisely there that I had placed such confidence and high hopes.

Johann Goethe

He told me further, that I was to go to Wetzlar and Ratisbon as well as to Vienna, and thence towards Italy, although he repeatedly mentioned that Paris should first be seen, because after coming out of Italy nothing could be pleasing.

These tales of my future youthful travels, often as they were repeated, I listened to eagerly, the more since they always led to accounts of Italy, and at last to a description of Naples. His otherwise serious and dry manner seemed on these occasions to relax and quicken, and thus a passionate wish awoke in us children to participate in the paradise he described. . . .My grandfather and grandmother's house stood in the *Friedberg*-street, and appeared to have been formerly a fortress; for, on approaching it, nothing was seen but a large gate with battlements, which were joined on either side to the two neighboring houses. On entering through a narrow passage, we reached at last a tolerably broad court, surrounded by irregular buildings, which were now all united into one dwelling. We usually hastened at once into the garden, which extended to a considerable length and breadth behind the buildings, and was very well kept. The walks were mostly skirted by vine trellises; one part of the space was used for vegetables, and another devoted to flowers, which from spring till autumn adorned in rich succession the borders as well as the beds. The long wall erected towards the south was used for some well-trained espalier peach-trees, the forbidden fruit of which ripened temptingly before us through the summer. Yet we rather avoided this side, because we here could not satisfy our dainty appetites; and we turned to the side opposite, where an interminable row of currant and gooseberry bushes furnished our voracity with a succession of harvests till autumn. Not less important to us was an old, high, wide-spreading mulberry-tree, both on account of its fruits, and because we were told that the silk-worms fed upon its leaves. In this peaceful region my grandfather was found every evening, tending with genial care and with his own hand the finer growths of fruits and flowers; while a gardener managed the drudgery. He was never vexed by the various toils which were necessary to preserve and increase a fine show of pinks. The branches of the peach-trees were carefully tied to the espaliers with his own hands, in a fan-shape, in order to bring about a full and easy growth of the fruit. The sorting of the bulbs of tulips, hyacinths, and plants of a similar nature, as well as the care of their preservation, he entrusted to none; and I still with pleasure recall to my mind how diligently he occupied himself in inoculating the different varieties of roses. That he might protect himself from the thorns, he put on a pair of those ancient leather gloves, of which three pair were given him annually at the Piper's Court, so that there was no dearth of the article. He wore also a loose dressing-gown, and a folded black velvet cap upon his head, so that he might have passed for an intermediate person between Alcinous and Laertes.

All this work in the garden he pursued as regularly and with as much precision as his official business; for, before he came down, he always arranged the list of causes for the next day, and read the legal papers. In the morning he proceeded to the Council House, dined after his return, then nodded in his easy

The Aesthetic Self

chair, and so went through the same routine every day. He conversed little, never exhibited any vehemence, and I do not remember ever to have seen him angry. All that surrounded him was in the fashion of the olden time. I never perceived any alteration in his wains-cotted room. His library contained, besides law works, only the earliest books of travels, sea voyages, and discoveries of countries. Altogether I can call to mind no situation more adapted than his to awaken the feeling of uninterrupted peace and eternal duration.

But the reverence which we entertained for this venerable old man was raised to the highest degree by a conviction that he possessed the gift of prophecy, especially in matters that pertained to himself and his destiny. It is true he revealed himself to no one, distinctly and minutely, except to my grandmother; yet we were all aware that he was informed of what was going to happen, by significant dreams. He assured his wife, for instance, at a time when he was still a junior Councillor, that on the first vacancy he would obtain the place left open on the bench of the *Schoffen*; and soon afterwards when one of those officers actually died of apoplexy, my grandfather gave orders that his house should be quietly got ready prepared on the day of electing and balloting, to receive his guests and congratulators. Sure enough, the decisive gold ball was drawn in his favor. The simple dream by which he had learned this, he confided to his wife as follows: He had seen himself in the ordinary full assembly of Councilmen, where all went on just as usual. Suddenly, the late *Schöff* rose from his seat, descended the steps, pressed him in the most complimentary manner to take the vacant place, and then departed by the door.

Something like this occurred on the death of the *Schultheiss*. They make no delay in supplying this place, as they always have to fear that the Emperor will at some time resume his ancient right of nominating the officer. On this occasion, the messenger of the Court came at midnight to summon an extraordinary session for the next morning; and as the light in his lantern was about to expire, he asked for a candle's end to help him on his way. "Give him a whole one," said my grandfather to the ladies, "he takes the trouble all on my account." This expression anticipated the result—he was made *Schultheiss*; and what rendered the circumstance particularly remarkable was, that although his representative was the third and last to draw at the ballot, the two silver balls first came out, leaving the golden ball at the bottom of the bag for him.

Perfectly prosaic, simple, and without a trace of the fantastic or miraculous, were the other dreams, of which we were informed. Moreover, I remember that once, as a boy, I was turning over his books and memoranda, and found among some other remarks which related to gardening, such sentences as these: "To-night N. N. came to me and said ----" the name and revelation being written in cipher; or "This night I saw ----" all the rest being in cipher, except the conjunctions and similar words, from which nothing could be learned.

It is worthy of note also, that persons who showed no signs of prophetic insight at other times, acquired, for the moment, while in his presence, and that by means of some sensible evidence, presentiments of diseases or deaths which were then occurring in distant places. But no such gift has been transmitted to any of the children or grandchildren, who for the most part have been hearty people, enjoying life, and never going beyond the Actual. . . .

Channeling the Religious Sentiments

It will be taken for granted, that we children had among our other lessons, a continued and progressive instruction in religion. But the Church-Protestantism imparted to us was, properly speaking, nothing but a kind of dry morality: ingenious exposition was not thought of; and the doctrine appealed neither to the understanding nor to the heart. For that reason, there were various secessions from the Established Church. Separatists, Pietists, Herrnhuter (Moravians), Quiet-in-the-Lands, and others differently named and characterized sprang up, all of whom were animated by the same purpose of approaching the Deity, especially through Christ, more closely than seemed to them possible under the forms of the established religion.

The Boy heard these opinions and sentiments constantly spoken of; for the clergy as well as the laity divided themselves into *pro* and *con*. The minority were composed of those who dissented more or less broadly, but their modes of thinking were attracted by originality, heartiness, perseverance, and independence. All sorts of stories were told of their virtues and of the way in which they were manifested. The reply of a certain pious tinman was especially noted, who, when one of his craft attempted to shame him by asking "who is really your confessor?" answered with great cheerfulness and confidence in the goodness of his cause,—"I have a famous one—no less than the confessor of King David."

Things of this sort naturally made an impression on the Boy, and led him into similar states of mind. In fact, he came to the thought that he might immediately approach the great God of Nature, the Creator and Preserver of Heaven and Earth, whose earlier manifestations of wrath had been long forgotten in the beauty of the world, and the manifold blessings in which we participate while upon it. The way he took to accomplish this was very curious.

The Boy had chiefly kept to the first article of Belief. The God who stands in immediate connection with nature, and owns and loves it as his work, seemed to him the proper God, who might be brought into closer relationship with man, as with everything else, and who would take care of him, as of the motion of the stars, the days and seasons, the animals and plants. There were texts of the Gospels which explicitly stated this. The Boy could ascribe no form to this Being; he therefore sought Him in His works, and would, in the good Old Testament fashion, build Him an altar. Natural productions were set forth as images of the world, over which a flame was to burn, signifying the aspirations of man's heart towards his Maker. He brought out of the collection of natural objects which he possessed, and which had been increased as chance directed, the best ores and other specimens. But the next difficulty was, as to how they should be arranged and raised into a pile. His father possessed a beautiful red-lackered music-stand, ornamented with gilt flowers, in the form of a four-sided pyramid, with different elevations, which had been found convenient for quartets, but lately was not much in use. The Boy laid hands on this, and built up his representatives of Nature one above the other in steps, so that it all looked quite pretty and at the same time sufficiently significant. On an early sunrise his first worship of God was to be celebrated, but the young priest had not yet settled how to produce a flame which should at the same time emit an agreeable odor. At last it occurred to him to combine the two, as he possessed a few fumigating pastils, which diffused a pleasant fragrance with a glimmer, if not with a flame. Nay, this soft burning and exhalation seemed a better representation of what passes in the heart, than an open flame. The sun had already risen for a long time, but the neighboring houses concealed the East. At last it glittered above the roofs, a burning-glass was at once taken up and applied to the pastils, which were fixed on the summit in a fine porcelain saucer. Everything succeeded according to the wish, and the devotion was perfect. The altar remained as a peculiar ornament of the room which had been assigned him in the new house. Every one regarded it only as a well-arranged collection of natural curiosities. The Boy knew better, but concealed his knowledge. He longed for a repetition of the solemnity. But unfortunately, just as the most opportune sun arose, the porcelain cup was not at hand; he placed the pastils immediately on the upper surface of the stand; they were kindled, and so great was the devotion of the priest, that he did not observe, until it was too late, the mischief his sacrifice was doing. The pastils had burned mercilessly into the red lacker and beautiful gold flowers, and as if some evil spirit had disappeared, had left their black, ineffaceable footprints. By this the young priest was thrown into the most extreme perplexity. The mischief could be covered up, it was true, with the larger pieces of his show-materials, but the spirit for new offerings was gone, and the accident might almost be considered a hint and warning of the danger there always is in wishing to approach the Deity in such a way. . . .

In my time I had been confided to the religious instruction of a good old infirm clergyman, who had been confessor of the family for many years. The *Catechism*, a *Paraphrase* of it, and the *Scheme of Salvation*, I had at my fingers' ends, I lacked not one of the strongly proving biblical texts, but from all this I reaped no fruit; for as they assured me that the honest old man arranged his chief examination according to an old set form, I lost all pleasure and inclination for the business, spent the last week in all sorts of diversions, laid in my hat the loose leaves borrowed from an older friend, who had gotten them from the clergyman, and unfeelingly and senselessly read aloud all that I should have known how to utter with feeling and conviction.

Johann Goethe

But I found my good-will and my aspirations in this important matter still more paralyzed by a dry, spiritless routine, when I was now to approach the confessional. I was indeed conscious to myself of many failings, but of no great faults; and that very consciousness diminished them, since it directed me to the moral strength which lay within me, and which, with resolution and perseverance, was at last to become master over the old Adam. We were taught that we were much better than the Catholics for this very reason: that we were not obliged to acknowledge anything in particular in the confessional, nay, that this would not be at all proper, even if we wished to do it. This last did not seem right to me; for I had the strangest religious doubts, which I would readily have had cleared up on such an occasion. Now as this was not to be done, I composed a confession for myself, which, while it well expressed my state of mind, was to confess to an intelligent man, in general terms, that which I was forbidden to tell him in detail. But when I entered the old choir of the Barefoot Friars, when I approached the strange latticed closets in which the reverend gentlemen used to be found for that purpose, when the sexton opened the door for me, when I now saw myself shut up in the narrow place face to face with my spiritual grandsire, and he bade me welcome with his weak nasal voice, all the light of my mind and heart was extinguished at once, the well-conned confession-speech would not cross my lips; I opened in my embarrassment the book which I had in hand, and read from it the first short form I saw, which was so general, that anybody might have spoken it with quite a safe conscience. I received absolution, and withdrew neither warm nor cold; went the next day with my parents to the Table of the Lord, and, for a few days, behaved myself as was becoming after so holy an act.

In the sequel, however, there came over me that evil, which from the fact of our religion being complicated by various dogmas, and founded on texts of scripture which admit of several interpretations, attacks scrupulous men in such a manner, that it brings on a hypochondriacal condition, and raises this to its highest point, to fixed ideas. I have known several men who, though their manner of thinking and living was perfectly rational, could not free themselves from thinking about the sin against the Holy Ghost, and from the fear that they had committed it. A similar trouble threatened me on the subject of the communion, for the text that one who unworthily partakes of the Sacrament *eateth and drinketh damnation to himself*, had, very early, already made a monstrous impression upon me. Every fearful thing that I had read in the histories of the middle ages, of the judgments of God, of those most strange ordeals, by red-hot iron, flaming fire, swelling water, and even what the Bible tells us of the draught which agrees well with the innocent, but puffs up and bursts the guilty,—all this pictured itself to my imagination; and formed itself into the most frightful combinations, since false vows, hypocrisy, perjury, blasphemy, all seemed to weigh down the unworthy person at this most holy act, which was so much the more horrible, as no one could dare to pronounce himself worthy, and the forgiveness of sins, by which everything was to be at last done away, was found limited by so many conditions, that one could not with certainty dare appropriate it to oneself.

This gloomy scruple troubled me to such a degree, and the expedient which they would represent to me as sufficient, seemed so bald and feeble, that it gave the bugbear only a more fearful aspect, and, as soon as I had reached Leipzig, I tried to free myself altogether from my connection with the church. How oppressive then must have been to me the exhortations of Gellert, whom, considering the generally laconic style with which he was obliged to repel our obtrusiveness, I was unwilling to trouble with such singular questions, and the less so as in my more cheerful hours I was myself ashamed of them; and at last left completely behind me this strange anguish of conscience, together with church and altar. . . .

The confidence which new friends repose in each other usually develops itself by degrees. Common occupation and tastes are the first things in which a mutual harmony shows itself; then the mutual communication generally extends over past and present passions, especially over love affairs; but it is a lower depth which opens itself, if the connection is to be perfected; the religious sentiments, the affairs of the heart which relate to the imperishable, are the things which both establish the foundation and adorn the summit of a friendship.

The Christian religion was wavering between its own historically positive base and a pure deism, which, grounded on morality, was in its turn to lay the foundation of ethics. The diversity of characters and modes of thought here showed itself in infinite gradations, especially when a leading difference was brought into play by the question arising as to how great a share the reason, and how great a share the feelings could and should bear a part in such convictions. The most lively and ingenious men showed themselves, in this instance, like butterflies, who, quite regardless of their caterpillar state, throw away the chrysalis veil in which they grow up to their organic perfection. Others, more honestly and modestly minded, might be compared to the flowers, which, although they unfold themselves to the most beautiful bloom, yet do not tear themselves from the root, from the mother stalk, nay, rather through this family connection first bring the desired fruit to maturity. Of this latter class was Langer; for, although a learned man, and eminently versed in books, he would yet give the Bible a peculiar pre-eminence over the other writings which have come down to us, and regard it as a document from which alone we could prove our moral and spiritual pedigree. He belonged to those who cannot conceive an immediate connection with the great God of the universe; a mediation, therefore, was necessary for him, an analogy to which he thought he could find everywhere, in earthly and heavenly things. His discourse, which was pleasing and consistent, easily found a hearing with a young man who, separated from worldly things by an annoying illness, found it highly desirable to turn the activity of his mind towards the heavenly. Grounded as I was in the Bible, all that was wanted was merely the faith to explain as divine that which I had hitherto esteemed in human fashion,—a belief, the easier for me, since I had made my first acquaintance with that book as a divine one. To a sufferer, to one who felt himself delicate, nay, weak, the gospel was therefore welcome, and even though Langer, with all his faith, was at the same time a very sensible man, and firmly maintained that one should not let the feelings prevail, should not let oneself be led astray into mysticism, I could not have managed to occupy myself with the New Testament without feeling and enthusiasm.

In such conversations we spent much time, and he grew so fond of me as an honest and well-prepared proselyte, that he did not scruple to sacrifice to many of the hours destined for his fair one, and even to run the risk of being betrayed and looked upon unfavorably by his patron, like Behrisch. I returned his affection in the most grateful manner; and if what he did for me would have been of value at any time, I could not but regard it, in my present condition, as worthy of the highest honor. . . .

Scarcely had I compelled my friend hither, who would rather have been in the open country by the stream, among men, than he playfully assured me that I showed myself a true German. He related to me circumstantially, out of Tacitus, how our ancestors found pleasure in the feelings which nature so provides for us, in such solitudes, with her inartificial architecture. He had not been long discoursing of this, when I exclaimed, "Oh! why did not this precious spot lie in a deeper wilderness! why may we not train a hedge around it, to hallow and separate from the world both it and ourselves! Surely there is no more beautiful adoration of the Deity than that which needs no image, but which springs up in our bosom merely from the intercourse with nature!" What I then felt, is still present to me; what I said, I know not how to recall. This much, however, is certain, that the undetermined, widely-expanding feelings of youth and of uncultivated notions are alone adapted to the sublime, which, if it is to be excited in us through external objects, formless, or moulded into incomprehensible forms, must surround us with a greatness to which we are not equal.

All men, more or less, feel such a disposition of the soul, and seek to satisfy this noble necessity in various ways. But as the sublime is easily produced by twilight and night, when objects are blended, it is, on the other hand, scared away by the day, which separates and sunders everything, and so must it also be destroyed by every increase of cultivation, if it be not fortunate enough to take refuge with the beautiful, and unite itself closely with it, by which both become equally undying and indestructible.

The brief moments of such enjoyments were still more shortened by my meditative friend; but when I turned back into the world, it was altogether in vain that I sought, among the bright and barren objects around, again to arouse such feelings within me; nay, I could scarce retain even the remembrance of them. My heart, however, was too far spoiled to be able to compose itself; it had loved, and the object was snatched away from it; it had lived, and life to it was embittered. A friend who makes it too perceptible that he designs to form you, excites no feeling of comfort; while a woman who is forming you, while she seems to spoil you, is adored as a heavenly, joy-bringing being. But that form in which the idea of beauty manifested itself to me, had vanished far away; it often visited me under the shade of my oak trees, but I could not hold it fast, and I felt a powerful impulse to seek something similar in the distance. . . .

The Image of the Daemonic

We have seen in the course of this Biography how the child, the boy, the youth has endeavored by different ways to approach the super-sensual, first looking with an affection to natural religion, then clinging closely with love to a positive one; further, by concentrating himself makes trial of his own powers, and joyfully gives himself up to the general faith. Whilst he roamed to and fro in the middle spaces of these regions, sought and looked around him, he was met by much which did not seem to belong to either of them, and he believed that he saw more and more distinctly that it is better to turn away one's thoughts from the Immense and Incomprehensible.

He thought that he discovered in Nature, animate and inanimate, with soul and without soul, something which was only manifested in contradictions, and therefore could not be grasped under one conception, still less under one word. It was not godlike, for it seemed unreasonable; not human, for it had no understanding; not devilish, for it was beneficent; not angelic, for it often showed malicious pleasure. It resembled chance, for it exhibited no consequence; it was like Providence, for it hinted at connection. Everything which limits us seemed by it to be penetrable; it seemed to sport in an arbitrary fashion with the necessary elements of our being; it contracted time and expanded space. Only in the impossible did it seem to find pleasure, and the possible it seemed to thrust from itself with contempt.

This principle, which seemed to step in between all other principles, to separate them and to unite them, I named Daemonic, after the example of the ancients, and of those who had become aware of something similar. I sought to save myself before this fearful principle, by fleeing, as was my custom, behind an image.

Among the special parts of the history of the world, which I studied with care, were the events which afterwards made the United Netherlands so famous. I had diligently examined the sources, and sought as far as possible to instruct myself at first hand, and to represent everything all living before me. The situation appeared to me in the highest degree dramatic, and as the principal figure, about whom the others grouped themselves most happily, Count Egmont came before me, whose human and chivalric greatness pleased me most.

Johann Goethe

But for my purpose it was necessary to transform him into a character possessing such qualities as would adorn a youth better than a man in years, an unmarried man better than the father of a family, one who was independent rather than one who, though freely minded, is limited by various relations.

When I had now in my thoughts made him youthful and liberated him from all conditions, I gave him boundless love of life, unlimited self-confidence, the gift of attracting all men to himself, and so of winning the favor of the people, the silent attachment of a princess, the spoken one of a child of Nature, the sympathy of a prudent statesman, and of gaining over to himself the son of his greatest adversary.

The personal bravery which distinguishes the hero is the basis on which his whole life rests, the ground and soil from which it sprung. He knows no dangers, and is dazzled by the approach of the greatest. Through enemies who surround us perhaps we strike our way through, but the nets of state policy are harder to break. The Daemonic element, which is in the play on both sides, in the conflict of which the lovely goes under and the hated triumphs, and then the prospect that out of this a third will spring, which will correspond to the wish of all men, this it is which has procured for the piece, not, indeed, at its first appearance, but later and at the right time, the favor which it now enjoys. And so here, for the sake of many beloved readers, I will anticipate myself and, as I do not know if I can come to speak of it again, will express something of which I became convinced later on.

Although that Daemonic element can manifest itself in all corporeal and incorporeal things, indeed even in animals expresses itself most remarkably, yet it stands especially in the most wonderful connection with man, and forms a power which, if not opposed to the moral order of the world, yet crosses it so that one may be regarded as the warp and the other as the woof.

For the phenomena which are hereby produced there are numerous names; for all philosophies and religions have endeavored in prose and poetry to solve this riddle, and finally to settle the thing which still remains for them henceforward unassailed.

But the Daemonic element appears most fearfully when it comes forward predominatingly in some man. During my life I have been able to observe several, partly near and partly at a distance. They are not always the most excellent men either as regards intelligence or talents, and they seldom recommend themselves by goodness of heart; but a tremendous power issues from them, and they exercise an incredible dominion over all creatures, indeed, even over the elements, and who can say how far such influence will extend? All united moral powers are of no avail against it; in vain all the more enlightened part of mankind make them suspect as either deceivers or deceived, the mass will be attracted by them. Seldom or never do contemporaries find their equals, and they are to be overcome by nothing but by the universe itself with which they began the struggle, and from such remarks that strange but monstrous proverb may have arisen: *Nemo contra Deum, nisi Deus ipse.*

From these loftier reflections I return to my own little life for which also strange events were at hand, clothed at least with a demoniac appearance. From the summit of the Gotthard, turning my back on Italy, I had returned home, because I could not give up Lili. An affection which is based on the hope of mutual possession, of an enduring life union does not die out at once; nay, rather it is nourished by the consideration of the reasonable desires and honest hopes which one cherishes.

It lies in the nature of the thing that in such cases the maiden becomes reconciled sooner than the youth. As the descendants of Pandora, to beautiful children the desirable gift has been allotted of charming and enticing, and more through Nature, with half-purpose, than through affection, and indeed with malice, of gathering men around them, whereby they often run the risk, like the magician's apprentice, of being frightened by the flood of their admirers. And then at last a choice must be made, one must be exclusively preferred, one must lead home the bride.

And how accidental is that which gives a direction to the choice and determines the selecting maiden. I had renounced Lili from conviction, but love made me suspect this conviction. With the same idea Lili had taken leave of me, and I had entered upon the beautiful journey to distract my mind, but it actually produced the opposite effect.

As long as I was absent I believed in the separation, but did not believe in the permanent parting. All memories, hopes, and wishes had a free play. Now I came back, and as the reunion of those who freely and joyfully love one another is a heaven, so the meeting again of two persons separated only on rational grounds is an intolerable purgatory, a fore-court of hell. When I came back into the neighborhood of Lili, I felt all those misunderstandings doubled which had disturbed our relations; when I came once more before her it lay heavy on my heart that she was lost for me. . . .

All this indeed I did not reject, but my planless nature could not wholly harmonize with the purposeful way of my friend; I enjoyed the pleasant feeling of the moment, Lili's image hovered before me waking and dreaming, and mingled with everything else which could have pleased or distracted me. But now I summoned before my soul the seriousness of my great travelling undertaking, and decided in a gentle and agreeable way to set myself free, and in a few days to continue my journey farther. . . .

My father had laid out for me a fine plan of travel, and had given me a little library which should prepare and guide me on the spot. In leisure hours I had had no other entertainment hitherto, even on my last little journey in the coach I had thought of nothing else. Those glorious objects, which from youth up I had got to know through narratives and imitations of all sorts, gathered

Johann Goethe

283

themselves before my soul, and I knew of nothing more desirable than to approach them while I withdrew decidedly from Lili.

Meanwhile I had dressed myself and walked up and down in my room. My serious hostess entered. "What am I to hope?" she cried. "Dearest," said I, "say no more to me, I have decided to return; the grounds for this I have weighed by myself, to repeat them would be fruitless. The resolution must be taken at last, and who shall take it but he whom it most concerns."

I was moved and so was she, and there was a violent scene, which I ended by ordering my servant to engage the post-coach. In vain I begged my hostess to calm herself, and to transform the jesting departure which I took of the company the evening before into a real one; to consider that it was to be regarded as a visit, a postponement for a short time, that my Italian journey was not given up, my return that way was not precluded. She would hear of nothing, and disquieted me still more, deeply moved as I was. The coach stood before the door, everything was packed, the postilion let sound the usual signs of impatience; I tore myself away; she would not let me go, and brought forward all the arguments of the present with so much art that, finally impassioned and inspired, I shouted out the words of Egmont: "Child! Child! No more! Lashed as by invisible spirits the sun steeds of time go on with the light car of our destiny, and nothing remains for us but bravely and composedly to hold fast the reins, and now to the right, now to the left, from a rock here, from a precipice there to avert the wheels. Whither is he going, who knows? Scarcely can he remember whence he came!"

Suggestions for Further Reading

Anon., "Famous Autobiographies," *Edinburgh Review*, CCXIV (1911), pp. 331-56.

Arnold Bergstraesser, *Goethe's Image of Man and Society* (Chicago: Henry Regnery, 1949).

_____, editor, *Goethe and the Modern Age* (Chicago: Henry Regnery, 1950). Contains a valuable essay by Albert Schweitzer.

Berthold Biermann, *Goethe's World as Seen in Letters and Memoirs* (New York: New Directions, 1949).

Robert K. Bishop, "A Preliminary Note on Goethe and Andre Gide," *Modern Language Notes*, LXIV (1949), pp. 326-29.

Ernst Cassirer, *Rousseau, Kant, Goethe*, translated by James Gutmann (Hamden, Conn.: Shoe String Press, 1961).

Kurt Robert Eissler, *Goethe: A Psychoanalytic Study, 1785-1786* (Detroit: Wayne State University Press, 1963).

The Aesthetic Self

Barker Fairley, "Nietzsche and Goethe," *Bulletin of the John Rylands Library*, XVIII (1934), pp. 298-314.

Robert Herndon Fife, "The Problem of Individual Freedom in the Humanists and in Goethe," *Germanic Review*, VII (1932), pp. 291-319.

Henry C. Hatfield, *Aesthetic Paganism in German Literature, from Winckelmann to the Death of Goethe* (Cambridge, Mass.: Harvard University Press, 1964).

Walter A. Kaufmann, "Goethe's Faith and Faust's Redemption," *Monatshefte*, XLI (1949), pp. 365-75.

Ludwig Lewisohn, *Goethe: The Story of a Man* (New York: Farrar, Straus and Giroux, 1949).

Eudo C. Mason, *Goethe's Faust: Its Genesis and Purport* (Berkeley, Calif.: University of California Press, 1967).

Joseph McCabe, *Goethe: The Man and His Character* (Philadelphia, J. B. Lippincott, 1912).

Walter Naumann, "Goethe's Religion," *Journal of the History of Ideas*, XIII (1952), pp. 188-199.

Theodor Reik, *Fragment of a Great Confession: A Psychoanalytic Autobiography* (New York: Citadel Press, 1965).

William S. Rogers, "Gide and Goethe," *Publications of the English Goethe Society*, XVIII (1949), pp. 68-83.

George Santayana, *Three Philosophical Poets: Lucretius, Dante, Goethe* (New York: Doubleday, 1953).

Albert Schweitzer, *Goethe: Four Studies by Albert Schweitzer*, translated by Charles R. Joy, (Boston: Beacon Press, 1949).

John A. Walz, "Increase Mather and Dr. Faust. An American 'Faust-splitter'," *Germanic Review*, XV (1940), pp. 20-31.

Soren Kierkegaard

Journals

*He has found what the great philos-
opher . . . desired, but did not
find: that archimedean point from
which he could lift the whole world,
the point which for that very reason
must lie outside the world, outside
the limitations of time and space.*

Soren Kierkegaard, existential philosopher and dialectician of subjectivity, was born in Copenhagen on May 5, 1813, the seventh child born to Michael and Ane Kierkegaard, his father's second wife. The circumstances of his parents' marriage are crucial to an understanding of his own religious sensitivity. A year following the death of his first wife, Michael Kierkegaard, a frustrated sheepherder, married Ane, a servant girl in the Kierkegaard household, and less than five months later the first child was born. Kierkegaard's discovery of the circumstances of his parents' marriage was a "great earthquake . . . the terrible revolution which suddenly forced upon me a new and infallible law of interpretation of all the facts. Then I suspected that my father's great age was not a divine blessing but rather a curse. . . . There must be a guilt upon the whole family, the punishment of God must be upon it . . ." Thus his father's own belief that a curse rested upon the family gained currency with Soren as well. It seemed substantiated by the fact that by 1834 Kierkegaard's mother and five of the seven children had died, four of the deaths occurring between 1831 and 1834.

In 1838, as a result of his father's death, Kierkegaard resolved to complete his degree in theology at the University of Copenhagen, a course of study which he had begun in 1830. In July 1840 he completed his degree and two months later became engaged to Regine Olsen. A year later he broke off the engagement, evidently because he felt he could not marry Regine without first revealing to her the secret of his father's sin or the curse upon the family. In breaking his engagement to Regine, however, Kierkegaard became clearer about his vocation. Through his engagement he had learned that he was destined to become the exception to the commonplace, that "the curse which rests upon me is never to be allowed to let anyone deeply and inwardly join themselves to me." Out of this experience, this awareness of his exceptionality, he found the language to talk about radical individuality. In his view, authentic Christianity is not mediated through the collective but through the individual—the single isolated individual. His task was to tease men into becoming religious by aiding them to become authentically singular.

In the years which followed the broken engagement until his death at the age of 42, Kierkegaard's writings and public career were directed toward chronicling the dialectic of authentic existence. His vocation was to stage a public drama through which the masses—the rulers of the age—would come to an awareness of their spiritual bankruptcy. Like Newman, Kierkegaard saw the emergence of mass society, at the expense of all other types of authority, to be the problem of the age. He envisioned his work to be that of "translating the masses into individuals." This could be done only through a depiction of the stages on the way toward radical individuality, namely, the life-styles of aesthetic naturalness, ethical judgment, and religious sensitivity. As Kierkegaard confesses in the selection which follows, the question of his vocation hinged on his finding "the idea for which I can live and die." Living with that imperative is what it means to be a Christian.

It has been said that no one prior to Soren Kierkegaard had given as much intensity and personal involvement as he to the exploration of subjectivity. If that be the case, then his *Journals* is an extremely important contribution to the cultivation of self-consciousness.

Journals

1835

July 29. As one goes from the inn through Sortebro across the bare fields that run along the coast, about a mile and a quarter to the north one comes to the highest point in the district, to Gilbjerg. It has always been one of my favourite places. And as I stood there one quiet evening, as the sea struck up its song with a deep and calm solemnity, whilst my eye met not a single sail on the vast expanse of water, and the sea set bounds to the heavens, and the heavens to the sea; whilst on the other side the busy noise of life subsided and the birds sang their evening prayer: the few that are dear to me came forth from their

From Soren Kierkegaard, *The Journals of Soren Kierkegaard*, edited and translated by Alexander Dru (New York: Harper Torchbooks, 1958). Reprinted by permission.

graves, or rather it seemed to me as though they had not died. I felt so content in their midst, I rested in their embrace, and it was as though I were out of the body, wafted with them into the ether above—and the hoarse screech of the gulls reminded me that I stood alone, and everything vanished before my eyes, and I turned back with a heavy heart to mix in the busy world, yet without forgetting such blessed moments.—I have often stood there and looked out upon my past life and upon the different surroundings which have exercised their power upon me; and the pettiness, which is so often the cause of the numerous misunderstandings separating minds which if they properly understood one another would be bound together by indissoluble ties, vanished before my gaze. Seen thus in perspective only the broad and powerful outline showed, and I did not, as so frequently happens to me, lose myself in the moment, but saw everything as a whole and was strengthened to understand things differently, to admit how often I had blundered, and to forgive others.

As I stood there, without that feeling of dejection and despondency which makes me look upon myself as the enclitic of the men who usually surround me, and without that feeling of pride which makes me into the formative principle of a small circle—as I stood there alone and forsaken, and the power of the sea and the battle of the elements reminded me of my own nothingness, and on the other hand the sure flight of the birds recalled the words spoken by Christ: Not a sparrow shall fall to the ground without your Father: then all at once I felt how great and how small I was; then did those two mighty forces, pride and humility, happily unite in friendship. Lucky is the man to whom *that* is possible at every moment of his life; in whose breast those two factors have not only come to an agreement but have joined hands and been wedded—a marriage which is neither a *marriage de convenance* nor a *mésalliance* but a tranquil marriage of love held in the most secret chamber of man's heart, in the holy of holies, where there are few witnesses but where everything proceeds before the eyes of Him who alone witnessed the marriage in the Garden of Eden—a marriage which will not remain unfruitful but bears blessed fruits, as may be seen in the world by an experienced observer; for like cryptogams among plants, they withdraw from the notice of the masses and only the solitary inquirer discovers them and rejoices over his find. His life will flow on peacefully and quietly and he will neither drain the intoxicating cup of pride nor the bitter chalice of despair. He has found what the great philosopher—who by his calculations was able to destroy the enemy's engines of war—desired, but did not find: that archimedean point from which he could lift the whole world, the point which for that very reason must lie outside the world, outside the limitations of time and space.

Gilleleie, August 1, 1835. What I really lack is to be clear in my mind *what I am to do,* not what I am to know, except in so far as a certain understanding must precede every action. The thing is to understand myself, to see what God really wishes me to do; the thing is to find a truth which is true for *me* to find *the idea for which I can live and die.* What would be the use of discovering so-called objective truth, of working through all the systems of philosophy and of being able, if required, to review them all and show up the inconsistencies within each system;—what good would it do me to be able to develop a theory of the state and combine all the details into a single whole, and so construct a world in which I did not live, but only held up to the view of others;— what good would it do me to be able to explain the meaning of Christianity if it had *no* deeper significance *for me and for my life;*—what good would it do me if truth stood before me, cold and naked, not caring whether I recognized her or not, and producing in me a shudder of fear rather than a trusting devotion? I certainly do not deny that I still recognize an *imperative of understanding* and that through it one can work upon men, *but it must be taken up into my life,* and *that is* what I now recognize as the most important thing. That is what my soul longs after, as the African desert thirsts for water. That is what I lack, and that is why I am left standing like a man who has rented a house and gathered all the furniture and household things together, but has not yet found the beloved with whom to share the joys and sorrows of his life. But in order to find that idea, or better still, in order to find myself, it is no use throwing myself still further into life. And that is just what I have done hitherto. That is why I thought it would be a good thing to throw myself into the study of the law so as to develop my sharpness of mind in the complications of life. Here was a great mass of detail in which I could lose myself; here perhaps I might be able to work out a complete whole from given facts, an organum of theft, following up its darker side (and here a certain spirit of association is also extremely remarkable). I therefore wanted to be a barrister so that by putting myself in another man's role I could, as it were, find a substitute for my own life, and find distraction in outward change. That was what I lacked in order to be able *to lead a complete human life* and not merely one of the understanding,[1] so that I should not, in consequence, base the development of my thought upon—well, upon something that is called objective—something that is in any case not my own, but upon something which grows together with the deepest roots of my life, through which I am, so to speak, grafted upon the divine, hold fast to it, even though the whole world fell apart. *That is what I lack and that is what I am striving after.*

It is the divine side of man, his inward action, which means everything, not a mass of information; for that will certainly follow and then all that knowledge will not be a chance assemblage, or a succession of details, without system and without a focusing point. I too have certainly looked for such a centre. I have looked in vain for an anchorage in the boundless sea of pleasure and in the depth of understanding; I have felt the almost irresistible power with which one

---

[1] For otherwise how near man is to madness, in spite of all his knowledge. What is truth but to live for an idea? Ultimately everything must rest upon a postulate; but the moment it is no longer outside him, and he lives in it, then and only then does it cease to be a postulate for him.

pleasure reaches out its hand to the next; I have felt the sort of meretricious ecstasy that it is capable of producing, but also the *ennui* and the distracted state of mind that succeeds it. I have tasted the fruit of the tree of knowledge, and often delighted in its taste. But the pleasure did not outlast the moment of understanding and left no profound mark upon me. It seems as though I had not drunk from the cup of wisdom, but had fallen into it. I have searched with resignation for the principle of my life, by trying to believe that since all things proceeded according to unalterable laws things could not be otherwise and by dulling my ambition and the antennae of my vanity. And because I could not adapt everything to my own mind I withdrew, conscious of my own ability, rather like a worn-out parson resigning with a pension. What did I find? Not my Self, which was what I was looking for (thinking of my soul, if I may so express it, as shut in a box with a spring-lock which external circumstances, by pressing upon the lock, were to open).—And so the first thing to be decided was the seeking and finding of the Kingdom of Heaven. But just as a heavenly body, if we imagine it in the process of constituting itself, would not first of all determine how great its surface was to be and about which other body it was to move, but would first of all allow the centripetal and centrifugal forces to harmonise its existence, and then let the rest take its course, similarly, it is useless for a man to determine first of all the outside and afterwards fundamentals. One must know oneself before knowing anything else (γνῶθι σεαυτον). It is only after a man has thus understood himself inwardly, and has thus seen his way, that life acquires peace and significance; only then is he rid of that tiresome, ill-omened fellow-traveller, the irony of life, which shows itself in the sphere of understanding, bidding true understanding begin with ignorance (Socrates) like God creating the world out of nothing.

Although I am still far from having reached so complete an understanding of myself, I have, with profound respect for its significance, tried to preserve my individuality—worshipped the unknown God. Warned by a premature apprehension I have tried to avoid coming in too close contact with those phenomena whose power of attraction would perhaps exercise too great an influence upon me. I have tried to master them, studied them individually and examined their importance in men's lives, but at the same time guarded against going, like the moth, too near the flame. I have had but little to win or lose from the ordinary run of men. Partly because everything which occupies them—so-called practical life—only interests me slightly; partly because the coldness and lack of interest with which they treat the more profound and spiritual emotions in man have estranged me still further. With few exceptions my associates have not exerted any particular influence upon me. A life which is not clear about itself inevitably displays an uneven surface; they have stopped short at particular facts and their apparent disharmony; they were not sufficiently interested in me to try to resolve them in a higher agreement or to perceive the inner necessity of it. Their opinion of me was therefore always one-sided, and I have, as a result, alternately

The Aesthetic Self

laid too much or too little weight upon their pronouncements. I have now withdrawn from their influence and their possibly misleading effect upon the compass of my life. And so I stand once again at the point where I must begin my life in a different way. I shall now try to fix a calm gaze upon myself and begin to act in earnest; for only thus shall I be able, like the child calling itself "I" with its first conscious action, to call myself "I" in any deeper sense.

But for that patience is necessary, and one cannot reap immediately where one has sown. I shall bear in mind the method of the philosopher who bade his disciples keep silence for three years, after which time all would come right. One does not begin feasting at dawn but at sunset. And so too in the spiritual world it is first of all necessary to work for some time before the light bursts through and the sun shines forth in all its glory. For although it is said that God allows the sun to shine upon the good and the wicked, and sends down rain upon the just and the unjust, it is not so in the spiritual world. And so the die is cast—I cross the Rubicon! This road certainly leads me *to strife;* but I shall not give up. I will not grieve over the past—for why grieve? I will work on with energy and not waste time grieving, like the man caught in the quicksands who began by calculating how far down he had already sunk, forgetting that all the while he was sinking still deeper. I will hurry along the path I have discovered, greeting those whom I meet on my way, not looking back as did Lot's wife, but remembering that it is a hill up which we have to struggle.

Sept. "What!" he said to himself, "the man who penetrates his brother's most secret thoughts, does not that fatal gift bring him to the frightful condition which came upon the Wandering Jew, who wandered through the gay tumult of the world without joy, without hope, without pain, in dull indifference, which is the *caput mortuum* of despair, as though through a dreary and disconsolate desert?"

Oct. 9. The same thing happens to Christianity, or to becoming a Christian, as to all radical cures; one puts it off as long as possible.

Oct. 13. There is a curious connection between Protestantism and the modern political point of view: it is a struggle for the same thing, the sovereignty of the people, which is why it is also interesting to note that the real royalists—in so far as they have not got one view on one subject and an essentially different one on another subject, which in an individual should both be based upon the same principle—lean towards Catholicism.

The real beauty of Lemming's playing (he is a Danish musician; I heard him at the University Club) was that he *stroked* the guitar. The vibrations became almost visible, just as when the moon shines on the sea the waves become almost audible. . . .

1841

My Lord God, give me once more the courage to hope; merciful God let me hope once again, fructify my barren and infertile mind.

My doubt is terrible.—Nothing can withstand it—it is a cursed hunger and I can swallow up every argument, every consolation and sedative—I rush at 10,000 miles a second through every obstacle.

It is a positive starting point for philosophy when Aristotle says that philosophy begins with wonder, not as in our day with doubt. Moreover the world will learn that the thing is not to begin with the negative, and the reason why it has succeeded up to the present is that it has never really given itself over to the negative, and so has never seriously done what it said. Its doubt is mere child's play.

For the rights of understanding to be valid one must venture out into life, out on the sea and lift up one's voice, even though God hears it not, and not stand on the shore and watch others fighting and struggling—only then does understanding acquire its *official sanction*, for to stand on one leg and prove God's existence is a very different thing from going on one's knees and thanking him.

My relation to "her"
August 24, 1849. Infandum me jubes, Regina,
renovare dolorem

Regine Olsen—I saw her first at the Rørdams. I really saw her there before, at a time when I did not know her family. (In a certain sense I feel a responsibility towards Bollette Rørdam. Earlier on she made a certain impression upon me and I perhaps the same impression upon her; but in all innocence, purely intellectual.)

Even before my father died I had decided upon her. He died (Aug. 9, 1838). I read for my examination. During the whole of that time I let her being penetrate mine.

In the summer of 1840 I took my theological examination.

Without further ceremony I thereupon called at their house. I went to Jutland and even at that time I was perhaps fishing for her, *e.g.* by lending them books in my absence and by suggesting that they should read certain passages.

In August I returned. The period from August 9 till the beginning of September I used in the strict sense to approach her.

On September 8 I left my house with the firm purpose of deciding the matter. We met each other in the street outside their house. She said there was nobody at home. I was foolhardy enough to look upon that as an invitation, just the opportunity I wanted. I went in with her. We stood alone in the living room. She was a little uneasy. I asked her to play me something as she usually did. She did so; but that did not help me. Then suddenly I took the music away and closed it, not without a certain violence, threw it down on the piano and said: "Oh, what do I care about music now! It is you I am searching for, it is you whom I have sought after for two years." She was silent. I did nothing else to make an impression upon her; I even warned her against myself, against my melancholy. When, however, she spoke about Schlegel I said: "Let that relationship be a parenthesis; after all the priority is mine." (N.B. It was only on the 10th that she spoke of Schlegel; on the 8th she did not say a word.)

She remained quite silent. At last I left, for I was anxious lest someone should come and find both of us, and she so disturbed. I went immediately to Etatsraad Olsen. I know that I was terribly concerned that I had made too great an impression upon her. I also feared that my visit might lead to a misunderstanding and even harm her reputation.

Her father said neither yes nor no, but he was willing enough as I could see. I asked for a meeting: it was granted to me for the afternoon of the 10th. I did not say a single word to persuade her. She said, Yes.

I immediately assumed a relation to the whole family, and turned all my virtuosity upon her father whom, moreover, I have always loved.

But inwardly, the next day I saw that I had made a false step. A penitent such as I was, my *vita ante acta*, my melancholy, that was enough.

I suffered unspeakably at that time.

She seemed to notice nothing. On the contrary her spirits were so high that once she said she had accepted me out of pity. In short, I have never known such high spirits.

In one sense that was the danger. If she does not take it more to heart, I thought, than her own words betray: "if she thought I only came from force of habit she would break off the engagement at once"; if she does not take it more to heart, then I am saved. I pulled myself together again. In another sense I must admit my weakness, that for a moment she vexed me.

Then I set my whole strength to work—she really gave way and precisely the opposite happened, she gave herself unreservedly to me, she worshiped me. To a certain extent I myself bear the guilt of that. While I perceived the difficulty of the position only too clearly, and recognized that I must use the maximum of strength in order if possible to burst through my melancholy, I had said to her: "Surrender to me; your pride makes everything easier for me." A perfectly true word; honest towards her, melancholy and treacherous towards myself.[2]

And now of course my melancholy woke once more. Her devotion once again put the whole "responsibility" upon me on a tremendous scale, whereas her pride had almost made me free from "responsibility." My opinion is, and my thought was, that it was God's punishment upon me.

I cannot decide clearly what purely emotional impression she made upon me. One thing is certain: that she gave herself to me, almost worshipping me, asking me to love her, which moved me to such an extent that I was willing to risk all for her. How much I loved her is shown by the fact that I always tried to hide from myself how much she had moved me, which however really has no relation to the passions. If I had not been a penitent, had not had my *vita ante acta*, had not been melancholy, my union with her would have made me happier than I had ever dreamed of being. But in so far as I was what, alas, I was, I had to say that I could be happier in my unhappiness without her than with her; she had moved me and I would have liked, more than liked, to have done everything for her.

But there was a divine protest, that is how I understood it. The wedding. I had to hide such a tremendous amount from her, had to base the whole thing upon something untrue.

I wrote to her and sent her back the ring. The letter is to be found word for word in the "psychological experiment." With all my strength I allowed that to become purely historical; for I spoke to no one of it, not to a single man; I who am more silent than the grave. Should the book come into her hands I wanted her to be reminded of it.

What did she do? In her womanly despair she overstepped the boundary. She evidently knew that I was melancholy; she intended that anxiety should drive me to extremes. The reverse happened. She certainly brought me to the point at which anxiety drove me to extremes; but then with gigantic strength I constrained my whole nature so as to repel her. There was only one thing to do and that was to repel her with all my powers.

During those two months of deceit I observed a careful caution in what I said directly to her from time to time: Give in, let me go; you cannot bear it. Thereupon she answered passionately that she would bear anything rather than let me go.

I also suggested giving the appearance that it was she who broke off the engagement, so that she might be spared all offence. That she would not have. She answered: if she could bear the other she could bear this too. And not unsocratically she said: In her presence no one would let anything be noticed and what people said in her absence remained a matter of indifference.

---

[2]To some extent she suspected my condition, for she often answered: "You are never happy; and so it is all one to you whether I remain with you or not." She also once said to me that she would never ask me about anything if only she might remain with me.

The Aesthetic Self

It was a time of terrible suffering: to have to be so cruel and at the same time to love as I did. She fought like a tigress. If I had not believed that God had lodged a veto she would have been victorious.

And so about two months later it broke. She grew desperate. For the first time in my life I scolded. It was the only thing to do.

When I left her I went immediately to the Theatre because I wanted to meet Emil Boesen. (That gave rise to what was then said in Copenhagen, that I had looked at my watch and said to the family that if they had anything more in their minds would they please hurry up as I had to go to the theatre.) The act was over. As I left the stalls Etatsraad Olsen came up to me and said "May I speak to you?" We went together to his house. "It will be her death, she is in absolute despair." I said "I shall calm her down; but everything is settled." He said, "I am a proud man and I find it difficult to say, but I beg you, do not break with her." He was indeed a noble-hearted man; I was deeply moved. But I did not let myself be persuaded. I remained with the family to dinner. I spoke to her as I left. The following morning I received a letter from him saying she had not slept all night, and asking me to go and see her. I went and tried to persuade her. She asked me: "Are you never going to marry?" I answered, "Yes, perhaps in ten years time when I have sown my wild oats; then I shall need some young blood to rejuvenate me." That was a necessary cruelty. Then she said, "Forgive me for the pain I have caused you." I answered: "It is for me to ask forgiveness." She said: "Promise to think of me." I did so. "Kiss me," she said. I did so but without passion. Merciful God!

And so we parted. I spent the whole night crying on my bed. But the next day I behaved as usual, wittier and in better spirits than ever. That was necessary. My brother told me he wanted to go to the family and show them that I was not a scoundrel. "If you do so I will put a bullet through your head," which is the best proof of how deeply concerned I was. I went to Berlin. I suffered greatly. I thought of her every day. Until now I have kept my promise and have prayed for her at least once and often twice a day, in addition to the other times I might think about her.

When the bonds were broken my thoughts were these: either you throw yourself into the wildest kind of life—or else become absolutely religious, but it will be different from the parsons' mixture.

I only remained in Berlin six months. Actually my intention was to remain away a year and a half. The fact that I came back so soon must have attracted her attention. And indeed it did, and she waited for me after Mynster's sermon on the first Sunday after Easter. But I rejected her advances. My intention was to repel her. I did not want her to think that I had been thinking of her whilst I was away. Moreover I knew from Sibbern that she herself had said that she could not bear seeing me. Now that was not the case as I truly saw; but I was obliged to think that she could not bear speaking to me.

For the rest, it would seem she took the most decisive step in her life under my auspices. Shortly before her engagement to Schlegel she discovered me in a

Church. I did not avoid her look. She nodded to me twice. I shook my head. That meant "You must give me up." She nodded again and I nodded in as friendly a manner as possible. That meant "You have retained my love."

Then, after she had become engaged to Schlegel (1843), she met me in the street and greeted me in as friendly and confiding a way as possible. I did not understand her, for I had not heard about the engagement. I only looked enquiringly at her and shook my head. She certainly thought I knew about the engagement and was asking for my approval.

When the banns of marriage were published (1847) I was present in the church.

1841

Oct. 25. . . . You say, "What I have lost or rather what I have deprived myself of," what I have lost, oh, how should you know or understand it. When it is mentioned the best thing you can do is to remain silent—and how should anyone know it better than I who have made the whole of my tremendously reflective soul into as agreeable a frame as possible for her pure depths—my dark thoughts—my melancholy dreams, my brilliant expectations—and above all my inconstancy, in short all that brilliance by the side of her depths—and when I reeled from looking down into her infinite devotion, for there is indeed nothing so infinite as love—or when her feelings did not sink into the depths—but danced above in the easy play of love—

What I have lost, the only thing I loved; what I have lost, in the eyes of men my word of honour; what I have lost, what I still and always shall, and without fearing that shock, stake my honour, my happiness, my pride in—being faithful. . . . Yet at the present moment as I write this, in a cabin shaken by the double movement of a steam-packet, my soul is as shaken as my body.

And in the one case in which I so much desired to act, it is melancholy to see myself assigned as my only activity what is usually left to women and children—to pray.

You say: she was beautiful. Oh what do you know about it; I know it, for her beauty cost me tears—I myself bought flowers with which to adorn her, I would have hung all the adornments of the world upon her, though only as they served to bring out all the hidden beauty within—and as she stood there in all her array—I had to go—as her joyful look, so full of life, met mine—I had to go—and I went out and wept bitterly.

How great is womanly devotion.—But the curse which rests upon me is never to be allowed to let anyone deeply and inwardly join themselves to me. God in heaven knows how often I have suffered when with childish glee I thought out a plan which I thought would really please her, and then had to make it a principle never to carry out anything in the joy of the moment, but wait until understanding and shrewdness had forbidden it, for fear of drawing her nearer to me. My relation to her may, I truly believe, be called unhappy love—I love her—I own her—her only wish is to remain with me—her family implore it—it is my greatest wish—and I have to say no. In order to make it easier for her I will, if possible, make her believe that I simply deceived her, that I am a frivolous man, so as if possible to make her hate me; for I believe that it would always be more difficult for her if she suspected that the cause was melancholy—how like are melancholy and frivolity.

How my pride is humbled because I am not able to return to her. I had set all my pride on being faithful to her, and yet I dare not be so. I am not accustomed to besmirching my honour—it has always been a point of honour with me to remain faithful. And yet in her eyes I am a deceiver, and that is the only way of setting right again what I have done wrong. I have held my ground with a terrible consistency, in spite of all my own inner desires, for I do not heed the outward temptations of men who would interfere with me. And yet there is still a fear which tortures me. Supposing she really becomes convinced that I deceived her, supposing she falls in love with someone else, which I must naturally wish for in many ways—supposing she then suddenly discovers that I really loved her, that I had done so out of love for her, inwardly convinced that it must end badly or that with the greatest joy in the world, and thanks to God, I would share my happiness with her and not my sorrow—then the last would be worse than the first.

I saw a pretty girl to-day—but it does not interest me any more—I do not wish it—no husband can be more faithful to his wife than I am to her. At the same time it is good for me; those little romances distracted me a good deal.

Passion is the real thing, the real measure of man's power. And the age in which we live is wretched, because it is without passion. If, as the good Jonas Olsen wrote in that memorable note, he really could hate as none has hated before, then I should consider myself fortunate in having been contemporary with him, fortunate in having become the object of that hate—that is a real fight.

Here in Berlin a Demoiselle Hedevig Schulze, a Viennese singer, plays the part of Elvira. She is quite pretty, and acts her part vigorously—in her movements, stature, dress (black silk dress, bare neck, white gloves), she bears a striking resemblance to a young lady I once knew.

... And when God wishes to bind a man to him he calls his most faithful servant, his most trustworthy messenger, and it is sorrow, and says to him: hasten after him, overtake him, do not leave his

Soren Kierkegaard

side (... and no woman can attach herself more closely to the man she loves than sorrow). ...

This is how I have understood myself in my entire literary work.

I am in the profoundest sense an unhappy individuality which from its earliest years has been nailed fast to some suffering or other, bordering upon madness, and which must have its deeper roots in a disproportion between soul and body; for (and that is what is extraordinary) it has no relation to my mind. On the contrary, perhaps because of the strained relation between soul and body my mind has received a tensile strength that is rare.

An old man, himself prodigiously melancholy (wherefore I shall not write down) had a son in his old age upon whom the whole of that melancholy descended in inheritance—but at the same time he had such an elasticity of mind that he was able to conceal it, and because his mind was essentially, eminently sound his melancholy could never obtain power over him, but neither was he able to throw it off, at the most he was able to bear it.

A young girl (who with girlish pride set gigantic forces in motion, and let me suspect a way out from what was begun through a sad mistake, a way out, a way of breaking off our engagement, for at first she only let the forces be suspected as though she did not care in the least about it) put a murder on my conscience; at the most solemn moment, a troubled father solemnly repeats the assurance that it would be the girl's death. Whether she was merely a chatterbox or not does not concern me.

From that moment on I dedicated my life with every ounce of my poor ability to the service of an idea.

Although no lover of confidants, although absolutely averse from talking with others about my inmost self, I nevertheless think and thought that it is the duty of man not to skip such a factor as that of seeking the advice of another man; only it must not become a foolish confidence, but a serious and official communication. I have therefore consulted my doctor as to whether he thought that the discord between the psychical and the physical could be resolved so that I might realise the universal. He doubted it. I asked him whether he thought that acting through my will my mind was capable of reforming and transforming that fundamental disproportion; he doubted it; he would not even advise me to set my whole will power in motion, of which he had some idea, lest I should burst everything asunder.

From that moment I made my choice. That sad discord with its attendant suffering (which without doubt would have driven most of those with sense enough to understand it to suicide) I have always looked upon as my thorn in the flesh, my limit and my cross; I have looked upon it as the high price at which Almighty God sold me an intellectual power which has found no equal among my contemporaries. That does not puff me up for *I am already ground to dust*; my desire has become to me a bitter pain and a daily humiliation.

The Aesthetic Self

Without being able to appeal to revelations or anything of the kind, I have understood myself in having to stress the universal in a botched and demoralised age, in making it lovable and accessible to all others who are capable of realising it, but who are led astray by the age to chasing after the unusual and extraordinary. I have understood my duty like the man who, being himself unhappy, so long as he loves man, desires only to help others who are capable of being happy.

But since my task was, at the same time, a humble and a pious attempt to do something good in reparation for what I have done wrong, I have been particularly observant that my effort should not serve the cause of vanity, that above all I should not serve the idea and the truth in such a way as to obtain worldly advantage from it. I am therefore certain that I have worked with true resignation.

During my work I have also constantly believed that I learnt to understand better and better God's will in regard to me: that I bear the agony with which God laid the reins upon me and so perhaps achieve the exceptional.

My merit in literature is that I have set forth the decisive qualifications of the whole compass of existence with such dialectical clarity and so originally as has not, so far as I know, been done in any other literature; neither have I had any books to help me nor upon which to draw for advice. Secondly, the art with which I have communicated it, its form, its logical accomplishment; but no one has time to read and study seriously and to that extent my production is for the moment wasted, like putting exquisite dishes in front of peasants.

End of Report

Berlin, May 5-13, 1846. As I have already said, it will be a long time before the man who opposes the masses can win sympathy over to his side, *i.e.* before anyone will understand the reality of the struggle.

Socrates, in my opinion, is and remains the only reformer I know. The others I have read about may have been enthusiastic and well-meaning, but they were at the same time decidedly narrow-minded.

When a man, particularly in adversity, proves himself to have been beautifully constructed, like some fine old instrument, so that with each new adversity not only are the strings unharmed but a new string added, that is a sign that the grace of God is upon him.

God looked upon me in my conscience, and now it is impossible for me to forget that he sees me. And because God looked upon me I had and have to look towards God.

From birth (or from one's earliest years) to be thus marked out as a sacrifice, to be thus painfully placed outside the universal, so that absolutely everyone would have compassion on one (for whilst other men are busy complaining of men's lack of compassion, such a man is only too certain of it): is the beginning of the demoniacal in a man. Now all depends upon whether such a man is bad—or good. If he is bad he becomes a Gloucester, hating and cursing life, raising himself above the universally human. If he is good then he will do everything for other men, his life as a sacrifice will bring him melancholy satisfaction, yet his life, too, has a condition which he makes, or even if he makes no conditions with God he nevertheless thanks God if he is successful: to be able to hide his wretchedness, to avoid becoming the object of compassion. Of all sufferings none is perhaps so great as to be marked out as the object of compassion, none which tempts man so strongly to rebel against God. It is commonly thought that such a man is dull and of limited intellect, but it would not be difficult to show that this is the secret which lies behind the lives of some of the greatest minds in history. But it is kept hidden, and that can be done, for it is as though God were to say to such a man, so long as he makes use of his outstanding gifts in the service of the good: I do not wish you to be thus humbled before men, to be abandoned in your unmerited misery, but where I am concerned it will help you to be conscious of your nothingness.

The majority of men are subjective towards themselves and objective towards all others, terribly objective sometimes—but the real task is in fact to be objective towards oneself and subjective towards all others.

June 9. In a certain sense my whole misfortune lies in this: had I not had means it would never have been possible for me to preserve the terrible secret of my melancholy. (Merciful God, my father too was terribly unjust to me in his melancholy—an old man who put the whole weight of his melancholy upon a child, not to speak of something even more frightful, and yet for all that he was the best of fathers.) But then I should never have become the man I have become. I should have been *compelled* either to go mad or to break through. As it is I have succeeded in making a *salto mortale* into a purely spiritual existence. But then again in that way I have become completely heterogeneous from mankind in general. What I really lack is the physical side and all the assumptions that go with it. . . .

Aug. 14. Curiously enough the journey to Berlin is still in my thoughts. But I cannot go. A man has applied to me regarding the sale of my house. He came so opportunely, really so inexplicably opportunely that I cannot appreciate it enough. In such circumstances I dare not go away. If he were to come in my absence it would distress me indescribably.

Aug. 16. And so the decision is taken; I remain at home. To-morrow the manuscript goes to the printer.—In order to reassure myself that it was not in any way a possible dislike for all the pother connected with going on a journey which prevented me, I have, with my habitual suspiciousness of myself, begun a course of baths which I knew to be very distasteful to me. . . .

I now feel the need of approaching nearer to myself in a deeper sense, by approaching nearer to God in the understanding of myself. I must remain on the spot and be *renewed inwardly*. It is quite a different thing from the possibility of setting forth upon a journey abroad of some length, perhaps at the end of the autumn. But it must not bear the impress of emotion or the concentrated excitement of a little expedition to Berlin.

I must come to closer grips with my melancholy. It has until now lain deep down and the tremendous intellectual strain has helped to keep it down. That my work has profited others, that God has approved it and helped me in every way is sure enough. Again and again I thank him for having done infinitely more for me than I ever expected. My consolation is that although no man has any merit before God yet he has nevertheless looked with approval upon my efforts, and that with his assistance I have borne my terrible suffering to the very end. I know within myself before God that my work as an author, my willingness to obey his sign, to sacrifice every earthly and worldly consideration, will soften for me the impression of what I have personally done wrong. Just because I began my literary activity with a heavy conscience I have taken the greatest care to make it so pure that it might be a small repayment of my debt. That purity, that integrity, that industry is what seems to be madness in the eyes of the world. I know that God looks upon it otherwise, and that it does not follow that my work is so pure in his eyes that I can praise myself for it before him.

But now God wishes things otherwise. Something is stirring within me which points to a metamorphosis. For that very reason I dare not go to Berlin, for that would be to procure an abortion. I shall therefore remain quiet, in no way working too strenuously, hardly even strenuously, not begin on a new book, but try to understand myself, and *really think out the idea of my melancholy together with God here and now*. That is how I must get rid of my melancholy and bring Christianity closer to me. Hitherto I have defended myself against my melancholy with intellectual work, which keeps it away—now, in the faith that God has forgotten in forgiveness what guilt there may be, I must try to forget it myself, but not in distraction, not at a distance from it but in God, I must see to it that in thinking of God I learn to think that he has forgotten it, and thus myself learn to dare to forget it in forgiveness. . . .

1848

My years of penitence are fast running out. I have nothing to complain of; I understand with God why I suffer—and give thanks. I live, and with God's help

I shall die in the belief that when death has carried me away (and this cannot happen before, or else it would not be penitence to the end) he will place the imprint of providence upon my life, so that it will help men to become aware of God, and to see how thoughtlessly they hinder themselves from leading the highest life, a life in communion with God.

I feel a longing to say nothing more except Amen. I am overwhelmed by gratitude for all that providence has done for me. How is it possible for things to go so well? Poetically speaking, I can only say that there is nothing which has happened in my life of which I cannot say, that is the very thing which perfectly suits my nature and disposition: I lack nothing. I was unhappy in my love; but I simply cannot imagine myself happy unless I were to become a different person altogether. But in my unhappiness I was happy. Humanly speaking, I am saved by one already dead, my father; but I simply cannot imagine myself having been saved by someone living. And so I became an author in exactly the way which suited the latent possibilities of my nature; and then I was persecuted—oh, had that been wanting my life would not have been mine. There is melancholy in everything in my life, but then again an indescribable happiness. But in that way I became myself through God's indescribable grace and support and, as I am almost tempted to say, by his special favour, if that did not mean less to me than the blessed thought, which I believe and which brings me such perfect peace: that he loves all men equally. I have, quite literally, lived with God as one lives with one's father. Amen.

If I could be reconciled with her, that would be my one wish, and a heartfelt joy. But her marriage rests upon me. If I were to give her any certainty as to how she was and is loved, she would regret her marriage. She is held together by the thought that however much she may have seen in me, admired me and loved me, I behaved meanly to her. She was not religious enough to stand by herself with an unhappy love—I have never dared to help her directly, that has cost me suffering enough.

I owe everything, from the beginning, to my father. When, melancholy as he was, he saw me melancholy, his prayer to me was: Be sure that you really love Jesus Christ. . . .

From now on the human race will no longer be led on by prophets and judges but forced back by martyrs, who will run headlong against that human discovery, progress. Otherwise there can be no progress: in intensity. The problem is set, once and for all; there is nothing further to add. The thing is to become more inward.

The result of human progress is that everything becomes thinner and thinner—the result of divine providence is to make everything more inward. . . .

The Aesthetic Self

1849

My misfortune, or the thing that made my life so difficult, is that I am strung a whole tone higher than other men, and where I am and what I am about does not have to do with the particular, but always also with a principle and an idea. At the best, most people think which girl they ought to marry; I had to think about marriage. And so in everything.

Now the same thing is happening to me. At the best, most people consider what occupation they are to take up; now I am in the midst of the stream, of the struggle with ideas and questions of principle whether, from a Christian point of view, there should be official Christian offices.

What makes me unpopular is not so much the difficulty of my works as my own personal life, the fact that in spite of all my endeavours I do not achieve anything (the finite teleology), do not make money, do not get a position, am not decorated, but achieve nothing all along the line, and am despised into the bargain. Now in my opinion that is what is great about me, if indeed there is greatness. But it costs me many a struggle and great efforts, for I too am flesh and blood—and yet that is exactly why I am misunderstood and ill-treated. . . .

1852

My Life's Course

In frightful inner suffering I became an author.

And so I was an author year after year, I suffered too for the idea, in addition to what I suffered within me.

Then came 1848. That helped. There came a moment when overcome with blessedness I dared say to myself: I have understood the highest. In truth, that is not given to many in every generation.

But almost at the same time something new rushed upon me: the highest of all is not to understand the highest but to act upon it.

I had certainly been aware of that from the very beginning, and I am therefore something other than an author in the ordinary sense. But what I was not so clearly aware of was that, by having means and being independent, it was easier for me to give existential expression to what I had understood.

When I understood this I was ready to declare myself a poet, namely because I have had means, which has made action easier for me than for others.

But it all comes to this, that the highest is not to understand the highest, but to act upon it, and be it noted, with all stress upon it. Then I understood properly for the first time that "Grace" must be introduced or else men are stifled just as they are about to begin. But "Grace" must not be introduced in order to hinder endeavour, no, it comes again in the form: the highest is not to understand the highest but to act upon it.

Soren Kierkegaard

The Difficulty with Our Age

June 4. The fact that enthusiasm lies beyond "reason," that is the goal of the struggle.

But oh, for the man who has to awaken that enthusiasm there can be no question of being understood in his own age. Everywhere nothing but these half-experienced, blasé, individualities, who when quite young had a dash of enthusiasm, but who when still almost as young became reasonable. They are so far from allowing themselves to be carried away that on the contrary they immediately supply an envious opposition, and instead of taking part—think they ought simply to "observe" the enthusiastic person, hoping that it will culminate in his either becoming reasonable or ending badly.

Have you seen a boat aground in the mud, it is almost impossible to float it again because it is impossible to punt, no punt-pole can touch bottom so that one can push against it. And so the whole generation is stuck in the mud banks of reason; and no one grieves over it, there is only self-satisfaction and conceit, which always follow on reason and the sins of reason. Oh, the sins of passion and of the heart, how much nearer to salvation than the sins of reason.

About Myself

June 19. Understanding myself to be fundamentally different from others, also with a thorn in the flesh, I became an author in great inner suffering.

Thus I had held out year after year in spite of suffering, and in spite of the new sufferings: a rabble's persecution: I can never thank God enough for what has been done for me.

Then came 1848. I was lifted up to a height which I had never before known, and perfectly understood myself in what had gone before, and the past. So I understood my task to be, or I thought of it in this way: to give myself entirely in a pure intellectual enthusiasm to the task of making it clear what Christianity is—yet without defining unconditionally my relation to Christianity, on the other hand to endure everything for the idea in intellectual enthusiasm.

That is how I understand it and myself in my difference. I wished to go into the country in order to stress it even more clearly.

However, that did not happen at once, a suspicion awoke in me, and my worries began. Whether, the first time the cares of life grew really serious, whether I should not regret having so decisively missed the possibility, which always remained to me, of getting a position in the Church. Whether it was warrantable both in regard to the Church and mankind, whether I could not whip things up so that I became the stumbling-block for Christianity. Then the thought of her awoke again strongly in me. . . .

From the moment I gave up the idea of going into the country I suffered greatly and in ways which I have never otherwise known: cares and misfortunes in all the small things of life, all of which has been increased by financial anxieties. I have certainly prayed for some time past for education, and those particular cares grew greater after that time. But I have certainly developed.

And now I have returned to the point I was at in 1848 but with a higher understanding. Once again I have been strongly reminded of my difference, and reminded of what I had almost forgotten, that I cannot take ecclesiastical office. Ordination is an obstacle to me. Moreover my idea was rather to get a position at a seminary. And so I understand myself in being different. On the other hand I have a direct relation to Christianity so that what I may suffer in the future does not belong under the rubric of intellectual enthusiasm for the question "what is Christianity" (that was how I understood my task in 1848), but under that of suffering for the doctrine, so that in bearing it I have the direct support of Christianity. . . .

It is the "imitation of Christ" that must now be introduced—and I must be what I am, in being different from others. O my God, it was thou who didst hold thy hand over me so that in the long hours of anguish I should not go and take a step in the direction of becoming like others and thereby becoming guilty of procuring an abortion (to use the strong expression employed in one of the Journals of that date, to describe what I then feared), and furthermore embroiling myself in something which in time I should have discovered to hold nothing but worry, because I am not at home in it, and finally should incur a protest when I come into eternity.

The "imitation" must be introduced. But *without authority*, that is and remains my category.

That has moreover happened, for in *On my work as an author* and in the preface to *Two Discourses at communion service* and later in *For Self-examination* I declare myself to be a poet.

For "Grace" is the decisive point, but the "imitation" must be introduced; but I am not anxious about my ability or about others, therefore I am only "a poet"; yet my life has already expressed for more than being a poet, and expresses more if I remain different.

The polemical craft which is my natural characteristic and is inseparable from my very being is here again in place. For how ironical—there are 1000 parsons, *i.e.* teachers (which is something far higher than being merely a poet)—and I am only a poet.

O my God, how clearly it now all stands out before me, how endlessly much has already been done for me. It is not difference that I must pray myself out of, that is not the task, but alas, I shall never know security, which consists in being like others. No, I remain different. There I remain with thee—and verily I know its happiness; the only thing that has made me anxious was the thought that possibly the task was another, namely that I should escape from that unlikeness, a thought which may very well have been prompted by the wish to make my life secure.

So I also feel courage and happiness—not indeed with an ebullient joy as in 1848; but then anxiety for my livelihood was more remote—if I were free from that at the present moment I should once again rejoice, for otherwise everything is well. However, I have suffered so very much in the past year and had to consider everything so seriously that doubtless I am a good deal changed.

But even with the financial anxieties I have, and some idea of what I, with my knowledge of the world, can foresee of the rumpus which will ensue, I feel peaceful and happy, perhaps more definitely so and with a more tranquil confidence than in 1848. . . .

1854

About Myself

Among those who have been ordered out extraordinarily by providence not a few have had greater abilities, and greater learning, all perhaps greater zeal and ardour—but none, none has had a more difficult task, in all Christendom none.

To battle against princes and popes—and the nearer we come to our own times the truer this is—is easy compared with struggling against the masses, the tyranny of equality, against the grin of shallowness, nonsense, baseness and bestiality.

Outside Christianity Socrates stands alone—noble, simple and wise, you were indeed a true reformer. . . .

Suggestions for Further Reading

H. E. Allison, "Kierkegaard's Dialectic of the Religious Consciousness," *Union Seminary Quarterly Review*, Vol. XX (1965), pp. 225-233.

George E. Arbaugh and G. B. Arbaugh, *Kierkegaard's Authorship: A Guide to the Writings of Kierkegaard* (Rock Island, Ill.: Augustana College Library, 1967).

H. J. Blackham, *Six Existentialist Thinkers* (New York: Harper, 1952). Especially the first chapter.

Conrad Bonifazi, *Christendom Attacked: A Comparison of Kierkegaard and Nietzsche* (London: Rocklift, 1953).

Liam Brophy, "Kierkegaard: The Hamlet in Search of Holiness," *Social Justice Review*. Vol. XLVII, No. 9 (1955), pp. 291-292.

The Aesthetic Self

James D. Collins, *The Mind of Kierkegaard* (Chicago: Henry Regnery, 1965).

W. Richard Comstock, "Aspects of Aesthetic Existence: Kierkegaard and Santayana," *International Philosophical Quarterly*, Vol. VI (1966), pp. 189-213.

Migual de Unamuno, *The Tragic Sense of Life in Men and Peoples*, translated by J. E. Crawford Flitch (New York: Macmillan, 1921).

Louis K. Dupre, "The Constitution of the Self in Kierkegaard's Philosophy," *International Philosophical Quarterly*, Vol. III (1963), pp. 506-526.

Haakon Flottorp, *Kierkegaard and Norway: A Study of Inwardness in History with Illustrative Examples from Religion, Literature, and Philosophy* (New York: Columbia University dissertation, 1955).

Rudolph Friedmann, *Kierkegaard: The Analysis of the Psychological Personality* (New York: New Directions, 1950).

Marjorie Grene, *Soren Kierkegaard: The Self Against the System in Dreadful Freedom: A Critique of Existentialism* (Chicago: University of Chicago Press, 1948).

Ralph Harper, *The Seventh Solitude: Metaphysical Homelessness in Kierkegaard, Dostoevsky, and Nietzsche* (Baltimore: Johns Hopkins University Press, 1967).

Karl Jaspers, "The Importance of Kierkegaard," translated by Erwin W. Geissman, *Cross Currents*, II, 3 (1952), pp. 5-16.

Per Lönning, *The Dilemma of Contemporary Theology: Prefigured in Luther, Pascal, Kierkegaard, Nietzsche* (New York: Humanities Press, 1962).

Walter Lowrie, *A Short Life of Kierkegaard* (Princeton, N. J.: Princeton University Press, 1942).

E. M. Manasee, "Conversion and Liberation: A Comparison of Augustine and Kierkegaard," *Review of Religion*, XVII (1943), pp. 361-383.

Erik and Kirsten Skinhoj, "Kierkegaard in American Psychology," *Acta Psychiatrica et Neurologica*, XXX (1955), pp. 315-25.

Friedrich Nietzsche

Selected Autobiographical Writings

As I write this a madman is howling
in the next room, and I am howling
with him inside of me, howling for
my lost integrity, sundered from God,
Man and myself, shattered in body,
mind and spirit, yearning for two
clasped hands to usher in the great
miracle—the unity of my being.

In a manner unique in Western philosophical thought, the whole of Nietzsche's work reveals the life history of its author. In a real sense, all of his works are autobiographical, although it was not until the last 12 years of his life that he wrote autobiography self-consciously. The following selection draws on the two autobiographical works of these latter years, *Ecce Homo* (written in 1888 and two months prior to his mental breakdown) and *My Sister and I* (written during his incarceration in an asylum and left in the hands of another patient for safekeeping). Although written in a period of disorientation, these works do not depart radically from his earlier works. In these writings, he struggles with the decadence of European man, recognizing his own enslavement to that decadence. He recounts his anguished but ultimately unsuccessful efforts to regain his "lost integrity." And he views his incarceration in the asylum as the final absurdity, for he alone had struggled to rise above the sickness and spiritual poverty of his age. In these writings, therefore, he completes the personal confession and trenchant social critique begun in his earlier works.

In order to relate these autobiographical writings to his earlier personal history, we need to look at two critical friendships in his life, those with Richard Wagner and Lou Salome. Born in 1844, Nietzsche came from a long line of Lutheran pastors. His father, himself a pastor, died when Nietzsche was two years old. In the years following his father's death, he was the only male in a household which included his mother, grandmother, two aunts, and his younger sister Elisabeth (the subject of *My Sister and I*). At 20, Nietzsche embarked on the study of philology and in 1869 accepted an appointment as associate professor at the University of Basel.

After settling in Basel, Nietzsche met the composer Richard Wagner. He spent a great deal of time at Wagner's home in nearby Tribschen. In the course of the following three years, he found philology increasingly uninspiring and, influenced in part by Wagner, published *The Birth of Tragedy*. This book, which marked his emergence as a philosopher in the romantic tradition, was resented by his colleagues in philology. He remained in his position until 1879, however, when serious illness forced his resignation. Toward the close of his tenure at Basel, he broke with Wagner. In commenting later on his reasons for doing so, he charged Wagner with decadence: "I cannot bear ambivalence; ever since his return to Germany, he has lowered himself step by step to everything I despise—even anti-Semitism . . . Richard Wagner, outwardly the conquering hero, in reality a rotting, despairing decadent, suddenly dropped, helpless and broken, before the Christian cross." In Wagner, he saw the decadence of European culture itself. Wagner would "soon be viewed as a splendid vestige . . . a marvelous stranger on whose strength and beauty the fortune of earlier times depended." In contrast, Nietzsche viewed himself as the harbinger of a new age, as another kind of stranger "seeking the philosophy of the morning."

After his break with Wagner and his resignation from the University of Basel, Nietzsche began searching for a geographical climate in which he might thrive physically and mentally. He was in Rome, therefore, when he met the young Jewess Lou Salome, who assumes an extremely important personal and symbolic role in *My Sister and I*. Miss Salome became his pupil, but she was more than that to him. As Ivo Frenzel points out, "Nietzsche's feelings for Lou were intense; but as far as she was concerned, the friendship with the lonely wanderer was never more than a profound intellectual experience." Though she refused his proposals of marriage, he continued to speak of the spiritual union between them, a union which would issue in the birth of a spiritual son. Their friendship continued in this vein until Nietzsche's sister Elisabeth intervened. Her hostility and jealousy toward Miss Salome intensified by her husband's intense anti-Semitism, Elisabeth wrote her a scathing letter. Nietzsche's petulant response to Lou's angry protest ("What have I got to do with these bickerings?") marked the end of their friendship.

In the winter following his break with Lou, Nietzsche wrote *Thus Spake Zarathustra*. As he put it: "My noble Zarathustra was born." It was completed, therefore, in the wake of his friendship with the one who, as Frenzel says, "inspired him with the hope that his shattered life might be made whole again." Their friendship issued in his Zarathustra, a spiritual offspring. But his own life remained irretrievably shattered.

Ecce Homo

Why I Am So Wise

The happiness of my existence, its unique character perhaps, consists in its fatefulness: to speak in a riddle, as my own father I am already dead, as my own mother I still live and grow old. This double origin, taken as it were from the highest and lowest rungs of the ladder of life, at once a decadent and a beginning, this, if anything, explains that neutrality, that freedom from partisanship in regard to the general problem of existence, which perhaps distinguishes me. To the first indications of ascending or of descending life my nostrils are more sensitive than those of any man that has yet lived. In this domain I am a master to my backbone—I know both sides, for I am both sides. My father died in his six-and-thirtieth year: he was delicate, lovable, and morbid, like one who is preordained to pay simply a flying visit—a gracious reminder of life rather than life itself. In the same year that his life declined mine also declined: in my six-and-thirtieth year I reached the lowest point in my vitality,—I still lived, but my eyes could distinguish nothing that lay three paces away from me. At that time—it was the year 1879—I resigned my professorship at Bale, lived through the summer like a shadow in St. Moritz, and spent the following winter, the most sunless of my life, like a shadow in Naunburg. This was my lowest ebb. During this period I wrote *The Wanderer and His Shadow*. Without a doubt I was conversant with shadows then. The winter that followed, my first winter in Genoa, brought forth that sweetness and spirituality which is almost inseparable from extreme poverty of blood and muscle, in the shape of *The Dawn of Day*. The perfect lucidity and cheerfulness, the intellectual exuberance even, that this work reflects, coincides, in my case, not only with the most profound physiological weakness, but also with an excess of suffering. In the midst of the agony of a headache which lasted three days, accompanied by violent nausea, I was possessed of most singular dialectical clearness, and in absolutely cold blood I then thought out things, for which, in my more healthy moments, I am not enough of a climber, not sufficiently subtle, not sufficiently cold. My readers perhaps know to what extent I consider dialectic a symptom of decadence. . . . Having admitted all this, do I need to say that I am experienced in questions of decadence? I know them inside and out. . . . To look upon healthier concepts and values from the standpoint of the sick, and conversely to look down upon the secret work of the instincts of decadence from the standpoint of him who is laden and self-reliant with the richness of life—this has been my longest exercise, my principal experience. If in anything at all, it was in

From Friedrich Nietzsche, *Ecce Homo*, translated by Anthony M. Ludovici, and vol. XVII of *The Complete Works of Friedrich Nietzsche*, translated under the general editorship of Oscar Levey (1909-1911) (New York: Russell and Russell, and London: George Allen and Unwin, Ltd., 1964).

this that I became a master. To-day my hand knows the trick, I now have the knack of reversing perspectives: the first reason perhaps why a *Transvaluation of all Values* has been possible to me alone.

For, apart from the fact that I am a decadent, I am also the reverse of such a creature. Among other things my proof of this is, that I always and instinctively select the proper remedy when my spiritual or bodily health is low; whereas the decadent, as such, invariably chooses those remedies which are bad for him. As a whole I was sound, but in certain details I was a decadent. That energy with which I sentenced myself to absolute solitude, and to a severance from all those conditions in life to which I had grown accustomed; my discipline of myself, and my refusal to allow myself to be pampered, to be tended hand and foot, and to be doctored—all this betrays the absolute certainty of my instincts respecting what at that time was most needful to me. I placed myself in my own hands, I restored myself to health: the first condition of success in such an undertaking, as every physiologist will admit, is that at bottom a man should be sound. An intrinsically morbid nature cannot become healthy. On the other hand, to an intrinsically sound nature, illness may even constitute a powerful stimulus to life, to a surplus of life. It is in this light that I now regard the long period of illness that I endured: it seemed as if I had discovered life afresh, my own self included. I tasted all good things and even trifles in a way in which it was not easy for others to taste them—out of my Will to Health and to Life I made my philosophy. . . . For this should be thoroughly understood; it was during those years in which my vitality reached its lowest point that I ceased from being a pessimist: the instinct of self-recovery forbade my holding to a philosophy of poverty and desperation. Now, by what signs are Nature's lucky strokes recognised among men? They are recognized by the fact that any such lucky stroke gladdens our senses; that he is carved from one integral block, which is hard, sweet, and fragrant as well. He enjoys that only which is good for him; his pleasure, his desire, ceases when the limits of that which is good for him are overstepped. He divines remedies for injuries; he knows how to turn serious accidents to his own advantage; that which does not kill him makes him stronger. He instinctively gathers his material from all he sees, hears, and experiences. He is a selective principle; he rejects much. He is always in the own company, whether his intercourse be with books, with men, or with natural scenery; he honours the things he chooses, the things he acknowledges, the things he trusts. He reacts slowly to all kinds of stimuli, with that tardiness which long caution and deliberate pride have bred in him—he tests the approaching stimulus; he would not dream of meeting it half-way. He believes neither in "ill-luck" nor "guilt"; he can digest himself and others; he knows how to forget—he is strong enough to make everything turn to his own advantage.

Lo then! I am the very reverse of a decadent, for he whom I have just described is none other than myself. . . .

Friedrich Nietzsche

Why I Am a Fatality

I know my destiny. There will come a day when my name will recall the memory of something formidable—a crisis the like of which has never been known on earth, the memory of the most profound clash of consciences, and the passing of a sentence upon all that which heretofore had been believed, exacted, and hallowed. I am not a man, I am dynamite. And with it all there is nought of the founder of a religion in me. Religions are matters for the mob; after coming in contact with a religious man, I always feel that I must wash my hands. . . . I require no "believers", it is my opinion that I am too full of malice to believe even in myself; I never address myself to masses. I am horribly frightened that one day I shall be pronounced "holy". You will understand why I publish this book beforehand—it is to prevent people from wronging me. I refuse to be a saint; I would rather be a clown. Maybe I am a clown. And I am, notwithstanding, the mouthpiece of truth; for nothing more blown-out with falsehood has ever existed, than a saint. But my truth is terrible: for hitherto *lies* have been called truth. *The Transvaluation of all Values*, this is my formula for mankind's greatest step toward coming to its senses—a step which in me became flesh and genius. My destiny ordained that I should be the first decent human being, and that I should feel myself opposed to the falsehood of millenniums. I was the first to discover truth, and for the simple reason that I was the first who became conscious of falsehood as falsehood—that is to say, I smelt it as such. My genius resides in my nostrils. I contradict as no one has contradicted hitherto, and am nevertheless the reverse of a negative spirit. I am the harbinger of joy, the like of which has never existed before; I have discovered tasks of such lofty greatness that, until my time, no one had any idea of such things. Mankind can begin to have fresh hopes, only now that I have lived. Thus, I am necessarily a man of Fate. For when Truth enters the lists against the falsehood of ages, shocks are bound to ensue, and a spell of earthquakes, followed by the transposition of hills and valleys, such as the world has never yet imagined even in its dreams. The concept "politics" then becomes elevated entirely to the sphere of spiritual warfare. All the mighty realms of the ancient order of society are blown into space—for they are all based on falsehood: there will be wars, the like of which have never been seen on earth before. Only from my time and after me will politics on a large scale exist on earth.

If you should require a formula for a destiny of this kind that has taken human form, you will find it in my Zarathustra.

"And he who would be a creator in good and evil—verily, he must first be a destroyer, and break values into pieces.

"Thus the greatest evil belongeth unto the greatest good: but this is the creative good."

I am by far the most terrible man that has ever existed; but this does not alter the fact that I shall become the most beneficent. I know the joy of *annihilation* to a degree which is commensurate with my power to annihilate. In both cases I obey my Dionysian nature, which knows not how to separate the negative deed from the saying of yea. I am the first immoralist, and in this sense I am essentially the annihilator. . . .

In reality two negations are involved in my title Immoralist. I first of all deny the type of man that has hitherto been regarded as the highest—the *good*, the *kind*, and the *charitable*; and I also deny that kind of morality which has become recognised and paramount as morality-in-itself—I speak of the morality of decadence, or, to use a still cruder term, Christian morality. I would agree to the second of the two negations being regarded as the more decisive, for, reckoned as a whole, the overestimation of goodness and kindness seems to me already a consequence of decadence, a symptom of weakness, and incompatible with any ascending and yea-saying life. Negation and annihilation are inseparable from a yea-saying attitude towards life. . . .

But I have chosen the title of Immoralist as a surname and as a badge of honour in yet another sense; I am very proud to possess this name which distinguishes me from all the rest of mankind. No one hitherto has felt Christian morality beneath him; to that end there were needed height, a remoteness of vision, and an abysmal psychological depth, not believed to be possible hitherto. Up to the present Christian morality has been the Circe of all thinkers—they stood at her service. What man, before my time, had descended into the underground caverns from out of which the poisonous fumes of this ideal—of this slandering of the world—burst forth? What man had even dared to suppose that they were underground caverns? Was a single one of the philosophers who preceded me a psychologist at all, and not the very reverse of a psychologist— that is to say, a "superior swindler," an "Idealist"? Before my time there was no psychology. To be the first in this new realm may amount to a curse; at all events, it is a fatality: *for one is also the first to despise.* My danger is the loathing of mankind.

Have you understood me? That which defines me, that which makes me stand apart from the whole of the rest of humanity, is the fact that I *unmasked* Christian morality. For this reason I was in need of a word which conveyed the idea of a challenge to everybody. Not to have awakened to these discoveries before, struck me as being the sign of the greatest uncleanliness that mankind has on its conscience, as self-deception become instinctive, as the fundamental will to be blind to every phenomenon. . . . Christian morality is the most malignant form of all falsehood, the actual Circe of humanity: that which has corrupted mankind. It is not error as error which infuriates me at the sight of this spectacle; it is not the millenniums of absence of "goodwill," of discipline, of decency, and of bravery in spiritual things, which betrays itself in the triumph of Christianity; it is rather the absence of nature, it is the perfectly ghastly fact that

Friedrich Nietzsche

anti-nature itself received the highest honours as morality and as law, and remained suspended over man as the Categorical Imperative. Fancy blundering in this way, *not* as an individual, *not* as a people, but as a whole species! as *humanity*! To teach the contempt of all the principal instincts of life; to posit falsely the existence of a "soul," of a "spirit," in order to be able to defy the body; to spread the feeling that there is something impure in the very first requisite of life—in sex. . . . What! is humanity itself in a state of degeneration? Has it always been in this state? One thing is certain, that ye are taught only the values of decadence as the highest values. The morality of self-renunciation is essentially the morality of degeneration. . . .

Have you understood me? I have not uttered a single word which I had not already said five years ago through my mouthpiece Zarathustra. The unmasking of Christian morality is an event which is unequalled in history, it is a real catastrophe. The man who throws light upon it is a *force majeure*, a fatality; he breaks the history of man into two. Time is reckoned up before him and after him. The lightning flash of truth struck precisely that which theretofore had stood highest: he who understands what was destroyed by that flash should look to see whether he still holds anything in his hands. Everything which until then was called truth, has been revealed as the most detrimental, most spiteful, and most subterranean form of life; the holy pretext, which was the "improvement" of man, has been recognized as a ruse for draining life of its energy and of its blood. Morality conceived as Vampirism. . . . The man who unmasks morality has also unmasked the worthlessness of the values in which men either believe or have believed; he no longer sees anything to be revered in the most venerable man—even in the types of men that have been pronounced holy; all he can see in them is the most fatal kind of abortions, fatal, *because they fascinate*. The concept "God" was invented as the opposite of the concept life—everything detrimental, poisonous, and slanderous, and all deadly hostility to life, was bound together in one horrible unit in Him. The concepts "beyond" and "true world" were invented in order to depreciate the only world that exists—in order that no goal or aim, no sense or task, might be left to earthly reality. The concepts "soul," "spirit," and last of all the concept "immortal soul," were invented in order to throw contempt on the body, in order to make it sick and "holy," in order to cultivate an attitude of appalling levity towards all things in life which deserve to be treated seriously, i.e. the questions of nutrition and habitation, of intellectual diet, the treatment of the sick, cleanliness and weather. Instead of health, we find the "salvation of the soul"—that is to say a *folie circulaire* fluctuating between convulsions and penitence and the hysteria of redemption. The concept "sin," together with the torture instrument appertaining to it, which is the concept "free will," was invented in order to confuse and muddle our instincts, and to render the mistrust of them man's second nature! In the concepts "disinterestedness" and "self-denial," the actual signs of decadence are to be found. The allurement of that which is detrimental, the inability to discover one's own advantage and self-destruction are made into absolute qualities, into the "duty," the "holiness," and the "divinity" of man. Finally—to keep the worst to the last—by the notion of the *good* man, all that is favoured which is weak, ill, botched, and sick-in-itself, *which ought to be wiped out*. The law of selection is thwarted, an ideal is made out of opposition to the proud, well-constituted man, to him who says yea to life, to him who is certain of the future, and who guarantees the future—this man is henceforth called the *evil* one. And all this was believed in as morality! . . .

Have you understood me? Dionysus versus Christ.

Excerpts from My Sister and I

I had a dream last night. Or should I say a nightmare? A nightmare is something which rises out of the subconscious into the conscious, loaded with shock and unpleasantness, to punish or frighten us. But what happened to me last night was a presentiment frenzied with happiness. If I think of it as a nightmare it is because, unlike ordinary dreams, which rise and fall in shadow, this one was deep and clear, and still remains with me, instead of fading away.

It appeared to me that the last citadel of the enemy had fallen. The old woman—whom I have hated more and more intensely every day since childhood—was dead. With my own eyes I saw her locked in a wooden box, dropped into a hole in the ground covered with lime. I was at the cemetery with a group of dark, wailing people none of whose faces—except that of Elisabeth, half embraced at my side—I saw clearly. Did it stem from the malevolent visit they both paid me yesterday afternoon?

The dream went on from the cemetery into a carriage which brought my sister and me home (*where that could be I could only wonder*). In a long, clattery ride not a word passed between us. We sat huddled into each other and let the empty, bitter, futile years, marred for us by that tyrannous presence, melt down to their chemical elements. I felt the way the earth must feel when winter's ice gives way for the new crop of flora and vegetation. My heart ached with anticipation.

The same warmth must have welled up in Elisabeth, too. I surmised this, as we always do in dreams, in an emotional tide not as clearly directed as in life, but none the less real. Once when I stole a surreptitious look at her cold, handsome face I caught a faint smile in the corner of her mouth, which mounted swiftly to her wonderful luminous eyes. But for the presence of the driver (masked like the people at the funeral) I might have tried to kiss her.

From Friedrich Nietzsche, *My Sister and I* (New York: Bridgehead Books, 1951).

If a thought can be conveyed from one person to another in associated words conceived but not uttered, this was my first communication to Elisabeth upon reentering this dreamhouse (*so strangely familiar to me as it sits in my recollection*): *There are three empty beds in this house, and two of them shall remain unslept in for as long as I am able to influence you. . . .*

This thought would never occur to Elisabeth herself. Suggested to her, it would most certainly be reacted to violently and unfavorably. My sister's world is one of scattered sunlight and shadows, the sunlight of her true passions and the shadows of the false ideas with which the world has bewitched her. Under no circumstances can she be expected to function as definitely and as imperiously as I do. But the seed of the thought can be planted in her mind. With a sick brother, so badly in need of kindness and sympathy, who can tell what will happen?

But all that has passed between us (in our childhood years directly, and directly and indirectly later) she is neither my sister nor any of the other things—such as adviser and helper—which she would like me and the world to believe her to be. For me, Elisabeth is primarily a woman—the warm sunny harbor toward which my whole life gravitates. . . .

It first happened between Elisabeth and me the night our young brother Joseph died, though we had no idea that he was dying when she crept into my bed, pleading that it was cold where she was, and she knew how warm I always was. As a matter of fact, this was not true. Even in these early days, chills seized me and held on to me at the oddest and most unexpected times. And I was particularly cold that night. . . . All afternoon little Joseph had kept the household in turmoil with his screaming and gasping. . . . Suddenly I felt Elisabeth's warm little hands in mine, her hissing little voice was in my ear, and I began feeling warm all over. . . .

I have been a rebel against the universe, and the universe has wreaked its vengeance upon me. Tolstoy's notion that Love is at the heart of the cosmos has always caused the laughter in me to rumble. Now the laugh is on me.

Like Ulysses I stopped my ears with wax, bound myself to the mast of my ship and sailed out to meet the Sirens. But the Sirens did not shatter my ears with their song of love; my wax and my chains were useless against their wiles. For they had a more potent weapon than song to drive me out of my monastic cell into the delirium of frustrated love: instead of song they showered me with silence, the hailstorm of voiceless derision.

I have been fox-like in my guile, but Lou Salome and the other sirens have out-foxed me: they clung to their perilous rocks, and I have dashed my head against them. The golden radiance that falls from their hair weighs heavily upon me like a coffin-lid. I can no longer love and therefore can no longer live, like a petrified forest whose gray branches are crumbling into dust. All I fear is the

The Aesthetic Self

Lama's[1] evil eyes, for she must suspect that, given the strength and the opportunity to evade her, I would in some way try to turn my slow dying into a victory over death. How better than by revealing my inner collapse in hasty notes such as these? . . .

The great end of art is to strike the imagination with the power of a soul that refuses to admit defeat even in the midst of a collapsing world. Up to now my work has been artistic because of my refusal to cry out against my private doom. But now I bellow like a wounded bull who is tormented beyond animal endurance, and the Lama dreads such a revelation of me who have become synonymous with Stoic fortitude and indifference.

I have been broken on the wheel of Fate; I am dying in agony, but my dear sister already considers me dead and is only eager to save me for the deathless future, for the psychic immortality that Spinoza spoke about. She is already enjoying my immortality as famous men come here to pay their respects and to bring the flowers of flattery to my premature grave. She quotes my *Grave-Song* to them: *"Hail to you, will of mine! Only where there are graves are there resurrections."*. . .

What Moliere laughed at in order to keep from weeping Augier treated with solemn emphasis as befitted his bourgeois muse. When he makes his heroine say: *I have my mother's heart*, he emphasizes the impact of heredity which is as implacable as the *ananke* of antiquity pursuing the tragic hero to his doom.

I have my mother's heart: her hypocritical virtue held me in bonds of iron all her life and I could only break away by attempting the impossible, the continuation of the desperate love-relationship with my sister who was equally in the grip of my mother's false modesty. We dared to go to violent extremities because we did not dare to hope for a normal sex-relationship—because our Mother with her medusa-eyes turned our emotions into stone. This is the paradox of my existence: I have loved life passionately but have never dared to channel this love in the direction of normal erotic experience.

My mother's excess of modesty has poisoned the well-spring of my being. As I lost my father in early childhood, the waters of my life remained polluted without the necessary masculine chemicals to purify the source of my being. I have therefore inwardly raged against delicacy and modesty in women, and when Lou Salome stormed me with the full impact of her erotic nature I surrendered to her with a sense of infinite relief—and delight.

But alas, like Augier's heroine, *I have my mother's heart*. She bowed to the ascetic ideal of the Christian to escape from the torture of the flesh, and although I tried to build a new heaven on the body of my beloved, my mother's God filled my paradise with the dreams of self-accusation so that my heaven became a hell, and I was driven like Adam out of my primal Eden. Instead of

[1] His nickname for his sister Elisabeth.

transfiguration, I suffered crucifixion, and my *Zarathustra the Atheist* was merely Neitzsche-Jesus affirming Life on the Cross, though secretly in terror of existence.

I have never cherished my proud loneliness; I have hungered for the passionate love of a woman who could redeem me from the terror of a world that has witnessed the death of God. . . .

That virtues may exist it is necessary to legitimize the pleasures of the flesh for the austerity of the pillar saints is not piety but pathology. Lou Salome was modest in the truest sense of the word, for she set bounds to our passion and never permitted it to veer beyond the line of mutual enjoyment. We were never bored with each other, for she always kept a voluptuous reserve, a reservoir of feminine mystery that made her, like God, a source of infinite delight. . . . O Lou, my lost paradise, there is no return to Eden, to the bliss that was and is no more. Like the gigantic shadows that trail us in the night, the kisses of our beloved dissolve suddenly in the darkness, without a hint of their golden rapture, without a touch of moonlight to soften the rough edges of black despair. . . .

The winds die down, there is calm everywhere, but a mad storm rages in the heart, for the hour of death has arrived. O peace of men and places, O caves where souls may hide and find tranquil oblivion. O sweet refuge of mountains where Silence walks on feet of velvet and the brooks flow without a sound through raptures of quiet green! Why must my head split open with the roar of a thousand seas, I who loved the stillness of the mountains and walked alone through miles of utter silence? . . . .Oh Lou, this is my punishment: I choked love to death, and its ghost drowns me in a rush of waters. . . .

I had grown tired of the world from which I received nothing but abuse. Just as I had received the precious gift of love as a solace, it was snatched from me by the Vandal hands of my jealous sister. Even as the watchman who keeps guard over the purple towers of a city she kept guard over the purple towers of our incestuous passion.

Verily the love of a woman is a balm for the wounded soul, but incest is a closed garden, a fountain sealed, where the waters of life are dried up and the flowers bloom only to wither at the touch.

So I shrink inwardly into my despair, remembering nothing but the guilty kisses of her who blocked every exit to the life of love, dooming me to an all-consuming hatred for God, for Man and for myself which gathered round me like a formless dread, trapping me in self-terror, the fear of a man who has been unshadowed by the love that he has killed. . .

Let us love each other in unity of thought. The words ring in my brain like a bell, a bell of longing swung from a belfry in Tautenburg. Let us love each other. . . let us love. . . let us. . . love. . . .

The Aesthetic Self

I have never ceased to educate myself, and even at the brink of the grave, while still in the flux of change, my comment on life changes with the surrounding tempest of events. My brain is still at work and weaving complexities of thought, while my shroud is being prepared and I am about to be gathered to my ancestors.

While other writers have written about nothing except people falling in love, I have postponed this trifling subject to the last, but now this personal side of life takes full possession of me: not art, not science, not philosophy, but falling in love has usurped the whole landscape of my foundered being. There is no other thing to talk about but the love that eludes us and which we seek passionately like the sunken continent of Atlantis buried beneath the ocean of the world's hatred.

Self-centered, solitary and alone, my brain no longer reaches out for the life of art or ideas, but rides implacably towards the harbor of her arms amidst the howling winds and raging tides of being.

Oh Lou, let me surrender myself to my instincts of passion and bliss!—Alas, it is too late, too late: you are gone, and tomorrow I will already be dead!

I remember with reverence the father I never really knew, and I can think only with loathing of my mother, knowing as I do that there is nothing she would not do to bring me consolation and comfort. God does well to hide behind His peak on Mount Sinai. . . .

The impotence of Christian love led my sister into a desperate effort to fulfill herself in a dark and forbidden area of erotic expression. Trained by my mother to repress her natural sex-emotions, she discovered too late that her effort to dam up her erotic desires merely unleashed a torrent of dark, abnormal passions that rushed through her being in full flood till she became a destructive force of nature that broke through all barriers of morals and civilization. She began to love what she desired least, and I was flung into the treacherous undertow of her outlawed passions which sucked us into their tidal will.

. . . . It is best that the world should not know—at least in her lifetime—that Elisabeth played the same role in my life's drama as Augusta played in Byron's. Like Augusta, Elisabeth was a buffer and a shield against the maternal despot who smashed her lances of ridicule and stupidity against her counter-sarcasm until Elisabeth assumed the role of the maternal tyrant as soon as I began to show an interest in the fair sex. To maintain her dominance over me she seduced me into the sin of the Egyptians, thus making it possible for me to tear myself away from my sick Lutheran conscience, having matched Satan himself with my sin.

Friedrich Nietzsche

Byron too felt that he was the equal of Satan, his Calvinist conscience smashed on the rock of his certainty that he had passed beyond the greatest sinners—Manfred and Cain—and reached the ultimate in wickedness. Through Augusta he was enabled to sit next to the throne of His Satanic Majesty whom Schopenhauer ensconced in heaven. But Elisabeth puffed up my pride still more: I could not tolerate the Satanic compromise by allowing a Ruler to be above me and so I stood on my own head and became the Superman—the Monarch of the Universe. As I have written: "If there were Gods, how could I endure it to be not God! *Therefore* there are no Gods."

. . . The more I contemplated Elisabeth the more I admired Caesar Borgia. He was too strong, clever and unscrupulous to be the victim of a petticoat's fury. At Tautenburg when I was with Lou and asserting the blond beast in me by defying the Lama and the gossip-mongers in town, I entertained the pleasant thought of giving my sister the Borgia treatment, and even experimented with a variety of poisons. But of course my homicidal plan never went beyond the experimental stage. My Lutheran conscience vetoed my will to be *as fierce as a lion and as cunning as a fox*. I tried to be Machiavelli's Prince but instead I was *the little pastor*, afraid of the God whom I buried in my youth.

I often wonder whether I would have been more fortunate if I had decided to let Schopenhauer's mother instead of my own give birth to me. My mother has settled down here in Weimar as Schopenhauer's mother did (she wants to be near her sunken son), but here the resemblance in their characters ends, except that they were both dominant females to whom mother-love was a convenient hammer with which to pound subservience and doggish servility into their sons. . . . When Mama finally departs from this veil of tears and receives her reward, I shall borrow Schopenhauer's prayers of relief—the only praiseworthy thought in all his philosophy. . . .

Did God die by his own hand, disgusted with His pious worshippers who threw all their problems into His divine lap, being too cowardly and ignorant to handle them themselves? God the proud Stoic, killing Himself to retain His self-respect—that is bad news for Christians who were told by crackpots like Saint Paul and Luther that not good works but mere blind faith in Christ was enough for them to win eternal salvation.

Not I but Saint Paul and Luther were the great immoralists who taught pious Christians how to murder, lie and steal and avoid the vengeance of Jehovah. It was Saint Paul and Luther who thrust *good* Christians beyond good and evil, beyond the moral law, and preached salvation through the hocus-pocus of Christ's sacrificial blood. Ever since then they have been redeeming themselves through the blood of the Jew Jesus and millions of his fellow-Jews.

The Aesthetic Self

In the twentieth century, in a fit of nihilistic frenzy, they will turn all Europe into a butcher's slaughter-house and wash their sins white in the blood of Israel!

This is no mere fancy: Heine already has prophesied the coming debacle of Christian civilization, when the Germans dust off their old pagan gods and plunge the West into a terrible blood-bath! If God were actually alive He would not allow the twentieth century to happen. Therefore God must be dead. But how did he die? As a Stoic too proud to see His world botched up by so-called followers of Jesus; . . .

Elisabeth could not stomach the fact that Lou Salome was a Jewess, but God could not swallow the bitter truth that she [Elisabeth] was a Christian who worshipped the Prince of Peace by plotting pogroms with her wild-eyed anti-Semitic husband! So in a paroxysm of wrath and disgust He cut His throat with the jagged edge of a star and let His blood pour over the earth in a divine torment of remorse.

No, this version is too romantic—it smacks of Wagner and Wagnerism. Stendhal's explanation was more prosaic and more consistent with the truth. God, the mechanic, died a natural death—of heart disease! He left His world to His Son, who like me, knew nothing of mechanics, being a poet, a dreamer of wild dreams. The Son entered the cosmic workshop, scratched his head at the sight of the huge, complicated engine of existence, pulled the lever, and started the engine *in reverse*, causing mad havoc throughout the universe, filled with flying wheels and the debris of shattered machinery!

This is how it must have happened: not God but His Son is the cause of world chaos. God died of a heart attack and His Son got us into a cosmic fix.

Sometimes I think that His Son is Friedrich Nietzsche, who is now expiating his clumsy foolishness. He paralyzed the cosmos and now he himself is in the grip of paralysis!

After swallowing enough chloral hydrate to drown the agonies of the world, I said farewell to Lou Salome in my Zarathustra *Grave Song*, bursting like a choral volcano in hot, flaming music of grief for my best love driven away by those terrible hell-cats, Mama and the Lama, spawned out of the spitting malice of our homicidal age. . . .

If I had been inconsistent in my attitude towards the Jews and the Jewess who caused such havoc in my life, it is because I am a child of Luther whose pathology is a part of the madness of our age. The Jew is the European symbol of democracy, of people's power which he identifies with the will of God but which Luther and I see as the Devil's handiwork, the Devil who plots to sow confusion and anarchy in the world. And yet the Jew, with his aristocratic pride and infinite demands, his cultural imperialism that has shaken the foundations of our Roman world order, also appealed to Luther, the destroyer of the Roman Antichrist, as he appeals to me who as Antichrist have also identified myself with Jesus, the Jew, the spiritual Superman who flung his gage of defiance against the Roman world.

While I was with Lou Salome my centre of awareness moved from my head to my heart, and all the Lutheran contradictions in my nature fused to a single passion of love for the Jewish people and all peoples. I removed my intellectual blinkers and saw life from the focus of the organic womb, the mystical realm that lies below Science and therefore is above it, dominating the complex demands of our total nature. This priestess of Isis interiorized my knowledge; I began to know life as a living experience, as the harmonious blending of the Seen and the Unseen, as an artistic activity in tune with cosmic forces that filled me with the splendor and desolation of godlike existence.

She was the female John the Baptist who heralded the coming faith of Simplicity which shall unite the Within and the Without, the Centre and the Periphery, the body with the wind and Soul in the single matrix of the Womb. But having lost her I fell back upon my Lutheran devils, my divided being which can never reach out towards God, the Whole, and therefore assumes that God is dead. . . .

So I am God's widower! God is laughing up His cosmic sleeve at my foolish assumption.

As I write this a madman is howling in the next room, and I am howling with him inside of me, howling for my lost integrity, sundered from God, Man and myself, shattered in body, mind and spirit, yearning for two clasped hands to usher in the great miracle—the unity of my being. . . . O Cosmic Irony, O Devil-God of Schopenhauer! I brought together all knowledge into a single system of thought while my mind is splitting into a billion fragments, scattering into tiny grains of dust death! . . .

I sit frozen with terror. Who is knocking at the door of Macbeth? The Bishop of Hippo [St. Augustine] with his dead eyes comes to claim me as God claimed him, a sinner: *You have made us for Yourself, and our hearts are restless till they find rest in You*. No, no, this is a trick of some fiend who has barricaded himself in my brain and is shooting the arrows of a dead God into my collapsing world. I shall call a keeper—*Am I my brother's keeper?*—God's widower is haunted by the divine ghost he once mourned. . . .

Monica, Monica—why is the name of Monica crying in my sick brain? Ah, that is my mother, Augustine's mother of course—*Eternal Recurrence*! The Womb seeks me out to swallow me back into its vast Nothingness. Monica is dead, the Womb itself is dust, and thus ends "our most sweet custom of living together."

But if we cannot live together, how can we live at all? When Mama comes with her honey-cakes dipped in vinegar, I shall ask her this ultimate question upon which hang all the law and the prophets. To live together, to love together: is this the answer to the great riddle of Being? But it is too late: the Sphinx has

The Aesthetic Self

destroyed me because I did not answer in time. Dionysos has been torn to pieces by the wild Maenads—the Lama, Mama, and Lou!

Dionysos is bleeding to death. *Help, keepers, help*!

Suggestions for Further Reading

Hannah Arendt, "Tradition and the Modern Age," *Partisan Review*, XXI (1954), pp. 53-75. A discussion of Nietzsche, Marx, and Kierkegaard as indicators of the end of the era of pure philosophy.

Lewis White Beck, *Six Secular Philosophers* (New York: Harper, 1960), pp. 79-91.

Eric R. Bentley, *The Cult of the Superman: A Study of the Idea of Heroism in Carlyle and Nietzsche* (New York: J. P. Lippincott, 1944).

_____, "Modern Hero-Worship. Notes on Carlyle, Nietzsche, and Stefan George," *Sewanee Review*, LII (1944), pp. 441-56.

Heinz Bluhm, "Nietzsche's Early Religious Development," *The Germanic Review*, XI (1936), pp. 164-83.

Harold H. Borland, *Nietzsche's Influence on Swedish Literature with special reference to Strindberg, Ola Hansson, Heidenstam and Fröding* (London: Wettergren, 1957).

Frederick C. Copleston, *Friedrich Nietzsche, Philosopher of Culture* (London: Burns and Oates, 1942).

Arthur C. Danto, *Nietzsche as Philosopher* (New York: Macmillan, 1965).

Ivo Frenzel, *Friedrich Nietzsche*, translated by Joachim Neugveschel (New York: Pegasus Books, 1967).

Daniel Halevy, *The Life of Friedrich Nietzsche*, translated by J. M. Howe (New York: Macmillan, 1911).

William Hubben, *Four Prophets of our Destiny. Kierkegaard, Dostoevsky, Nietzsche, and Kafka* (New York: Macmillan, 1952).

Karl Jaspers, *Nietzsche. An Introduction to the Understanding of His Philosophical Activity*, translated by Charles F. Wallraft and Frederick J. Schmitz (Tucson, Ariz.: University of Arizona Press, 1965).

_____, *Nietzsche and Christianity*, translated by E. B. Ashton (Chicago: Henry Regnery, 1961).

Walter A. Kaufmann, *Nietzsche: Philosopher, Psychologist, Antichrist* (Princeton, N.J.: Princeton University Press, 1950).

_____, "Nietzsche's Admiration for Socrates," *Journal of the History of Ideas*, IX (1948), pp. 472-91.

_____, "Some Typical Misconceptions of Nietzsche's Critique of Christianity," *Philosophical Review*, LXI (1952), pp. 595-99.

Richard Kuehnemund, "Faust and Zarathustra in Our Time," *Germanic Review*, XV (1940), pp. 116-36.

Frederick R. Love, *Young Nietzsche and the Wagnerian Experience* (Chapel Hill, N.C.: University of North Carolina Press, 1963).

Karl Löwith, "Nietzsche's Revival of the Doctrine of Eternal Recurrence" in *Meaning in History* (Chicago: University of Chicago Press, 1949), pp. 214-222.

Otto Manthey-Zorn, *Dionysus: The Tragedy of Nietzsche* (Amherst, Mass.: Amherst College Press, 1956).

Charles Morris, "Nietzsche: An Evaluation," *Journal of the History of Ideas*, VI (1945), pp. 285-98.

Hugh A. Reyburn, *Nietzsche: The Story of a Human Philosopher* (New York: Macmillan, 1948).

Josiah Royce, "Nietzsche," *Atlantic Monthly* (March 1917), pp. 321-31.

William M. Salter, *Nietzsche the Thinker* (New York: Frederick Ungar Publishing Company, 1968).

August Strindberg

The Son of a Servant

*His new self revolted against
his old one, and for the rest of his
life they fought with each other
like an unhappy married couple
who cannot get a divorce.*

August Strindberg (1849-1912) is often called Sweden's greatest writer. In addition to having a formative influence on the development of drama in Sweden, Europe, and throughout the Western world, Strindberg was also a political satirist of rare skill who employed his novels, short stories, poems, and plays to ridicule established institutions and cherished traditions.

Most of his works are autobiographical. *The Son of a Servant*, subtitled *The Story of the Evolution of a Human Being*, recounts Strindberg's childhood and adolescent years, from 1849 to 1867. It is followed by *Storm and Stress*, the record of Strindberg's university years in Uppsala, 1867-1872, during which time he was influenced by the writings of Soren Kierkegaard, among others. *In the Red Room* covers the years from 1872 to 1875 and treats the beginnings of Strindberg's literary, journalistic, and editorial career. *The Author* is followed by *A Madman's Defense*, dealing with the years 1875 to 1887, when Strindberg's chief preoccupation was his first marriage. A number of other works are also chiefly autobiographical. *Inferno* covers the author's brush with insanity during the years 1894 to 1897. *Legends* carries on from *Inferno* and tells about the author's conversion to a creedless mystical religion. *Alone* follows another unsuccessful marriage in 1903, and gives glimpses of the subconscious of the solitary creative artist. Finally, *The Occult Diary* concerns itself with Strindberg's thoughts during the years 1896 to 1907. All are employed by

Strindberg to chart and interpret his spiritual odyssey, from the pietism of his earliest years to the free-flowing mystical outlook at which he finally arrived.

Strindberg's life was marked by upheaval and confusion. Never successful long in marriage, nor in retaining custody of his five children, Strindberg seems yet to have used every personal crisis as an occasion to explore his own psyche. In almost Kierkegaardian fashion, he was preoccupied with producing a description (or a grammar) of self-consciousness. At the same time, as the subtitle of *The Son of a Servant* indicates, he looked to evolution for the eventual disclosure of the true self. This meant that the events of his life as well as the people in it became instruments in his quest for a conscious identity which would not be threatened by the shifting tides of fortune or social and literary approbation. Each event became a means of self-disclosure, and each person came to play a part in an unfolding personal drama. The scenes were designed by the political climate of Sweden in the nineteenth century—a situation which found the poorer classes beginning to emerge from economic oppression—and are infused with religious themes from Swedenborg, alchemy, theosophy, and mysticism.

The first book in Strindberg's autobiography, *The Son of a Servant*, reconstructs much of Swedish social, political, economic, and religious life in the nineteenth century. It is particularly insightful regarding the way in which a Christian pietistic upbringing can influence adolescent life. The reader will notice that Strindberg has attempted to tell the story of his childhood and boyhood in terms of the perspective and attitudes which he had during that portion of his life. Some readers will feel that this was the only period in Strindberg's life in which he took religion seriously. Others may argue that the initial stages are so tinged with confusion that they do not deserve to be called a "religious phase." And others may see the entire life-sequence, as Strindberg himself did, as a kind of evolution toward greater religious maturity. Strindberg has made the materials available to document all of those responses, and the decision will rest upon what one regards religious sensitivity to be. In this context, as well as in the original historical setting, Strindberg's presence provokes the kind of controversy and discussion which quickly finds itself taking in all sides and incorporating all of the possible responses to fundamental religious questions.

The Son of a Servant

Childhood Memories

Childhood memories show clearly how our senses come to life, first taking in colours and movements, our senses responding to the slightest breath, how later our perceptions are directed mainly to what is striking and blatant, and only at the end to moral ideas, justice and injustice, cruelty and mercy.

The Aesthetic Self

Our memories lie in confusion, unformed and undefined, like pictures in a kaleidoscope. But when we turn the wheel, they merge together and form pictures, sometimes significant, sometimes not, all depending.

One day John sees some great big wonderful pictures of emperors and kings in blue and red uniforms, pictures the servant girls have hung up in the nursery. He sees another showing a building that is being blown sky-high, a building full of Turks. He listens to someone reading from a newspaper a description of flaming cannon balls being fired at towns and villages in a distant land. And he even remembers little details—his mother weeping at hearing how the poor fishermen were driven out of their burning cottages with their children. The pictures? Tsar Nicholas and Napoleon III. The rest of it? The storming of Sevastopol and the bombardment of the coast of Finland.

His father spends the whole day at home. All the tumblers in the house are placed on the window ledges. They are filled with sand in which candles are inserted. At night all the candles are lit. The rooms are warm and bright. And it is bright too in the Clara schoolhouse and in the church and in the vicarage. And the church is full of music.

The occasion? The celebration of King Oscar's recovery from a long illness.

A great uproar in the kitchen. Somebody is ringing the front doorbell, and his mother has been called out.

A man in uniform is standing there with a book in his hand, writing. The cook weeps, his mother supplicates and shouts, but the man in the helmet shouts even louder.

A policeman!

'The police!' The whole flat echoes with the cry. All day long they talk of nothing but the police. His father is summoned to the police station. To be arrested? No, but he has to pay a fine of three riksdalers and sixteen shillings banko, because his cook had emptied out the dishwater in the gutter in the daytime.

One afternoon he sees them lighting the lamps in the street. A cousin draws his attention to the fact that they have no oil and no wicks, but only a metal tube. These are the first gas lamps.

For many nights he lies in bed, without getting up by day. He is tired and sleepy. A harsh-voiced man comes to his bed, and says that he must not lay his hands outside the coverlet. They give him evil-tasting stuff with a spoon. He eats nothing. They whisper in the room, and his mother weeps. Then he is sitting up again at the window in the bedroom. Bells are tolling the whole day long. Green biers are carried across the churchyard. Sometimes a dark mass of people stand round a black chest. Gravediggers with their spades keep coming and going. He has to wear a copper plate suspended by a blue silk ribbon on his breast, and chew all day on a root. That is the cholera epidemic of '54.

One day he takes a long walk with one of the maids. He walks so long he becomes homesick and cries for his mother. The maid takes him into a house. They sit in a dark kitchen near a green water-barrel. He begins to think he will never see his home again. But they walk even farther, past ships and barges, past a gloomy brick house with long high walls behind which prisoners sit. He sees a new church, a new avenue lined with trees, a dusty country road with dandelions growing along its edges. Now the maid carries him. At last they come to a great stone building and close by a yellow wooden house with a cross, surrounded by a large garden with green trees. They see people dressed in white, limping, mournful. They reach a great hall filled with brown-painted beds. Nothing but beds with old women in them. The walls are whitewashed, the old women are white, the bedclothes are white. And the place smells bad. They pass by a great many beds and stop in the middle of the room at a bed on the right side. In it lies a woman younger than the rest, her black curly hair confined by a night-cap. She lies half on her back, her face is emaciated, and she wears a white cloth over her head and ears. Her thin hands are wrapped in white bandages and her arms shake ceaselessly inwards at the elbows so that her knuckles rub against each other. When she sees the child, her arms and knees tremble violently, and she bursts into tears. She kisses his head. The boy feels uncomfortable. He is shy and not far from crying himself. 'Don't you know Christine?' she says. 'I suppose you don't.' Then she dries her eyes again and describes her sufferings to the maid, who is handing her some food out of a basket.

The white old women now start to murmur and mumble, and Christine begs the maid not to show what she has in the basket, for the women are envious. So the maid slips a yellow riksdaler into the hymn book on the table. It's all so tiresome to the boy. His heart tells him nothing. It does not tell him that he has drunk this woman's lifeblood, blood that had been bought and sold. It does not tell him that he slept his best sleep on that shrunken bosom, that those shaking arms had cradled, carried, and dandled him. His heart tells him nothing, for the heart is only a muscle, pumping blood, indifferent as to the source it sprang from. But after receiving her last fervent kisses, after bowing to the old women and the nurse, and once again breathing freely in the courtyard after inhaling the close air of the sick-ward, he becomes somehow conscious of a debt, a misplaced debt, which can only be paid by eternal gratitude, a few bits of food, and a riksdaler slipped into a hymn book, and he feels ashamed at being glad to get away from the brown-painted beds and the suffering women.

She had been his wet nurse, who lay for fifteen years in the same hospital bed, suffering from spasms, wasting away, till she died there. Then a portrait of him in a schoolboy's cap was sent back to him by the directors of the Sabbatsberg infirmary, where it had hung during all those years in which the growing youth had only once each year given her an hour of his time—an hour of indescribable joy to her, to him an hour for easing his conscience a little. All he had got from her was rotten blood and twitching nerves, but he still felt he owed her a debt—a universal debt, not a personal debt, for she had only given him what she had been obliged to sell. The fact that she had been compelled to sell it

328   The Aesthetic Self

was the sin of society. But as a member of society he felt to a certain degree guilty.

Sometimes he goes into the churchyard. Everything is so strange there. Stone cellars with covers on which are printed letters and numbers. Grass that can't be walked on. Leafy trees that can't be touched. Uncle took a leaf one day but a policeman came over. The big building whose foot is always thrust in his way is a mystery to him. People go in and out of it. Songs and music are heard from inside. And there's always a ringing, a bonging, and a tolling. It's full of secrets. And in the east wall is a window with a golden eye—'That is God's eye'—He doesn't know what that means, but in any case it's a pretty big eye and must be able to see awfully far.

Under the big window is a cellar window with bars. Uncle shows the boys the shining coffins inside—'That's where the Nun of Clara Church lives.'—Who is that? He doesn't know, but it must be a ghost.

He finds himself standing in an enormously big room and doesn't know where he's supposed to be. It's very beautiful, with everything in white and gold. Music as if from a hundred huge pianos sings over his head, but he can't see any instruments or any players. The benches form a long avenue and down at the far end is a picture—out of the Bible probably. Two white people are lying on their knees, and they have wings, and there are two gilded candles. They must be the two angels with gilded candles who go through his house. And there stands a man in a red coat, and he is quiet and his back is turned. The people are leaning in their benches as if they were asleep.—'Take off your caps,' says Uncle, 'and hold them in front of your faces.'—The boys take a look around and close by they see a strange stool, painted brown, and on it are two men in grey robes with cowls over their heads. They have iron chains on their feet and hands, and guards are standing next to them.

'Thieves,' whispers Uncle.

John hates it in there—strange, inexplicable, cruel, harsh—and also very cold. His brothers must feel the same way for they ask Uncle if they can go. They go out right away.

Incomprehensible—that's his impression of the cult that is supposed to reveal the simple truths of Christianity.

Cruel—crueller than the gentle teachings of Christ.

The part with the thieves was the worst. Iron chains—and those coats! . . .

His Mother's Death

Life now lay open before the young man. The pressures were off him, and no doubt he would have sailed smoothly through life if circumstances had not combined to take the wind out of his sails.

August Strindberg

After passing through twelve confinements, his mother had been weak for a long time. Now she was obliged to keep to her bed, and she got up only occasionally. She became moody and cranky. If she was contradicted, her cheeks would turn red. The previous Christmas she had had a violent argument with her brother regarding the pietist lay preachers. At dinner the latter had praised *Fredman's Epistles* as being more profound and richer in ideas than the sermons of the pietists. John's mother flared up and became hysterical. But this was only a symptom of her illness.

Now, while she was still able to get up, she began to mend the children's linen and clothes and to clean out all the drawers. She often talked to John about religion and other transcendental matters. One day she showed him some gold rings.

"You boys will get these when Mama is dead," she said.

"Which is mine?" asked John without stopping to think about death. She showed him a plaited girl's ring with a heart on it. It made a deep impression on the boy, who had never owned anything made of gold, and he often thought of that ring.

About that time a nurse was hired for the children. She was young and good-looking, didn't say very much, and sometimes smiled in a critical sort of way. She had served in a count's mansion in Garden Street, and probably thought that she had come into a pretty shabby house. She was supposed to look after the children and supervise the housemaids, but she was on almost intimate terms with the latter. There were now three servants—a housekeeper, a manservant, and a girl from the country. The girls had their boy friends, and they all had a good time in the kitchen, which sparkled with copper and tin ware. There was eating and drinking, and John and his brothers were often invited in. They were called 'sir' by the boy friends who toasted them and drank their health. Only the manservant stayed away. He thought it was 'vulgar' to act like that while the mistress of the house lay ill. The home seemed to be dissolving and disintegrating, and John's father had had money difficulties with the servants since his mother had been obliged to stay in bed. But she remained loyal to the servants to death, instinctively assuming they were right. And they took advantage of her partiality. It was strictly forbidden to excite the patient, but the servants intrigued against each other, and against the master of the house. One day John had melted some lead in a silver spoon. The cook blabbed to his mother; she was furious and told his father. But his father was only annoyed with the telltale. He went to John and said in a friendly way, as though he were compelled against his own wishes to make a complaint: 'Now you know you shouldn't melt lead in silver spoons. I don't care about the spoon; that can be repaired. But that devil Frederica has upset Mother. Don't tell the girls when you have done something stupid. Tell me and we'll straighten it out.'

For the first time he and his father were friends. He loved him when his father treated him as an equal.

One night while he was asleep his father's voice awoke him. He started up. The room was dark. Through the darkness he heard a deep trembling voice. 'Boys, you must come to your mother's bed—she's dying.'

He felt as if he had been struck by lightning. He sweated drops of ice and shivered all over as he pulled on his clothes. His eyes were wide open and streaming with tears, making the lamp flame look like a red bladder.

They stood round the bed and wept for an hour. Two hours. Three hours. The night crept on. His mother was unconscious and recognized none of them. The death struggle began—rattling in the throat and cries for help. The smaller children were not aroused. John sat and thought of all the bad things he had done. He could find nothing to weigh against them. After three hours he stopped crying. His thoughts wandered here and there. Death was so final. What would it be like with no mother around? Empty, desolate. No comfort, nothing to take her place. Only the deep gloom of misery. There must be some ray of hope or happiness. His glance fell on his mother's dresser with a plaster statuette of Linné holding a flower in his hand. There was the only good thing that would come from the bottomless well of unhappiness: he would get the ring. He could see it on his hand now. "This is in memory of my mother," he would be able to say, and he would weep at the thought of her. But he could not stop thinking how fine it would look.

Disgusting! Who could think such thoughts at his mother's deathbed? A boy drunk with sleep? A child who cried himself dry? Goodness no, an heir! Was he more avaricious than others? Was he born stingy and grasping? No, for then he would never have told anyone about something that was buried so deep within him. But all his life he could never forget it. It kept turning up in his mind, and whenever he thought of it during a sleepless night or when he was tired after work, he felt the blood rise to his cheeks. Then he would examine himself and his conduct and would punish himself as the lowest type of humanity. Not until he was older and had come to know a great number of men and had studied the mechanics of thought did he find out that the brain is a strange object that goes its own way, and that all men are alike in leading a double life: the one that can be seen and the one that can't, the one revealed by the thoughts they speak and the other by the thoughts they think.

But at this point he only knew that he was bad. And when he learned about pietism and heard the pietists talk about fighting evil thoughts, he realized that he had many evil thoughts. Where had they come from? What caused them? Original sin and the devil, said the pietists. He went along with them on that because he didn't want to be held responsible for his ugly thoughts. Yet all the same he could not help but think he was responsible. He had not yet heard about determinism and man's lack of free will. The determinists would have told him, 'That was no bad thought, my boy; it was a healthy thought. You were only trying to make a painful time as painless as possible. Every heir, rich and poor alike, has thought the same way—and, mark you, must have thought that way according to our knowledge of the way man thinks. The self-denying Christian moralists, the pillar saints with their heads in the clouds, call all thoughts evil that are based on self-preservation. But that is unwholesome, for the first and most holy duty of the individual is to protect himself, as far as that is possible without causing harm to others.'

But his entire upbringing was in accordance with the inferior conception of the world that prevailed then, oriented as it was towards a fixed heaven and a fixed hell. Some deeds were considered evil, others good. The former were to be punished, the latter rewarded. For example, it was considered virtuous to mourn one's mother deeply, regardless of how the mother might have treated one as a child. To be endowed with stable and durable feelings was considered a virtue. Those whose feelings were of a different kind were considered less virtuous. The unfortunate ones who noticed this lack in their character wanted to change and improve themselves. The result was that they were hypocritical towards others and dishonest with themselves. However, we have now reached the stage where sensitivity or emotionalism is regarded as a weakness; in older times it would have been called a vice.

French still has the same word *vice* for both vice and defect. A surplus of emotion and imagination, which serves only to conceal the truth, is now viewed as belonging to a lower stage of development, to savages, children and women. It is about to be buried and ploughed under like the crops of a farm exhausted through over-cultivation, and a new era of clear thinking is knocking at the door.

John was a quadroon with romanticism, pietism, realism, and naturalism in his bloodstream. Therefore he never became anything but a patchwork.

Certainly John thought about other things than that miserable ring. It was only a momentary distraction, two minutes out of months of sorrow. When at last there was stillness in the room, and his father said, 'Mother is dead,' he was not to be comforted. He shrieked like a drowning man. How can death bring such profound despair to those who believe they shall meet again? Faith has a rough time of it during those moments when there before one's eyes a personality is so thoroughly destroyed and annihilated.

John's father, who was generally as imperturbable on the outside as an Icelander, softened now. He took his sons by the hands and said, 'God has visited us. Now we have to stick together like friends. People go about thinking they can take care of themselves, not needing anyone. Then comes the blow, and then we see how we all need one another. Let us be sincere and understanding with each other.'

John felt a momentary relief from his sorrow. He had found a friend, a strong, wise, manly friend whom he could admire.

White sheets were now being hung up at the windows of the house in sign of mourning.

'You don't have to go to school, if you don't want to,' said his father.

'If you don't want to!' That meant his father recognized he had a will of his own.

Then came the aunts, cousins, relations, nurses, old servants, all calling down blessings on the dead. All offered their help in making the mourning clothes—there were four small and three older children. Young girls sat by the sickly light that fell through the sheeted windows and sewed while they conversed in undertones. It was strange and mysterious, and the period of mourning brought a whole chain of peculiar experiences with it. Never had the boy been the object of so much sympathy, never had he felt so many warm hands stretched out to him nor heard so many friendly words.

On the next Sunday his father read one of Wallin's sermons on the text 'She is not dead, but sleepeth.' With what extraordinary faith he took these words literally, and how well he understood how to open the wounds and heal them again! 'She is not dead, but sleepeth,' he repeated cheerfully. The mother did indeed sleep there in the cold parlour, but no one expected to see her wake up.

The time of burial approached, and a plot in the cemetery was purchased. His father's sister-in-law helped to sew the suits of mourning. She sewed and sewed. The old mother of seven penniless children, the once rich burgher's wife, sewed for the children of the marriage her husband had cursed. One day she stood up and asked her brother-in-law to speak with her privately. She whispered with him in a corner of the room. The two old people embraced each other and wept. Then John's father told them that their mother would be laid in their uncle's family grave. It was distinguished by a much-admired monument in the New Cemetery consisting of an iron pillar surmounted by an urn. The boys knew that this was an honour for their mother, but they did not understand that her burial there marked the end of a family quarrel and that justice had been done, after her death, to a good and conscientious woman who had been despised for having become a mother before she was legally married.

Now the house radiated with peace and reconciliation as they all tried to outdo one another in acts of friendliness. They smiled understandingly at each other, avoided disturbing each other, and anticipated each other's wishes.

Then came the day of the funeral. After the coffin had been screwed shut and was being carried through the hall, filled with mourners dressed in black, one of John's little sisters became hysterical. She cried and flung herself into his arms. He picked her up and hugged her as if he were her mother and wanted to protect her. When he felt how her trembling little body clung close to him, he felt stronger than he had for a long time. Comfortless himself, he could bestow comfort, and as he quieted her he himself grew calm. It was only the black coffin and the crowd of people that had frightened her. The smaller children hardly missed their mother. They did not cry for her and soon forgot her. The tie between mother and child is not formed overnight but only through long

August Strindberg

333

personal acquaintance. John's real sense of loss lasted for scarcely a quarter of a year. He mourned for her indeed a long time, but that was more because he wished to go on living in that frame of mind. It suited his natural melancholy disposition, which seized upon this period of mourning for his mother as a convenient way of expressing itself. . . .

Shattering Religious Icons

Parallel with the strong reactionary current of pietism ran that of the new rationalism, but in the opposite direction. Christianity, which at the close of the preceding century had been relegated to the class of myths, was again received into favour, and since the Christian Church enjoyed the protection of the state, those who supported the restoration could not prevent themselves being reinoculated by Christian dogmas. But in 1835 Strauss's *Life of Jesus* made a new breach, and even in Sweden fresh water began to trickle into the dried-up wells. The book was made the subject of legal action, but upon that foundation the whole work of the new reformation was built up—by self-made reformers, as is always the case, since the other kind do not reform at all.

Pastor Cramér had the honour of being the first in this movement. As early as 1859 he published his *Farewell to the Church,* a popular but well-informed criticism of the New Testament. He set the seal of sincerity on his belief by seceding from the State Church and resigning his office. His book produced a great effect, and although the writings of Ignell had a wider vogue among the theologians, they did not reach the younger generation. In the same year there appeared Rydberg's *The Last Athenian.*

The influence of this book was lessened by its being hailed as a literary success and thereby transplanted to the neutral territory of belles-lettres. A deeper impression was made by Rydberg's *What the Bible Tells Us about Christ* in 1862, which signalled the Ragnarök of the theologians. Renan's *Life of Jesus* in Ignell's translation took young and old by storm and was read in the schools along with Cramér, which was not the case with Rydberg's book. Then came Boström's attack on the Doctrine of Hell (1864), and with that the door was opened to rationalism or free thought, as it was called. Boström's work, which was not really important, had a great effect because of his reputation as a professor at Uppsala and as a former tutor to the Royal Family. The courageous man was willing to risk his good name, something no one after him has had to do, since it is no longer dangerous to be a freethinker or to work for freedom of thought.

In short, everything conduced to undermine John's faith. One little puff and down it went like a house of cards. He met a young engineer who was a lodger in Fanny's house. He watched John a long while before he made any approaches. John respected him, since he was supposed to have a good head, and he probably was also somewhat jealous. Fanny knew the two men would meet, and warned John what would happen. She said the engineer was an extremely interesting man, brilliant but dangerous. Finally John was introduced to him. He was a strongly-built man from Värmland, with rough, candid features, and a childlike laugh—when he did laugh, which wasn't often—a quiet laugh rather than a roar. They were soon on familiar terms. The first evening only a slight skirmish took place between them. The subject was Faith and Knowledge.

'Faith must master reason,' said John, echoing Krummacher.

'No,' replied his friend. 'Reason is a divine gift, which raises man above the brutes. Shall man lower himself to the level of the brutes by throwing away God's divine gift?'

'There are things,' said John, echoing Norbeck, 'that we can certainly believe without demanding proof. We believe the calendar, for example, without having any real knowledge of the movement of the planets.'

'Yes,' answered his friend, 'we believe it because our reason does not revolt against it.'

'But,' said John, 'in Galileo's time they revolted against the idea that the earth revolves around the sun. "He is possessed by a spirit of contradiction," they said. "He just wants to be different." '

'We don't live in Galileo's age,' replied his friend, 'and the enlightened reason of our time rejects the Deity of Christ and everlasting punishment.'

'We cannot dispute about these things,' said John.

'Why not?'

'They are beyond the powers of reason.'

'Just what I said two years ago when I was a believer.'

'Have you—were you a pietist [läsare]?'

'Yes, I was.'

'Hm! And now you have peace of mind?'

'Yes, I have peace of mind.'

'How did you manage that?'

'Through a preacher I learned to recognize the true spirit of Christianity.'

'You mean you are a Christian?'

'Yes, I acknowledge Christ.'

'But you don't believe that he was God?'

'He never said so himself. He called himself God's son, and we are all God's sons.'

Fanny interrupted the conversation, which was typical of religious discussions about 1865. John's curiosity was aroused now. There were then, he said to himself, men who did not believe in Christ and yet had peace. But mere criticism could not shatter the religious icons in his mind; the *horror vacui* held him back until the works of Theodore Parker fell into his hands. These sermons without Christ and hell were just what he needed. And such fine sermons they were. It must be admitted that he read them in extreme haste, and that he was

August Strindberg

most anxious that his friends and relatives should enjoy them too so that they would not criticize him. He confused the disapproval of others with his own bad conscience and was so accustomed to consider others right that he fell into conflict with himself.

But Christ the Inquisitor came tumbling down; and the election of grace, the punishments of Judgment Day, all collapsed as though they had been tottering for a long time. He was astonished at how quickly it happened. It was like taking off clothes he had outgrown and putting on new ones.

One Sunday morning he went with the engineer to Haga Park. It was spring. The hazel bushes were in bloom and the anemones were out. The weather was fairly clear, the air soft and dewy after a night's rain. They talked about freedom of the will. The pietists [*läsare*] refused to take a definite stand on the subject. No one, they said, had the power to become a child of God of his own free will. The Holy Spirit must come to one. Predestination. John wished to be converted but he could not be. He had learned to pray, 'Lord, create in me a new will.' But then how could he be held responsible for his evil will? Yes, he could, answered the pietist, through the Fall. For when man, originally endowed with free will, chose evil, posterity inherited this evil will, which became perpetually evil and ceased to be free. And man could be delivered from this evil will only through Christ and the workings of grace and the Holy Spirit. The new birth did not depend upon his own will but on the grace of God. In other words, he was not free. But even though he was not free, he was still held responsible. There was the false conclusion.

The engineer was a nature worshipper, and so was John. Now just what is this nature worship that is regarded at the present time as so hostile to culture? A relapse into barbarism, say some. A healthy reaction against over-culture, say others. When man discovers society is a living arrangement based on error and injustice, when he perceives that, in exchange for petty advantages, society suppresses too forcibly every natural impulse and desire, when he sees through the illusion that he is a demigod and a child of God and realizes he is simply a kind of animal—then he flees from society, which was built on the notion of man's divine origin, and goes out into nature to find himself. Here he feels in his proper environment as an animal, sees himself as a figure in the landscape, and beholds his origin—the earth and the meadow. He sees as in a living compendium the interdependence of all creation—the mountains that have become soil, the sea that has turned to rain, the plains that are crumbled and levelled hills, the woods that have risen from the hills and the lakes. He views the ocean of air that he and all living creatures breathe, he hears the birds that live on insects, sees the insects that fertilize the plants, beholds the animals on which he himself lives. He feels at home. And in our time with its scientific point of view, a solitary hour with nature, where one can see all of evolutionary history in living pictures, can be the only satisfactory substitute for divine service. But our optimistic

The Aesthetic Self

evolutionists prefer to spend an hour in a dark meeting hall in some narrow city street where they can spew forth their denunciations against the social organization that they both despise and admire. They praise it as the highest stage of development but wish to overthrow it on the grounds that it is irreconcilable with the true happiness of the animal. They wish to reconstruct and develop it, some of them say. But reconstruction cannot take place without completely razing the present society—and they say they don't want any halfway measures. Are they not admitting, then, that the present society is a case of misdirected evolution, simultaneously hostile both to culture and to nature?

They say that the social community is, like everything else, a product of nature, and that culture is nature. Yes, but it is the worst aspect of nature, nature on a sidetrack, working against its own goal—happiness.

At any rate, it was the nature worship of that time and of John's forerunner, the engineer, which revealed to him the defects of civilized society and prepared the way for the new view of man's origin. Darwin's *Origin of Species* had appeared as early as 1859, but its influence had not yet penetrated the intellectual world very deeply, much less had it been able to fertilize other minds. Everyone was spouting Moleschott, and materialism was the watchword of the day. Armed with this and with his geology, the engineer pulled to pieces the Mosaic story of the creation. But he still spoke of the Creator; he was a theist and saw God's wisdom and goodness reflected in his works.

While they were walking in the park, the church bells in the city began to ring. John stood still and listened. He heard the terrifying bells of Clara Church that had rung throughout his melancholy childhood; he heard the bells of the Adolf-Fredrik Church that had frightened him into throwing himself on the bleeding breast of the Crucified; he heard the bells of St. John's that on Saturdays, when he was in Jacob School, had announced the end of the week.

A gentle, southerly breeze bore the sound of the bells out from the city, and it echoed under the fir trees, warning him, threatening him.

'Are you going to church?' asked his friend.

'No,' answered John, 'I'll never go to church any more.'

'Well, follow your conscience,' said the engineer.

It was the first time that John had remained away from church. He was defying both his father's orders and the voice of his own conscience. He grew excited, inveighed against religion and the tyranny of the family, talked of the church of God in nature, and was carried away by the new gospel that proclaimed salvation for all, happiness and the good life to all. Then suddenly he became silent.

'You've got a bad conscience,' said his friend.

'That's right,' said John. 'One should either not do what one will regret, or not regret what one has done.'

'The latter is better.'

'But I regret it anyway! Regret doing the right thing, because I know it's not right to play the hypocrite in this old temple of idols. My new conscience tells me I am right and my old one tells me I am wrong. I'll never have any peace of mind again.'

And he never did. His new self revolted against his old one, and for the rest of his life they fought with each other like an unhappy married couple who cannot get a divorce. . . .

As one age made room for another, the Jews smiled as they observed these Christians, who had tried for two thousand years to make a red hell of this green earth and who now for the first time realized that the teachings of Christ constituted a subjective personal doctrine, well suited to the spiritual needs of its author and his suffering fellow men under the Roman Empire, but one that had to be adapted to fit new conditions. Being positivists by nature and having lived through one epoch after another without participating in the Christian experience, the Jews now saw the Christians themselves razing Christendom. And how they smiled when it came crashing down. That was the Jew's vengeance, and that was his function in European culture.

In 1865 young John, still trembling from his stigmatization, worn to the bone in his struggle against the flesh and the devil, his ears still aching from church bells and psalm singing, entered the brightly lit theatre in the company of daring young men of high rank and good breeding. And from the centre of the dress circle he saw the paintings of the happy pagan world spread out before him and heard music, fresh, ingenuous music, music with a certain *gemüt*—Offenbach was born in Germany—melodious, spirited. Merely the overture by itself made him laugh. And what came after that! The temple ritual behind the veil reminded him of the baking of the Communion bread in the parish kitchen. Thunder turned out to be a sheet of black iron. The god who ate the sacrifice offered up to him was Carl John Uddman. The goddesses—three beautiful actresses. The gods on high—invisible stage directors. The whole antique world went out the window. All those gods and goddesses and heroes who had been hallowed in the schoolbooks came tumbling down from their pedestals. Greece and Rome, which were always treated as the source of all culture, were exposed and brought down to the level of everything else. All on the same level! Democracy in action! And John felt another few pounds of oppression lifted from his back, and the fear and despair of not being able to 'raise himself in the world' vanished. Then came the part about the joy of life. Human beings and gods paired off helter-skelter without asking anybody's permission. The gods helped young girls flee from old men; the priest stepped down from the temple where he had grown tired of deluding people and, with a crown of laurel leaves around his perspiring forehead, danced the cancan with the hetaerae. That was fair play, strictly aboveboard. It all struck him like the word of God. There was nothing to criticize, nothing to object to. It was perfect the way it was. Was it

The Aesthetic Self

unwholesome? No. But as for applying it to life itself—he had no desire to do that. It was only a play, something unreal, and his point of view was then, and would always be, aesthetic. What did aesthetic mean: So much could be smuggled in under the cloak of that word, so many concessions and compromises could be made. It meant it wasn't a matter of life and death; on the other hand it didn't mean it was to be taken as a joke. It was very vague. The *Decameron* glorified vice and sin, but its aesthetic value was great. What kind of value was that? Ethically the book was damnable; aesthetically it was praiseworthy. Ethics and aesthetics! Here was a new, double-bottomed magician's box from which one could pull forth gnats or camels, as one wished. . . .

Playing the Clergyman's Role

During a visit to the pastor's house, John happened to mention to the assistant or curate his idea of entering the clergy. Since the senior pastor no longer preached because of old age and general infirmity, the curate was the only one who delivered sermons. He found the work a burden and kept his eye peeled for young graduates who were eager to make their debuts as preachers. Now he asked John whether he felt like delivering a sermon.

'But I haven't graduated yet.'

'Doesn't make any difference.'

'Really? Well, let me think about it.'

The curate did not let him consider long. He said that many students and graduates had preached here before, and that the church had won a certain amount of fame because the great actor Knut Almlöf had preached there in his youth.

'You mean Almlöf who's playing Menelaus? In *La belle Hele'ne*?'

'Exactly!'

That did it! Out came the Bible, a book of homilies was borrowed, and John promised to have his trial sermon ready by Friday.

Imagine! Only a year after his Confirmation, he would be climbing into the pulpit to preach, and the royal secretary and the baron and all the ladies and gentlemen would humbly and devoutly give audience as he spoke. How suddenly he had come through—no clerical examination, not even a college degree—and soon he would be borrowing a gown and bands and turning the hourglass and praying the Lord's Prayer and reading banns. His head began to swell, and he walked home feeling a foot taller, fully conscious that he was no longer a boy.

But when he got home he began to have afterthoughts. He was a freethinker. Was it honourable to play the hypocrite? No, no! But must he give up the sermon? That would be too great a sacrifice. Fame beckoned. And would he not perhaps be able to sow a few seeds of free thought?

August Strindberg

339

Yes, but still he would be dissembling. Always seeing the selfish motives behind an act, he could not avoid considering the intentions of the doer rather than the good or bad consequences of the deed. His preaching could be of service to others; it would not hurt them to hear something new and true, and therefore he—Still it was not honest. He could not get around that. He went to the baroness and unburdened his conscience.

'Do you believe that preachers believe all they say?' she asked.

That was the preachers' affair, said John. As for himself, he couldn't do it.

Finally, he went by horse to the curate's house and laid his cards on the table. The curate appeared cross and upset at having been confided in.

'You believe in God, don't you? Then why in the name of Jesus fuss about it?'

'Yes, of course, I do.'

'Very well! Just don't talk about Christ. Bishop Wallin never mentioned the name of Christ in his sermons. But don't make a fuss about it. And keep me out of it.'

'All right. I'll do the best I can,' said John, glad to have kept his honour intact and his ambitious hopes alive.

They had a drink and a bite to eat, and the matter was settled.

There was something good about sitting in front of his books and homilies and hearing the royal secretary ask for him. And to hear the maid answer: 'The tutor is busy writing his sermon.'

Now he had the text to think about. It was for the seventh Sunday after Whitsuntide, first year, and the complete text read as follows. 'Jesus said, Now is the Son of man glorified, and God is glorified in him. If God be glorified in him, God shall also glorify him in himself, and shall straightway glorify him.'

That was all. He turned the sentence this way and that but could make no sense of it. 'Pretty thick.' But it touched the most delicate point—the Deity of Christ. If he could find the courage to explain that away, it would certainly be a heroic accomplishment. The prospect fascinated him, and with Theodore Parker's help he composed a prose poem on Christ as the Son of God, and then put forward very cautiously the assertion that we are all God's sons but that Christ is His chosen and beloved Son, with whom He was greatly pleased and to whose teachings we must listen. But that was only the introduction, and the gospel is read after the introduction. Now what should he preach? He had already pacified his conscience by plainly stating his views regarding the Deity of Christ. He glowed with excitement, he swelled with courage, and he felt that he had a calling to fulfill. He would draw his sword against dogmas, against the doctrine of election, against pietism. It was his mission.

When he came to the place where, after reading the text, he should say, 'The text we have read gives us occasion for a short time to consider the following subject,' he wrote. 'Since the text of the day provides no further occasion for remark, we will, for a brief while, consider what is of greater

The Aesthetic Self

importance.' And then he would deal with God's efficacious grace in conversions.

Thus he would be making a double attack: one against the custom of preaching from the text, and another against the Church's teaching on the subject of election.

First he dealt with conversion as a serious matter that required sacrifice and depended on the free will of man (he was not quite clear about that). Then he went through the doctrine of election, and finally flung open for all the doors of the kingdom of heaven: 'Come unto me, all ye that labour and are heavy laden.' Publicans and sinners, whores and governors, all would go to heaven, including the thief and the robber. 'Today shalt thou be with me in paradise.' That is the gospel of Christ for all, and no one should assume that the key to the kingdom of heaven is committed to him and imagine that he alone is the child of God (that was a hit at the pietists), but the doors of grace are open to all and everyone. Everyone!

He was very much in earnest as he wrote all this, and he felt like a missionary.

On Friday he betook himself to the church and read certain passages of his sermon from the pulpit. He chose the most harmless ones. Then he repeated the prayers while the curate stood under the choir gallery and shouted, 'Louder! Slower!' He passed the test, and he and the curate had a drink and a bite to eat.

On Sunday the church was full of people. John put on his gown and bands in the vestry. For a moment he thought the whole thing was ridiculous. Then he was seized with anxiety. He prayed to the only true God for help, now that he was to draw the sword on His behalf against age-long error, and when the last notes of the organ were silent, he entered the pulpit with confidence.

Everything went well. But when he came to the passage, 'Since the text of the day provides no further occasion for remark,' and saw a movement among the faces of the congregation, which looked like so many white smudges, he trembled. But only for a moment. Then he plucked up courage and read his sermon in a fairly strong and confident voice. When he neared the end, he himself was so moved by the beautiful truths he proclaimed that he could scarcely see the writing on the paper for tears.

He took a deep breath, and read through all the prayers till the organ began to play and he left the pulpit. The curate thanked him and added, 'But—I say—one shouldn't depart from the text. Wouldn't do. My, my, my, suppose the Church Consistory heard of it. But I'm sure no one noticed it. Let us hope not.' As for the contents of the sermon, he had no objections to make.

They had dinner at the pastor's house, and John played and danced with the girls, and he was the hero of the day.

'It was a great sermon,' said the girls. 'So short.'

'You read much too fast. And you skipped one of the prayers.'

'You have to crawl before you can walk,' said the curate. . . .

Weaknesses and Strengths

That summer he remained at home and gave lessons on a grand scale. With the money earned he hoped to go to the university at Uppsala in the autumn and do graduate work. The clergy no longer attracted him. He had put that behind him, and besides it went against his conscience to take the ordination vow.

That summer he slept with a girl for the first time. He felt terribly disappointed, like so many others have done.—So that was all there was to it!—The funniest thing about it was that it happened right across from the Bethlehem Church. But why had it not happened sooner? So many years of anguish and anxiety would have been spared him, so much strength and energy saved. In any event, things were quite calm and peaceful afterwards, and he felt healthy and happy, as if he had fulfilled a duty.

In the autumn he went to Uppsala. Old Margaret packed his suitcase, and put in cooking utensils, and a knife and fork and spoon. Then she made him borrow fifteen crowns from her. His father handed him a case of cigars and told him to help himself. John had eighty crowns tucked away, which he had earned from tutoring, and which would have to get him through the first term at the university.

The doors to the big wide world stood open for him and he had the ticket in his hand. All he had to do was walk in. All!?

'A man's character is his fate.' That was a standard, widely held saying at that time. Now that John was about to go out into the world and seek his destiny, he spent many leisure hours trying to cast his horoscope by studying his character. He thought it was already complete. Society respects and honours certain people as men of character, men who have sought and found their positions in life, assumed the parts they will play, worked out the bases for their behaviour and their actions, and who from then on act that way automatically.

A man with a so-called character is a very simple piece of mechanism: he has only one posture from which to carry on the extremely complicated business of life, and he has decided to hold one definite opinion on any given matter for the rest of his life. And in order not to be accused of 'lacking character,' he never changes this opinion, however foolish or impossible it may be. It follows that a man of character must be just a very ordinary man and, one might say, a little stupid. A man of character and an automaton seem to be pretty much the same thing. Dickens's famous characters are mere puppets, and stage characters have to be automatons. And a well-drawn character is equivalent to a caricature. Moreover, a man of character is supposed to know what he wants. But who knows what he really wants? One wants or doesn't want, that's all. The moment one attempts to ponder over what one's will is seeking, then one's will usually ceases to function. In society and in life one must always weigh the consequences of one's deeds for oneself and for others; that is, one must ponder and reflect. He who acts on the spur of the moment is an unwise man, a selfish man, a naive, unconscious man; and it is he who gets ahead in life because he does not consider the trouble he makes for others but sees only the advantages he gains for himself.

Having acquired the habit of self-examination from Christian soul-searching, John began to wonder if he had the kind of character or personality suitable for a man who wanted to make his way in the world.

He remembered that the housemaid he had whipped for having uncovered his body while he was asleep had exclaimed, 'That boy's got character!' What did she mean by that? She had seen that he was enough of a man of action to go out into the park after he had been treated insultingly, cut a switch and whip her with it. If he had done the ordinary thing and squealed to his parents, then she would have thought he was a coward. But his mother, who was alive then, had had another opinion. She called him revengeful. There he already had two points of view on the same question. Naturally he shared the one that was less honourable, since he believed more in that. Revenge? No, it was punishment, wasn't it? But did he have the right to punish? Right? Who was right? Parents always took revenge, didn't they? No, they chastised and punished. Then they must have some other right that he didn't have, and that meant there were two rights.

Yes, he must indeed be revengeful. Once by Clara churchyard a boy had said for all to hear that John's father had stood in the pillory. That was an insult to the whole family. Since John was weaker than his opponent, he called up his reserves and got his elder brother, who could fight, to join him to even the score in the blood feud by bombarding the boy with snowballs. In fact they more than got even because they also beat up the culprit's younger brother. The poor fellow was comparatively innocent, but they just didn't like his looks.

That was only good old-fashioned blood vengeance with all its symptoms. What else should he have done? Run and squealed to the teacher? No, he never did that. Well, then he must be revengeful; that was all there was to it. And that was a serious charge. He began to consider the matter more closely. Had he revenged himself on his father or his stepmother for the injustices they had done him? No, he had chosen to overlook them and to retire to his own corner.

Had he revenged himself on his teachers at Clara School by sending them boxes full of stones as Christmas presents? No! Was he really so severe towards others? Was he splitting hairs when he judged their conduct towards him? Lord, no! He was easy to get along with, gullible, and could be talked into anything as long as he wasn't pressured into it, or oppressed. By promising to swap, his schoolmates had tricked him out of his herbarium, his insect collection, his chemical apparatus, his Wild West books. Had he demanded payment or insulted them? No; he felt ashamed on their account and let it pass. At the end of one semester the father of a boy whom John had been teaching forgot to pay him. He felt ashamed to remind him, and it was not till half a year later that, at the instigation of his own father, he asked to be paid.

There was a peculiar trait in his character that made him identify with others, suffer for them, and feel ashamed for what they did. If he had lived in the Middle Ages, he would have stigmatized himself.

If one of his brothers behaved boorishly or stupidly, John blushed. In church he heard a boy's choir sing terribly out of tune. He crawled down in the pew and ached with shame.

Once, in fighting with a schoolmate, he managed to give him a good hard jab in the chest, but when he saw the boy's face distorted with pain, he burst into tears and reached out his hand to him. If anyone asked him to do something that he really couldn't bring himself to do, he suffered with that person, knowing that a wish or need was going unfulfilled.

He was cowardly and would listen to anyone rather than see him go away angry with him. He was still afraid of the dark, afraid of dogs, horses, and strangers. But he could also be courageous if necessary, as, for example when he rebelled in school over his final examinations, and when he rose up against his father.

'A man without religion is a mere animal,' said the old copybooks. Now that it has been discovered that animals are the most religious of creatures, and that he who has knowledge does not need religion, the practical worth of religion has been significantly reduced. By constantly placing the source of his strength outside himself, in God, John had lost faith in himself. God had gobbled up his ego. He prayed always, and at all hours, when he was in need of something. He prayed in school when he needed an answer; he prayed at the card table when he needed good cards. Religion had corrupted him by educating him for heaven instead of earth; the family had ruined him by training him for family life instead of for society; and school merely prepared him for the university instead of for life.

He was weak and irresolute. When he bought tobacco, he would ask his friend what kind he should buy, and then he would waver between Hope tobacco and Coat of Arms tobacco and finally pick Chandeloup. That's how he became a pawn in the hands of his friends: he wanted to be liked in order to lessen his fear of the unknown; having friends made him feel stronger.

He was a prey to capricious moods. One day, when he was a tutor in the country, he came into the town in order to go out with Fritz. When he got into town, he stayed in, lying in bed at home, debating with himself for hours on end whether he should go to Fritz or not. He knew that Fritz was expecting him, he himself wanted to see him, and yet he did not go. The next day he returned to the country and wailed and moaned in a letter to Fritz, trying to explain his behaviour. But Fritz refused to put up with his whims and got angry.

But for all his weakness he sometimes was aware of enormous resources of strength, which made him feel capable of anything. When he was twelve his brother brought home a French boys' book from Paris.

'We'll translate that and bring it out for Christmas,' said John.

And they actually did translate it, but as they did not know what further steps to take, nothing came of it.

An Italian grammar fell into his hands and he learned Italian.

When he was a tutor in the country, where there was no tailor, he undertook to alter a pair of trousers. He opened the seams, altered and stitched the trousers, and pressed them with the huge stable key. And he also repaired his own shoes.

When he heard his sisters and brothers play in a quartet, he was never satisfied with the performance. He wanted to jump up, snatch the instruments from them, and show them how it ought to be played.

When he practised singing, he would use the 'cello and pick out the tune on that. If only he knew what the strings were called!

John had learned to speak the truth. Like all children, he told little white lies in self-defense or in answer to impertinent questions, but he found a brutal enjoyment, in the middle of a conversation in which everybody was dallying with the truth, in saying straight out what everyone was actually thinking. At a ball, where he was very taciturn, his dancing partner asked him if he liked dancing.

'No, not at all.'

'Then why are you dancing?'

'Because I'm darn well forced to.'

Like all boys he had stolen apples, which didn't bother him at all. He made no secret of it. It was a time-honoured custom, wasn't it?

In school he had never done any real harm. Once, on the last day before the close of the term, he and some other boys had broken off all the clothes pegs and torn up some old exercise-books. He was the only one who got caught. But it was only a bit of mischief, an outburst of wild joy, and was not taken seriously.

Now, when he was passing judgment on himself, he began to collect other people's opinions to see what they made of him. He was amazed at the range of opinions. His father thought him hard; his stepmother, malicious; his brothers, eccentric. Every maid in the house had a different opinion of him. One of them liked him and thought that his parents treated him badly. Fanny at first thought he was tender and sensitive. His engineer friend regarded him at first as a likable child. Friend Fritz considered him melancholy and impulsive. His aunts thought he had a good heart; his grandmother that he had character; his girl at Stallmästergarden naturally idolized him; and his teachers didn't know what to make of him. He was rough with those who treated him roughly, decent towards those who treated him decently. And his friends? They never said what they thought of him. Compliments were never exchanged; only insults and blows and slaps.

August Strindberg

John asked himself whether it was he or the opinions of him that were multifarious. Was he false to himself and others, showing a different face to different people? His stepmother could tell him all about that. Whenever she heard anything good about him, she always said he was putting on an act.

Yes, but who didn't? She herself was friendly with her husband, stern with her stepchildren, soft with her own child, deferential to the landlord, arrogant with the servants. She bowed before the pietist clergy, smiled at the powerful, sneered at the powerless.

That was the 'law of accommodation,' which John still did not know about. It was a part of human nature, the instinct to adapt oneself—based partly on calculation and partly on unconscious or reflex actions. A lamb to one's friends, a lion to one's enemies.

But when is one true to oneself and when false? And where is the self—which is supposed to constitute one's character? Here and there and every place at once. One's ego is not a unit in itself; it is a conglomeration of reflexes, a complex of urges, drives, instincts, alternately suppressed and unleashed.

Because of the many strains of blood within him, the conflicting elements in his family, the wealth of experience he had gained from books and a busy life, young John was a rich mixture of all sorts of material, but all disorganized. Since he had no fixed situation, he was still looking for the role he was to play. That's why he was still characterless.

He had not been able to decide which of his impulses must be restrained and how much of his ego should be and must be sacrificed for the sake of the social organization that he was preparing to enter.

If he had really been able to view himself objectively, he would have found that most of the words he used were borrowed from books or from schoolmates, his gestures from teachers and friends, his facial expressions from relatives, his temperament from his mother and wet nurse, his tastes and inclinations from his father, perhaps from his grandfather. His face bore no resemblance to either of his parents. Since he had not seen his grandparents, he could not judge whether there was any resemblance to them. What did he possess, then, that was his in and by itself? Nothing. But there existed in his soul-complex two fundamental characteristics, which were to be crucial to his life and his destiny.

Doubt. He could not accept ideas without questioning them, developing them, combining them. In that respect he could not be an automaton, nor be enrolled as a member of organized society.

Sensitivity to pressure. That's why he tried to lessen this pressure first by rising in the world and secondly by criticizing and exposing the higher level to show that it was not so high after all and consequently not really worth striving for.

So he stepped out into the world! To evolve, change, develop—and yet to remain for ever the same as he was.

The Aesthetic Self

Suggestions for Further Reading

Robert Brustein, "Male and Female in August Strindberg," *Tulane Drama Review,* VII, 2 (1962), pp. 130-74.

Carl E. W. L. Dahlstrom, *Strindberg's Dramatic Expressionism* (Ann Arbor, Mich.: University of Michigan Press, 1930).

Charles Irving Glicksberg, *The Self in Modern Literature* (University Park, Pa.: Pennsylvania State University Press, 1964).

Alrik A. Gustafson, *A History of Swedish Literature* (Minneapolis: University of Minnesota Press, 1961).

Eric O. Johannesson, "The Problem of Identity in Strindberg's Novels," *Scandinavian Studies,* XXXIV, 1 (1962), pp. 1-35.

Franklin S. Klaf, *Strindberg: The Origin of Psychology in Modern Drama* (New York: Citadel Press, 1963).

Charles R. Lyons, "The Archetypal Action of Male Submission in Strindberg's *The Father,*" *Scandinavian Studies,* XXXVI, 3 (1964) pp. 218-32.

Brita M. E. Mortensen and Brian W. Downs, *Strindberg: An Introduction to His Life and Work* (Cambridge, Eng.: Cambridge University Press, 1949).

Evert Sprinchorn, "Notes" to August Strindberg, *The Son of a Servant* (London: Jonathan Cape, 1966), pp. 205-23.

Axel Johan Uppvall, *August Strindberg: A Psychoanalytic Study with Special Reference to the Oedipus Complex* (Boston: Gorham Press, 1920).

André Gide

Journals

I have lived as a man torn asunder. But how can it be explained that this cohabitation of extremes in me led not so much to restlessness and suffering as to a pathetic intensification of the sentiment of existence, of life?

André Gide, one of the great masters of French literature, was born in Paris in 1869. His father was a professor of Roman law at the Sorbonne—Protestant, bourgeois, and cultured. His mother was of Norman ancestry, Roman Catholic, and wealthy. From childhood André displayed an interest in classical culture and lived in the manner of the genteel class. He attended the Ecole Alsacienne and the Lycee Henri Quatre, passing his baccalaureate exams in 1889. He read Latin and Greek easily and was fluent in German, Italian, and English.

Two events in Gide's childhood and early adolescence are of special importance. First, Gide's father died when the boy was 11 years of age. Then, when he was 13, he found his cousin Madeleine Rondeaux weeping while kneeling in prayer. Madeleine had discovered that her mother had been unfaithful to her father but had resolved not to tell anyone about this fact. André fell in love with Madeleine and married her in 1895. Much of his writing—including *Strait Is the Gate* and *The Immoralist*—describes their relationship.

In 1893-1894, while on a trip to North Africa, Gide discovered his innate tendency toward homosexuality. During this same period, while away from Paris, he decided to provide an alternative to traditional morality by substituting a self-cultivated ethic for conventional codes. His feeling of antipathy toward convention reached its highest intensity during World War I, at which time Gide worked for the Red Cross and then in convalescent hospitals for wounded soldiers, when he decided that the emergence of one's true self requires a negation of the past. His written work from 1920 on is given to the conflicts between his great adoration of his wife and his homosexual tendencies, his disposition toward aesthetic pleasures and his aspiration to asceticism, his Protestant upbringing and his love for all things human, and his predilection for "the pleasures of the flesh" and his devotion to more highly disciplined pursuits.

His very extensive *Journals*—kept until his eightieth year—record that conflict. In terms of religious consciousness, one can find in the *Journals* the several stages in the transition from the view that the human depends upon the divine to the awareness that the realization of God depends upon the aspirations and humanistic energies of man. In his last years, Gide apparently took the next step in his journey toward enlightenment. He declared that in order to be what man needs to be, one has to abandon reliance upon a deity. But in addition to recording a personal odyssey, Gide's *Journals* serve as a treasury of commentary on continental ethical attitudes, literature, and philosophy in the late nineteenth century and the first half of the twentieth century.

In terms of "the religious personality" André Gide's *Journals* serve as a documentary of a quest to discover the true self. Gide seeks to secure that self by discovering the source of harmony which lies beyond any forms of contrariety, either personal or cultural. In the selection which follows, the reader may trace that quest over a span of some 60 years. The selection is formed by excerpts from the *Journals* which treat a constellation of religious subjects. It illustrates very explicitly the interdependence of a developing self-consciousness and a developing religious consciousness. Both are construed by means of aesthetic categories.

Journal
1889-1949

1890

January. . . .My pride is constantly being irritated by a thousand minute slights. I suffer absurdly from the fact that everybody does not already know what I hope some day to be, what I shall be; that people cannot foretell the work to come just from the look in my eyes. . . .

End of November. Thinking of one's salvation: egotism.

The hero must not even think of his salvation. He has *voluntarily* and *fatally* consecrated himself, unto damnation, for the sake of others; in order to manifest.

Rule of Conduct: Pay no attention to *appearing. Being* is alone important.

And do not long, through vanity, for a too hasty manifestation of one's essence.

Whence: do not seek to *be* through the vain desire to *appear*; but rather because it is *fitting* to be so. . . .

1891

10 June. . . . One should want *only one thing* and want it constantly. Then one is sure of getting it. But I desire everything and consequently get nothing. Each time I discover, and too late, that one thing had come to me while I was running after another. . . .

(Early August). My mind was quibbling just now as to whether one must first be before appearing, or first appear and then be what one appears. . . .

Perhaps, my mind said, we *are* only in so far as we *appear.*

Moreover the two propositions are false when separated:

1.   We *are* for the sake of appearing.
2.   We *appear* because we are.

The two must be joined in a mutual dependence. Then you get the desired imperative: *One must be to appear.* . . .

Uzès, 29 December. O Lord, I come back to thee because I believe that all is vanity save knowing thee. Guide me in thy paths of light. I have followed tortuous ways and have thought to enrich myself with false goods. O Lord, have pity on me: the only real good is the good thou givest. I wanted to enrich myself and I impoverished myself. After all that turmoil I am poorer than ever. I remember my former days and my prayers. O Lord, lead me as thou didst in thy paths of light. O Lord, keep me from evil. May my soul again be proud; my soul was becoming ordinary. Oh, may those early struggles and my prayers not be in vain. . . .

31 December. . . .The fear of not being sincere has been tormenting me for several months and preventing me from writing. Oh, to be utterly and perfectly sincere. . . .

1892

3 January. . . . A man's life is his image. At the hour of death we shall be reflected in the past, and, leaning over the mirror of our acts, our souls will recognize *what we are.* Our whole life is spent in sketching an ineradicable portrait of ourselves. The terrible thing is that we don't know this; we do not think of beautifying ourselves. We think of it in speaking of ourselves; we flatter ourselves; but later our terrible portrait will not flatter us. We recount our lives and lie to ourselves, but our life will not lie; it will recount our soul, which will stand before God in its usual posture. . . .

11 January. I am torn by a conflict between the rules of morality and the rules of sincerity.

Morality consists in substituting for the natural creature (the old Adam) a fiction that you prefer. But then you are no longer sincere. The old Adam is the sincere man.

This occurs to me: the old Adam is the poet. The new man, whom you prefer, is the artist. The artist must take the place of the poet. From the struggle between the two is born the work of art. . . .

Munich (second day), 12 May. . . . In any event, egoism is hateful. I am less and less interested in myself and more and more in my work and my thoughts. I no longer wonder every day and every hour if I am worthy of my God. But that is a great error; one must be capable of reflecting even the purest things. . . .

1893

Montpellier, March. . . . which gave to my sorry joys, to each one of them all the bitterness of sin.

. . . and my greatest joys have been solitary and laden with care.

I lived until the age of twenty-three completely virgin and utterly depraved; crazed to such a point that eventually I came to seek everywhere some bit of flesh on which to press my lips.

Paris, end of April. And now my prayer (for it still is a prayer): O my Lord, let this too narrow ethic burst and let me live, oh, fully; and give me the strength to do so, oh, without fear, and without always thinking that I am about to sin!

It now takes as great an effort to let myself go as it used to take to resist.

That ethic of privation had so thoroughly established itself as my natural rule of conduct that the other is now very painful and difficult for me. I have to urge myself to pleasure. It is painful for me to be happy. . . .

(August). Before leaving I reread all of my journal; I did so with inexpressible disgust. I find nothing in it but pride; pride even in the manner of expressing myself. Always some form of pretentiousness, claiming either to be profound or to be witty. . . .

The desire to compose the pages of this journal deprives them of all worth, even that of sincerity. They do not really mean anything, never being well

Andre Gide

enough written to have a literary value. In short, all of them take for granted a future fame or celebrity that will confer an interest upon them. And that is utterly base. Only a few pious and pure pages satisfy me now. What I dislike the least in my former self are the moments of prayer. . . .

13 September. Rule of Conduct: Originality; first degree.

I omit the lower degree, which is mere banality; in which man is merely gregarious (he constitutes the crowd).

Therefore: originality consists in depriving oneself of certain things. Personality asserts itself by its limitations.

But, above this, there is a still higher state to which Goethe achieves, the Olympian. He understahds that originality limits, that by being personal he is simply anyone. And by letting himself live in things, like Pan, everywhere, he thrusts aside all limits until he no longer has any but those of the world itself. He becomes banal, but in a superior way.

It is dangerous to try to achieve too early that superior banality. If one does not absorb everything, one loses oneself completely. The mind must be greater than the world and contain it, or else it is pitifully dissolved and is no longer even original. . . .

Montpellier, 10 October.   . . . Whereupon, ceasing to call my desires temptations, ceasing to resist them, I strove on the contrary to follow them. Pride seemed to me a less desirable thing. In that splendid egoism full of religion, I now saw, perhaps wrongly, only restrictions and limitations. Self-abandon struck me as a superior wisdom; it seemed to me that I would find in it greater profit for my soul. This was, I am well aware, still a form of egoism, but a newer, more curious form and one that satisfied in me more potential powers. I maintain that expression: satisfy potential powers; this had now become my rule of conduct; I wanted to live powerfully. O beauty! O desires! How skilfully you distracted my soul! That was the time when every smile diverted it; I used to smile myself and was never serious; I abhorred sorrow and protested against my inclinations toward sympathy. What more need I say? What I had begun with effort a charm or habit made me continue without restraint. Yet the habit of asceticism was such that in the beginning I had to force myself toward joy and it was with difficulty that I smiled; but how short a time those efforts lasted! Was I not following, meanwhile, perfectly natural laws? This occurred to me from the fact that, to live happily, I had perhaps only to let myself go. I say 'perhaps' because I am not quite sure; yet I had the *naïveté* to be amazed at first; wasn't this exactly what I had wanted: simply to let myself go? . . . I was like a sailor who drops his oars and lets himself drift; at last he takes the time to look at the shores; while he was rowing he saw nothing. My will, so constantly stretched taut, relaxed at present without any function. At first I experienced a mild discomfort; then even that disappeared, melting into the infinite charm of living, and of living carelessly. This was the great rest after the long fever; my former anxieties became incomprehensible to me. I was amazed that nature was so beautiful, and I called everything nature. . . .

1894

13 October. O Lord, I must hide this from everyone else, but there are minutes, hours even, when everything in the world strikes me as without order and lost, when every harmony that my mind has invented disintegrates, when the very thought of the pursuit of a higher order is a bore to me, when the sight of poverty upsets me, when my old prayers and my former pious melancholy rise into my heart, when the passive virtue of the humble man again seems to me the most beautiful. . . .

To create an antagonism between two parts of your nature, to make of yourself an enemy of nature, can perhaps flatter pride and contribute to poetry, but it is not *reasonable*. A clear understanding of God makes one want to follow the direction of things, the direction of oneself. That is much more difficult than resisting the current and at least calls for more wisdom. It presupposes intelligence, which is in no wise necessary to resistance. And serving God without intelligence (when you have intelligence) amounts to serving him with only a part of yourself. . . .

1905

24 August. Nothing is consistent, nothing is fixed or certain, in my life. By turns I resemble and differ; there is no living creature so foreign to me that I cannot be sure of approaching. I do not yet know, at the age of thirty-six, whether I am miserly or prodigal, temperate or greedy . . . or rather, being suddenly carried from one to the other extreme, in this very balancing I feel that my fate is being carried out. Why should I attempt to form, by artificially imitating myself, the artificial unity of my life? Only in movement can I find my equilibrium. . . .

1 September. I am again losing my footing; I am letting myself be carried along by the monotonous current. A great drowsiness benumbs me from my awakening until evening; games occasionally shake it off, but I am gradually losing the habit of effort. I compare what I am to what I once was, to what I should have liked to be. If only . . . but no, everything becomes soft in such an easy existence. Sensual pleasure permeates everything; my finest virtues are dissipated and even the expression of my despair is blunted.

How can I call absurd a rule of conduct that would have protected me against this? At one and the same time my reason condemns it and calls out for it in vain. If I had a father confessor, I should go to him and say: Impose upon me the most arbitrary discipline and today I shall say it is wisdom; if I cling to some belief that my reason mocks, this is because I hope to find in it some power against myself.

As soon as a healthy day comes along, I shall blush at having written this. . . .

1911

Whether he be named St. Paul, Luther, or Calvin, I see him as beclouding the whole truth of God. . . .

At times I deeply regret living in an epoch when respect is so rarely shown and so difficult. Not everyone can do without it with impunity. 'My mind was naturally inclined toward veneration,' Goethe (or at least his translator) says somewhere. If curvatures of the mind were as obvious as those of the spine, I know more than one that would not dare show itself in conversation, etc. . . .

'Levelling is not God's work and every proper man must have moments in which he is tempted to weep over that work of desolation.' (Kierkegaard.). . .

1912

Cuverville, 7 June. I consider detestable all moral teachings that are not dictated by the love of humanity—but I tell you that these counsels are dictated by the love of humanity and that, through the apparent and resolute severity of that voice, I feel stirring a great suffering love, that only the dryness of your hearts, O sceptics and rationalists, prevents you from recognizing.

30 June. Beethoven's ample phrase. Absurd habit I had got into of letting the breath drop in the middle. It should swell with a single *inspiration* from one end to the other. It is just a fortnight ago that I became convinced of this (I should even say: that I became aware of it) and I am striving to correct myself to give nuances to the content of the phrase. Important progress.

11 November. From day to day I put off and carry a little farther into the future my prayer: may the time come when my soul, at last liberated, will be concerned with God! . . .

1916

18 January. While writing to Ghéon, I reread the fifteenth chapter of the Gospel according to St. John and these words are suddenly illuminated for me with a frightful light:

The Aesthetic Self

'If man abide not in me, he is cast forth as a branch, and is withered; and men gather them, and cast them into the fire, and they are burned.'

Truly was I not 'cast into the fire' and already a prey to the flame of the most abominable desires? . . .

19 January. Everything in me calls out to be revised, amended, re-educated. The trait I have most trouble struggling against is my sensual curiosity. The drunkard's glass of absinthe is not more attractive than, for me, certain faces encountered by chance—and I would give up everything to follow them. . . . Why, to be sure this involves such an imperious urge, such an insidious, such a secret counsel, so inveterate a habit that I often wonder if I can escape it without outside aid.

'I have no man, when the water is troubled, to put me into the pool.' (John, v, 7.). . .

Sunday, 23. Yesterday evening I yielded, as one yields to an obstinate child—'to have peace'. Lugubrious peace; darkening of the whole sky. . . .

25. . . . I read in Rutherford (Vol. II, p. 113) a passage about the devil and hell that just happens to back up my thought wonderfully: 'The shallowest of mortals is able now to laugh at the notion of a personal devil. No doubt there is no such thing existent; but the horror at evil which could find no other expression than in the creation of a devil is no subject for laughter, and if it do not in some shape or other survive, the race itself will not survive. No religion, so far as I know, has swelt like Christianity with such profound earnestness on the bisection of man—on the distinction within him, vital to the very last degree, between the higher and the lower, heaven and hell. What utter folly is it because of an antique vesture to condemn as effete what the vesture clothes! Its doctrine and its sacred story are fixtures in concrete form of precious thoughts purchased by blood and tears.'

For several days now I have been striving to free myself from the Foyer, to cease being interested in it. I have great difficulty in doing so, and the time I spend trying to interest myself in something else (not to say in myself) is put to poor use, almost lost. And since Saturday I have been again assailed by abominable imaginings, against which I am defenceless; I find no refuge anywhere. At certain moments, sometimes for hours, I wonder if I am not going mad; everything in me yields to my mania. Yet I strive to organize the struggle. . . . What patience and what deception it would take! . . .

Sunday, 30. If I had to formulate a credo, I should say: God is not behind us. He is to come. He must be sought, not at the beginning, but at the end of the evolution. He is terminal and not initial. He is the supreme and final point toward which all nature tends in time. And since time does not exist for him, it is a matter of indifference to him whether that evolution of which he is the summit follows or precedes, and whether he determines it by propulsion or attraction.

It is through man that God is moulded. This is what I feel and believe and what I understand in the words: 'Let man be created in our image.' What can all the doctrines of evolution do against that thought?

This is the gate through which I enter into the holy place, this is the series of thoughts that lead me back to God, to the Gospels, etc. . . .

Will I some day succeed in setting this forth clearly?

For a long time already I have believed this without knowing it, and now it becomes clear in me through a series of successive illuminations. The reasoning follows. . . .

1917

1 November. At moments it strikes me, and as if in a sudden flash, that I have only a little time still to live, and that this is why I take such a lively interest in everything I read, that everything I see seems so beautiful to me, and that I enjoy life so completely. . . .

16 November. The thought of death pursues me with a strange insistence. Every time I make a gesture, I calculate: how many times already? I compute: how many times more? and, full of despair, I feel the turn of the year rushing toward me. And as I measure how the water is withdrawing around me, my thirst increases and I feel younger in proportion to the little time that remains to me to feel it.

18 November. The above lines will seem prophetic if I am to die in a short while; but I shall be really ashamed if it is given to me to reread them fifteen years from now. If I could simply not know or forget my age, how little I should be aware of it! I ought never to remind myself of it except to urge myself to work. . . .

One of the Herouard sons, the youngest of those who are in military service, has just been killed. Em. went this morning to Cuverville to attend the funeral service for Georges's deputy mayor, old Crochemore. As people were preparing to leave the church, an old woman began to shout in a high-pitched voice:

'There's God! There's God!'

Em., who is afraid of crazy people, ran out terrified, while her neighbor reassured her:

'Don't be afraid, Mam Gille! She's seized like that every time.'

And for some time we amuse ourselves by imagining the panic caused by the arrival of God in the church. . . .

The Aesthetic Self

. . .I have never been able to renounce anything; and protecting in me both the best and the worst, I have lived as a man torn asunder. But how can it be explained that this cohabitation of extremes in me led not so much to restlessness and suffering as to a pathetic intensification of the sentiment of existence, of life? The most opposite tendencies never succeeded in making me a tormented person; but rather perplexed—for torment accompanies a state one longs to get away from, and I did not long to escape what brought into operation all the potentialities of my being. That *state of dialogue* which, for so many others, is almost intolerable became necessary to me. This is also because, for those others, it can only be injurious to action, whereas for me, far from leading to sterility, it invited me to the work of art and immediately preceded creation, led to equilibrium and harmony.

It must, however, be recognised that, for a number of souls, which I consider among the best-tempered, happiness lies not in comfort and quietude, but in ardour. A sort of magnificent using up is all the more desirable to them since they are constantly being renewed by it and do not so much suffer from the wearing away as they rejoice in their perpetual recreation. As for me, I can tell you that I have never so keenly felt myself growing old as in that very quietude to which your rule of conduct invites one, but which you are less likely to achieve the more earnestly and nostalgically you strive to attain it. Your belief in the survival of souls is nourished by the need of that quietude and your *lack of hope* of enjoying it in life.

Shall I tell you what keeps me from believing in eternal life? It is that almost perfect satisfaction I enjoy in effort itself and in the immediate realization of happiness and harmony.

I was like the prodigal son who goes squandering his possessions. And that imponderable treasure which the slow virtue of my fathers, from generation to generation, had patiently accumulated on my head, no, I was not unaware of its value; but the unknown I could hope for by renouncing it seemed to me even more precious. The words of Christ rose up luminously before me like the column of fire that guided the chosen people in the night, and in the heavy darkness in which I decided to adventure I kept repeating to myself: 'Sell all your goods and give them to the poor.' My heart was filled with apprehension and joy, or more exactly: with the apprehension of my joy. For, thought I, it is not a question of interpreting the divine words to attain complete happiness; it is a question of accepting them without reservations, of understanding them 'in spirit and in truth'; and then at last, and then above all, to put them into practice, for, as it is said in the Gospel, 'every one that heareth these sayings of mine and doeth them not. . . '

I began then to seek out which, among the thoughts, opinions, and tendencies of my soul and mind that were most familiar to me, were the ones that I most certainly derived from my ancestors, from my upbringing and puritan formation, which at first had constituted my strength, from that sort of moral atmosphere in which I was beginning to stifle. And doubtless, pushing that relinquishment to the extreme, to the absurd, I should have ended up in complete impoverishment—for 'what have you that you have not received?'—but yet it was complete impoverishment that I coveted as the truest possession. Resolved to give up in this manner every personal possession and convinced that I could not hope to dispose of everything except on condition that I possessed nothing in my own right, I repudiated every personal opinion, every habit, every modesty, my very virtue, as one throws off a tunic in order to offer an unveiled body to the contact of the wave, to the passing winds, to the sun. Strengthened by these abnegations, I soon felt my soul only as a living will (yes, this is the way I defined it to myself), palpitating, open to all comers, like unto everything, impersonal, a naive confusion of appetites, greeds, desires. And if perhaps I had been frightened by the disorder into which their anarchy led me, was I not able to reassure myself at once by recalling these words of Christ: 'Why should you be troubled?' I surrendered then to this provisional disorder, trusting in a more sincere and natural order that would organize itself, I thought, and believing moreover that the disorder itself was less dangerous for my soul than an arbitrary and necessarily artificial order, since I had not invented it. Divine ray! I exclaimed, isn't what is opposed to you above all that false wisdom of men, made up of fear, lack of confidence, and presumption? I resign everything to you. I surrender myself. Drive out all shadow from me. Inspire me.

Considering later on that nothing separates one more from God than pride and that nothing made me prouder than my virtue, I began to detest that very virtue and everything on which I could pride myself, everything that allowed me to say: I am not like you, common run of men! And I am well aware that this excess of renunciation, this repudiation of virtue through the love of virtue itself, would appear as merely an abominable sophistry to the pious soul who reads me. Paradox or sophistry that thence forth bent my life, whether or not the devil prompted it I shall examine later on. It is enough for me to say for the moment that I advanced boldly on this path that was so new. What am I saying: path? Every step I took forward was a venture into the unknown. . . .

. . .I never *am*; I am *becoming*. I am becoming the person that I believe (or that *you* believe) I am. There is in every human being a little bit of the irresistible and a great deal of as you will. And even the share of irresistible can be reduced.

(It is easier to think this at the age of fifty-eight than at twenty.)

If it is still fanciful at the age of sixty to think you know yourself thoroughly; it is dangerous at twenty to try to know yourself thoroughly.

My desire, doubtless, is sincere; but my desire to overcome it is no less so. But that is not the important thing, and it matters little to me to weigh the authenticity of one or the other. The important thing is to know whether I am

The Aesthetic Self

right to try to overcome that desire, whether I am struggling out of fear or virtue, out of fear of others or of myself, etc., etc. Questions, moreover, that I never ask myself any more. The novelist who makes his hero ask himself these things one after another is not following truth; or else his hero is mere hypocrite. One begins instinctively by solving all these questions; one asks them of oneself only later on and only if one is a quibbler. They do not so often precede action as they substitute for it.

The sentence that begins with: 'I know myself. . . ' always ends with a negative. 'I know myself: I. . .not. . . . ' . . .

20 October. My grandmother Rondeaux, likewise, had saved up for the end the best of what she had to say, the last instructions and recommendations she wished to leave with her children. When she felt that the solemn hour was approaching, she gathered them all round her, but at that moment was seized with a paralysis of the tongue and, instead of a sublime speech, could only utter a tremendous scream. Such a loud scream, Albert told me as he related this recollection, that it was heard all the way to the end of the garden. This took place at La Mivoie.

That is perhaps what lies in store for me if I delay too much.

I cannot be satisfied with Roger Martin du Gard's absolute nihilism. I do not sidestep it, nor repulse it, but intend to go beyond it, to pass through it. It is beyond, that I want to rebuild. It strikes me as monstrous that man should need the idea of God in order to feel steady on earth; that he should be forced to accept absurdities in order to construct something solid; that he should recognize himself incapable of demanding of himself what religious convictions obtained from him artificially, so that he lets himself go to nothing as soon as his heaven is empty.

The best thing Sisyphus can do is to leave his rock alone and to climb up on it in order to 'dominate the situation'. But, for this, it is still essential that the rock should be of good quality. How many of these young writers, who make so much of their writings, are pushing only a cardboard rock, or have nothing to lift but a bookcase.

This image of Sisyphus is very good, but I believe I have already used it. It's a pity. But it is better to use it twice than to let it be lost.

23 October. All the thoughts that desire once nourished, all the anxieties it provoked, ah, how difficult it becomes to understand them when the source of lust dries up! And how can one be surprised by the intransigence of those who have never been led by desire? . . . It seems, with the coming of age, that one had somewhat exaggerated its demands and one is astonished to see younger men letting themselves still be tormented. The waves subside when the wind drops; the whole ocean falls asleep and reflects the sky. Knowing how to wish for the inevitable, this is all wisdom. All the wisdom of the aged. . . .

6 November. I am an unbeliever. I shall never be an ungodly man. . . .

1931

. . . It is no longer a matter of restoring ruins, but of building anew on a ground that must first be tested. Everything must be questioned, doubted again; nothing must be accepted but the authentic, from which all mysticism is banished. I mean by mysticism: any blind belief.

16 June. Evolution of my thought? Without a first Christian formation (or deformation), there would perhaps have been no evolution at all. What made it so slow and difficult was the sentimental attachment to what I could not cast off without regret. Even today I still have a sort of nostalgia for that mystical and ardent climate in which my being was then inflamed. I have never again recaptured the fervour of my adolescence, and the sensual ardour in which I subsequently delighted is but its ridiculous imitation. At least so it appears to me, now that my senses are ageing. Oh, how easy it would be for me, even today, to write emotional remarks on the subject that my reason would disown tomorrow! Nothing is easier than to stir to emotion when one does not hesitate to talk nonsense. It is illusion that permits the lyricism of childhood. My whole effort has been to achieve in myself a happiness that could do without being illusory.

Then, to be sure, my youth had much to do with it; the wild beating of a new heart; my love. . . . I could nourish that religious fervour only with what soon appeared to me as *inadmissible.* . . .

5 August. A man 'in whom is no guile'. I know no other which, more than this word of the Gospel, has dominated my life. It seems to me pretentious to say so. But, young as I then was, yes, that is what I inscribed in my mind. It seems to me today that 'sincerity' and the effort to achieve it *in oneself* are contained therein. . . .

1937

Cuverville, 13 May. . . . I see nothing but distress, disorder, and madness everywhere; but justice mocked, but the right betrayed, but falsehood. And I wonder what life could still bring me that matters. What does all this mean? What is it all going to lead to, and the rest? Into what an absurd mess humanity is sinking! How and where is escape?

But how beautiful the last rays were this evening, gilding the beech grove! . . . Alas, for the first time I am not associating myself with the spring! And now, those pathetic songs of birds, in the night. . . .

The Aesthetic Self

14 May. I did well to write those lines, yesterday. It purged me. This evening I feel quite reconciled with the universe and with myself.

27 June. To feel oneself an exceptional being; I sobbed with fright when I first made that discovery, but I had to resign myself to it, and already I had sufficiently accepted the exceptional not to be very much surprised when I had to become aware of it likewise in sexual matters. No, my surprise came rather, later on, from discovering that, in this domain at least, the exceptional (I mean: what was presented to me as such) was, after all, rather frequent.

The feeling of the exceptional I experienced, still quite young, upon noting that often I did not react as others did; as the common run of others. And try as one might later on to humiliate oneself, to depreciate oneself, to want to be vulgar, to refuse oneself to every distinction, to try to melt into the mass and like it, one remains none the less a creature apart. That feeling of differentiation the child may feel while still very young and by turns with sorrow, even with anguish, and very rarely with joy.

28 June. I see less well and my eyes become tired more quickly. I hear likewise less well, I tell myself that it is probably not bad that there should withdraw from us progressively an earth one would have too much trouble leaving—that one would have too much trouble leaving all at once. The wonderful thing would be, at the same time, to get progressively nearer to...something else. . . .

1942

Sidi-bou-Said. As soon as I had realized that God was not yet but was becoming and that his becoming depended on each one of us, a moral sense was restored in me. No impiety or presumption in this thought, for I was convinced at one and the same time that God was achieved only by man and through man, but that if man led to God, creation, in order to lead to man, started from God; so that the divine had its place at both ends, at the start and at the point of arrival, and that the start had been solely in order to arrive at God. This bivalvular thought reassured me and I was unwilling to dissociate one from the other: God creating man in order to be created by him; God the end of man; chaos raised up by God to the level of man and then man raising himself up to the level of God. To accept but one of them: what fear, what obligation! To accept but the other: what self-satisfaction! It ceased to be a matter of obeying God, but rather of instilling life into him, of falling in love with him, of demanding him of oneself through love and of achieving him through virtue.

8 June. Science, to be sure, progresses only by everywhere substituting the *how* for the *why*. But however remote it may be, there is always a point at which the two interrogations meet and fuse. To achieve man. . .billions of centuries would not have sufficed if chance alone had contributed. However anti-finalist one may or can be, one encounters here something unacceptable, unthinkable; and the mind is forced to admit a propensity, and inclination encouraging the groping, vague, and unconscious progress of matter toward life and consciousness; then, through man, toward God.

9 June. But how slow God is in becoming! . . .

La Marsa, 12 June. The time is approaching, and I feel it quite close, when I shall have to say: I must give up. . . .

31 December. Doubtless I no longer cling much to life, but I have this fixed idea; *to last.* To make myself and my dependencies last a little while longer: linen, clothing, shoes, hope, confidence, smile, graciousness; make them last until the farewell. In view of this I am becoming economical, parsimonious of everything in order that none of this should give out ahead of time, through great fear that this war may be drawn out, through great desire and great hope to see the end of it.

1947

. . .Faith moves mountains; yes, mountains of absurdities. To faith I do not oppose doubt, but affirmation: what could not be is not.

Hence I shall refuse to consider finality in nature. According to the best advice, I shall everywhere substitute, systematically, the *how* for the *why*. . . .

Those ideas which one first thought one could not possibly do without. Whence great danger of basing one's moral comfort on false ideas. Let us check, let us verify first. Once the sun turned around the earth, which, as a fixed point, remained the center of the universe and focal point of God's attention. . . . And suddenly, no! It is the earth that turns. But then everything is upset! All is lost! . . . Yet nothing is changed but *the belief*. Man must learn to get along without it. First from one, then from another, he frees himself. Get along without Providence: man is weaned.

We have not reached this point. We have not yet reached this point. It requires much virtue to achieve that state of total atheism; even more to remain there. The 'believer' will probably see in it nothing but an invitation to license. If this were so, hooray for God! Hooray for the sacred falsehood that would preserve humanity from collapse, from disaster. But cannot man learn to demand of himself, through virtue, what he believes demanded by God? Yet he must nevertheless get to this point; some, at least, must, to begin with; otherwise the game would be up. That strange game that we are playing on earth (unintentionally, unconsciously, and often unwillingly) will be won only if the idea of God, on withdrawing, yields to virtue, only if man's virtue, his dignity, supplants God. God has ceased to exist save by virtue of man. *Et eritis sicut dei.* (Thus it is that I want to understand that old word of the Tempter—who, like God, has existence only in our minds—and see in that offer, which has been characterized for us as fallacious, a possibility of salvation.)

God is virtue. But what do I mean by that? I should have to define; I cannot do so. I shall manage to do so only subsequently. But I shall already have accomplished much if I remove God from the altar and put man in his place. Provisionally I shall think that virtue is the best the individual can obtain from himself.

God lies ahead. I convince myself and constantly repeat to myself that: He depends on us. It is through us that God is achieved. . . .

Get along without God. . . . I mean: Get along without the idea of God, without a belief in an attentive, tutelary, and retributive Providence . . . not everyone can achieve this. . . .

1948

8 June. . . . The worst is allowing people to think: 'Yes, since the Nobel Prize, Gide has *become distant.*' After that there remains nothing but to go and drown or hang oneself. And it so happens that since the warmth has returned, I have ceased to have any desire to do so. But before that, on certain days, I felt as if already completely detached; this, however, held me back: the impossibility of getting anyone to understand, to accept, the real reason for a suicide; at least, this way I shall be left alone and in peace. But go away on a trip . . . already on the steps of the train, what a relief to feel out of reach, liberated! But go where? I think of that little hotel that Alix told me about (I noted it down) in a fishing village on Lago di Garda. If only I were sure of finding room there. . . . Constantly called upon, I must put off from day to day; and constantly I hear the wildest of the Fates whispering in my ear: you haven't much time left.

3 September. These last days of life seem the most difficult to live through; but this must be an illusion, for one has only to leave it to time, and to gravity. . . .

An extraordinary, an insatiable need to love and be loved, I believe this is what dominated my life and urged me to write; an almost mystical need, moreover, since I consented to its not being satisfied during my lifetime.

Torri del Benaco, 7 September. I believe I am sincere in saying that death does not frighten me much (I am constantly thinking of it); but I see the summer go by with a sort of despair.

Never before had I seen such a long series of such beautiful, such splendid days. . . .

Paris, 15 December.   Last words. . . . I do not see why one should try to pronounce them louder than the others. At least I do not feel the need of doing so.

1949

. . . I have already written, I don't recall where, that there is probably no word of the Gospel which I earlier or more completely adopted, subordinating my being to it and letting it dominate my thoughts: 'My kingdom is not of this world.' So that 'this world', which, for the mass of human beings, alone exists—to tell the truth, I do not believe in it. I believe in the spiritual world, and all the rest is nothing to me. But that spiritual world, I believe that it has existence only through us, in us; that it depends on us, on that support which our body provides it. And when I write: 'I believe that. . .' there is no question whatever of an act of faith. I say: 'I believe' because there is no other way of expressing the establishment, by my reason, of that obvious fact. What have I to do with *revelations*? I want to appeal solely to my reason—which is the same and was the same at all times and for all men.

Beneath which sprawls at ease my constant sensuality.

I believe that there are not two separate worlds, the spiritual and the material, and that it is useless to oppose them. They are two aspects of one and the same universe; as it is useless to oppose the soul and the body. Useless is the torment of the mind that urges them to war. It is in their identification that I have found calm. And that the spiritual world prevails in sovereign importance is a notion of my mind, which depends intimately on my body; both conspire and agree in order to achieve harmony in me. I will not and cannot try to subject and subordinate one to the other, as the Christian ideal aims to do. I know by experience (for I long strove to do so) what it costs. On whichever side, the body or soul, victory inclines, the victory is artificial and temporary and we have eventually to pay the expenses of the conflict.

27 May.   Accumulation of days in the hospital; vague mass of more than a month; hesitating between better and worse. Succession of days filled almost solely with reading. Sort of desert morass with the daily oasis, charming beyond all hope, of the regular visits of the incomparable friend that, during this long period of purgatory, Roger Martin du Gard was for me. His mere presence already provided me a link with life; he forestalled all the needs of my mind and body; and however gloomy I might have been before his coming, I soon felt quite revived by his remarks and by the affectionate attention he paid to mine. I do not know whether I could ever have been more aware in the past of the

The Aesthetic Self

ineffable blessing of friendship. And what an effacement (even excessive) of his own interest, of himself! No, no! Religion achieves nothing better, or so naturally. . . .

4 June. Some days it seems to me that if I had at hand a good pen, good ink, and good paper, I should without difficulty write a masterpiece.

10 June. Hugo enjoys rhyming two diphthongs, one counting as two syllables, the other as one. I note in passing:

> *Qu'un vin pur fasse fete aux poulardes friandes!*
> *Et que de cet amas de fricots et de viandes. . .*

I had noticed others.

Suggestions for Further Reading

James G. Brennan, *Three Philosophical Novelists: James Joyce, André Gide, Thomas Mann* (New York: Macmillan, 1964).

Jean P. L. Delay, *The Youth of André Gide* (Chicago: University of Chicago Press, 1963).

Denis De Rougement, *The Myths of Love*, translated by Richard Howard (London: Faber and Faber, 1963). Especially pp. 163-188.

Eugene H. Falk, *Types of Thematic Structure: The Nature and Function of Motifs in Gide, Camus, and Sartre* (Chicago: University of Chicago Press, 1967).

Wallace Fowlie, *André Gide: His Life and Art* (New York: Macmillan, 1965).

Albert J. Guerard, *André Gide* (Cambridge: Harvard University Press, 1951).

James C. McLaren, *The Theatre of André Gide: Evolution of a Moral Philosopher* (Baltimore: Johns Hopkins Press, 1953).

Harold Marsh, *Gide and the Hound of Heaven* (Philadelphia: University of Pennsylvania Press, 1952).

Justin O'Brien, *Portrait of André Gide: A Critical Biography* (London: Secker and Warburg, 1953).

George D. Painter, *André Gide: A Critical Biography* (London: Weidenfeld and Nicholson, 1968).

Vinio Rossi, *André Gide: The Evolution of an Aesthetic* (New Brunswick, N.J.: Rutgers University Press, 1967).

Lawrence Thomas, *André Gide: The Ethic of the Artist* (London: Secker and Warburg, 1950).

Helen Watson-Williams, *André Gide and the Greek Myth: A Critical Study* (Oxford: Clarendon Press, 1967).

Paul Tillich

On the Boundary

*. . . there remains a boundary for
human activity which is no longer a
boundary between two possibilities
but rather a limit set on everything
finite by that which transcends all
human possibilities, the Eternal.*

Paul Johannes Tillich, often described as "an apostle to the skeptic" because of his lifelong interest in defending Christian theology as well as religious studies as legitimate substantive fields, was born in Germany on August 20, 1886, the son of a Prussian minister. He received his academic training in a number of German universities, earning the Ph.D. degree from Breslau in 1911 and a degree in theology from Halle in 1912. During the war, from 1914 to 1918, Tillich was a chaplain in the German army, and he then began his teaching career, becoming professor of philosophy at the University of Frankfurt in 1929. He was ousted from his professorial post by the Nazi regime and, upon invitation from Reinhold Neibuhr, journeyed to America in 1933 to become a member of the faculty of Union Theological Seminary in New York. His career in America was both brilliant and large and emanated from a number of outstanding universities. While at Union Seminary Tillich also taught philosophy at Yale. In 1955 he moved to Harvard and in 1962 became Nuveen Professor of Theology at the University of Chicago. On two occasions, in 1963 and 1965, Tillich was visiting professor of religious studies at the University of California, Santa Barbara. He died in Chicago on October 22, 1965. It has often been said that no other theologian, with the possible exception of Reinhold or Richard Niebuhr, had more influence in shaping religious attitudes in post-war America.

Tillich was a comprehensive thinker who used art, science, psychology, and philosophy as keys to the human quest for meaning. For him every creative and cultural phenomenon held the promise of further interpretation, for each could disclose something diagnostic about the human situation. Then, through his "method of correlation," Tillich referred the human question to answers which came through corporate revelatory experience. He contended that all human questions, when raised under the auspices of "ultimate concern," could be seen in relation to a symbolic representation of the Christian faith. The schema was clearly dependent upon existentialist philosophy. Tillich thus both provided the language for referring the human question to the validity of existence, and indicated that the answer to the question would require personal decision and faith.

One of the purposes of Tillich's intellectual endeavors was to restore to man a sense of harmony in his relationships with nature, culture, and the Judaeo-Christian religious tradition. That harmony, Tillich felt, had been broken by the passing of an earlier life-view or world outlook. The evidence of its passing was reflected in man's inability to effect any of these three relationships in personally satisfying ways. Tillich's efforts to restore order and meaning led him to a full-scale symbolic reinterpretation of nature, culture, and the Western world's dominant religion. But it also disciplined him personally to find his stability in those attitudinal places—the "boundaries" as he called them—from which disorder, dissonance, and disharmony could be overcome. He writes of his inner compulsion to mediate contrarieties and transcend alternatives in the autobiographical sketch which follows.

An Autobiographical Sketch

Temperamental Boundaries

When I was asked to give an account of the way my ideas have developed from my life, I thought that the concept of the boundary might be the fitting symbol for the whole of my personal and intellectual development. At almost every point, I have had to stand between alternative possibilities of existence, to be completely at home in neither and to take no definitive stand against either. Since thinking presupposes receptiveness to new possibilities, this position is fruitful for thought; but it is difficult and dangerous in life, which again and again demands decisions and thus the exclusion of alternatives. This disposition and its tension have determined both my destiny and my work.

In the shaping of a child's character, one should not ascribe too much importance to the characters of its parents. There are, however, parental and

From Paul Tillich, *On the Boundary. An Autobiographical Sketch* (New York: Charles Scribner's Sons, 1966). Reprinted by permission of the Estate of Paul Tillich.

The Aesthetic Self

ancestral traits that do recur rather strikingly in children and later descendants, and perhaps cause deep conflicts in them. Whether this is more a matter of heredity or of the impressions of early childhood is an open question. Nevertheless, I have never doubted that the union of a father from Brandenburg and a mother from the Rhineland implanted in me the tension between eastern and western Germany. In eastern Germany, an inclination to meditation tinged with melancholy, a heightened consciousness of duty and personal sin, and a strong regard for authority and feudal traditions are still alive. Western Germany is characterized by a zest for life, love of the concrete, mobility, rationality and democracy. Though neither set of characteristics was the exclusive property of either parent, it was through my parents that these conflicting traits influenced the course of my inner and outer life. The importance of such parental legacies is not that they determine the course of one's life, but that they define the scope and supply the substance out of which critical decisions are drawn.

Without this double inheritance my position on the boundary would be hard to understand. My father's influence was dominant, in part because of the early death of my mother. Consequently the character of my mother's world asserted itself only through constant and deep struggle with that of my father. In order for the maternal side of my makeup to express itself, outbreaks, often extreme, were necessary. Classical composure and harmony were not part of my heritage. This may explain why Goethe's classical traits were alien to me, and why the pre- and post-classical periods of Greek antiquity were more assimilable than the classical. This tension also accounts in part for certain premises underlying my interpretation of history: the choice of the line moving forward and towards a goal rather than the classical premise of the self-enclosed circle; the idea that the struggle between two opposing principles constitutes the content of history; the theory of dynamic truth, which holds that truth is found in the midst of struggle and destiny, and not, as Plato taught, in an unchanging "beyond."

Between the ages of four and fourteen I lived in a small town near the Elbe, where my father was the leading minister and the superintendent of the church district. In the small towns of many parts of Germany, the typical resident is the "farmer-burgher"—a townsman, usually well-to-do, who manages a fairly good-sized farm from his town residence. Towns of this kind have a decidedly rustic character. Many of the houses have yards, barns, and gardens attached to them, and it is only a few minutes' walk out into the fields. Cattle and sheep are herded through the streets morning and evening. Nevertheless, these are real towns with civic rights and traditions as old as the Middle Ages. The gates of the town wall open on to narrow streets with serried rows of houses and shops. The sheltered, protective quality of the town with its hustle and bustle, in contrast to the eeriness of the forest at night and the silent fields and sleepy hamlets, is one of the earliest and strongest of my childhood impressions.

Paul Tillich

Visits to Berlin, where the railroad itself struck me as something half-mythical, heightened these memories and developed in me an often overpowering longing for the big city. This affected me later in many ways; it came to philosophical expression in the essays "Logos und Mythos der Technik" and "Die technische Stadt als Symbol" (The Technical City as Symbol).

This attraction to the city saved me from a romantic rejection of technical civilization and taught me to appreciate the importance of the city for the development of the critical side of intellectual and artistic life. Later on, I arrived at a vital and sympathetic understanding of Bohemianism, a movement that is possible only in large cities. I also learned to appreciate esthetically both the fantastic inner activity and the physical size of a city. Finally, I acquired firsthand knowledge of the political and social movements concentrated in a large city. These experiences and their lasting effect on me—the myth of the city, so to speak—are largely responsible for the popularity of my book *The Religious Situation*.

My ties to the country, however, are even stronger. Nearly all the great memories and longings of my life are interwoven with landscapes, soil, weather, the fields of grain and the smell of the potato plant in autumn, the shapes of clouds, and with wind, flowers and woods. In all my later travels through Germany and southern and western Europe, the impression of the land remained strong. Schelling's philosophy of nature, which I read enthusiastically while surrounded by the beauty of nature, became the direct expression of my feeling for nature.

The weeks and, later, months that I spent by the sea every year from the time I was eight were even more important for my life and work. The experience of the infinite bordering on the finite suited my inclination toward the boundary situation and supplied my imagination with a symbol that gave substance to my emotions and creativity to my thought. Without this experience it is likely that my theory of the human boundary situation, as expressed in *Religiöse Verwicklichung*, might not have developed as it did.

There is another element to be found in the contemplation of the sea: its dynamic assault on the serene firmness of the land and the ecstasy of its gales and waves. My theory of the "dynamic mass" in the essay "Masse und Geist" (Mass and Spirit), was conceived under the immediate influence of the turbulent sea. The sea also supplied the imaginative element necessary for the doctrines of the Absolute as both ground and abyss of dynamic truth, and of the substance of religion as the thrust of the eternal into finitude. Nietzsche said that no idea could be true unless it was thought in the open air. Many of my ideas were conceived in the open and much of my writing done among trees or by the sea. Alternating regularly between the elements of town and country always has been and still is part of what I consider indispensable and inviolable in my life. . . .

370   The Aesthetic Self

Boundaries between Reality and Imagination

The difficulties I experienced in coming to terms with reality led me into a life of fantasy at an early age. Between fourteen and seventeen, I withdrew as often as possible into imaginary worlds which seemed to be truer than the world outside. In time, that romantic imagination was transformed into philosophical imagination. For good and for ill, the latter has stayed with me ever since. It has been good in that it has given me the ability to combine categories, to perceive abstractions in concrete terms (I would almost say "in color") and to experiment with a wide range of conceptual possibilities. It has been of doubtful value insofar as such imaginative ability runs a risk of mistaking the creations of the imagination for realities, that is, of neglecting experience and rational critique, of thinking in monologues rather than dialogues, and of isolating itself from cooperative scientific effort. Whether good or bad, this imaginative tendency (plus certain other circumstances), prevented me from becoming a scholar in the accepted sense of the word. Amongst intellectuals of the twenties there was a kind of aversion against the scholar in the restricted sense of "expert."

Imagination manifests itself, among other ways, in a delight in play. This delight has accompanied me all my life, in games, in sports (which I never took as more than play), in entertainment, in the playful emotion that accompanies productive moments and makes them expressions of the sublimest form of human freedom. The romantic theory of play, Nietzsche's preference for play as opposed to "the spirit of gravity," Kierkegaard's "esthetic sphere," and the imaginative element in mythology were always both attractive and dangerous to me. Perhaps it was an awareness of this danger that drove me more and more to the uncompromising seriousness of prophetic religion. My comments in *Die sozialistische Entscheidung* (Socialistic Decision) about the mythological consciousness were a protest not only against the ultimate lack of seriousness in nationalistic paganism, but also against the mythical-romantic element not conquered in myself.

Art is the highest form of play and the genuinely creative realm of the imagination. Though I have not produced anything in the field of the creative arts, my love for the arts has been of great importance to my theological and philosophical work. At home my father maintained the musical traditions associated with the evangelical ministry. He himself wrote music. Like most German Protestants, however, he cared little for architecture and the fine arts. Since I am not artistically inclined and only later gained an appreciation of the visual arts, my longing for art was directed toward literature. This was in line with the humanist tradition in education at the *Gymnasium*. Schlegel's classical German translation of Shakespeare became particularly important for me. I

Paul Tillich

identified myself (almost dangerously) with figures like Hamlet. My instinctive sympathy today for what is called existentialism goes back in part to an existential understanding of this great work of literature. Neither Goethe nor Dostoievsky had a similar effect on me. I came to know Dostoievsky too late in my life. Goethe's work seemed to express too little of the boundary situation in the Kierkegaardian sense; it did not then seem to be existential enough, although I have revised this judgment in my maturity. Even after my infatuation with Hamlet, which lasted for some time, I preserved the capacity for complete identification with other creatures of poetic fancy. The specific mood, the color as it were, of certain weeks or months of my life, would be determined by one literary work or the other. Later this was especially true of novels which I read infrequently but with great intensity.

Literature, however, contains too much philosophy to be able to satisfy fully the desire for pure artistic contemplation. The discovery of painting was a crucial experience for me. It happened during World War I, as a reaction to the horror, ugliness and destructiveness of war. My delight even in the poor reproductions obtainable at the military bookstores developed into a systematic study of the history of art. And out of this study came the experience of art; I recall most vividly my first encounter—almost a revelation—with a Botticelli painting in Berlin during my last furlough of the war. Out of the philosophical and theological reflection that followed these experiences, I developed some fundamental categories of philosophy of religion and culture, viz., form and substance. It was the expressionist style emerging in Germany during the first decade of this century and winning public recognition following the war and the bitter struggle with an uncomprehending lower middle-class taste that opened my eyes to how the substance of a work of art could destroy form and to the creative ecstasy implied in this process. The concept of the "breakthrough," which dominates my theory of revelation, is an example of the use of this insight.

Later, when expressionism gave way to a new realism, I developed my concept of "belief-ful realism" from a study of the new style. The idea of "belief-ful realism" is the central concept of my book, *The Religious Situation*, which for that reason is dedicated to an artist friend. My impressions of various representations of individuals and groups in Western art gave me the inspiration and material for a lecture, "Masse und Persönlichkeit" (Mass and Personality). My growing preference for the old Church and her solutions to such theological problems as "God and the World," "Church and State," was nourished by the deep impression made on me by early Christian art in Italy. The mosaics in the ancient Roman basilicas accomplished what no amount of studying church history could have done.

This vital experience of modern painting also opened the way for an appreciation of modern German literature, as represented by Hofmannsthal, George, Rilke, and Werfel. I was most deeply impressed by the later poetry of

Rilke. Its profound psychoanalytical realism, mystical richness, and a poetic form charged with metaphysical content made this poetry a vehicle for insights that I could elaborate only abstractly through the concepts of my philosophy of religion. For myself and my wife, who introduced me to poetry, these poems became a book of devotions that I read again and again.

Intellectual Interests

I never doubted—nor did anyone else—that I was destined to a life devoted to intellectual rather than practical matters. I was about eight when I first wrestled with the idea of the Infinite. In school and in my pre-confirmation instruction, I was fascinated with Christian dogmatics; I devoured popular books on philosophy. My education in the humanistic tradition and my enthusiasm for the language and literature of the Greeks strengthened this disposition toward the theoretical. I fully agreed with Aristotle's contention, as expressed in the *Nichomachean Ethics*, that pure contemplation alone offers pure happiness. My inward struggles with the truth of traditional religion also helped keep me within the domain of the speculative. In the religious life, however, contemplation implies something other than philosophical intimations of Being. In religious truth, one's very existence is at stake. The question is: to be or not to be. Religious truth is existential truth; to this extent it cannot be separated from practice. Religious truth is *acted*, as the Gospel of John says.

It soon became clear, though, that a one-sided devotion to contemplation was based on the same escape from reality as my flight into literary fantasy. As soon as I recognized this danger and was confronted with practical tasks, I threw myself into them with complete ardor—partly to the advantage and partly to the disadvantage of my intellectual pursuits.

My university studies were followed by two years of parish work and four years as a field chaplain on the Western front. After the war I spent a brief period in church administrative work. My theoretical studies were severely restricted, though not entirely interrupted, during these years of practical activity. This time of immersion in practical problems, however, did not shake my basic devotion to the theoretical life.

The tension between theory and practice was heightened at the outbreak of the revolution. For the first time, I became very much alive to the political situation. Like most German intellectuals before 1914, I had been rather indifferent to politics. Our consciousness of social guilt had not expressed itself politically. It was during the collapse of imperial Germany and the revolution of the last year of World War I that I began to understand such issues as the political background of the war, the interrelation of capitalism and imperialism, the crisis of bourgeois society, and the schisms between classes. The tremendous pressure of the war, which had threatened to obscure the idea of God or to give it demonic coloration, found an outlet in the discovery of the human responsibility for the war and the hope for a refashioning of human society. When the call to a religious socialist movement was sounded, I could not and would not refuse to heed it. At first we worked only on theoretical problems of "religion and socialism." But the goal of our work was political, and we were thus inevitably faced with problems of practical politics which often conflicted with theoretical positions.

Ever since the last years of my secondary education, I wanted to be a philosopher. I used every free hour to read those philosophical books that came by chance into my hands. I found Schwegler's *Geschichte der Philosophie* (History of Philosophy) in the dusty corner of a country preacher's bookshelf, and Fichte's *Wissenschaftslehre* (Theory of Science) on top of a wagon load of books on a Berlin street. In a state of boyish excitement, I bought Kant's *Critique of Pure Reason* from a bookstore for the immense price of fifty cents. These works, especially that of Fichte, introduced me to the most difficult aspects of German philosophy. Discussions with my father, who was an examiner in philosophy on the committee which examined students for the ministry, enabled me from the beginning of my university career to carry on discussions with older students and young instructors about idealism and realism, freedom and determinism, God and the world. . . . Partly through the accident of a bargain purchase, and partly through an inner affinity for his work, I came under the influence of Schelling. I read through his collected works several times, and eventually made his work the subject of my dissertations for the degrees of doctor of philosophy and licentiat of theology.

During this time I also studied Protestant theology, and at the conclusion of my studies I became an assistant pastor in various parishes of the "Old Prussian United Church." My most important theological teachers were Martin Kähler and Wilhelm Lütgert, both of Halle. Kähler was a man whose intellectual ability and moral and religious power were overwhelming. As a teacher and writer he was difficult to understand. In many respects he was the most profound and most modern representative of the nineteenth-century theology of mediation. He was an opponent of Albrecht Ritschl, a proponent of the theological doctrine of justification, and a critic of the idealism and humanism from which he was himself intellectually descended.

I am indebted to him primarily for the insight that he gave me into the all-embracing character of the Pauline-Lutheran idea of justification. On the one hand, the doctrine of justification denies every human claim before God and every identification of God and man. On the other hand, it declares that the estrangement of human existence, its guilt and despair, are overcome through the paradoxical judgment that before God the sinner is just.

. . . I managed to reconcile the doctrine of justification with radical historical criticism by developing an interpretation of the idea of justification

The Aesthetic Self

that has been of the greatest importance to me, both personally and professionally. I applied the doctrine of justification to the sphere of human thought. Not only human acts but human thinking as well stand under the divine "No." No one, not even a believer or a Church, can boast of possessing truth, just as no one can boast of possessing love. Orthodoxy is intellectual pharisaism. The justification of the doubter corresponds to the justification of the sinner. Revelation is just as paradoxical as the forgiveness of sins. Neither can become an object of possession.

It was the work of Schelling, particularly his late thought, which helped me relate these basic theological ideas to my philosophical development. Schelling's philosophical interpretation of Christian doctrine opened the way, I thought, to a unification of theology and philosophy. I confess that even today I find more "theonomous philosophy" in Schelling than in any of the other German idealists. But not even he was able to achieve a unity of theology and philosophy. World War I was disastrous for idealistic thought in general. Schelling's philosophy was also affected by this catastrophe. The chasm that he had seen but soon covered up again opened itself anew. The experience of those four years of war revealed to me and to my entire generation an abyss in human existence that could not be ignored. If a reunion of theology and philosophy is ever to be possible it will be achieved only in a synthesis that does justice to this experience of the abyss in our lives. My philosophy of religion has attempted to meet this need. It consciously remains on the boundary between theology and philosophy, taking care not to lose the one in the other. It attempts to express the experience of the abyss in philosophical concepts and the idea of justification as the limitation of philosophy. . . .

Between Two Lands

My writing this self-portrait in an alien country is a destiny that, like all true destiny, represents freedom at the same time. The boundary between native land and alien country is not merely an external boundary marked off by nature or by history. It is also the boundary between two inner forces, two possibilities of human existence, whose classic formulation is the command to Abraham: "Go from your home . . . to the land that I will show you." He is bidden to leave his native soil, the community of his family and cult, his people and state, for the sake of a promise that he does not understand. The God who demands obedience of him is the God of an alien country, a God not bound to the local soil, as are pagan deities, but the God of history, who means to bless all the races of the earth. This God, the God of the prophet and of Jesus, utterly demolishes all religious nationalism—the nationalism of the Jews, which he opposes constantly, and that of the pagans, which is repudiated in the command to Abraham. For the Christian of any confession, the meaning of this command is

Paul Tillich   375 indisputable. He must ever leave his own country and enter into a land that will be shown to him. He must trust a promise that is purely transcendent.

The real meaning of "homeland" varies according to the situation of the individual. It may be the land of his birth and his national community. Occasionally, "physical emigration" may be demanded. But the command to go from one's country is more often a call to break with ruling authorities and prevailing social and political patterns, and to resist them passively or actively. It is a demand for "spiritual emigration"—the Christian community's attitude toward the Roman Empire. The path into an alien country may also signify something wholly personal and inward: parting from accepted lines of belief and thought; pushing beyond the limits of the obvious; radical questioning that opens up the new and uncharted. In Nietzsche's words, it means moving into "the land of our children" and out of "the land of our fathers and mothers." It is a temporal, not a geographical, emigration. The alien land lies in the future, the country "beyond the present." And when we speak of this alien country we also point to our recognition that even what is nearest and most familiar to us contains an element of strangeness. This is the metaphysical experience of being alone in the world that existentialism takes as its expression of human finitude.

In every sense of the word, I have always stood between native and alien land. I have never decided exclusively for the alien, and I have experienced both types of "emigration." I began to be an "emigrant" personally and spiritually long before I actually left my homeland.

My attachment to my native land in terms of landscape, language, tradition and mutuality of historical destiny has always been so instinctive that I could never understand why it should have to be made an object of special attention. The overemphasis of cultural nationalism in national education and intellectual productivity is an expression of insecurity about national ties. I am convinced that this overemphasis occurs in individuals who come from the boundary—either externally or internally—and who feel obligated, therefore, to justify their patriotism to themselves and to others. They are also afraid to return to the boundary.

I have always felt so thoroughly German by nature that I could not dwell on the fact at length. Conditions of birth and destiny cannot really be questioned. We should instead ask: What shall we do with this which is given in our lives? What should be our criterion for evaluating society and politics, intellectual and moral training, cultural and social life? Accidents of birth do not constitute answers to such questions, because the questions presuppose them. If the presuppositions are mistaken for the answers we find ourselves caught in the vicious circle that today is praised as national feeling, although it testifies to a lack of confidence in the strength of our national substance and leads to a terrible emptiness of national life. . . .

I tried to lay bare the anthropological roots and political consequences of nationalism. The experience of World War I was crucial for my position. It revealed the demonic and destructive character of the national will to power, particularly for those who went to war enthusiastically and with a firm belief in the justice of their national cause. Consequently, I can only view European nationalism as an instrument for the tragic self-destruction of Europe even though—or perhaps because—I realize that nationalism is inevitable. . . .

In this world, national as well as international peace depends on the power to restrain the violators of peace. I am not speaking in justification of a national will to power; but I recognize the necessity for interconnected forces, behind which there must be a power capable of preventing the self-destruction of mankind. Today the idea of "mankind" is more than an empty notion. It has become an economic and political reality; for the fate of every part of the world depends on the fate of every other part. The increasing realization of a united mankind represents and anticipates, so to speak, the truth implicit in a belief in the Kingdom of God to which all nations and all races belong. Denying the unity of mankind as aim includes, therefore, denying the Christian doctrine that the Kingdom of God is "at hand." I was happy to discover on the boundary of this new continent where I now live, thanks to American hospitality, an ideal which is more consistent with the image of one mankind than that of Europe in her tragic self-dismemberment. It is the image of one nation in whom representatives of all nations and races can live as citizens. Although here too the distance between ideal and reality is infinite and the image is often deeply shadowed, nonetheless it is a kind of symbol of that highest possibility of history which is called "mankind," and which itself points to that which transcends reality—the Kingdom of God. In that highest possibility, the boundary between native and alien land ceases to exist.

Summing Up

Many possibilities of human existence, both physical and spiritual, have been discussed in these pages. Some things have not been mentioned, although they are part of my biography. Many more things have been left untouched, because they do not belong to the story of my life and thought. Each possibility that I have discussed, however, I have discussed in its relationship to another possibility—the way they are opposed, the way they can be correlated. This is the dialectic of existence; each of life's possibilities drives of its own accord to a boundary and beyond the boundary where it meets that which limits it. The man who stands on many boundaries experiences the unrest, insecurity, and inner limitation of existence in many forms. He knows the impossibility of attaining serenity, security, and perfection. This holds true in life as well as in thought, and may explain why the experiences and ideas which I have recounted are rather fragmentary and tentative. My desire to give definitive form to these thoughts has once again been frustrated by my boundary-fate, which has cast me

Paul Tillich

on the soil of a new continent. Completing such a task to the best of my ability is a hope that becomes more uncertain as I approach fifty. But whether or not it is to be fulfilled, there remains a boundary for human activity which is no longer a boundary between two possibilities but rather a limit set on everything finite by that which transcends all human possibilities, the Eternal. In its presence, even the very center of our being is only a boundary and our highest level of accomplishment is fragmentary.

Suggestions for Further Reading

James Luther Adams, *Paul Tillich's Philosophy of Culture, Science, and Religion* (New York: Harper and Row, 1965).

D. Mackenzie Brown, *Ultimate Concern: Tillich in Dialogue* (New York: Harper and Row, 1965).

Lewis S. Ford, "The Three Strands of Tillich's Theory of Religious Symbols," *Journal of Religion*, Vol. 46 (January 1966), Pt. 2, pp. 104-130.

Charles W. Kegley and Robert W. Bretall, editors, *The Theology of Paul Tillich* (New York: Macmillan, 1952).

David Kelsey, *The Fabric of Paul Tillich's Theology* (New Haven, Conn.: Yale University Press, 1967).

Walter Leibrecht, editor, *Religion and Culture: Essays in Honor of Paul Tillich* (New York: Harper and Row, 1959).

Robert P. Scharlemann, *Reflection and Doubt in the Thought of Paul Tillich* (New Haven, Conn.: Yale University Press, 1969).

"Symposium on Tillich's Theology," *Theology Today*, Vol. XV (April 1958), pp. 36-83.

Paul Tillich, *Biblical Religion and the Search for Ultimate Reality* (Chicago: University of Chicago Press, 1955).

_____ , *The Courage to Be* (New Haven: Yale University Press, 1952).

_____ , *Dynamics of Faith* (New York: Harper, 1957).

_____ , *The Future of Religions*, edited by Jerald C. Brauer (New York: Harper and Row, 1966).

_____ , *The New Being* (New York: Charles Scribner's Sons, 1955).

_____ , *The Protestant Era* (Chicago: University of Chicago Press, 1948).

_____ , *Systematic Theology* (Chicago: University of Chicago Press, 1951-1963).

The Aesthetic Self

_____, *Theology of Culture*, edited by Robert C. Kimball (New York: Oxford University Press, 1959).

Gustave Weigel, "Contemporaneous Protestantism and Paul Tillich," *Theological Studies*, Vol. XI, No. 2 (1950), pp. 177-202.

_____, "The Theological Significance of Paul Tillich," *Gregorianum*, Vol. XXXVII, No. 1 (1956), pp. 34-54.

Author Index